MY TWO WARS

BOOKS BY MORITZ THOMSEN

MY TWO WARS

THE SADDEST PLEASURE:
A JOURNEY ON TWO RIVERS

THE FARM ON THE RIVER OF EMERALDS

LIVING POOR

MY TWO WARS

MORITZ THOMSEN

INTRODUCTION BY PAGE STEGNER

STEERFORTH PRESS

SOUTH ROYALTON, VERMONT

For information about permission to reproduce
selections from this book, write to:
Steerforth Press L.C., P.O. Box 70, South Royalton, Vermont 05068.

Library of Congress Cataloging-in-Publication Data
Thomsen, Moritz.
My two wars / Moritz Thomsen. -- 1st ed.
p.   cm.
ISBN 1-883642-06-X
1. Thomsen, Moritz.   2. World War, 1939-1945--Aerial operations, American.
3. World War, 1939-1945--Personal narratives, American.   4. United States.
Army--Biography.   5. Bomber pilots--United States--Biography.
6. Thomsen, Charles, d. 1959.   I. Title.
D790.T518   1996
940.54'4973--dc20

Manufactured in the United States of America

FIRST EDITION

INTRODUCTION

ONE SEPTEMBER AFTERNOON in 1972 I was sitting in my office in the Peace Corps building in Quito, Ecuador trying to listen to the Watergate hearings on Armed Forces Radio, when a well-proportioned man of medium height and indeterminate age came through the door and sprawled in the chair by my desk. He was wearing a pair of stained khaki pants, a black wool shirt with several buttons missing, sneakers with no socks. His face was tanned and weather-creased; his work-scarred hands rough and heavily stained by nicotine. In spite of his down-at-the-heels appearance, he had that look of aristocratic intelligence so often conferred on men of very strong character and worldly experience, and from a single glance it was perfectly clear that he was something other than the poor laborer his sartorial presence suggested. "My name is Moritz Thomsen," he said. "I read your two novels and that mercifully brief but splendid book on Vladimir Nabokov and I wanted to come by and meet you."

I was, I confess, mildly astonished. My slim volume of lit/crit on Nabokov's English fiction probably sold no more than four or five thousand copies, mostly to libraries, and I couldn't imagine how he had come by it — or for that matter, by the even worse-selling novels. But mainly I was astonished because here was the living author of *Living Poor,* a book I regarded then (and now) as the most impressive and original piece of work ever to have come out of Kennedy's inspired experiment in screwing up exotic cultures — here he was, slouched beside my desk and offering up what was clearly sincere praise for my little accomplishments, conversing with me about "those idiots," Lionel Trilling and Mary McCarthy and their tedious exegesis of *Lolita,* discussing issues of point of view and voice in my own fiction, and wanting to know what I was working on now. Could he read it? Would I come down to his farm in Esmeraldas for a visit?

What an absolutely astute, discerning, and utterly charming man. Naturally, I invited him home for dinner. He paused, expressed concern that the hole in the rear of his trousers revealed the absence of his underwear, then opined his shirttails would probably cover the indignity.

"How could you *forget* your underwear?" I asked, greatly amused.

"Forget? Actually, I'm not sure I own any," he said.

I abstract this initial encounter because it set the tone for a friendship that lasted for nearly twenty years, even though I never saw Moritz again after I left Ecuador in 1973. He was one of the most self-effacing and modest men I ever met, enormously informed for a supposedly reclusive expatriate, and always a brilliant storyteller. If his sense of humor was often black to the point of morbidity, it was a quality offset by his bright passion for music and books and the craft of writing, especially other people's writing, and by his fascination with the idiosyncrasies of human behavior, especially his own. Endlessly disparaging of his talents and the magnitude of his accomplishments, he could rise to inspired heights of eloquence in his condemnation of all agents, editors, and critics (whom he regarded as a kind of literary Gestapo) who maliciously failed to appreciate or understand his work. "Of course," he would say, subsiding in his chair, "the bastards are probably right."

For a time after I left Ecuador, Moritz and I corresponded regularly, then irregularly, then again, during the last year of his life, almost monthly. I knew he was in poor health because he alluded now and then to the crippling emphysema that prevented him from walking two blocks to buy eggs for his dinner, but most of his communication was about two manuscripts he was trying to sell (always followed by a blast at editors, reviewers, the publishing industry, the literary establishment, his agent), and then in January of 1991 he wrote that his old World War II pilot had come to visit him, and he had sent back copies of both manuscripts with him to be forwarded to me. I got them in mid-February, and so informed Moritz. Late in March he wrote me a long letter from which I excerpt the following.

A couple of months or years ago you wrote me that my old pilot had sent you the war ms., that you would read it immediately . . . This is awful suspenseful kind of talk building up unbearable expectations. . . .

Come on, Page; I can take it, though I suspect that your silence suggests that you have been struck dumb with the awfulness of the finished product . . . Tell me Page, I am ready now to start reworking if you can suggest some easy ways to do it. . . .

As usual nothing new going on down here except torrential rains, strikes, tear gas attacks, dope wars, kidnappings, bestiality, and no water.

In the meantime, Page, Jesus, man, write me, will you. If you can't bear the ms. just write and tell me. I'll understand (HAH).

—M.

I quickly wrote him that I had *indeed* read the first manuscript, *My Two Wars,* and that far from being struck dumb by the awfulness of the product I thought he had written another masterpiece, almost — but that because he had eschewed most forms of punctuation (in particular, the comma), and because he hadn't changed the ribbon in his typewriter since Richard Nixon resigned from office, it had taken me a while to decipher it. I also told him that I didn't think most readers were going to be as obsessed with his hatred of his father (the first war) as he was, and that the point behind the episodes recounted in this opening part of the book became redundant. I feared that readers might wear out before they got to the second war, which I thought was the best narrative account ever written of an imperfect and fragile human soul caught up in the air war over Germany during World War II. It's all vintage Thomsen, I told him — intensely personal, totally honest, immensely funny, ironic, cynical, compassionate, confessional. But I thought he either had to cut back on Daddy, eliminate Daddy, integrate Daddy, or use Daddy to better frame the entire book and give it shape.

In May I got another long letter, from which I again excerpt.

> Well, I read your letter 6 times and thought shit, what Page envisions instead of my rewrite #16 is the original plan . . . I can't remember why I changed that except that last dinner where I get kicked out of the house was so long, and boring for an ending, but maybe you are right — or 80% right, and I'm going to try, and if it works, thank you.

A month later he wrote that he had gotten the manuscript out, read page one, and put it away again. "The material is too repellent to mess with anymore." He sounded exhausted and depressed, which I attributed, in part, to a bad review of *The Saddest Pleasure* in the *London Times Literary Supplement* that he said had "devastated" him. Characteristically, he undermined his devastation by concluding, "Had I not written the Goddamn book I might very well have written almost the same review — and been just as bitchy too."

On August 16th he wrote to say that he had tried the revisions once more, but just wound up sending a letter to his agent saying he couldn't get together the strength to rewrite when there was absolutely no interest from a publisher. He signed off, "Page, I am half sick and will write you again in a few days. Thanks again, kid, I have put you through hell but how else does one get ahead except walking on the backs of his betters." Ah, Moritz.

Twelve days later he was dead, though I didn't get the word until mid-September. Moritz's close friend and Quito resident, Mary Ellen Fieweger, wrote to a number of his acquaintances and admirers, and the circumstances surrounding his death as she depicted them in her account seem right out of one of his own narratives, almost as if he's scripted his won postmortem. With Ms. Fieweger's permission I quote (with the exception of one irrelevant paragraph), her summary of the events as she wrote them to the poet Robert Peterson.

18 September 1991

Dear Mr. Peterson,

I took the liberty of opening your letter to Moritz as he isn't around to read his own mail anymore. Moritz died on August 28. Though the official cause of death was listed as coronary thrombosis, he came down with cholera about two weeks earlier. He refused to go to a hospital and, during the last forty-eight hours, refused any and all treatment, including IVs, painkillers, and oxygen. I think he was ready to die, and determined to do it the way he had chosen to live most of his adult life. He died poor, with a disease that affects only the poor.

His body was cremated, a wish he expressed a number of times over the years. This took place at the only mortuary concern in Guayaquil offering that particular service, Los Jardines de Esperanza, at the southern edge of the port city. To get to the Gardens of Hope, you have to travel an unpaved, winding road lined with garbage dumps and surrounded by shanty towns. No doubt Moritz would have appreciated this touch, as well as the fact that because the oven was broke and the part needed to repair it could not be found, cremation was delayed for thirty-six hours, cause for concern in a tropical country where embalming is not practiced. He would also have appreciated the fact that while the search for parts and the repair itself was going on — the search was in vain; someone finally improvised something — he was charged an hourly rental rate for the shabby mourning room where he rested in a chipped and dented coffin adorned with flowers rusting at the edges, accompanied by a pathetic band of five — Ester Prado, her children Ramon and Marta, one of her sisters, and me — not counting the quack of a doctor who during the past year made house calls during which she shot him up with vitamins and assured him that he was in her prayers day and night, these calls coinciding, according to Moritz, with each new financial crisis that came her way. It wasn't until she presented me with a bill for services rendered that I understood the good doctor's solicitousness: those hours at the cemetery appeared on the bill; Moritz was covering one last financial crisis for her. Finally, Moritz would no doubt have appreciated that, on the little signboard they put up at the entrance to mourning rooms — this particular signboard also rusting at the edges — his name was spelled wrong: MONITZ.

I don't expect to meet ever again a human being as honest, as good as Moritz was. Sometimes he was hard on those around him, but he was always much harder on himself. He lived his convictions quietly, daily, the hardest way, I think, to live convictions. In *Living Poor* he wrote, "You can't move in too close to poverty, get too involved in it, without becoming dangerously wounded yourself." People I took to meet Moritz, who had read his books and wanted to know the writer, were often shocked by his material surroundings (or, better, lack thereof) and later asked why he lived that way. After his death a friend suggested that his life was his way of teaching us something. I don't think he intended to teach anyone anything, he was too modest to assume he had anything to teach. But that's what he did, maybe in spite of himself.

Moritz was often lonely, especially after he moved to Guayaquil because of his emphysema and no longer had a circle of friends visiting daily. He said the hardest thing about being an expatriate was that everybody eventually left. Letters, especially those from friends, meant more to him than you probably imagined. He pulled them out when I went to visit and asked me to read them. Sometimes, if the post office was on strike or there had been no mail, he pulled the same letter out on several visits, just to hear it again. I was one of the few people who didn't leave, in good part because Moritz was here. After he moved to the coast, I flew down about once a month. During the last couple of years, as his emphysema got worse, and he left his apartment less and less (during the last six months I don't believe he went out a single time, not even to see the movies he wanted to see, because the effort involved in getting from the table he sat and worked and read at to the front door — five paces, maybe — was monumental), he very reluctantly began asking me to do things. He hated being dependent, even in little things, and I don't think I ever succeeded in convincing him that, dammit, he wasn't a burden, that there were people, like me, who felt eternally in his debt just because they had been privileged to know him, to become a friend, to read his books. Did Moritz tell you that during the last year of his life he had begun to make notes for a new book, called "From My Window"? It was going to be a wonderful, sad book about what he had witnessed while sitting at his window, breathing in lead emissions and other contaminants, observing life in the heart of downtown Guayaquil. Moritz is going to be missed by a lot of people, and the books he might have written by a lot more.

Sincerely,
Mary Ellen Fieweger

When a U.S. citizen lives for over twenty years in a Latin American country and dies leaving no immediate family and no will, the settling of the "estate" becomes a bureaucratic nightmare of unimaginable proportions — even when there is very little to disperse in the way of personal property. The manuscript of *My Two Wars* sat on my desk for almost four years while the tangled business of resolution went on; then, in May of 1995, Steerforth Press managed to track down Moritz's only heirs, his niece and nephew, and obtain permission from them to publish the book.

Asked by Steerforth to act as its "editor," I was faced with a complicated choice in my editorial capacity — whether to just clean up the typos, misspellings, and punctuation and leave the text unaltered, or whether to actually execute some of the textual changes that Moritz and I talked about in our letters. I don't know what textual doctrine or bibliographic protocol demands in cases like this, but have determined to remain happily ignorant. In the end I went with what I felt Moritz would have wanted me to do.

The only major change to the manuscript is the translocation of one thirty-page scene. Taking my cue both from Moritz's letters and from a paragraph in the manuscript itself, I moved that "last dinner where I get kicked out of the house" episode to the end of the book where it was located in his original plan, and where it seems to rightfully belong. It is anything but too "long and boring for an ending"; it is, in fact, a highly dramatic denouement that brings the book full circle and ties the knot in the double helix of the two wars.

Here and elsewhere throughout the manuscript the language has been left untouched, except where Moritz himself inserted penciled changes or deletions. I have imposed "chapter" breaks at various points throughout the narrative, even though only a few were indicated, because no obvious purpose was served by four hundred pages of undivided text and readability was greatly enhanced by their inclusion.

And finally, because Moritz sent me in his last letter "a special carton of several 1000 hand-crafted commas carved from pure, aged Yak butter, and in those earth tones that the true Mongolodophile finds so ravishing," I have used four or five hundred of them to supply punctuation where it was often . . . overlooked.

I trust you will forgive me these intrusions, Moritz; never ask an old crony for his opinion.

—Page Stegner
Santa Cruz, California

MY TWO WARS

THIS IS A BOOK about my involvement with two outrageous catastrophes — the Second World War and my father. Neither left
physical scars that could help authenticate my presence — either in that
war which killed a hundred million or as part of an odd family dominated by a man who tended to lose control under pressure — but scars
presuppose wounds, and who needs them? They are the two big wars of
my life, lost, I suppose as all wars are, as all wars are the seedbeds of future
wars. These two, being contiguous, are closely connected in my mind,
but though I think I could not write about one without writing about
the other, I fear I have failed to connect them properly in these pages. In
the end, having given in for a time to hot feelings, it seems I've written
two books within one cover. This is like cooking and serving a hunter's
stew and a sunshine cake in the same bowl. It has been possible to write
about the war with that calmness that long distancing brings to the resurrection of old horrors. But time has not separated me from those
childish and neurotic obsessions, those memories of my father and the
home he made. I begin to write about him and find my voice going
shrill, my body trembling with fifty-year-old angers. Old emotions still
cramp my fingers, old injustices still march through my dreams, there is
something still unsettled between us.

One day some fifteen years ago I was invited to have dinner with a
friend. He had a young son who made extravagant demands upon his
parents and who was regarded by all who watched him tyrannize that
house as a truly insufferable monster. That evening just before we sat
down at the table I observed a typical family drama: the little six-year-
old boy comes strolling down a hall, and his father, hidden in a doorway,
pops his head out and says "Boo." The boy starts, and then, embarrassed
at having revealed his fright, becomes as stern as a hanging judge.
"Daddy," he cries, stamping a foot. "You are a bad daddy. Don't you ever

do that again, bad Daddy. I am going to tell Mama about this." The father admits that he acted stupidly, apologizes for it, and we go in to dinner.

Though I would never have dared to accuse my father until I was almost old enough to vote, I am now reminded of that angry little fellow who, so unlike me, saw himself as a paid-up member of a democratic family whose dignity was not to be trifled with. Those of us who watched this brat having his endless tantrums and demanding justice are incredulous, but delighted, to know that he has grown into a remarkably fine, healthy, and loving young man bursting with talents, enthusiasms, and high expectations. Watch, in the years to come, for the name of Carlos Arango to appear carved high and deep on monuments to goodness or greatness.

Patiently watch the six-year-old monsters that you know, the little child stars who dominate and produce havoc in the houses of your friends and inspire you to hesitate for just a second when invited to share a meal. The chances are that, purged of their resentments, they will grow up into well-adjusted adults, a pleasure to be around. It is those little well-brought-up angels with their hands folded quietly in their laps who do not swing their legs, do not speak unless spoken to, who call you sir or ma'am and bow or curtsey cutely when introduced, they are those ones whose lives will one day go off like hand grenades. There is a kernel of truth in the stupid generality that the children of missionaries, raised up on biblical wisdom and taught to suppress selfish or spontaneous inclinations, will tend to appear in later life as streetwalkers, alcoholics, radio evangelists, or manic-depressives with suicidal tendencies.

I think of that kid, Carlos, because suddenly I stand in his place, allowing myself, not without a certain satisfaction, to be swept up in old angers and the need to cry out about them. In my case the situation is grotesquely comical; I am not six years old but seventy-two, and my father has been dead for seventeen years. An unkind judge might decide that this obsessive concentration on the past is an unhealthy thing. Of course it is. Might not a kinder judge point out that every writer's material is necessarily a harvesting of his own life? Besides, people under the compulsion to write may be more than normally eccentric, may even be, like whores, drunks, and pickpockets, the grown-up battered children of bad daddies.

Like a carpenter who can't make a good joint but, knowing what one is, keeps trying, let me strain however ineptly to connect my two themes — war and father. The connection truly exists, though it may be difficult for anyone to fully believe the following pages, desperately constructed out of ancient memories to make a marriage that will sound authentic. Surely one thing is true: in that psychological game where one must immediately say the word that another word brings to mind, as *hot* or *good* will automatically trigger the words *cold* and *bad,* so to me the words *family* or *father* instantly transform themselves into the word *war.*

I was born during the Civil War, and my first days were spent within fifty yards or so of one of its last and greatest battles. Yanks and Rebs, bleeding, yelling, sweating, dying, waving flags, running into the mouths of smoking cannons, grasping their stomachs as they fell, swarmed over the dry hills behind the house my father had rented in Hollywood, the immortal hills that D. W. Griffith used for the filming of his epic, *Birth of a Nation.* My mother had vivid memories of that summer as I nursed at her breast and she stood in the dry grass, smelling gun-smoke, flinching at the cannons' booms. She knew, she said, that she was watching cinematic history, in spite of the fact that she was unaware of the new filming techniques that were being invented daily before her eyes. I, of course, remember nothing of that battle, nor of the other vicious war that began about the same time and ended five years later in a scandalous divorce. Remembered or not, the family war, the booming of cannon, the rushing here and there in the back yard, the heady sweetness of my mother's milk, may have put into my bloodstream the first intimations that life is a bloody conflict and that just beyond the screen door there are people behind tree trunks, behind the birdbath and the sundial and the high dead summer grass, crouching there with knives in their hands, their faces contorted with rage.

It was a few years later that I began to associate bloodthirsty war with the German disposition to worship it. My father's friends, still young but demobilized, returned from Europe with their lungs destroyed by mustard gas or their youthful enthusiasm for beer drinking grown into a destroying passion to live in a perpetual alcoholic stupor. There were scandals as men of promise went down the drain or shot themselves. German spiked helmets, sadistically ugly; brutal pistols, iron crosses, bayonets joined the other toys in my bedroom — the teddy bears, the woolen dog on wheels I still dream about, the Tinkertoys, the magic lantern that lit up a whole wall, the stereopticon that took double-imaged postcards and made them three dimensional and allowed me to study closely Japanese gardens, pools, and temples. In 1917, when I was two, my father in a madness of patriotic fervor begged and begged my grandfather to use his influence to have him accepted by the army. After a year of barracks life, disenchanted, he used that same influence to get himself discharged. There was a rumor I first heard when I was twelve, that he had come back home with gonorrhea, but having recently learned about the connection between the social diseases and whores, I was too horrified to keep this information and immediately forgot it — until much later when I got a certain satisfaction as I added it to the list of all the other things I held against him.

Everything between my mother and father except the subconscious awareness that they were engaged in a mortal combat is missing from my memory. Everything. Each one lives separate in my mind as though they had never met. To be more precise — no memory of them together, little memory of them apart. My father was the man who jiggled me on his knee when he came to visit from time to time; he lived in California, I lived in Seattle. At Christmas he jiggled me on his knee dressed in a red suit filled out with pillows and spun glass whiskers; slightly terrifying. As for my mother, she simply disappeared one day when I was five or so. I was sent with a nurse to live in Grandmother's house, and I have only the faintest memory of my mother, who appeared three times outside the window where I slept. She was dressed in long white angel robes and glittered in the darkness, sustained by small sparkling wings that hummed like eggbeaters, her face anguished by the screen that separated us. How strange, then, that at age ten or eleven when I was finally allowed to spend a week with her, but had almost no memory of her at all, I immediately picked her out of a large crowd waiting on the Sausalito dock where the ferry from San Francisco had delivered me, and where I had been put by my furiously jealous stepmother who refused to say good-bye.

In the house of my grandparents, full of aunts and cousins (two houses, really, since my grandmother wintered in Altadena), my first memories were born. My first wisdom, almost esoteric for its being secret and publicly unacknowledged, was bedrock fundamental: relations between family members were warlike and terrible. Being small and semi-invisible I moved at will within the combat zone, saw sisters furious with one another kissing and smiling, saw my father greeted warmly by family members who a minute before had screamed that his behavior was outrageous. Two of my four aunts, who had been married for their money by scoundrels, only saved their husbands from prison by obtaining the divorces that my grandfather demanded to replace the stolen funds. Oh, that place of hidden passions, broken hearts, tears and screams behind closed doors and in midnight rooms. During the first years of the 1920s it seemed that the lives of everyone in the family had come unraveled. There was a constant stream of monumental tragedies with lives being ruined and brought to the brink of suicide, so that while in the outside world nothing showed but high-held heads, brave smiles, and constant attendance at parties, those hidden crises occasionally burst out of the closets into the heart of the family circle where we were all gathered for dinner. It was in this house, solidly German and as bourgeois as three chapters out of *Buddenbrooks* (authoritarian in the way that only occurs where the head of the house wields unlimited power), that I modified my conviction that the synonym for family was war by adding the word German before the word family.

At the dinner table when passions took over and everyone began to scream and weep, to keep the grandchildren from having nervous fits the whole family switched into German. We didn't understand the details of why, for instance, Aunt Inga had begun to tear out her hair, but we confronted, with various degrees of curiosity, disgust, or fear, the essences of greed, hatred, or despair. The background music was in German.

By the time I was six I knew that German soldiers had hacked off the hands of Belgians, bayoneted children, and, swinging babies by the feet, dashed out their brains against trees, walls, kitchen tables. My grandfather, with his hair cut short in a military pompadour and his brisk greying mustache, looked to me exactly like Hindenburg. In an attic closet his Knight Templar's sword, sharp enough to cut off heads, its ivory handgrip shaped like a cross, waited.

At the dinner table it seemed to me that among my father and his sisters it was the one who screamed the loudest who won the battle—until my grandfather restored order. He was rich, and the thousand dollars a month he gave to each of his children (and the knowledge that he could cut them off) produced, after a minute of brutal summing-up in a voice as clipped, final, and furious as distant machine-gun fire, a frightful silence, as though everyone at the table had been struck dead with dum-dums. There was something awesome and magnificent about the power of a tyranny so overwhelming that it canceled out like a tidal wave the impulse to judge it as moral or immoral. His children loved him out of pure terror. I almost made it to the end without ever having been the victim of his rage, but just a few months before he died I forgot to take Grandmother to church. He met me at the front door and he told me what he thought of me. It was terrible, and it was all true, and I stood there pissing in my pants and went upstairs shaking so violently that a phonograph record I picked up (side three of Stravinsky's *Rite of Spring*) fell and broke. I was sixteen when that happened, fifty-six years ago, but thinking about it now my eyes fill with tears; he knew what an asshole I was.

It is curious that I saw myself as part of a German family, for we were not Germans but Danes, at least according to the chauvinistic Seattle gossips during the First World War who mocked the family's new money and the social pretensions of my aunts. And who whispered that we had become Danes overnight at about the same time that the *Lusitania* sank, American symphony orchestras stopped performing Wagner, and the bottom dropped out of the wiener and sauerkraut market. Both my grandparents had come from an ambiguous area. Schleswig-Holstein was a rural countryside as flat as Holland and swarming with cows and the incredibly blond children who milked them. Were they Germans or Danes? It was claimed by both countries and had been invaded time and time again by Germans.

On an early evening in February of 1934 when I was nineteen years old, in a blinding moment of revelation while I watched my father drinking beer in a Munich beer hall, I made that final connection between him and the war. Even more depressing, I began to see a connection, badly hidden in the folds of the American flag, between the goofy right-wing conservatism in the fanatic wing of the super-rich Republicans and German Fascism with its brutal and simplistic solutions. Sitting at a good German table made of solid oak, drinking good

German beer out of ceramic tankards, I suddenly realized that war was coming, that it was inevitable, that it was almost upon us, and that in all probability I would be one of its victims.

To explain our presence in that beer hall — which was a highly unlikely place to be considering that my father had just lost all his money and was staggering on the lip of bankruptcy — I must digress and scratch a little into family history.

When he was twelve years old my grandfather, with everything he owned tied up in a large handkerchief, plus bread and cheese for three days, left Tondern, a farming village in Schleswig-Holstein, and set out to make his fortune. He went to sea; the year was 1858. The family stories claim that he left to remove that one-too-many mouth from his father's table, left without even a coat to protect him from the cold. How many times as a spoiled rotten brat did I hear that story? By the time he was twenty-one he was captain of a sailing vessel. He left the sea at twenty-five because his cousin said she would never marry a man who would be gone ten months of every year. They married and went to America. He worked in Maine as a day laborer, in the meat-packing plants of Chicago for a dollar a day, someplace further west as a miller in a flour mill. He had a son who died. By thirty he had saved enough money to buy a wagon with a team of horses, a plow and a harrow, a rifle, and the other necessities — a list so modest and heartbreaking that one can't even imagine it. He went by wagon with my grandmother and homesteaded in Kansas or Nebraska. A few years later — with nothing behind him but endless eighteen-hour days, the wind and sun of high summer, the howling blizzards rushing down from the Arctic circle, the *loneliness* — he had doubled his money. Perhaps he was worth three thousand dollars.

One day his luck changed; or God, looking down on all those faceless and suffering immigrants scattered and isolated over the immensity of the western prairies, picked him out to play jokes on. That day, just before the harvest, a terrible wind, a blinding fury of hail, swept across the wheat fields — until it came to grandfather's property line. Then the wind died, the hail turned into a gentle rain, until thirty minutes later, on the *other* property line, the wind and the hail began again, leaving a few hundred acres of standing grain in the middle of a general devastation. That act of grace was only the beginning, a little blat of trumpets announcing the main theme — that he was now being cherished, and on the basis of his own dreams, not God's, about being rich as Danish royalty.

He moved to Spokane with ten thousand dollars and bought a half interest in a flour mill. A year later he bought out his partner, and ten years after that owned or was building new mills in Tacoma, San Francisco, Portland, and Kobe, Japan. My God, but it was easy to make money, and he was a man whose talents precisely matched his dreams. The flour mills were the beginning. By the time he was fifty he had spread out into everything: grain, timber, gold, fishing. He owned a chain of cracker factories, fattened five thousand hogs on Seattle garbage, made porcelain toilets, ran a sand and gravel business, dug dry oil wells on the Olympia peninsula, started to build a railroad from Acapulco to Mexico City.

In 1922, to pull the date out of a hat, B.C. Forbes, Hearst's financial editor and the father of his more famous son, Malcolm, came to our house for dinner for a week running. I dimly remember a man with huge horn-rimmed glasses that made him look like a dumb owl, and remember that I didn't like him because of his resemblance to my uncle Jim, whose name, ever since he stole money from the brokerage firm where he had once worked, was no longer mentioned in the house. Mr. Forbes was writing a book about Men Who Are Making the West. I have forgotten who else was included in that book except for Stanley Dollar, one of the heroes of this story, and Giannini, that Bank of America fellow. Strange that I've forgotten; we had at least twenty copies of the book lying around the house for years, though in truth I only read Grandfather's chapter, for it was the only one that read like a fairy tale with shipwrecks, Chinese pirates, sharks, etc. My mother always insisted that the mythology surrounding Grandfather's early life had all been invented by Mr. Forbes. "I never heard a word about Father's going to sea until that Mr. Forbes showed up," she told me. "What I heard, once, was he milked cows and dug potatoes in Maine when he left Tondern. The truth is, nobody talked about his humble beginnings. The girls were ashamed; they didn't want to remember they'd played naked in the dust outside a sod hut, especially when the riffraff, the eastern fortune hunters, came wooing. Plus a genuine French prince who truly loved your Aunt Tree, I think, but Father said no, no gott damn princes."

Grandfather loved America, the energetic and optimistic pioneering men of his time, and the laissez-faire capitalism of the century's early years when almost anything you wanted to do was legal. The West Coast with its untouched riches of fish, timber, wheat, cattle, and minerals, the Orient just over the horizon, and gigantic Alaska just to the north, all this convinced him that only some kind of an idiot could live in Washington without making a million. What he hated were the things that put limits to his powers to create wealth. It was obvious to him that building a factory that gave jobs to hundreds was noble work, and that workers who did not understand their partnership in this holy enterprise were probably Jewish or Russian anarchists to be rooted out, clubbed down, and sent back to Czarist serfdom. The 1917 general strike in Seattle, organized by the IWW, might well have killed off my grandfather with a raging heart seizure. He hated the IWW and the new labor unions which would one day unite and bring down the world of business men, the visionary men who were creating American prosperity and the modern world. How could those little brown brothers, Cubans and Filipinos, resist our disinterested and Christian impulses to civilize them? What ungrateful savages.

When Henry Ford announced that he would pay his workers five dollars a day, Grandfather, in newspaper interviews, denounced him as a traitor to his class. How could you set a basic wage and promise to pay it to an unproved worker? Yet for all the narrowness of his vision he loved working men; in the flour mills, in the cracker factories, he knew every man by name. His love was, I suppose, as mad as the love of an old-time plantation owner for his slaves.

He distrusted flashy dressers, men who wore cufflinks, spats, or derbies, men, in fact, who wore hats of any kind. He mocked college graduates for their timorous self-confidence and their snobbishness, mocked the sons of inherited wealth who listened to highbrow music, wore wrist-watches, smoked cigarettes, danced in the afternoons at tea dances. Look at their weak faces or their skinny wrists, listen to those fake eastern accents — men who had never done a day's work in their lives. Degenerates. He would never raise a son like that. He detested secretly the fops who wooed his daughters, and it is possible that at times he grew tired of his daughters' bright social chatter and their solemn reverence for Wagner. He was honest, gruff, unpretentious, respected; to his

peers and to the shameless politicians of the day who courted him, a diamond in the rough. Though in his old age he had come to reflect a dying
breed of entrepreneurs with their rugged individualism, their insensitivity to social injustice, and their labor phobias, he died before he
became a caricature. Unlike my father, who embraced all of his father's
prejudices, one thought of Grandfather in other than political terms. He
was bigoted and Republican but I saw him as an American of his times, a
flawed but original giant. My father I saw as some kind of fanatic nut, his
philosophy mired back there someplace around 1900. Grandfather was
an empire-builder when building empires was considered noble work.
Father continued to worship the discredited imperial dreams that helped
lead us to moral disaster and that resulted finally in a majority of citizens
crazy and confused enough to freely vote into office men like Nixon
and Reagan.

Two of the last newspaper articles in the scrapbooks my father kept
about Grandfather chart him from the apex of his financial trajectory to,
very soon after, his plunge into comparative poverty. The first is a photograph of my father smiling broadly as he poses on the steps of the train
from New York, underneath a headline that reads, "Bringing home the
bacon." The year is 1927, I believe, and the article reports that Grandfather has just sold the Pacific Coast Biscuit Company to National Biscuit
for twelve million dollars. Half is in cash, half is in National Biscuit stock.
My father had the check photographed and passed it around the dinner
table one night. I remember vividly my father's ecstasy, and feeling that I
held something holy in my hands, and having to conquer the impulse to
run with it.

The second is a photograph of my grandfather sitting at his big mahogany desk downtown. He too is smiling, but it is a smile to make you
weep, the dazed smile of a clubbed man hiding his despair, the awful
smile of an old man who no longer understands. It is 1932, three years
after the stock market crash, the factories are closed, ten million unemployed are questioning the American dream, worthless farm produce
that hungry people can no longer afford rots on farms — sacks of wheat
with the sacks worth more than what they hold, hogs and cattle worth
less than their ticket to the slaughterhouse. Above the article about my
grandfather the headline reads, "Losses twenty-two million; still smiling."

Before 1929 people had thought of Grandfather as a business genius; afterward, when no one was a business genius, they talked about the fantastic luck that had allowed him to become so rich so fast. In the days of the five-cent Hershey bar and the six-hundred-dollar automobile, a million dollars represented true wealth. He did have genius, but what good is genius without luck? And part of genius is knowing how to sit astride and ride one's luck when it is running well, loose, and wild. Truly, what was more stunning than the good luck that made him rich in forty years was the bad luck that took so much of it away in less than a thousand days.

Genius or not, even a genius is not always right. Some of his last advice to my father (who tried to take it) almost ruined his life. National Biscuit was worth around eighty dollars a share. "Hang on to National Biscuit until it goes to a hundred," Grandfather said. And my father, buying on margin, took all his money and all that he could borrow, and finally at the end all that he could steal from his sisters and his children, and bought National Biscuit. One of the vivid memories of my high school years is built around the ringing of the telephone at about six each morning just after the New York stock exchange opened. My father's broker. The stock had dropped again, and he needed another thousand dollars to preserve the equity. Between the first telephone call and the last, National Biscuit went from eighty to something around thirty-three, and my father to all intents and purposes was wiped out.

Breakfast was not a pleasant time.

Grandfather was also less than prophetic concerning the future of radio, or if he was aware of radio's potential he scorned it for the products that it sold. He believed in real things, things you could see or feel — bags of flour, boxes of cookies, sacks of fish meal, sawed lengths of fir or cedar. How could you hold your head up after selling something as invisible as time, minutes of sound loaded with lying promises? It was not only as dishonest as prostitution but it was also a cheap trick that would enchant the public for a while and then fade away. In one of his dealings that had gone bad he had found himself, almost without knowing it, owner of a small radio station. He had no interest in this toy and gave it to my father as a present, as in earlier years he had bought him racing cars. My father loved gadgets, tricky things that performed in unexpected ways. One of the great pleasures of his later years was a necktie he had ordered through the mail that had painted on it in fluorescent paint, "Kiss me in the dark, baby." It was supposed to glow in the dark but didn't, though he never believed us as we sat at the table with the lights off peering toward the dark shape at the head of the table.

For a few years the radio station delighted him. He moved the main studio into the lobby of the building where he had his offices, and put in a big, double-paned, soundproof window so that people waiting for the elevator could share in the excitement of this fantastic invention that sent out into the world the great music of the day — Guy Lombardo, Ted Lewis, Al Jolson, Russ Columbo, and Bing Crosby, a friend of my father's from public school days in Spokane. A tall skinny kid looking for his first job in radio presented himself to my father and was hired. He was the principal announcer and newscaster, rushing out into the afternoon streets just before broadcasting the news to find it in the headlines of the *Seattle Times*. I watched him a few times and thought that he was enjoying himself too much to be taken seriously, for it hadn't occurred to me then that one might love one's work. A few times, feeling very smart, though now I can't imagine why, I would call him up, identify myself, and have certain music dedicated to certain friends, feeling a little jolt of pleasure when my name was mentioned and knowing that it was echoing for that instant in thousands of houses.

Forty years later, when my father in his seventies had become shamelessly eccentric and spent a couple afternoons a week writing scurrilous letters to eminent people, accusing them of everything from atheistic godless communism to sodomy, he remembered his first radio announcer who had become transfigured with time into Chet Huntley, a liberal and highly respected commentator. "If I had known back then what I know now," my father had written him, "that you would turn into a do-gooding, communist, ass-kissing sob sister, I would have put you into a sack and drowned you like a sick pup. Good night, Chet." This was the typically high-spirited treatment that anyone in public life who was not slightly to the right of a John Bircher might receive. It did not quite measure up to my father's letter to Robert Kennedy after he had read a gossip columnist's report that Mr. Kennedy, while vacationing in Acapulco, was seen on the beach in pink swimming trunks. It was this letter, I believe, that inspired the FBI one day to surround the house, call my father out, and interview him, hands on pistols ready to draw. It was a long letter that began, "Dear Bobby: I think it's just too precious for words of you to wear those yummy pink swimming trunks. You must have looked just darling, and I'll bet all the men on the beach just went crazy."

Grandfather spent the last fifteen years of his life trying to teach my father how to replace him when the time came. Little by little he transferred his authority, or, since he was always there, pretended to. His affairs were so complicated, and he had delegated so little real power to his other employees that in the last of the flush years, when the two of them had to attend a meeting or sign papers in another city, they would travel on different trains so that an accident would not kill them both and leave affairs in impossible disarray. Carrying out this plan made him feel richer than he was. He had read, or Mr. Forbes had told him, that royalty and the Rockefellers traveled thus, and playing with fate in this way may have fed his subconscious desire for immortality, his never expressed but deeply felt suspicion that his money and the power of his money would live after him. He was like a ship's captain teaching a first mate secret and special tricks for navigating in the oceans of the world. But how do you prepare someone to bring a ship safe to port when torpedoes go off amidships, a typhoon strips off the superstructure, fires break out in the engine room, and the sailors mutiny — all at the same time? Of course, it wasn't only my father's ship that was sunk beneath him during those awful years when good times were just around the corner.

Grandfather died in 1932. A little over a year later my father, being cared for by the same doctor who had cared for the dying Thomas Wolfe when he was in Seattle, was signed in for bed rest and sedation in a private sanitarium. The year it took to put him there must have been, of the many bad years, the worst of his life. He judged himself by a single criterion: it was his net worth that gave value to his life and made him worthy of respect. And so, finally, when he was not worth much of anything but the new house he had built and fifty thousand dollars of paid-up life insurance premiums, he thought of himself as a worthless failure and was frequently tempted to put a bullet through his head for the satisfaction of collecting his insurance and being rich again.

He had caught that fatal disease that can only spread by handling large amounts of money, and that once caught, destroys happiness forever. For this is the curse of wealth — that having it is no guarantee of happiness, and that losing it, one mourns forever. The loss of what one once had produces a sadness that is never alleviated by feelings of gratitude for what one still has — the children, the secret bank account, the years that lie ahead for becoming rich again. The scar of having lost everything, the empty feeling that one scarcely exists, becomes, with time, a permanent insecurity, a vulnerability, a castration. There is scarcely a day for the rest of one's life when one cannot be suddenly brought low by having to face the knowledge of one's nakedness before malignant possibilities.

It was powerful enough in my father's case to make him, in his later years when he was rich again, half long for death where he could no longer be threatened or his wealth diminished. He never felt safe again after the great Crash, and in the fifteen years before his death he began, with increasing dedication, to collect silver dollars — never very many, but more than he could lift. He had them hidden in a secret room which one entered by a ladder after removing the floor of a small closet just behind the armchair where he watched television. He sat there for years growing old, and I was one of the few who knew that, far more than watching television, he was guarding those boxes of dollars hidden in the earth below him, like some Germanic troll out of Wagner's *Siegfried*.

In the years immediately after Grandfather's death — those years my father had probably been waiting for so that he could prove deserving of the power that had been left him — he lost almost everything. He lived under intolerable pressure and he reacted to his bad luck with an amazing lack of grace. He became the principal actor in a melodrama that encompassed the world. He shook, shrieked, sulked, wept, and raged; his need to be comforted was insatiable, but from those who might have been expected to give him solace or understanding he was little by little isolated by his passionate self-pity and his need to drag us all into the maelstrom of his defeat. In a way, I suppose, we *were* to blame. Just the sight of my face, perhaps vacant or smiling, perhaps intent on the funny papers, could, since it was obvious that I shared nothing of his despair, start him boiling with sarcasms, wild fingers clawing at his eyes like an amateur Oedipus. In the end it wasn't only his money and the money he was pledged to administer and protect for his sisters that he lost, but their belief in him, our belief in him. Within six months his mother and father died, his sisters and his children began avoiding him, and he quarreled with his only close friend over a few dollars, a quarrel that wasn't patched up for thirty years. At the end of that phase of his life, when he lay for months locked in a darkened room, he was absolutely alone. A man who desperately needed sympathy, he received none at all.

The single act that drove him over the edge into madness was his wife's repudiation of him. She, who more than any of us had been the victim of his obliterating self-absorption, by her closeness to his irrationalities had become almost equally insane. Driving into town with her one morning, my father had for the hundredth time ritualistically threatened to kill himself. My stepmother, her voice trembling with exasperation, suggested that he put up or shut up. "Do it, sweetheart," she cried. "Do it and stop talking about it all the time." I think that no one can live for any length of time with a woman as small-minded and unimaginative as my stepmother without being tempted at frequent intervals to swing a fist into her confused and stubborn face, but I believe that this was the only time that he ever gave in to the impulse. It was an immediate response, lightning quick, a hard, despairing blow, a wide untargeted strike from the driver's seat. Three or four days later he came home in the evening to find half the furniture in the house hauled away, and the following day he read in the paper that he was being sued for divorce and half his money, which in her stupidity or her rapaciousness or her fury she estimated at approximately three million dollars. If he didn't have that much, nor had he ever had anything like that much, it was, I guess, the value she put on her assaulted dignity.

I suspect that it was not so much love for this second woman as the terror of losing the little half of what was left of his money that made him fight so hard to get her back, that even made it easy for him, when everything else had failed, to go insane for a while. Perhaps pity for his madness would bring her back. In one sense going nuts was no more than a strategic device, but playing at madness can be as dangerous as swimming in whirlpools, and one can't always get out when the water turns icy. He needn't have lost the dignity of his saneness with such shameless abandon, for his wife, once she had freed herself from the constant uproar of marriage to him, once she was divorced and discovered my father's true and pathetic net worth, found in that simple peace of separation that she was bored. She had lost what she realized now had become her true life's work — revenge against this man who had turned her life into a twisted form of pain. Within two years she agreed to marry him again, for certain monetary considerations, and she spent the remaining thirty-five years of her life driving him as permanently batty as he had permanently driven her. It was a marriage then, this new one, of true and constant dedication, one to the other, a marriage of pure and mutual loathing. No one who knew them would deny that in their concentration on each other, which was like the unsleeping vigilance of two sharpshooters waiting for a bit of flesh to glisten in the underbrush, there was at times a certain sad and disgusting beauty.

And so finally they were married again, though for years I didn't know this or even that they had been divorced. My father, freed from some of his demons, appeared once more in the business world. He went back to managing what was left of Grandfather's investment company, but he did it timidly and without confidence in his own judgment, walking through life now in a kind of terror, like a man without defenses moving through strange territory that he realizes is hostile. His doctor suggested that he was still not strong enough to confront a depressed world that seemed intent on self-destruction.

2

RATHER LATER THAN SOONER THEN, we have come almost to-Munich and the beer hall there and the end of a little story that with more skill I could have made move faster.

One day early in 1934, my father runs into Stanley Dollar, or goes to his office in San Francisco to talk about the shipment of flour to Japan and China, or receives Mr. Dollar in his own office in Seattle. The Dollar line, the President line, the American Mail line — I never knew its real name, if it had one, that fleet of circumnavigating steamships. But Mr. Dollar was the guiding power, though his company like so many others around him was swirling down and away into bankruptcy, and just barely sustained in those years by a mail contract with the United States government.

Now a semi-invented but essentially truthful conversation that will make everything clear:

"It's sad and terrible about the old gentleman," Mr. Dollar says. "He had a good full life, but in the world of business he was irreplaceable."

"Ah, yes, the governor. We're lost without him. But I console myself that he passed away without having to see all his life's work turning to dust. He was spared a lot of that."

"But you still have the mills, and people will always need bread. Unfortunately, for what I'm selling there's not much demand these days."

"Yes," my father says, "the country's gone to hell, we're falling into communism. There's no more niceties. That fucking Harry Bridges, that goddamn Roosevelt, how I detest those radical sons of bitches." There is a little silence while my father gets control of himself. "Listen, Stanley," he says finally, "what you should do is advertise. I've got me a fine radio station that covers the whole Seattle area: Tacoma, Bellingham. Let me sell you some time. We'll work you up a live-wire presentation, a real nice campaign, and I'll guarantee you results."

"We've got no money for that, Charlie," Mr. Dollar says, and he studies my father for a moment. "Now, listen, my boy, and I'm going to talk to you like a father — what *you* should do is hop on one of our ships and take a little trip around the world. Forget everything for a while, recover your perspective. Did you know that you can travel these days for less than it costs to stay at home?"

"No money, no money, cleaned out," my father says. "I'll tell you the truth, Stanley, I'm just about broke, hardly know where the next meal's coming from." My father's eyes swell and film over; his voice has begun to tremble, dissolve.

"Charlie, I've heard you're thinking of putting yourself out to pasture for a while. And now it strikes me that perhaps we can do business. Like the Injuns, Charlie, a barter — six oyster shells for a strip of deer hide, a totem pole for a bearskin and a pile of smoked salmon bellies."

"Keep talking, Stanley," my father says. "You've got the floor and I'm listening."

Is it all clear now, shipmates?

While Chet Huntley, or a reasonable facsimile, begins selling luxury trips around the world on radio station KPCB, my father, his newly again married bride, and his two utterly charming teenage children (going through at the time a snotty, snobby, asshole phase) take off for Yokohama and all points west with four free tickets and seats at the captain's table. This whole nine-month episode, more grim than great for the awful closeness into which we were forced, takes on the overtones of surrealism. There wasn't an ocean liner in the world large enough to isolate my only half-cured father from the constant sight of his detestable children, and to complicate things we were not halfway across the Pacific, with the Aleutian Islands shining in the sun like ice cream cones, before my father got it into his head that my stepmother, that poor sexless creature who loved only Jesus, was committing hanky-pankies with ship's officers, unmarried passengers, and the aging homosexual who came to her cabin each morning to make up the bunk. Of course, the oddest thing of all was the trip itself. Though we were treated as very special people for the boatloads of flour that had been shipped to the Orient, we were in truth almost as poor as the fifty-year-old Chinese messboy who served us.

Which reminds me: for that whole trip, Seattle to New York, through all the mysterious cities of the East, through India, Colombo, Egypt, across brass-colored seas boiling in the sun, at every meal, the one at noon and the one at seven, I ordered a curried something — a curried lamb, a curried chicken, a curried fish. I won't call this a digression because it may have been one of the factors in my father's angers. Waiting for me to order the same thing twice a day must have made his teeth grind, must have made him want to start snorting with disgust. But my God, those curried plates were good, and the little bowls of peanuts, shredded coconut, chutney, chunks of pineapple that came with them. The memories of that trip we took more than fifty years ago have for the most part faded into the perfume of those Indian dishes, the hot richness of food that got streams of sweat rolling down my face. But made my soul smile.

Now we come to the part of the trip that my father hated, for money would have to be spent. We left the ship and the free meals, and like princes turned into pumpkins, tourist class and hungry, boarded a train out of Mussolini's Rome and headed north across the Alps to Hitler's Germany, to Grandfather's Tondern in Denmark.

The first night in Munich, we went to Munich's prime attraction, a five- or six-story block-square building known then as the world's largest beer hall. Each floor of that building, from the outside as plain and practical as a department store, was, if I am remembering truly, divided into three or four large rooms. Each room had been got up with simple-minded music hall fakery to represent its international intentions and to charm with hints of distant places the working-class Germans who had been too poor for years to travel except in short leather pants and hiking boots, salami butts stuffed into back pockets. Here is one room: a German beer garden set in an Italian August (rows of tables below latticework arbors of plastic clustered grapes as large as oranges, as purple as wounded flesh; hanging piles of empty Chianti bottles; waiters who sing the old O Sole Mios that make one hate memories of childhood. Another: a German beer parlor in Japan (paper parasols; woodcuts of Kabukis, Fuji, browsing deer; waitresses in geisha outfits, grossly healthy German frauleins dressed as dolls). No more; my imagination has broken down.

Except for the room my father has selected — a German beer hall in

Germany. It was the largest and the plainest of them all, a very large, high-ceilinged place filled with long tables and benches. On the walls that ran the length of the building were hung hundreds of battle flags, flags in all colors, artistically tattered, dramatically aged with Clorox (or something) to ape ancient campaigns, to capture past time itself. It was as phony as a grade C movie starring the producer's alcoholic and over-weight mistress, blinded by true love to her defects and determined to finish the picture without money if necessary. The flags drooped there like great dead rags in the still, dead air, but with all the merciless heart-break of old triumphs and defeats that could only make sense to German blood. The room was full. We searched for a table and finally joined a dozen young men dressed poorly in dark students' suits or leather jackets or as falsely got up as the battle flags: Nazi warriors with black boots, black belts, and blood red stabs of color at neck and shoulders. Some of the men sat with their arms around the waists of incredibly handsome women with hair like gold and cheeks flaming from the bitter outside cold — the snow-cold streets and the flow of moving air from the dark fir forests and the Bavarian ski slopes.

We ordered beer, all except my stepmother, who thought drinking was sinful and knew that if God had wanted us to drink beer He would have mentioned it in the Bible, though even there you could be fooled, for hadn't some evil heretic slipped in the word *wine* where the original Hebrew had been, as all her congregation knew, *grape juice*. She isolated herself from us with her distaste and, scowling, observed German con-duct which she probably hoped would prove to be licentious.

The beer came in large ceramic tankards, brought by fast-moving waiters as adept as acrobats. The foam beneath the hinged metal tops on the tankards was thick and yellow, and the beer as we wallowed into it with our noses through the suds was as rich and nourishing as meat and potatoes. The three of us, perhaps because the beer was so good, drank in the hum and hubbub of this hall of flags and warriors, impressed with the military correctness and reserve of the men and the formal joy they took in this simple tribal gathering, as though they sought warmth or consolation from the harshness of a German winter or the harshness of a German past.

But it wasn't the past that brought them together now, but the future.

Suddenly, like a switch being thrown — and one is not so much blinded by the glaring light as by what the light reveals — they began to sing, first one table, then another, then the whole flag-draped hall: words that I didn't understand but that plainly spoke of manly virtues — courage, sacrifice, blood, and brotherhood. It was the quick joining together that gave a brutal grandeur to whatever they were saying, its strength in the passion of the crowd's single emotion. I began just tentatively to feel uneasy, as though we had stumbled upon a private German ritual involving shameful truths and whose object was to reveal new and violent facets of man, new and violent solutions for a tottering and corrupt Europe. If this martial music suggested danger, it was also in its power beautiful, as beautiful as the young men and women who at this moment were allowing me to share their passion. I could feel myself, against convictions that I thought I strongly held, being gathered up and absorbed into this masculine world. I knew that fascism was a sickness, a madness of mobs, but when it was turned into spectacle — bright sound, crowd rhythms and responses, the vigor of young bodies — it enchanted the senses like the swell of lust that one feels for the beauty of a woman who is obviously a whore and possibly carries death in her embrace.

The singing grew stronger, more disciplined, more together; it filled the room. Tankards, their metal tops snapped shut, pounded on the tables, boots pounded on the floor, the flags on their standards trembled, and the faces of the men became sternly joyous, abstracted, fulfilled. But in the sameness of their expressions, which held an incipient brutality, less interesting, like an endless row of stamped-out and identical lead soldiers; it was the faces of the German women which now inspired and reflected a half-secret truth — not the intentions of their men to redeem past humiliations, to make a German world, to march again — but their own fanatic desire to revel in the chaos and suffering that lay ahead.

I had seen that same look on the faces of my handsome aunts, all of them determined to move the family out of the decent merchants' class that my grandfather had climbed to and into an American aristocracy based on money and cultural sophistication — money to be spent on the education of their children in exclusive schools; on books, music, original and daring art; on the development of sensibility and discrimination.

My aunts had the faces of the young women who in those years were marching in the streets for the right to vote and who, out of political convictions, had begun to smoke in the semi-public ambience of restaurants. They were dedicated to the ideal of creating a freer world.

And so, since I loved my aunts, and shared in the face of my father's disgust their belief in art and in its power to replace a God that I no longer believed in (and that I suspect they didn't either), I found a justification in the faces of these German women pounding their beer mugs in Nazi rhythms, for they had the same kind of dedicated beauty that had moved me in Seattle. They too had been transfigured by a cause larger than themselves.

For about five minutes, with my feet tapping to the music that was overwhelming my better judgment, I stood at the gateway to this Nazi hell, pulled toward it by my pounding blood and the body's longing for communion with these oceanic emotions that give form and meaning to existence. For the five minutes that I became a Nazi, I did it to the glory of its virile power, accepting everything I knew about it; knowing that the shop windows of Jews in Berlin were being smashed by surly mobs of brown-shirted louts and their owners clubbed down in the streets; knowing that artists and scientists were fleeing the country; that organized chaos was being planned; that a nasty Hitler with a magic voice and a corrupt band of neurotic followers was seducing a whole nation into a bacchanal. We had known it for years; Hitler himself told us what was coming, and so we had known it without believing, and now we were beginning to believe in some of the changes that he had promised to bring. But just as we recognize some possibility of goodness beneath the filthiness of unbroken house dogs or the cruelty of boys who stone sparrows and rip the wings from insects, so for that short time I judged Nazi barbarism as a simple adolescent phase, a petty reaction to the international humiliation of the first war's defeat. With time the brutality would shrivel away, leaving something strong and noble.

It was my father, all unknowing, who saved me. Now, in the beginnings of my joy, I glanced across the table to where he sat and saw him stripped of his disguises, saw him as I guess he saw himself (as I was beginning to see myself), responding to the call of that still-German blood pounding in the veins. Tears stood in his eyes, his cheeks were flushed, and on his face, made placid as a cow's in his surrender, was that terrible look of one overwhelmed by a new possibility: that without thought but responding simply to the most primitive emotional impulses, one could live a better, a happier life, as free of inner doubts, questionings, or the agonizing stabbings of conscience as any natural animal. It was the look of the true believer, the newly born-again fundamentalist Christian who has received and accepted the Christian message, "Don't think, don't think; only believe." He had never been far from his truth, that it is only the unexamined life that is worth living. But now for the first time, perhaps, he saw the consequences and its rewards.

He had successfully resisted the patient and unending efforts of his sisters to polish his manners and turn him into a social creature at ease in the bourgeois world of money and fashion. In fact, like Grandfather, he detested the men who sat in drawing rooms or symphonic halls or on the boards of museums as little more than sexual neuters, and so now when I saw with what ease and rapidity he had surrendered to the promise of grandeur implied by the women in the beer hall, I realized that though their faces glowed as brightly as my aunts' in the fervor of their dedication to gracious living, there was really no connection between the two groups of women except as I had united them in imagination. All my life my father had been so wrong about so many things that I was inclined to find virtues in the things he hated, and to find proofs of his flawed judgment in the much smaller list of the things he liked. So now, automatically, I separated myself from my feelings, thinking, "My God, just look at him; if he loves this music and the pounding of boots and the intense and dedicated fanaticism of these big-boned women, then there must be something very wrong here. Why is he so moved?" Looking into myself I saw that it was the lure of criminality and the repudiation of democracy and the simple animal beauty of mob power; and as soon as the spectacle was opened up to critical examination and to the realization that the emotions it produced were morbid and fraudulent, the whole thing turned into a kind of repellent theater.

If I have dragged out for an uncommonly long spell the two or three beers we drank that evening, and the fierce, banal drama of the sieg heils and the blood-red flags, I've done so out of the emotion of the times, and for the miracle of having been able to accept and so quickly reject the fascist poison. It is one of the clearest memories of my life. Much later it occurred to me that in a way that little hour had put a period to my childhood, and from that time on I began to feel that I must become the principal character in my own life.

And it was certainly from that moment, facing German passion, that it became apparent we were rushing toward another war.

Ignoring chronology, straining to connect my two themes, war and father, brought me to write about the middle 1930s and the collapse of Grandfather's dynasty. But it was not only the loss of a great fortune that paralyzed and destroyed my father; he was as destroyed making it as he was losing it. That evening in a Munich beer hall when family and history were symbolically united made a powerful impression, but one that fades to smoke when compared with some earlier family dramas. So before jumping ahead again to 1945, I must go back to the crazy boom years of the middle 1920s, an era almost truly defined in the mention of the bootleggers, the first big touring cars and the paving of American highways, the gin parties, the silly irrelevance of songs like "Yes, we have no bananas" and "Barney Google with his goo goo googly eyes."

3

I T WASN'T TRUE, of course, but one remembers the 1920s as a time of euphoria when everyone wanted to dance, everyone wanted to make whoopee, when everyone who wasn't yet rich was going to be. In my adolescent world, at any rate, I didn't know anyone but Grandmother's servants who were not rich. Even the bootleggers who delivered cases of bathtub gin and Canadian whiskey to my father's house or to my grandfather's kitchen door drove the immense and speedy Stutzes or Packards that my father favored. Now women had begun to dominate large areas of the social scene, or was it simply that, moving into the years of sexual torment, it seemed so to me? I was sexually moved to a kind of hysteria by the liberated middle-aged ladies of twenty-five or so who smoked in restaurants, crossed their legs and showed their stockings rolled at the knees, and blatantly painted their scarlet Clara Bow lips in little baby pouts. I took Grandfather's side when he roared that his daughters would not smoke in his presence or in his house, and was even tempted to tell on them when they wandered out of the house to the Ford coupes that they had bought and hidden halfway up the block, because not only did Grandfather not want to see women with cigarettes hanging out of their mouths, he didn't want to see them sitting behind the wheels of cars either.

My father was captive to his times, and if he wasn't quite rich yet in 1926, he must have felt like it — or believed it was simply a matter of time, of months, before he would be. Now, newly married to his second wife, he hired a young architect to invent the house and gardens that would interpret him and refute the sisters who scorned his lowbrow tastes. Some years before, he had bought ten acres of land just outside the city, half of it zoned for housing, half for farming. He began to spend weekends walking through the brush with Mr. Shay, the architect. My father had never liked the English for their cool foppish voices, their limp elegance, but Mr. Shay must have had a passion for them, or at least for the grandeur of their country houses and the intimate and informal nature of their best gardens. He came to my father, finally, with the complete plans that would turn him into an instant aristocrat — the long, brick, slate-roofed manor house with centuries of tradition hinted at in the leaded windows, the exposed oak beams of the high two-storied baronial hall with the dimensions of a basketball court, the basement barroom fitted with chains set into the walls, skulls lit up from inside, all the usual barroom crap including an unplanned dampness and the stink of mildew.

Outside, it was all swimming pools, rose gardens, rock gardens, hothouses, dog kennels, tennis and badminton courts, acres of lawn, acres of forest primeval. To anchor this first low-grade Disney World in reality, the architect designed a family crest and named the whole production "Wildcliffe." (My sister and I, when it was time to goad Father from boarding school or camp, would ask him in letters how things were going in Ye Wildee Cliffe.) Everyone, I think — the architect, my father's sisters, his mother — cautiously went into the choreography of appropriate steps that a great landowner might take in this dance with privilege: in the evenings to stroll through the gardens (popping, I suggested, the blooms from their stems with a riding crop, like a screen villain), on cool Sundays to pot rare African violets in the hothouse or laze in the grape arbor contemplating God's generosity, the ever-upward-tending price of stocks, or the sensitivity that comes with wealth.

It was all of it the stuff of dreams, the vulgar backdrop for the years of unhappy melodrama that followed. It was the last of the boom years' big houses — or at least for the next forty years, when once again new money but the same bad taste would build for a million dollars what my father had built for a hundred thousand — a house so big that there was never any question of being able to sell it. At his death it went to a spastic society to be used as a rest home or a hospital.

When everything was built and set in motion (even a sundial that only counted the happy hours), when all the cooks, maids, and gardeners boiled, dusted, clipped, my father was still not absolutely happy with his role. He kept going. He tried to set his personal stamp on things by setting out three-foot-high plaster of paris dwarfs in the rhododendrons, brilliantly painted Snoopys, Droopys, Poopeys, etc. He ordered a dozen enormous ceramic urns from his toilet factory, he built doll houses in the woods, and inside he hung the walls with paintings of Jack Dempsey and noble collies done on black velvet, and in the upstairs hallway original oil paintings by commercial artists of pretty calendar girls which had been commissioned by the lithograph company that printed the Snow Flake cracker boxes for the biscuit factories.

When he had done what he could he found that it was still just a little too genteel. It was nice, he liked it, but it was someone else's dream. He began to stand at the edge of the hill, where everything behind him had been tamed and landscaped, and stare down the slope of Ye Wildee Cliffee toward the untouched farmland, and he began to dream his own dream finally, the dream of a peasant with ten thousand years of Danish farming in his blood. Now, in his free time, he changed into farm clothes and rushed down into the muck of the bottom land, into this patch of immensely rich but water-saturated soil. And, authentic at last, he began to create a five-acre domain that would, until he died, exist at the very center of his passions. He built a barn with dovecotes under the roof for pigeons, with stalls for a cow, a horse, a pen for a pig, a pen for a goat. Later, he built a row of four long chicken houses which he filled with twenty thousand white leghorns. On the farmland he experimented with mint, oats, hay, and finally blueberries, a crop that lost him several thousand dollars a year for the rest of his life, but a loss that could be manipulated to soften the blow of income taxes. He began blindly, instinctively, because the farm animals were only the fairy tale stage, and he had to go through the children's book of his fantasies before he could get serious.

The billy goat stage was short and mean. Father bends over one day like a character in the funny papers and makes a billy goat target of his ass. Billy goat charges and butts my father head first into a steaming pile of cow dung. Father takes an axe handle and breaks off one of billy goat's horns. And he was with us for another year or so, a hateful, terrorized, stinking creature with the devil's own whiskers who pissed into his own mouth and then made terrible grimaces of ecstasy with rubbery goat lips. His eyes were yellow, absolutely cold, absolutely mad; he lived on for one thing, I think: he wanted another chance at my father's ass.

My father's affair with the pigeons was not a love story either. After a time, when he had hundreds of birds prettily cooing beneath the roof and the flashing of iridescent wings circling the area, a veterinarian, ex-plaining the high mortality among the chickens, pointed out that the pigeons in their travels were bringing home all the local diseases. For months we listened to the crack of father's shotgun and hated him for the destruction, the sad fluttering down, the broken wings, the starving orphaned squabs.

It was Grandmother who helped him with gifts that tried to dignify his intentions. She bought a horse — no, not a horse, a polo pony — to live in the horse stall. She bought fruit trees and the cuttings of rasp-berries and exotic Luther Burbank hybrids. And one day she came to lunch and gave my father an expensive purebred collie bitch — the first of the aristocratic dogs that would make up the Missy dynasty: Missy number one.

It is difficult for me to date precisely the rise and decline of my fa-ther's new country life. He probably moved into that enormous brick pile sometime in 1927, which in a way was like moving into the castle shortly before it was dynamited: so many things happened in the very short time between the glory of the flush years and the market crash. Who in 1928 could have imagined that within four years my father would be renting this house to a Texas millionaire while he lived alone in a two-room apartment? I remember a night in the house, with every-thing still squeaky new, when a Mr. Frederick Beers and his young daughter came to dinner. He was the president of the National Biscuit Company from New York, and I was terrorized into my best behavior, realizing out of secret hints that millions of dollars were involved and that if I farted at the table or knocked over my glass of water or got fresh with the plump little girl in the pongee dress from De Pinna's (like the ones my sister wore and hated) I could expect to be beaten to death.

It was 1928 and then it was 1929 and we were really rich and then the market crashed, the sky darkened with storm clouds, and Grandfather and Father were both gutshot but didn't yet know it. And scarcely knew it a year later. Now the four long chicken houses were full of chickens and my father had hired an old friend, a stockbroker, to take care of the chickens and crate the eggs because then, in 1931, it was hard to find a job. My father began yelling that he couldn't take the pressure and wanted to kill himself, and every night it seemed we had creamed chicken, carrots, and mashed potatoes for dinner. That was the year he was made a director of the Seattle First National Bank, the year he bought a black Cord sedan, beautiful but menacing with its sleek George Raft mafioso lines. Chicken every night because he wanted to save on the grocery bill, a gangster sedan because he wanted to put up a good front.

Every so often, when the chickens molted, grew lazy, and lost interest in laying eggs, my father sold them as fryers and replaced them one house at a time with day-old chicks from a hatchery. One Sunday afternoon, a month after new chickens had been delivered to the nearest of the hen houses, someone — my father or his employee — failed to close the door tightly, and Missy with her long nose pushed it open and found herself in Paradise. I don't know how long it took but she was efficient and sometime later when my father went into the hen house to admire his babies he found that they had all been killed — five thousand dead chickens scattered through the litter, proud Missy wagging her tail to greet him.

Terrible screaming, bad words that in those days people didn't use, terrible howling of a terrified dog floated up to us from the bottom land. I had never heard my father yell quite so loudly; I raced down the hall and burst into my stepmother's bedroom. "What's wrong? What's happening?" I yelled. My stepmother stood in an open window staring down toward the screams and curses and the wailing dog. Her face was wild and she did not speak, although her lips were moving as though she were praying. The hen house was hidden by trees but after a time my father appeared, walking backward and dragging the dog by her hind feet. When she tried to nip or lick his hands he clubbed her flat. Near a barbed wired fence he took a short loose roll of wire and twisted one end of it around the dog's head; then he wrapped her body to the fence so that she stood upright but immobilized. He disappeared but returned immediately with the bodies of a dozen dead chickens, and he strung these around the dog's neck, a necklace of dead birds, all the time yelling and kicking at the howling dog. "What's happened is Missy's killed some chickens," I said. "So why doesn't he just kill Missy?" I started to cry. My stepmother was saying something, the same words over and over, and I can't remember now if she said "the old sea bastard" or "the old sea slug," only that she sounded out of her head but that her words, like church ritual, were insanely appropriate.

My father went to the barn finally; the dog, fastened to the fence as though she had been nailed there, did not move or cry until my father appeared with the shotgun, and the dog, covered with mud, feathers, blood, and her own shit, began to howl. And my father, wanting to kill her slowly, I suppose, steadily cursing, stood ten yards or so away and fired three times into the shuddering carcass.

The pigeons exploded out of their nests in the barn's roof and circled in a small panic below a darkening sky around the dead dog. My father stood there without moving for a very long time.

Within a year the hen houses were all empty; eggs in the market sold for less than it cost to produce them; the manager of the business quarreled with my father and disappeared out of our lives to join the growing lines of the unemployed. The wind tore pieces of tar paper from the hen house roofs, someone (guess who) threw rocks through the windows, the sliding doors slipped from their runners, a band of skunks took possession of the space below the floor, marsh weeds — nettles and wild grass, fireweed and dwarf willow — grew up in the space between the houses. Within a year my stepmother, one eye blackened, fled the house and sued for divorce. My grandparents died one after the other, the family businesses faltered and staggered on the brink. My father had a breakdown and disappeared into a sanitarium, and his country manor was rented out at a thousand dollars a month. If all this fractured, transposed, and hysterical family history is confusing, don't worry about it; I'm confused myself. These blows against my father's resilience that happened sixty years ago in those years between the wars, happening very fast and in a senseless order, have, in a large degree, lost their reality. For me, as it happened, it was drama; I had little capacity to share his suffering. In those years too, being young, I scarcely existed even in my own mind as much more than a rather unimportant extension of my father, a little something that belonged to him — a musical instrument, for example, upon which he might choose to blow out a few notes from time to time.

And I wasn't alone in seeing myself in this way. In his mind too, I was his — something belonging to him like his wife, his beer stock, his swimming pool.

He came back from the sanitarium, remarried his wife, and tried to reconstruct his life. It was too soon, and he met Mr. Dollar and we postponed his destiny for a year and went around the world. We had been back in Seattle for little more than six months, father back in harness and trying to manage family affairs, when he blew it all again. It turned out that it wasn't only his children and his wife that he felt he owned, but his sisters as well. At any rate he regarded his sisters' interests as being of less importance than his own, believing he had the right to use their money to save himself. He must have been desperate to the point of irrationality because he was almost immediately caught out. Terrible whispered threats within the family, threats involving criminal behavior. Father turned into an eight-year-old boy. He had to sell the last of his National Biscuit stock and turn over his share of Grandfather's inheritance to re-pay the loan his sisters had made to him without their knowledge.

At that time the flour mill in Portland was losing money and father went down to reorganize the mill. While he was gone my aunts called a special board of directors' meeting, and a few days later he received a short note informing him that, because of his health, it had been decided to replace him. One of my cousins would be taking over, they appreci-ated all that he had done to try to keep the investment company solvent, the times were very difficult, a few years of rest. . . .

I rush over this part of my father's life because I know so little about it. A short time before he had thrown all my clothes out of my bathroom window (again), and had forbidden me the house. I almost never saw him for he had forced me into the revolting situation of having to go to work, and I lived and worked in another city. (I loaded boxcars with sacks of flour in the Tacoma mill for four-forty a day. The day after my father was fired, I was too.)

Fired, my father hid in his country house and brooded. Fired, I went mountain climbing for four months, read Mann's *Magic Mountain* while camped by hidden Cascade lakes, and then, my life changed, went back to the university, to Columbia. I had decided to become a famous short story writer, and I arrived in the city the day that Hitler's panzers moved into Poland.

This final family scandal, leaving wounds that never healed, was some-thing that so depressed my father he could scarcely discuss it. When he did I found that I disbelieved him, for in his version he was generous and noble and his sisters were suspicious, greedy, with claws like scalpels. I found the truth in my aunts' silence: they felt no need to defend themselves, and wished only to put behind them an episode which could have grown into a public scandal. His disgrace, his fall, was so mysterious that it may have been more than two years later when, without thinking, one of my aunts mentioned in a casual way that not only had my father robbed his sisters but he had robbed his children, too.

"You mean me?" I cried. "But how much?"

"It's hard to tell," my aunt said. "I think he used your money to buy your clothes and to pay your school tuition. But I would judge that he owes you more than thirty thousand dollars."

"Why that little skunk," I said, beginning to laugh.

"I spoke to him about this," my aunt said. "He promised to pay you back."

"Oh, sure," I said. "Sure, sure, sure."

4

M Y FATHER, who all his life was prejudiced in varying degrees against Catholics, Jews, Baptists, Negroes, Mexicans, Italians, and all people who were short and swarthy, had a full bag of racist jokes. For a year or so when I was eight or nine this had been one of his favorites:

> Old Abraham Levi leans a ladder against his house and tells his son to climb it. His son obeys. "Higher," Abraham calls and his son climbs higher. "Now," Abraham says, standing at the bottom of the ladder and holding out his arms, "jump into Papa's arms." The son jumps, Abraham steps back, and the boy smashes into the cement sidewalk. "But, Papa, why?" the boy asks, bloody and weeping. "Let that be a lesson to you, my boy," Abraham Levi says. "Don't ever trust anybody, not even your own father."

My father would roar with laughter, and I would smile politely, but by the age of eight or nine that story was a lesson, not a joke. I would no more have thought of leaping into his arms from a ladder's bottom rung than from the top ledge of a ten-story building. Still, wary as I was at times, he fooled me, and I would find myself dropping through space and cursing myself for a fool.

In the summer of 1941 my sister, in her own revolt against bourgeois decency, married a San Francisco artist who painted large abstractions in pure bright colors that worked together and by some miracle sometimes turned into living presences which, when hung on a wall, could change the whole mood of a room into a celebration. It was not rewarding during the Depression to practice high art, but my brother-in-law hung on and was saved from starvation when he was offered the directorship of the WPA art program in Oakland. He organized the Oakland artists, a rather politicized bunch who painted clenched fists, red flags, and marching workers. Everyone was passionate about the Spanish Republicans; everyone had a friend in the Lincoln Brigade. My brother-in-law-to-be tried to respond to social injustice and to the increasingly radicalized fury of the intellectuals, but his heart wasn't in it. He talked about Trotsky and the brotherhood of man, he painted murals in the post offices up and down the Sacramento Valley: pastel pigs, farmers with pitchforks organizing, migrant workers bowed down under heavy baskets of grapes or pale tomatoes, but there was no passion in his presentation. He was interested in something else.

He was obsessed with color, perpetually and newly stunned by its power to influence the emotions; the way that two or more colors when put side by side would either fight each other to the death or enhance one another like flawless people in a perfect friendship. There were colors that cured; colors that drove people mad; colors on a battleship that made it almost impossible to hit, or on a tiger, impossible to see; colors on your girl's dress that made you want to turn away with disgust; whore colors; colors for suicides; honeymoon colors, powerful as aphrodisiacs. He claimed that Matisse used color with as much intuitive daring as a race car driver and was the greatest painter of the century, "like a juggler keeping ten balls in the air at the same time." He once told me in a drunken moment that he was my implacable enemy because I had criticized a color in one of his paintings and called it "dirty."

That my sister would marry an artist instead of a steady red-blooded stockbroker or the owner of a Ford agency was one of the two crosses my father packed around for thirty years. He claimed that she had married out of her class to mock him, just as he claimed that I was a liberal Democrat only in order to sadden and shorten his life, to humiliate him to the point he couldn't look his friends in the eye. Bad enough that she had married an artist; worse still, one at the beginning of his career and only moderately successful; worst of all, a Mexican artist who, when my father was raging, was referred to as "the little Mex." He had gained this distinction in my father's mind when he discovered what he always believed was his daughter's most closely guarded secret: that in 1940 her husband had mixed colors and painted in large areas for Diego Rivera when that communist traitor who had insulted great men like John D. Rockefeller had been commissioned to paint a mural for the San Francisco World's Fair.

I had nailed together his other cross and thrown it upon his back when I had announced in my typically arrogant way that I intended to be a writer. "Three generations from shirtsleeves to shirtsleeves," my father said. "Listen to me, neither of you will come to any good."

My father, like a great Republican elephant, never forgot anything that might later be used against someone. He carried grudges that grew more sinister each year. An example: When Coolidge gave his inaugural address in 1925 and it was broadcast, it was the first coast to coast radio transmission in the history of the world, a technical miracle that I wanted desperately to hear. I was a nine-year-old American who wanted to be part of history. But on that day, because my writing was so cramped and illegible (almost as disgraceful as my father's), I had been sent to my room to write out one thousand times "Write with the wrist not with the fingers," all to be done in fat flowing country rube Palmer method script. "Please, I want to hear President Coolidge." "Do as you're told and go to your room." "But this is history, this is important. I want to hear Coolidge." "Enough of your insolence. You get up and go to your room. *Or else.*" "But it's coast to coast, the new president talking from Washington, DC." "I'm going to count to three, young man, and if you're not out of this room —. One — two —." "Oh, go to hell," I screamed and left the room. And sat at the top of the stairs listening through the static and the fading signal to that thrilling moment, a moment our teacher had told us was as important as the first Pony Express.

I was almost fifty years old when I was reminded, as he went down the inevitable unchanging list of my flaws and insolences, that even as a child I had had no respect. And that the day Coolidge gave his inauguration speech, a day he remembered as though it were yesterday, I had told him to go to hell.

For ten or twelve years after my sister wantonly repudiated her middle-class origins by marrying into Bohemia my father never wrote to her without including an example or two of his own art work, for he too had suddenly become an abstract artist. He used the backs of old envelopes or lined notebook paper, penciling the whole space into small squares which he then filled in with colored crayons. In homage to the Dadaists, if he had ever heard of them, each drawing was titled: Spring Morning in the Coal Mine, One Hung Low Strikes Back, Nine Cats on a Ten P.M. Fence. The work was neat, the colors evenly applied, lines clean as Mondrian's — all meant to prove that any goddamn fool could be an artist and engage in this stupid childishness. Maybe for a month or so it was almost even a little bit funny, but twelve years of it, twelve years of the same joke that was meant to wound? Finally, my sister, glancing at another letter with accompanying art work, would groan and without reading it file it away in the wastebasket.

In 1956 it was my turn to be mocked.

He was sixty-six, getting old, and he probably thought that nothing much new was apt to disturb the tranquil flow of what he called his "sunset years," two words that were programmed to fill his eyes with tears. So if he was going to do what he had promised himself for years to do — write down the story of his life — he had better do it while he could, while he still had the wit and slyness to rewrite history, the memory of every single person who had treated him badly. His plans to recreate the past were, though on a more modest scale, as creative as Stalin's. He wanted to clean up his past so that all of us, instead of regarding him as an irrational and menacing figure, would finally understand and love him. What had been the catalyst, what had really triggered his resolve and set him to work, was hearing me say years after the war that the experience of combat had done something to my brain, my creative faculties or my capacity to concentrate.

"For God's sake, the war's been over for ten years. It's time to pull yourself together, stop feeling sorry for yourself, and do what you're trained to do."

"You got mad when I said I wanted to write, you get mad when I say I can't write."

"Do what you're trained to do, that's what I say. When I think of the money we spent giving you an education; thousands of dollars down the drain; and you end up hosing down hog pens in California, up to your ass in debt, not a suit of clothes to your name. My God, not even a *necktie.*"

Every couple of years after the war, as long as they felt up to it, my father and his second wife would leave home when the winter rains began in November and set sail for a couple of months, heading for tropical and sun-dappled ports. And now this year, halfway through such a trip, from Penang or Kobe came a letter and a snapshot. He is sitting on the deck of a ship, naked to the waist in the hot shine of a blazing sun; behind him the ocean burns and sparkles. Barrel-chested, short, heavily muscled arms, greying hair cut close, he is, at sixty-five, in wonderful condition. Slightly overweight, but only slightly gross, he is the personi-fication of what he claims is his philosophy: "I want to live my life so I can look a man in the eye and tell him to go to hell."

And the letter:

> When we hit the hot weather I stripped down for action as the photo shows, took my little Royal out onto the deck and went to work. Hardly stopped for lunch. In eighteen days worked up almost a hundred pages so except for fitting in the photos and writing the captions, my book is done — Memoirs of Yours Truly. All it took was a little determination, a little get up and go, just sat down and stuck with it, and can't see there is any big deal about writing a book. You just decide to do it then you do it, a question of guts I would say. You think of something and put it down and that reminds you of something else and you put that down and so it goes. When you aren't reminded of anything you type out The End. What's so hard about that with all your training, a good typewriter, etc.

A couple of months after his return from wherever he went, he sent me by mail a belated Christmas present, one of three copies of the book. Bound in black Morocco, ninety-eight pages of single-spaced narrative, and as the publishers say, Lavishly Illustrated, it was, until you plunged into the horrors of the text, a not unimpressive achievement. It was only after I had read his work that I realized how much he had to hide — and amazingly, how much of what he should have tried to hide he revealed as a proof of his manly stance toward life. Something to be described in bloody detail. To put it briefly: except for dates and place names his ver-sion of his life had almost nothing in common with the life I am giving him in these pages. His version was blatantly fictitious, based roughly on his youthful readings in *Horatio Alger, Tom Sawyer* and *The Young Execu-tive's Leadership Guide.* The early Huck Finn section deals extensively with the wide gap-toothed irresistible smile, the freckled nose, the frogs in the pocket, and fails to mention the day in his middle teens when he killed the two cats. If this was something he had forgotten why did he leave twenty-five thousand dollars in his will to the first man to invent a contraceptive for cats?

Two months before he died he mentioned things which indicated that he had poisoned his life with other brutal cruelties which he had never been able to forget. He had, however, forgotten about them when writing his memoirs.

This simplistic rendering of the life he wished he had led had quite the opposite effect from what he had hoped to achieve. His grandchildren were not even allowed to know that it existed, and instead of forgiving him, my sister and I, when we would get together, quoted him with outrage, laughing hysterically, pounding the table, almost unable to believe that he could so lamely dismiss or ignore the years of his tyranny. "Listen to this," my sister would scream, rifling through the pages. "He's talking about 1932, 1933. 'I guess I might have been a little hard to get along with in those years.'"

"When he wouldn't say a word at the dinner table for a month at a time, when he tore all the pictures of El Vera's family off the walls after he counted her family pictures and his family pictures and she won, when he threw all my clothes out the window. Yeah, Dad, you might have been just a little hard to get along with."

"Of course, in a sense it's true," my sister said. "He wasn't any harder to get along with in 1933 than any other year you'd care to mention . . . When did Missy die?"

On the other hand, some of the strange things he felt obliged to mention illuminated with a new weird light stretches of time that I had always, if I thought about them at all, felt I understood — pieces out of my life that I was forced now to rebuild with new material. Those years between mothers, between my real one and the false one who replaced her, were one of those times full of gaps; the year we moved back into the house and tried once more to imitate family life with the beautiful but stupid young woman my father married is spotted with strange memories out of which, trying to understand, I invented my own explanation. Before that I had lived for four years with my grandmother — six months in Seattle, six months in Altadena, California; now I was back with my father, glad at first, then less and less so.

We had scarcely settled in when the whole tone of the place became as programmed toward physical fitness as a boxer's training camp. In the mornings, still half asleep, still in pajamas, to a phonograph record — no, to a whole album of phonograph records made by a madman named Walter Kamp who counted off numbers and yelled at us to straighten our spines, to twist and stretch — the four of us, father and his little bride, his son and his daughter, did chin-ups, roll-overs, torso-wiggles, leg-bends, and a dozen other ridiculous and demeaning calisthenics. The bride soon bowed out but the children were not allowed to sleep while the old man sweated. Punching bags appeared, not one but two — one for the attic, one for the basement. Fanatic. On Sundays we took long walks, or slid down thousands of beautiful moss-stained cedar steps that dropped through a hillside park shaded almost to night by acres of Douglas fir, to the Madrona swimming beach with its municipal bathhouse and its chilling waters already contaminated, I imagine, by the leakage of the local septic tanks.

I thought for years that this hearty emphasis on physical fitness, which lasted for almost a year, had been introduced into our lives to combat the effeminizing influence of Grandmother's world where, surrounded by women devoted to social grace and the development of sensibility, I must have struck my father as an insufferable proto-esthete. He could hardly bear to acknowledge a son who preferred reading a book to going out into the street with a football and getting the shit knocked out of him. The reason I believed this strenuous regime had been designed to toughen me up was that he told me so, and who, being eight or nine years old, wouldn't believe a father so newly come back into his life? If I had been a brighter kid I might have figured out when I had to stand on a chair to reach the punching bags, that while they had been my Christmas presents, they gave my father more delight that they gave me. I didn't like to hit them, since I did it so ineptly; I didn't like the sweaty leather smell; but I liked the music that they made. Mornings and evenings the house would throb in a magic way to the machine-gun popping of a punching bag and the quick, brutal, educated blows like drumbeats of fists attacking leather, blows and echoes: the trembling house.

I was forty years old when I received that other disappointing Christmas present, my father's book of memoirs, and within it another explanation for that period of vaguely grotesque athletic activity that now, seen from my father's point of view, revealed the past in a dark, sad, terrible light.

The year of the punching bags and the crazy voice of Walter Kamp counting out cadence while I struggled to come awake and my red-faced father pulled at my blankets between knee-bends became, twenty-five years later and with new information, nothing more than the last small part of a long, complicated drama.

Because at the beginning of my old age I had written to my mother, who was then very old indeed, saying that I intended finally to fight back, to come out swinging, that I hoped by writing about my father to get him out of my dreams, and would she, if she could, please write me something about his good qualities. "He must have had some," I wrote, "or then I'd have to ask you why you married him. I'm not promising to treat him fairly, but I can promise that I'll treat him more fairly than he ever treated any of us."

"Charley's good qualities?" my mother wrote back. "Well, he had beautiful blue eyes. And when you were young he loved you very much. If I think of anything else I will let you know." And then she plunged into the longest letter I ever received from her, or from anyone else for that matter — thirty pages of passionate invective, so charged, so immediate that I kicked myself for having stirred her mind to remember again such painful things.

I quote a couple of passages:

> During the war in 1916 I worked for the Red Cross driving an ambulance. In the big Seattle general strike Charley joined the vigilantes against the IWW. He said IWW meant I won't work. In the family they said, "Charley shoots them down, and Dolly picks them up." I don't know which of us they were making fun of, but your grandfather really did hate the labor unions. The Red Cross ran a canteen on 3rd Avenue for the soldiers. We served them coffee and donuts and in the afternoons from three to five we danced with them to a funny little phonograph. Charley was insanely jealous. Dancing with a soldier I would look up and see your father out in the street, his face up against the window. We still lived with your

grandmother though we'd been married for three years. I wasn't
even given an allowance. When I had to buy a dress your Aunt Anna
went with me and helped me pick it out. I was from the wrong side
of the tracks and no doubt would buy something vulgar. We lived in
that house treated like children. Your father told me: "I forbid you to
dance with those yahoos. I saw them pawing you, you didn't do a
thing, you loved it." "My God, Charle." I said. "It's almost eighty
years since Lincoln freed the slaves. Don't keep treating me as
though you own me. There's a war on; we have to do something for
the boys." "Does that include whoring?" he said, crying with rage.
You were a year old then. Your grandmother hired a nurse to look
after you; she didn't even talk it over with me first. Mother was an
angel, but she had no right to hire a woman to look after you as
though I weren't capable myself.

Later in the week another tea dance as we called them then. And
there is Charley out there in the street peering through the window
as we dance with the soldiers. When I go home that evening he has
been there and gone. He took a razor or scissors, took all my dresses
out of the closet and one by one cut them into ribbons. I've often
wondered if as he cut and slashed he imagined me inside those
clothes. I've wondered how he could stay in a rage so long. It must
have taken him at least an hour.

I left him and took you with me and went to stay with my sister.
Do you remember your Aunt Dora? I don't suppose you do. She
had a lovely voice and sang on the Orpheum circuit; your father
said she was a slut because she traveled around with actors and
comedians and magicians. He wouldn't have her in the house. Or
my mother either for that matter. There was still a lot of prejudice
against the Irish in those days, though I'll never understand why in
the case of your father's family who were just one generation
removed from being Danish peasants, Danes out of the bogs. There
was terrible pressure put on me to come back. Even your
grandfather begged me with tears in his eyes. I made him promise
that we would live in our own house, replace all my clothes, give me
a decent allowance. I didn't speak to your father about any of this. I
didn't trust him. I did it all through your grandfather who was angry
enough with Charley to have killed him. When your grandfather

promised something he kept his word. Do you remember the 3515
East Marion house, a sweet little white Colonial house above the
lake with a wonderful view of Mount Rainier? In the evenings it
was pink, you could almost reach out and touch it. You were a baby
there. Your sister was born there. Remember the bush outside the
front door covered with big bunches of pink blooms like snowballs?
You loved those flowers, and one day you picked them all off and
made a pile. One day you walked on a bee, and you ran into the
house crying, "A bee stepped on me, a bee stepped on me." Oh my,
but you were cute.

At eighty-two, two years later, and in one of the last of the letters in
which my mother chose to reminisce, she wrote:

We called the house in Altadena "mother's cottage," but actually it
was bought for your Aunt Wilhelmina who had a terminal case of
tuberculosis. The doctor recommended a warm dry climate where
she could spend the winters. While they were looking for the house
they sent her down to stay with me in Hollywood. Your father was
sales manager of the Los Angeles plant and we'd rented a little house
out by the lot where they were filming *Birth of a Nation*. Day and
night there were guns and cannons going off, smoke creeping down
the hillside, soldiers running around and waving flags practically in
our backyard. You were just a baby and can't possibly remember.
Your father caught the war fever for a time. He was married with
dependents but he used his influence to get in — and a year later
when he was tired of it, to get out. While he was gone Wilhelmina
came, a lovely girl, the nicest by far of all your aunts. She played
Chopin, Beethoven, all the romantics like a professional, to make
you weep.

They brought Wilhelmina to me, and it was just a tiny rented
bungalow, and all of them could see, but no one in that family
thought to buy another bed for your aunt to sleep on. I couldn't,
your father hardly sent me enough to live on, so all that winter I
slept beside that dying woman. It's just temporary, they said. We've
found a lovely place in Altadena, it won't be long. They spent a
hundred thousand dollars on a house with a beautiful garden where

she could spend her last months surrounded by beauty. But a little precise detail like your own bed to sleep in, no, that didn't occur to any of them. The insensitivities of the very rich or in this case, the vulgar thoughtlessness of people who have become rich too fast — and all of them, all the girls, and including your father, that fancy European education. My God, learning how to be 19th century dukes and duchesses. I've never forgiven them for that. Everyone knew then that tuberculosis was terribly contagious. God, I must have been a stupid child. Why did I take it? Do you remember your Aunt Wilhelmina? Probably not, you were just two when she died. She would stick her feet out at the end of the bed and you would play with her toes. How she loved you. She was a lovely person, over six feet tall, and with the radiant face of someone fated to die young.

When your father came down on furlough from Fort Lewis he would play with you for hours at a time. You had a little kitten and he would squeeze the halves of walnut shells over his paws and then set him on the bare oak floor to watch him sprawl and fall, to listen to him cry. I knew about that other thing with the cats so I didn't dare say anything. You laughed along with him not knowing that what he was doing was wicked.

"What other thing about the cats?" I wrote, hardly daring to know. What I had always held against him most was the brutal way he had killed the collie.

My mother wrote, "If you don't know why should I be the one to have to tell you. He's dead now, it happened over seventy years ago. It was your Aunt Anna who told me, who saw it and hated him ever after. In Seattle when he was fifteen, sixteen, he wired two cats together by their tails and hung them over a clothes line, then he sat there on the back steps and watched them tear each other to pieces. My God, don't put that in the book, son, don't drag up all that old muck. At any rate, don't ask me to remember any more. The past is past. Or at least that's where we try to keep it."

Just as there are empty spaces in my memories, so in my father's recollections he moves from one year to another between enormous blanknesses. It is not surprising, of course, that he does not mention razoring his wife's dresses to ribbons or hanging up cats to watch their agonies. What is surprising is that until my mother left him, he scarcely mentions her in his memoirs, as though fifty years later she is still too devastating a force and he, through all the years of his life, too vulnerable, too close to tears, to hold her in his mind. Until he comes to that time when he destroys her, or tries to, and all his reticences boil away.

5

I T IS IMPOSSIBLE FOR ME to use my father's memoirs to describe the
first twenty years of his life. The Samuel Clemens estate would sue me
for copyright infringement. When he was eight or nine he was sent to
Europe with his sisters to be expensively educated but before this break
with his semirural past, which must have been cruelly traumatic, he
attended public schools in Spokane. He admits on one page of his memoirs that he was a bully. "I used to get beat up every day on the way
home from school. Then one day I fought back and won and after that
I beat up on everybody. I was the head of a gang that terrorized that
neighborhood."

In his late teens and early twenties he had been one of Seattle's more
flamboyant playboys, a word I think that was then seldom used in Seattle.
His sisters and then his father described him as a gutter drunk. He ran
with a crowd that included Bill Boeing, a man whose passions changed
from racing cars to airplanes while my father's stayed focused on beer,
racing cars, and wrecking them. I think that for a time Mr. Boeing was
interested in my mother, who worked as a secretary in the Cadillac
agency and was, along with a half dozen others, "the most beautiful
woman in Seattle." To some degree my father led a double public life.
He drank and broke the traffic laws and brawled in the local whorehouses with the sons of prominent men — louts, I suppose, very much
like himself, not quite sons of the pioneers anymore, but still exuding a
frontier exuberance. He was not comfortable with the foppish Eastern
fortune hunters who hung around his house and offered themselves,
their names, and their social position to the impressionable, the perhaps
delightfully raw but desirable daughters of the newly rich. Gradually
he spent more and more time with the politicians and the traveling
salesmen in the downtown saloons. For one campaign (what did he do?
— bribe drunks, steal ballot boxes?) he helped a friend get elected as

Seattle's chief of police. He got out of politics, he writes, because "politics was too dirty even for me."

And now the memoirs begin to get vague and crazy. In two pages rushing through time he wrecks his racing car, talks Grandmother into buying him another, promises Grandfather not to race it himself, races it himself, wrecks it, and is thrown out of the house. A friend gives him a job on a boat going to Alaska to trade beads or rum or something to the Eskimos; it is a trip that nets his friend two hundred thousand dollars and my father only experience, plus a little bunch of badly made unsalable walrus-tusk cribbage boards. He makes another trip to Alaska and unloads freight off the boats in Nome toward the end of the gold rush, and most of the money he makes this time is from the canned goods he steals out of the ships' holds.

For a year he plays at life, denied entrance to his father's house, but getting by somehow with money slipped to him by his weeping, still adoring mother, who meets him surreptitiously in boarding houses or cheap hotels — and the money he borrows (and forgets to repay) from that beautiful girl in the Cadillac agency who will a few years later become my mother.

Out of nowhere on an otherwise tranquil day he is suddenly subjected to the whirlwind. It will prove to be one of the great and terrible watershed moments of his life, though perhaps, fainting, he comes away too stunned by the experience to immediately understand it. Reading between the lines of a short, vague, mysterious entry you are led to understand that his youth, his way of living, his whole sense of himself came to an end in a single day — that he was once more summoned before his father late on a Saturday afternoon in his deserted downtown offices. It was the last judgment: he went in, trembling, a cocky little wastrel; he staggered out a man, in a manner of speaking, a kind of zombie who for the rest of his life would be a shadow on the wall, aping the movements of his father through intricate financial dances, aping the dark cut of his father's suits and that weird nineteenth-century laissez-faire manifest destiny bullshit which wasn't very old-fashioned yet in 1910, but would be soon enough.

Writing this almost twenty years after his death it occurs to me for the first time that long ago I might have made this simpleminded connection: that perhaps my father's constant anger, his assaults upon my dignity, his need to humiliate, to deprive, to dominate and degrade were nothing more than old stale copies, rickety constructions, old echoes of that day that had left him false to himself — a resentful, raging man driven by the laws of compensation to rage against his son, but without the talent to do it well. In the business world an impressive figure, director of banks, president of corporations, associations, but in fact a straw man, a frightened, insecure fellow who had to take over an enormous empire from his father without the talent to hold it together.

One Sunday morning I had been ground up fine by my grandfather's contemptuous anger; I knew his artistry, the royal rage of Persian or Mongolian despots who wield the power of life and death, who make stern, implacable decisions. And so it is easy to imagine that session (the big mahogany rolltop desk, the big cigar box made of teak, the pigeons on the windowsill, Puget Sound below the buildings — green islands in a blue sea); not the things that my father would remember, who probably felt on that day as if he had been thrust into the heart of an atomic meltdown where he was transformed by some devastating alchemy from one substance into another — or in his case, from one substance into the shadow of another. "The old governor sure set me straight that day," my father wrote. "I thank him every day of my life." Even the anger had been burned out of one level of his mind, and he is like someone thanking the bloody-handed man who stands before him with the castrating knife that has just civilized his passions.

He went to work for Grandfather, began to learn the business. A month of intense preparation and he was on his way to Acapulco to become the paymaster for the railroad that Grandfather was building to Mexico City. He hauled mule-loads of Mexican silver pesos to the work gangs in the rock cuts, three pesos a week per man, and not much later, from a Mexico suddenly aflame with revolution, he escaped at night with other gringos to a boat in the harbor. On the way north to Los Angeles he ate dog stew. "It wasn't half bad," he wrote.

Back in Seattle, and going through the farce of starting at the bottom, he sold soda crackers, graham crackers, hard candies, and chocolate-covered creams for the biscuit company. He must have been sensational, for within a year he was the sales manager in Los Angeles, and shortly after manager of all the sales managers, and then ascending into glory, vice-president, president; Grandfather, trying to loosen his grip on things, gave away titles and tried to stay away from the office, but he couldn't do it, and he continued to run the business in a nicely secret way that didn't too much humiliate my father.

In the memoirs ten years pass. Scarcely mentioned: his marriage, the little rented house in Hollywood, the white Colonial house above the lake that Grandfather bought him — and the most delightful events of all in all those years, the births of his two delightful children. Halfway down a page he remembers trading in a Stutz Bearcat for a sensational touring car, an HCS. And the rest of the page is empty; it is not a chapter break, this only pause in the whole book — more an anguished moment remembering something that washed his mind clean, memories that leave him momentarily naked.

And now, beginning at the top of a new page, smashing through generalities, he began to write with a stunned bravado, still too involved to keep to the matter-of-fact voice he was trying to use. (We have come to the edge of punching bag country.) "One day out of the blue," he began, "Dolly sued me for divorce. Even got a court order barring me from my own house. She fell in with a slick shyster lawyer who figured he could clean me out."

How many nights did he park his car up the street and watch that house which he was forbidden to enter? My father's absence opened the house up to the return of old friends who had been driven away by his jealousy; they came to console and celebrate. In the mild summer evenings, hidden in bushes, he watched people standing in the doorway and then, welcomed, disappearing inside where, he was sure, they would engage in unspeakable orgies. From the window the tinny sounds of phonograph fox-trots drifted. And creeping close he may even have smelled the perfume of bourbon and ginger ale and heard his children from the upstairs windows crying in their sleep, or screaming for glasses of water. I suppose he was scarcely in his right mind when he went to his friend, Bill Severns, the chief of police, and arranged to have the house watched and its rooms fitted with concealed listening devices.

Behind the house, at the edge of a rock garden, the former owner had built a hen house of lathe and wire. Old straw and chicken droppings turning to dust covered the floor; the wire netting sagged, the door sagged on hinges pulling loose; the earphones were concealed in a nest. Detectives outside the house, my father and his good friend the police chief standing through the night, ankle deep in chicken shit, week after week. After days of silence, over the sound of music carried on the secret wires, comes an electrical screech — the loud voice perhaps of a drunken man, a drunken woman, a dirty joke, a ribald toast, coarse laughter. The police chief fills a notebook, the cool nights of autumn arrive, and he says, "Charlie, let's call this charade off. Enough of standing around like this, another night or two and I'll be laying eggs. We've got enough, Charlie — we can nail her. In a court of law Dolly is not leading a moral life. I'll testify, I'll swear she's not a proper mother. And that fellow from Portland, and that fellow from Pacific Grove. No, I'd say the situation is unambiguous."

"Ah, poor little Dolly," my father wrote. "I had her cold; that was the end for Dolly."

"He came to me and we sat outside in that big touring car of his," my mother wrote me years later. "He showed me pages of so-called evidence all typed up. Bill Severns, the Seattle police, a private detective agency. He had a report on the free life my sister led. His father, he said, would pledge ten thousand dollars to fight me in the courts. 'Don't leave me, Dolly,' he cried. 'Oh, Charlie, it's all over, I can't come back.' 'If that's the way you want it,' he said. 'But if you fight me I'll get you on adultery. I'm going to divorce you, you're not divorcing me. Bill had the whole place wired; he'll testify on oath. Dolly, I'll make a scandal for you you'll never live down; I'll make you headline news up and down the coast. Or you can desert me, just leave quietly. No settlement; the children are mine.' 'You wouldn't,' I said. 'Oh, wouldn't I?' he said. What could I do?"

It was four or five years later that my father married the very pretty girl who worked as his secretary in the Portland flour mill. He opened up the Marion Street house again, and once more we awakened in the mornings to a pink and stupendous Mount Rainier floating at the end of the lake above the clouds; the punching bags and boxing gloves (unmentioned in my father's text) appeared; and on weekends he led us briskly through dark woods to cold water.

In that time between his divorce and his new wife he devotes some pages to business triumphs and an unconsciously funny description of his second courtship, written in the sentimental style of *True Romances,* and undoubtedly written to please this woman who would read it. But actually the wooing must have been a trial, for he moved into very close contact with a narrow, rigid, working-class family, none of whose lips had ever been sullied with alcohol and who believed that anyone who said God Damn was headed for the fires of hell. The woman he had chosen was sexually terrified, paralyzed by overheard hints concerning the sexual act which she had never dared imagine. She insisted that hands not wander, lips remain tightly pressed together when being kissed, and that she be delivered home before midnight, her hair still neatly arranged within the cloche hat. On Sunday mornings, before the picnics or the long drives my father had planned to separate her from the protective presence of her sisters, he went with her to her church, a brutally fundamental sect incestuously aligned with that religion of my grandmother's cooks and maids, the Holy Rollers. It was as stern and simpleminded as the religious philosophy my stepmother finally grew up into — and many years later proudly displayed on the bumper of her Chrysler convertible: "If you love Jesus, honk."

They were married, and after a horrifying honeymoon which must have suggested to them both that they had chosen foolishly, she was presented to her children, who had been instructed to love her and to call her Mother. We obeyed, feeling foolish when we used the word to this young woman who was almost a stranger, and we even loved her for a time, loved her at least as much as the endless string of women who had been hired to care for us, some of whom for secret tippling or petty thefts or religious mania had had to be let go, and who wept along with us as they disappeared forever out of our lives. No one is more class-conscious than the servants of the middle class, and I think my stepmother never had a cook or a maid who didn't loathe her for the inept way she concealed her poorly decent background.

Why did she marry my father? The explanation must lie in her own naiveté and the cleverness with which he concealed his shameful qualities and turned himself into a charmer. I doubt that she had the imagination to marry him for his money; the impulse, had it occurred to her, would have struck her as sinful. At the same time it is impossible to feel that sexual passion played any part in her decision. Children, thank God, are spared the awareness of their parent's sexual tensions, but I have always felt that from the beginning some terrible game was being played between them — my father with all his wit and cunning trying to get into her bed, my stepmother with all of hers, trying to keep him out there alone in his outdoor sleeping porch. When she divorced him for a time, seven years after marrying him, she told me in an atypical burst of confidence which embarrassed us both that "in bed he was like a bull," the identical sentence that my mother used years later while reminiscing.

We moved back into the little house that still held faint memories of a real mother (after five years now turning into an angelic presence who appeared in dreams and visions). And we listened to the music of the punching bags.

Three times a week for almost six months my father went to the YMCA at lunch time, took boxing lessons and sparred. And then one day he felt that he was ready. In the police reports he had the addresses of the two men whom he had to confront before he could begin his new life with his new wife. One morning he left Seattle and drove to Portland. "I went to his house about three," my father wrote.

It was Saturday and he was expected home at any time. I talked to his wife at the front door, introduced myself and told her the whole story, how he broke up my family. She listened and didn't say anything and then invited me inside to wait. I showed her the depositions and offered to let her read them; she said it wouldn't be necessary and that this wasn't the first time. I sat in the front room, she sat in the kitchen. She came in once and offered me coffee.

About six she came in to where I was sitting in the dark. She said, "His car just drove up; do whatever you want." I went outside and met him on the front walk and his wife called down from the top of the steps, "This is Mr. Thomsen from Seattle. You were a guest in his house, and I think he has it in his mind to kill you." "No," I said, "but almost." And I went at it, rushed him, he was too surprised to defend himself. I went for his face, I changed that bastard's face, broke his nose and then flattened it, went for his jaw and he had lost all his strength and I went for his eyes, his stomach, his heart. When his wife pulled me off he was kneeling in a pool of blood, both eyes smashed shut. She said, "That's enough, Mr. Thomsen. Now you're even. He broke up your family, now you've broken up his." And then as I was driving away she began to scream.

He drove south for half the night and slept for a few hours in a small hotel, perhaps near Ashland. By nine o'clock the next morning he was deep into California, and that afternoon he pulled up in front of a house in Pacific Grove and met the second man he had come to see. But once again he had to explain to a woman shocked into a deadly silence what he intended to do and why. How strange that neither of the women offered any resistance to the idea of their husbands being pounded into pulp.

The blows, the blood, the facial disfigurement, the man's cries for mercy were all so like the first confrontation that in spite of a new immediacy in the memoir's detail (written now with the sauce and precision of a sports writer on the old *Police Gazette*) there is no point in writing the same story twice. There was one new detail: the two small children who stood in the doorway frozen with terror, watching their father as he went down under my father's blows. I think this detail, which is almost too painful to hold in the mind, gave my father a particular satisfaction, for he was a man who understood that power was to be used and enjoyed, that power was to be made manifest, or what was the use of it? What he needed, and what he had thought about for the five years that he took to carry out his vengeance, was a crushing, an ultimate life-destroying humiliation for these two men who may or may not have held my mother in their arms. It is just as probable that writing down this account he was newly fulfilled, inspired to cheap eloquence as he looked ahead to that moment when his appalled children and grandchildren would read his words, would shudder at his stern power and would know that he was brave and noble.

The old muck.

All my later life I had lived with the conviction that what my father felt for my mother was a profound, implacable hatred, a wound on his life too painful to touch, and that whatever had happened was over and done with, and that the unspoken rule of never mentioning her name in his presence indicated that he was on the way to forgetting her, that for him, in some deep sense, my mother had to cease to exist. I had watched that hatred break out one day when I was sixteen, one late afternoon helping him clean feeders in one of his henhouses. Now I don't remember why, but we had begun to quarrel, and suddenly red-faced and trembling he had yelled something like, "You've always thought more of her than me, always loved that woman who deserted her children, that whore." For one of the few times in my life (I had certainly learned by the age of sixteen not to feel much of anything about anything) I lost control, raised my fists above him and panted out, tears gushing from my eyes, "You son of a bitch, I'll kill you." At that age I was already taller than he, though with one blow he could have knocked me through the henhouse wall, so in a sense there was a certain noble bravery in my threatening him, and he may have felt this, for as I towered over him ready to smash or be smashed, he began to smile, and something like admiration moved like a shadow across his face. It occurs to me now, fifty-seven years later and perhaps stretching the reality, a creative writer for a moment rather than a miner of family muck, that as we faced each other, my fury finally overpowering his, we had never been so close, nor ever would be again. This drama, which for many years seemed to me like the last scene in the last act of my father's hatred and repudiation, took place while five thousand white Leghorns watched us with scandalized eyes; now I can't remember a single chicken.

6

TWELVE YEARS AFTER MY FATHER DIED there came another ending to that old story that I thought had had an ending in the henhouse. In 1979 I had told my mother that I intended to write about him; after months of urging me not to she had become resigned to the idea and had sent me his last letter to her. When had they been divorced, 1921? How amazing then this letter written almost fifty years later, in 1969, only three or four months before my father's death. I have it someplace, lost now or filed away with other mice-nibbled papers, so I can quote hardly anything but the first sentence which impressed itself on me only for the magnitude of its hypocrisy, its monumental insensitivity, the sheer guts of this man who could so twist and ignore the past: "Dearest Dolly, I never begrudged you food, clothing, or shelter, I always took care of you so I never understood why you left me, there was always food in the kitchen, you always dressed real nice, my but you were pretty, we had that nice little house, Colonial because that was your favorite, but you walked out on me and I'll never understand."

The rest of the letter, and it is a long one for my father who was by then senile (single-spaced typing on both sides of a half-sized sheet), turns immediately into a passionate letter of love. "I never loved anyone but you, Dolly; it was only you all the years of my life." There hadn't been a day he hadn't remembered her, not a night he hadn't burned to hold her in his arms. Could she remember those nights on the beach at Three Tree Point, the room at the lodge at Lake Crescent, at Paradise Lodge? etc., etc. All in all it was pretty hot stuff for a seventy-nine-year-old geezer, and I was embarrassed reading it, as perhaps was my mother who had jotted at the margin of one impassioned and steamy paragraph, "The old goat."

My father owned apartment houses and for twenty years had hired a man to manage them. He was badly paid and ill-used and ended up as a kind of slave to my father's whims and rages, but being middle-aged and terrified of being unemployed in the Great Depression, he had stayed on confident in the promise of an ultimate reward — the promised generous bequest that would show up in my father's last will and testament and ease his last years. What he ended up with was an old wristwatch and a two-hundred-dollar bonus for each of his years of service (a settlement that so outraged the executors that they doubled his wages for all the years that he stayed on until the properties could be sold.) Now, in his last letter to my mother, he wrote that when she answered him, as he was sure she would (though she didn't), to send it to Mervin at the apartments and "whatever you do, don't write me here at the hospital or at home where El Vera could get her hands on it."

So all along it had been love instead of hatred that had confused his life. But how could one have told with him whose love was so easily expressed as rage or madness, whose emotions were so closely focused on his boy-sized but obsessive passions?

I read this confession out of the past and it clarified one of the funnier grotesqueries he had paraded to any of us visiting him in the hospital room where he finally died. There he had kept in constant contact with his wife (or she with him), and a half dozen times a day they spoke together on the telephone. They whined at each other back and forth, aping love, aping something. When they were ready to hang up an invariable ritual was performed. My stepmother would say, singing on three notes, "I luv oo," and my father, copying the intonations or trying to, with all the fading dignity of his years, would echo in baby talk this inane, this lying refrain. It was one of the customs she had introduced to housebreak him, just as she had insisted that he say in a falsely genteel way, "Thank you so much" instead of "Thank you." His subservience to her vulgarity reminded me of that last scene in *The Blue Angel* where Emil Jannings, destroyed by Marlene Dietrich, stands on the stage of a whorehouse crowing like a rooster. At the end that was how they said good-bye: "I luv oo." "I luv oo-oo."

My father would drop the phone into its cradle and say, "Bitch," and I would turn to watch the blue jays on the hospital lawn to keep from laughing in his face. Sometimes he would explain: he had, through the years, opened up seven or eight savings accounts in different banks and deposited ten thousand dollars in each, ready money he had planned to be used toward paying his death taxes. And now, "She found the saving books, she found them where I had them put away, she's got the money, the bitch, she's got the money hid." For now, no longer the straightforward but predictable irritant in his life that he had learned to live with, she had joined the rest of us — his children, his lawyers, and his doctors, who he knew were gathered around his failing body and waiting to pick his bones.

It was an accident that I was in Seattle just two days after he died and a day before his funeral. Seattle held terrible memories and in the last twenty-five years — a day here, a couple of days there — I hadn't spent much more that a few months in this city where every street, every park, every heartbreaking view of mountains and water confused me with anguish, rejection, and a longing for its beauty. It seemed to me a microcosm for the whole of my country, my America, which, after the war had become imperialist again in its wild thrust to suck up and consume all the richness of the world, and which in its passion to embrace a heartless and automated future had become a place rushing away toward irrelevance. It was a country that had repudiated it noble beginnings, turned its back on the realities of the world, the truths that would thrust into our consciousness the awareness of mankind's sufferings — its hunger, its sicknesses, its corruptions and injustices. We were a people so insulated from the stink of life that death, except on TV where it entertained children, was now the big obscenity, the only subject never mentioned in polite conversation. Why did no one turn away in anger or disgust from my father's dead face, the mourners who stood out of curiosity around the open coffin contemplating the undertaker's whorish art —the painted lips, the rouged cheeks, the silly smile of some elfish charmer who is just about to say, "Off to heaven but I've had a ball"?

Ever since I had lost my farm in California, I had lived in Ecuador on a beach in a bamboo shack among the poorest people in the world, a life freely chosen. By the age of fifty-five then, I had lived in two worlds: as a child and then a teenager, until the Depression changed things, I had lived among the rich. I sure as hell preferred living with the poor to living with the rich, though I would admit now that it was naive of me twenty years ago to find innate qualities of nobility or greatness of soul in people who lived in squalor, who lived without resources, naked in the hands of God. It was an illusion among many others that I hung on to for years. Having become, with fifteen million other farmers, newly superfluous to a ruthlessly automated agriculture, I had, by a miracle, ended up shocked back to life by watching poor people as they struggled against their luck. And as I came back to life I found that once more I was consumed with the desire to write.

My sister also, for reasons similar to my own (a distress with the growing fascist tendencies in America that Nixon seemed to epitomize), had chosen to live outside the United States. With her husband and her children she had gone to live in southern France. My four cousins who still lived in Seattle had long ago quarreled with my father and cut him out of their lives. They were not present in the church. Of the fragmented remnants of the Thomsen family only my aunt, a very old lady now and the only one of my father's sisters still living, came, more out of a sense of what was correct than out of love, to listen to the eulogies in the chapel of the Episcopalian cathedral that my grandmother had built as a memorial to her daughter, Wilhelmina, who had lain in the bed beside my mother in a Hollywood bungalow dying of tuberculosis. While my cousins with other names carried the taint of Grandfather's blood, I was now the only Thomsen left in the world, and I had sworn years before, perhaps as a joke, perhaps to insult my father, that in the cause of suffering humanity I would have no children, and that with my death the family name would also die.

My aunt and I had been delivered to the church in one of those outrageous, black, grotesquely enormous Lincolns reserved for heads of state, Mafia big shots, Wall Street manipulators, safely returned astronauts, and close kin of the rich but newly dead. Even my aunt who had her own Lincoln, a less pretentious model that because of her age she was no longer allowed to drive, was aghast. Sinking back into it one had the feeling that one could never fight one's way out.

Two rows of pews had been reserved for the family. The front row was empty except for a strange woman with badly combed hair who was very casually dressed in an old polo coat smudged with dirt and darkened with grime at the collar. I sat and watched people, mostly strangers to me and very old, as they walked to the altar and stared into the open casket. "Do you want to go up for a last look at your father?" my aunt asked. "No," I said, "Do you?" "No," my aunt said.

"Who is that woman in front of us?" my aunt whispered. She was very deaf and spoke too loudly. I shrugged and shook my head, but made uneasy by the dirty polo coat, studied the figure, which had begun to frighten me as it took on reality and came to me out of the past, vaguely familiar. And now, vaguely familiar, too, the painfully self-conscious body, holding herself in, stiff with stage fright, without a sense of presence and frightened as a child who is aware only of people staring at her. Suddenly I realized, and with a terrible shock, that, of course, it was my father's wife. "My God," I said. "It's El Vera."

It was frightening to see her alone and frozen into her awful stillness, almost unrecognizable for want of that something that had rushed out of her with my father's death — the hatred that had strengthened her to confront him, the anger that gave meaning to her years and the determination to outlast him. Well, she had won, but the victory would kill her (for she died only a very few months later and, according to a letter from my sister, who was prone at times to exaggerate, died mad and screaming in the room of a sanitarium whose walls were padded). Now, today, she was as empty, as careless, as irrelevant as a scarecrow stuffed with dead grass, as though she had lost her only authenticity, which had been made manifest by the man who had now abandoned her. And wasn't it probable that I had been unable to recognize her because I had never had the patience or wit or the basic kindness to see her as a person in her own right, but simply as the foolish woman my father had taken to be his wife? Some of us that day, even some who disliked her, must have been struck with fear and pity and guilt as she sat there stiff and unmoving, for she seemed to be waiting for nothing so much as for her own death.

We sat and waited and everything was more complicated than I had ever imagined. If from time to time, though less and less, I had anticipated his death with impatience, I had always thought of it from my point of view, not his — as that little area of increased freedom through which I would be able to move with the loss of his power over me. I had thought of his death still in the future as a time when I might, no longer judged, find it a little easier to breathe. The day before, newly arrived from Montana, I had stood in a window looking out over a city that I no

longer wished to love. A moment before I had walked into a friend's office and she had cried, "Well, thank God, but where have you been? The
police of all the states between here and Montana have been looking for
you. Your father is dead, the funeral is tomorrow, please call your aunt
immediately." It was an awesome moment, stunning for having come so
suddenly and for the emptiness I felt, so unlike the drama of liberation I
had been rehearsing. Empty, I stared out at a landscape of mountains
which in a single second moved closer, bathed in the golden light of air
thick with the smoke of September's forest fires. The summer snow on
the distant peaks glistened like bronze, and all the menace with which I
had invested this country that more truly belonged to my father instantly
dissolved, turned magic, dusted with smoke and pollen and nostalgia. In
a week I would be leaving it forever, but it was mine at last and the raw
material of dreams. My first thought was, "Shit, I'll have to buy a suit of
clothes, a dark tie, and now, right now, today." I thought, "A suit will cost
a hundred dollars; if he has cut me off with a dollar then I am making a
very bad business investment." I began to laugh; from the back it may
have looked as if I was sobbing. I wanted to make a joke about buying a
suit and then being disowned but decided this was not the time. I
thought, "No, he'd like to disown me but doesn't have the guts to make a
scandal. But if he did and I bought the suit it would only prove what he
always said, that I had no head for business."

I thought, "Well, now I can begin to live my life," but this was a
thought created out of emptiness, a slightly pompous artifact like a constructed line of not quite honest poetry — something made up to help
me feel released or a sense of freedom or a sense of the possibility of a
new beginning. How many times had I said at some critical juncture,
making drama, "Now, I can begin to live my life" or "Now everything is
going to change" and realized later that no one easily changes what he
has become — the sum of all of his days.

I thought, "But, you asshole, you don't feel anything, or what you do
feel is absolutely shitty; you're as big a bastard as he was."

Since returning from South America, since the day when I began visiting him in the hospital each afternoon in what I had defined to myself
at first as a final reconciliation, later realizing that this was impossible, I
had begun with apprehension to recognize aspects of my father in myself. Until then I had viewed my character with a certain complacency,

or at least with the feeling that my flaws were only my own. God's curse unto the third and fourth generation was spooky, but what did it have to do with me except to hint that God, like my father, was a tyrant and somewhat of a shit? From my father I had inherited the color of my eyes, the square, peasant's hands, perhaps even the tendency to find life tragic. And watching him through the years as he roared and smashed the people he loved, I found in my horror of family ties and in my terror of close relationships and what was, I was finally forced to recognize, an incapacity to love, something else my father had given me by example, if not through the threads of his DNA. In this respect I was more damaged than a black friend of mine who had grown up in a Detroit ghetto and who told me, "Until I was thirty-five I thought that making love always began with first beating the shit out of the woman." It never occurred to me that in addition to superficial traits I might also have, hidden and still sleeping, all the raw material for becoming as I aged a kind of pale, second-class doppelganger. How could I have thought it possible to become civilized by simply believing in and accepting everything my father hated? Simply put, I had always seen myself as the other side of the coin, as having saved myself, as having won my war with him by having made myself into his opposite.

But now I was almost fifty-five years old, and during that couple of weeks as I sat by the bedside of my dying father, I could feel growing within me like a long quiescent but awakening cancer those same qualities that I so detested in my father: impatience, rage, a suspicion and distrust of people's motives, an impulse to isolate myself in solitude, an impulse toward revenge.

Three months before he died he had wanted to buy me the suit of clothes, the very kind I was wearing now as we waited for the service to begin. I had left Ecuador in a state almost as close to nakedness as the people I had lived among; in San Francisco I bought bright new duds — a tweed jacket, grey flannels, murderously expensive Florsheims; after a few days I flew to Seattle.

I hadn't seen my father for four years; for over three years we had not even written to one another. I had joined the Peace Corps after I lost the farm and this was the final proof that my sympathies were oriented toward Moscow. "If you join that crazy bunch of radical do-gooders, those pinko Kennedy-lovers, don't be surprised when you read my will to discover you've been cut off at the pockets," he had told me. But he had been threatening me for years with the pocketless pants I would have to wear in my old age, and I had decided that at heart he was a conformist, a slave to the opinions of others, and that he could not bear, even though dead, to live on as a cruel and unjust man in the eyes of the public.

The hospital was in the country — long corridors like tentacles spread out to the compass points, one-storied, rooms with French doors, most of them locked but appearing as though they would slide open to the invitation of lawns, trees, birds, and clouds; at the building's center the head nurse in a hotel lobby and beside her a large empty room and a large television set, upon the surface of which demented faces argued in shades of orange, blue, or metallic greens, everything made insane and surreal by the absence of sound — or the sound from another room of a moaning woman. A nurse guided me that first day past endless rooms like honest love stories with unhappy endings — two bickering ancients to a room. "I wouldn't stay too long," the nurse said. "If he drops off just leave him; you'll be back tomorrow, I suppose. We keep him sedated be-cause he's pretty feisty, pretty creative, always trying to get away from whatever it is that's after him . . . Well, lookee here, Mr. Thomsen, just look who's come to see you." Baby talk.

I hardly recognized him, he seemed so small in the long high bed, and because with the hospital gown hiked up above his thighs he presented new parts of himself: wrinkled buttocks, a shriveled sex, the white hair on his belly. He was pale and thin, almost emaciated, his face vacant, as if he had left with his thoughts on a long faraway journey. When he saw me, when he finally recognized me, his face collapsed and he wept, but like a child who holds for no more than a moment the weight of his emotion. A couple of minutes later, as though I had never been gone, he drew me down to him to whisper that one of the nurses was going through his billfold in the night, that his lawyer was peeking over his shoulder at the list of his assets, that his doctor hadn't bothered to visit him in weeks. He asked me no questions; I told him no lies. On another bed by the glass doors another old man with a neatly trimmed mustache and wearing a dark silk dressing gown was glancing through a magazine. "He's an architect," my father said. "He groans in the night so I can hardly sleep. Goddammit Arthur, you groaned last night so I could hardly sleep." The two old men began a long, faintly humorous conversation between themselves, and I sat by the doors looking out the window at the birds. They talked and talked, and I went out into the corridor and walked up and down peering into the rooms where old ladies in pretty housecoats moved slowly in wheelchairs. When I came back the old architect was sleeping. My father looked at me for a long time. "I want to buy you a suit of clothes for Christmas," he said finally. "Let's try to make you look decent."

"Thanks," I said. "That's nice of you, but it's six months to Christmas, and besides I don't need new clothes; I just bought these."

"Those are new?" he asked. "You're dressed up like a kid, like a college freshman." I smiled, or tried to, and didn't say anything. "I want to see you dressed like a man with self-respect, a nice, dark, double-breasted suit, a nice red tie. You're not a professor, you know."

"No, and I'm not the president of Union Carbide either. To tell you the truth, I thought I looked pretty spiffy." Half an hour and he had begun jabbing at me and in an area where I was sensitive, for the clothes I wore reflected the way I saw myself. When I had been a farmer I dressed like one; now back from South America, with a book written and about to be published, I had chosen to dress like two writers who years before had taught me in New York — Oliver La Farge and Whit Burnett, eminent men, polished, knowing, elegant in Harris tweed jackets and soft English flannels. I had been young and idolized them, but now, beginning to be old, I was embarrassed, having written a single book, that anyone might think I now felt entitled to dress like a writer.

"Maybe even a double-breasted grey flannel," my father said. "But a nice dark grey."

"Look, I might as well tell you now — in about four months I'm going back to South America and try to farm. Back to the hot country, the rain forest."

"Well, that's all right, that's okay," my father said. It was an answer so placid, so essentially uninterested that I imagined him suppressing his impulse to make some sarcastic comment.

"Those jungle cockroaches, they can eat a suit of clothes over the weekend."

Maybe he hadn't been listening, maybe he hadn't understood, because now he said, following the same train of thought, "You get Mervin, no,

I'll talk to him, and he can go with you to Frederick and Nelson's and help you pick out a nice suit. You put it on my account."

I had come determined not to fight, to remain silent when he began to rant, to sit silently and smile. It would be a benign cruelty, like refusing to spar with a boxer who is crazy to mix it up and draw a drop or two of blood; it would be civilized insult if he had the wit to see it that way. And it looked like it would be easy to remain separated from all the undischarged emotion that he must have built up in the last few years — and from my own. The hospital with its elements of fantasy had soaked up a lot of my own emotion and like barely heard music or a shot of heroin or a blow on the head, had insulated me from my own feelings. Instead of being absorbed in the pathos of this old man who had finally lost his power, I had looked at the brightly painted walls, the old ladies in their wheelchairs, the crisp dresses of the nurses below their smiling, competent, cold faces, and the absolutely menacing way the glass walls seemed to separate everything, isolating all of the natural breathing world from the doddering stricken people. I had been thinking, "But purgatory is not where you go after you die, purgatory is where you go before you die."

And now my father, saying something that for a second I had barely understood, had suddenly put me into a rage; amazed, I found myself standing, trembling, and almost yelling at him in a furious and outraged voice. "Let me get you straight, okay? You want Mervin, your apartment manager, to take me by the hand, lead me downtown, and pick out a suit of clothes? Why, for Christ's sake? Because you think I shouldn't be let loose to do it alone? What the hell are you afraid of, the tremendous sums of money involved, that I'll take the money and piss it all away on bubble gum? Or do you think I'll buy a purple suit and grass-green trousers like a vaudeville clown? Maybe I'm just too stupid to be trusted alone to bring off an immensely complicated deal like buying a suit? Christ Almighty, I'm almost fifty-five fucking years old."

My father's eyes opened wide as though coming fully awake, as though I had shaken him out of his self-absorption. And seeing his shock beneath my anger I felt lifted up in a joyful release. I had hit him with some honest anger, something I had scarcely dared to do since that day twenty-five years before when I had come to him after the war and he had turned his back on me. It was like walking out of a dim room into the sun.

My father seemed about to say something and I interrupted him. "Look, do me a favor, no more about the clothes, okay? Forget the fucking clothes, okay? I'll buy my own clothes, okay?"

"Sure, that's okay," my father said. "That's fine." He looked at me with what I imagined later as the kind of confused admiration I had seen on his face that day in the henhouse when I had raised my clenched fists above his head. It was as though he recognized some part of himself in my anger, in the cruel need to hurt him if I could. In my petty meanness, in my joy over the power I now had over him, he might have felt, if only momentarily, our kinship, our common blood.

Later, on another day, I had half tried to apologize; late afternoon with the shadows of the trees stretched out across the lawn. I sat by his bed without speaking, safe behind my foolish smile.

"Christ," my father said, "you just sit there like a dummy. If you've got nothing to say you might as well leave."

"When we talk, we fight," I said. "So, I don't talk. Like that business about the suit; I should have kept my mouth shut."

"What did I do wrong?" my father asked. "The best schools, violin lessons, your own horse, a trip around the world. Now you're going to live with niggers."

The word, like a low blow, infuriated me; I had a strong desire to get up, curse him, and leave. Instead I sat there and smiled until I could find the words. "What went wrong?" I said finally. "Well, I'm going to tell you what went wrong, whether or not you believe Freud, your old buddy Frood. This is the way they handle the situation in Italy: the father is the head of the family, right? The big cheeseburger. What he says goes, his word law. And he's usually a tyrant, you know — God, a potbellied, screaming maniac. The boy lives in the house completely dominated by his old man, do this, do that, do it this way, you idiot; whatever the old man says, that's the way it is. The boy grows up; he might be thirty years old but the old man calls him boy, but anyway he grows up finally and wants to belong to himself, he wants to be free. So one day after a few drinks they begin to fight, I mean with fists, teeth, feet, they're screaming at each other because for the son it's to the death. For the old man it's simply long-delayed justice, so the son usually wins. And then the boy is free, the father goes out and sits under his grapes, he gets old, he becomes human, he asks his son's advice, they begin to be friends.

"Maybe," I said, beginning to laugh or cry. "Maybe that's what went wrong. I never beat the shit out of you." I felt sad and wonderful saying it.

My father smiled wanly. "That'll be the day. No, you were never man enough, I'd of broken you in two." This was all something he didn't want to think about; he picked up a magazine and stared at one of the pages; the smile faded and he looked as sad and vacant as I had ever seen him.

It is another afternoon, and I'm almost ready to leave for Montana. I'm driving his car now, and it seems to be enough mine that I've taken the liberty of scraping off the rear bumper sticker which said, "Thank God, this is a republic, not a democracy; let's keep it that way." I am sitting with my father, and though I can't remember clearly, this may be almost the last time that I would ever see him. He lies on the bed, legs bare, propped up into a half-sitting position with pillows. As usual we have said almost nothing to each other for twenty minutes or so, but even the tensions that these long silences produce have disappeared now. We are thinking our own thoughts, living our own lives; we have, I think, given up on each other.

And then my father says an amazing thing that makes my heart begin to pound and my body grow tense. "I want to tell you this. Something happened years ago that I can't forget; I can't get it out of my head, never could. I did something, you understand, something bad, something bad."

He stops talking, I think because he sees this as a confession and as a dialogue. He wants me to become involved in an exchange of emotions in which I may with a last kindness relieve him of his guilt. I am supposed to speak, he waits for me to speak, I can't. But I am not smiling. We stare at one another. I know exactly what he is going to say. I have known for thirty-five years that the day he killed the collie Grandmother had given him was the day some part of him had died, just as it had for me watching him do it. In his will he is leaving thousands of dollars to the Humane Society and a special prize of twenty-five thousand dollars to the man who invents a contraceptive for cats.

After a time my father says, "Do you remember that beautiful collie that Mother gave me, when was it, 1929, 1930? A couple of years after we moved out into the country."

"Yes," I said, "I sure do, I remember, and I know what you're going to say, I was there and saw you. And I swear to God, Father, I don't want to talk about it. I can't talk about it."

"I want to be forgiven," my father said.

I didn't say anything.

"I want to be forgiven," he said again, trying to make his voice stern, trying to turn his plea into an order that out of fear I would feel obliged to obey.

I didn't answer but got up, walked around his bed, and stood with my back to him looking out through the French doors over the wide green lawn and beyond the lawn to the tall flame-colored trees blazing in the Ecuadorian rain forest.

7

AN ALMOST-YOUNG EPISCOPALIAN MINISTER stood before my
father's casket and spoke a few unkind words. It was a brutal hon-
esty, a rudeness that mocked church politics, for we were gathered
together in a memorial chapel that was dedicated to the memory of my
father's sister, Wilhelmina, and had been largely paid for with Grandmother's money. The minister was the same man who a year or so before
had called my father and his wife fascists in a public church meeting.
Later he had been ordered by his bishop to apologize, had driven out
into the country, and standing at the back door had said, "I sincerely
want to apologize for calling you fascists in public . . . But Mr. Thomsen,
you are, you know. Both of you; you are fascists." Today his last words
in the chapel rather emphasized the wickedness of Man without mentioning any names. After the service my aunt and I sank back and
disappeared in the sybaritic extravagance of the funeral parlor's Lincoln
and drove behind my stepmother's identical model to the cemetery. The
final rituals were performed, those silly questions asked of death, "Where
is thy sting, thy victory?" And now my father, stripped of his flowers, his
bronze casket richly austere, was put into motion and, by hidden springs
and cables, in a disappearing act that mixed showbiz and theatrical magi-
cian's state-of-the-art technology with the comforts of the church and
the cruel and solemn reality of extinction, sank slowly, slowly into the
ground. Next to the abyss was a pile of raw earth artfully hidden by un-
rolled strips of plastic turf dyed super-bright in shades of Technicolor
green. Astroturf.

With the same emptiness, the same guilt at feeling so little upon hearing the news of his death, I endured this final rite. What I felt most was a
dull amazement that the celebration of death, which should have contained elements of awe and terror, should have been allowed to slip from
the hands of the church and been given over to the undertakers, those

bad choreographers, those men of vulgar taste. On the other hand, while I had been unmoved, it had been the kind of show that would have pleased my father, the magnificence of the casket alone a symbol of his noble life and his noble ending as a very rich and important business leader. He must have picked it out before he died; it was just a little heavier and a bit more expensive than my grandfather's coffin.

My father died in the fall of 1959 and, though I have had almost twenty years to come to terms with whatever it was that existed between us, I have never made that final peace that is called forgiveness. This was something that was outside my control, for while with time I could push him out of my thoughts, he continued to creep into my dreams. They are dreams I no longer remember except as dark poisonous things that sat on my chest and mimicked the more threatening aspects of his living presence. Then I stopped dreaming, he faded away, the past became the past; the jungles of Ecuador, as romantic as childhood gardens, let me live in the illusion that I was beginning life again and from the beginning. But forgetting my father was little more than a device to quiet a deep inner guilt that bothered me for my coldness toward him. There had never been a time since my freshman year in college when I hadn't thought that some day I must write about him. What a gold mine of fantastic stories, slapstick extravaganzas, tales that wandered at the edge of credibility. If there is one single factor that would make one want to write it is the conviction of being in possession of unique material — plus the desire to share it. What I had wanted to forget was not my father and the careless way he had handled his life, but the overcharged emotions he had laid on me that had warped my own life. Like a pail of muddy river water I put him aside until the impurities could settle out and I could see his essence in its transparency with some of the rage and blame sunk to the bottom.

And so about ten years after his death, when I thought I was distanced enough and beginning to want to write about the war and the years before the war, the memories of which, now that I was old, were blooming with the bright colors of nostalgia, once more I picked up and began to read my father's book of lying memoirs that I hadn't looked at in thirty-five years. In empty rooms or on deserted beaches or in the darkness of the awful early morning hours I began to reexamine my life. For the first time I tried to look at myself coldly. I had never understood my father, but if I were going to write about him I would have to try and see him in a new light. Half feeling that somehow I deserved it, I had never understood why he had hated me with such a sustained passion, and so I began to look at myself through his critical eyes, as though by understanding why he had been so perpetually critical and nagging, I could, by sharing his contempt, also share some of the blame for his rage.

To go back when you are almost seventy and resurrect yourself as a child, teenager, a college student, is an appalling and painful exercise. I became acquainted with a young man who, had I met him now, would have bored and vexed me. What a smart-ass, what a conceited, selfish, empty-headed, sex-driven, snobbish peer clone. I remembered him without pity, and relived forgotten episodes so shameful or squalid or stupid that even now, an old man, I had to shake my head in shame. Still, still, obnoxious as I must have been, as infuriating as I must have been to the adults doomed to share my space, I could not find traits that were not common to the young people I had grown up with. In other words, within narrow limits I had been no more disgusting than any other teenager brought up under the shadow of family wealth which made him feel that he was something special. Why then if I were no more infuriating than the average ridiculous middle-class whelp had I so displeased that man? Why, when my youth in many respects had been only as vapid and as wasted as his? I read and reread his memoirs, looking for a clue, but he had obliterated too many things; too many things were disguised or hidden. The chief impression I received, even acknowledging that the book was about him, was the realization of how small a part I had played in his life — especially considering what an overpowering presence he had been in mine. In that almost one hundred tedious pages of his I had been given a semi-starring role in a single paragraph, and I kept going back to it; it troubled me, for in the plainness and banality of his description, and even though his memory of that day was superficially almost identical with mine, I felt that something of importance had been left out.

Let me quote directly from his book. It will give you an idea of his literary style — which in moments of black depression I sometimes fear I may have inherited.

Well to go on with the story. We lived on the farm at Wildcliffe. Moritz was in the army and Wyllie was married and lived in Sausalito, California. Moritz as I said was in the army, he got in early so he could get it over with and get his army discharge. He was working toward this end when on Dec. 7th, 1941 the Jap bombing of Pearl Harbor came along. I remember it so well, I was just home from the hospital from my operation on my back. Moritz was home that Sunday morning when news of Pearl Harbor came over the air, we were all dumbfounded, the next day we were in World War #2. I remember Moritz walking up and down the long hall at our home, he walked and walked up and down and tears were in his eyes at times. I guess he knew what was ahead of him. Moritz was stationed at Fort Lewis, near Tacoma, and he used to come up and see us on weekends sometimes. Well, my back got well. It took weeks to learn to walk again, but I kept after it, walking on the front porch at home, hour after hour.

Oh, bad Daddy, you do have a way with words. But is that all you truly remember of that day that changed everything and which, in a convoluted and perhaps not entirely believable way, I believe I can pinpoint as the day you decided I would probably be more satisfactory to you as a dead son than as a live one?

7 December 1941. In world history it is one of the most awesome dates of the twentieth century. My father's flaccid account almost contradicts the popular notion that great historical moments are intensely remembered. Despite my father's memory of that day, almost like a blank page, I still believe it. Something happens in our minds at those cataclysmic moments when as individuals we are caught up in history. We take on some of the oversized qualities of the time; the smallest details become significant, the smallest details, etched into our memories. The memory of Roosevelt's death, Kennedy's assassination, the bomb at Hiroshima — our personal lives are closely woven into these events. It is as though only disaster can bring us to life, sharpen our senses, send the blood surging through our bodies. Universal disasters give us each, by concentrating the emotions, a temporary sense of being a part of the rolling earth. So it is comparatively easy to go back into the mind of that young man who answered to my name in 1941, but I may have to move

a lot of earth and build a shaky hypothesis or two to bring a little light into the state of my father's mind on that Sunday morning almost fifty years ago.

One of those Japanese bombs had exploded in my father's head; for a time everything was confused and chaotic. Of all the races in the world my father admired only the Chinese and Japanese; as he contemplated the news on the radio that morning he felt as though he were going insane. He was truly dumbfounded that morning, but perhaps in confessing his dumbfoundedness he was saying that for a few hours there was nothing much of anything in his mind but a tragic confusion.

In a sense my father had no opinions about much of anything until he had checked out his morning copy of the Seattle *Post Intelligencer.* This was a typical Hearstian production — yellow journalism; a combination of simplistic nineteenth-century jingoism and McKinley-type Republican bromides; today's opinions identical to yesterday's precisely reflecting my father's extreme and extremely old-fashioned political views. Hearst had hired the great brains of the times, and my father avidly read and quoted these brilliant pundits who had columns in this rag, intellectuals now completely forgotten or discredited: Louella Parsons, Walter Winchell, Arthur Brisbane, B.C. Forbes, Westbrook Pegler. They all knew which side the bread was buttered on, and they aped the Hearst philosophy, sometimes screaming even louder than the old man himself. They hated, just to name the first items that come to mind: Roosevelt and his wife, Eleanor; labor unions (especially the CIO and the coal miners' organization); the forty-hour week which effeminized the American worker; radical, bomb-carrying anarchist university professors; uppity minority groups; decadent England; godless Russia. And the sly, yellow, madly-copulating Oriental. Seattle, as the Gateway to the Orient, especially needed to be educated to the secret designs of the Yellow Menace, and about once a week columns or editorials appeared that quoted Napoleon's remark, "Beware of China when she rouses herself and begins to march." Queer, because most the time Hearst was writing about Japan. But really, what was the difference? Both races were yellow with slanty eyes, and oh my God, they were over there in their uncounted zillions — rousing, slowly rousing. Hearst featured political cartoons that starred evilly grinning Orientals with inch-thick glasses and enormous buck teeth and with long knives plunged into the backs of kindly old gentlemen in star-studded top hats and wide, red-and-white striped trousers. Those of us who in the late 1930s worshipped Steinbeck for his poetic and radical politics hated Hearst and continued to do so even after the madness of Pearl Harbor made him, in that respect at least, a kind of goofy but inspired prophet. He disgusted us even when he was right. But he was so rarely right. Poor old man, so confused between his beliefs in manifest destiny and isolationism, between the rosebud past and the terrifying future. My father was almost completely loyal to him, and carried the burdens of his hatreds and irreconcilable attitudes into irrational territory. But on one point he stood his ground. He had very strong feelings about the Japanese. The Japanese had made the family rich.

When my father was still a child and my grandfather's luck had begun to seem monstrous, Grandfather had begun to look toward the Orient. Standing on the rim of the Pacific with no west left, he still felt that burning westering lust. It probably occurred to him that if every Asian were to eat a pound of flour each year, all the wheat fields of the western states could not supply the demand. He went to Japan and came back with a Japanese butler-chauffeur who had been his cabin boy and who stayed with the family for years. He went back to Japan and built the first flour mill in that country, and each time he came back he brought fantastic presents — enormous stuffed turtles that my father rode across the floor, the gaping mouth-bones of man-eating sharks, that same stereopticon which later I would inherit and which put Japanese scenes into three dimensions so that you could walk into the picture and disappear. The chauffeur taught my father how to drive and how to care for cars. And when my father was allowed to go on camping trips, he and his friends and the baskets of food prepared by my grandmother were all delivered and picked up at the edge of the woods or the banks of some trout stream by the faithful Oriental.

I don't believe it was Grandfather who sent Perry with his gunboats to Japan to open up the country to American enterprise, but he followed close behind, and he made a lot of money. And then because he wasn't just lucky but smart as well, he realized he could do as well by selling wheat to the Kobe mill. His partner was a Mr. Nakamura. They became close friends, Grandfather sold him the property and, enflamed now with bigger passions closer to home, began to build his Mexican railroad.

This business in Kobe all took place years before I was born, but the warm friendship with Mr. Nakamura cast a golden oriental glow over those early years that I spent in my grandparent's house. The terms of the sale of the mill were scrupulously observed, the Japanese company flourished, Mr. Nakamura became a rich man who years later I believe, though I'm not sure about this, became involved with Frank Lloyd Wright in the construction of the Imperial Hotel. Out of his gratitude and admiration Grandmother's house began to fill with gifts: sets of ebony chairs carved in the shape of dragons; a silver punch bowl, lotus-shaped with dragons for handles and large enough to intoxicate fifty guests; an eight-foot-square rosewood chest that opened up like parting theater curtains and was filled with secret drawers; bolts of raw silk; mah jong sets in ivory and teak; Hiroshige woodcuts; sets of plates and bowls as thin and translucent as egg shells. How could my father have grown up in that house without being awed by the Japanese?

My father's momentary sense of confusion on the seventh of December 1941 was compounded of more elements than his ambiguous feelings about Japan and their surprise attack. In the first hour or so, dumbfounded, he may have constructed in the wildness of his imagination an equation that turned reality inside out: his prime enemy being Roosevelt, Japan had, by confronting this monster, automatically become the national savior. Republicans, the good old red-blooded kind with their secret fascist passions and their belief in simple solutions, sometimes hold pretty strange opinions before they are outfitted in straitjackets and given board and room at the local funny farm. Besides all that, my father did not have a subtle mind; but no, he figured out before the day was over that his fantasies were treasonous and that Japan would have to be brought to its knees. Maybe with luck, before those little paper houses flared up like burning garbage, certain samurai would succeed in assassinating Roosevelt; maybe in the first days of peace my father could send CARE packages to the Nakamura family.

My presence in the house that morning, combined with the news from Hawaii, focused his mind on another more pressing problem — me. He felt that I was slipping away from him. He was a man who hung onto everything; he could scarcely even bear to throw away an interesting newspaper and already had a couple of hundred pounds of sensational headlines piled in the attic that one day he would fit into scrapbooks, convinced that the Seattle Historical Society would, after his death, receive and treasure them. (It didn't.) He knew instantly, even as the Zeros were diving out of the sun behind Diamond Head, that it was war, and that the war was going to change everything, and that, imprisoned in a uniform but liberated into a world of adventure and violence and Great Events, I might develop a taste for independence. As with everything around him, he owned me and he felt, for my own good and his own satisfaction, that he had a right to control my future to the honor of my grandfather whose name I carried. But now I was twenty-five and had begun to display traits of restlessness and impatience. One day I might just walk out of his life and not come back, as I had always done before. In his eyes, being in the army gave me a spurious but threatening freedom, and when he hadn't seen me for a couple of months he may have imagined that I had escaped or was consciously trying to escape his domination.

Even greater than his desire to have power over me was his conviction that I needed taking care of. He knew that in matters of business (and really, what else mattered?) I was inept, a kind of financial half-wit. This was more than just partly true, for having lived until I was seventeen with the knowledge that everyone in the family was rich, I continued to feel rich and blessed even after the Depression had pretty much leveled us to the ground and my father had become a kind of high-class basket case. By that time it was too late; my philosophy was rooted. In my grandmother's house, surrounded by my aunts with their social aspirations, in the private school where I was taught to represent the noble qualities of my class, I learned that it was vulgar to talk about money or about God, that to be nakedly competitive showed a lack of self-confidence and the animal greed of a peasant, that when you cut an apple in half to share you always chose the smaller piece, that when you voted you put aside your own private interests and considered national needs. These were not all traits unworthy of being cultivated, though there was a degree of snobbishness involved, and they were ways of thinking that my father found decadent, repugnant, and unrealistic.

My classy aunts taught me by precept and example that it was mean to hang on to money, and that out of simple respect for your position, whether you could afford it or not certain standards were to be maintained. I spent every dollar I could lay my hands on — mostly on books and phonograph records — though the spendthrift sums I threw away did not average, after my grandmother's death, much more than ten or fifteen dollars a month. This was, of course, a considerable sum in the 1930s. So all right, I was a spendthrift, and yes, with the country sinking into despair and millions of unemployed standing in lines and fighting for fifty-cent-an-hour jobs, it must have been profoundly irritating to contemplate this idle shit hidden away in his room listening to long-haired music, Stravinsky or Roy Harris, on scratchy 78 rpm records that cost a dollar a piece. Or reading obscene books like Freud's *Interpretation of Dreams,* or a lying, muckraking, anarchistic, sour-grapes book about my father's heroes called *The Robber Barons.* Or the utter madness of *Finnegan's Wake* that sat on my table in a prominent place. Unread, unreadable.

I thought for many years that these aristocratic pretensions of mine had created the disgust he felt for the way it seemed that I was turning out, made him see me with such divided feelings. It was only years after he died — and years after I had accepted the idea that I had served him badly by not dying the hero's death which he could have exploited to give grandeur to his life — that I stumbled upon what lay like foundation stones as the basis for his confusion. It had nothing to do with my good manners. What he wanted for me, or rather, what he wanted me to be for him, was made up of two absolutely contradictory elements: he wanted a son he could own and he wanted a son worth owning, a catch-22 situation, because I could only be the kind of man whom he could look in the eye with love if I were strong enough to free myself from him and make my own life. If he could own me, if he could buy me for whatever price, then any price was too high. He was like a man mad with love for a woman who, in the moment that he robs her of her virginity, loses her value, transformed into a common street slut.

8

I HAD NOT JOINED THE ARMY to get it over with and get out. Not at all. In 1940 I had been drafted — and so quickly after the draft laws were passed that I sometimes thought of myself as the first draftee and the draft laws as a plot promulgated for the sole purpose of screwing up my life.

Before that Sunday morning in December then, I had already spent almost a year in the army. Nothing in the past but the books I had read had prepared me for barracks life in the fir-treed parks of Fort Lewis. Most such books are anti-war and so I knew that war was hell, that officers were martinets, and that endless, idiot drilling was not particularly stimulating. Now I began to learn that armies are like great, spreading amoebas which seem to operate without a central organizing brain. My little army, organized around a small group of play soldiers from Lompoc, California and rushing around to prepare us for combat, was constantly reinventing itself. I had no patience with its improvisatory blundering and no respect for a discipline that was so uncertain. All of us who were assigned to this artillery regiment were under the domination of the Lompoc sergeants, the Lompoc corporals, and the Lompoc Pfc.'s. General MacArthur himself would have hard-ass scrabbled in that outfit for a half-friendly sneer of recognition for his military qualities. The Lompoc farmers, they weren't civil, just sort of stupid, loyal to one another. We were dull-witted too, peaceful dolts who dreamed only of the private lives we wished to lead — instructed by equally uninvolved men with black stripes pinned to their sleeves. Teaching us to bayonet swinging sacks of straw while baring the teeth and shrieking like Fay Wray about to have her teats rubbed by King Kong. They made us yell, but they were as embarrassed as we were.

I decided after a couple of months, dressed in slightly too large khakis, assigned to an artillery outfit that had no artillery, learning to drill (at first) with a wooden gun, and being bombed in maneuvers with little bags of flour dropped from Piper Cubs, that in this soured circus atmosphere the only honest role would be that of a fool. It was my first creative show of independence in the army; I had no military ambitions and felt no need to order anyone to do anything. Like most draftees in 1940, I was not enthusiastic about the war that was being planned for us; on the contrary, I felt a kind of disgust with the corrupt and vacillating European leadership that had allowed Hitler to overrun the western nations. It was the few books I had read that helped me define my role. What else could I use but books? By rejecting my father's values I was in a sense a kind of blank page, a young man without a personality and without any discernible talents. It is even possible that I rejected the serious elements of army life because I was so ignorant, so inept at soldiering — as inept at soldiering as at everything else.

Camping alone on a high mountain lake in my nineteenth year, I had lain around camp when I wasn't fishing or chasing mountain goats and read *The Magic Mountain*. Turgid, slow-moving, incomprehensible, exquisitely boring, the only vaguely sexy part in a French I scarcely understood — for whatever reason it sent my Germanic blood into a boil. It made me want to be a writer. I read a sentence that went, something, something, something, "the justice of organic dissolution." And decided then and there, digging out a notebook from my pack, that I would keep a record of my thoughts and copy out new words and noble sentiments. Apparently I had no thoughts or noble sentiments, for at the end of the summer the notebook was empty except for the notation, "The juices of organic dissolution. Chased a billy goat down the shale under the Dollar Watch look-out." The young writer with nothing to write about. Back at the university I tried to think of plots for the short story course but was reduced to stealing plots from Chekhov and setting them in the Pacific Northwest, poor Russian peasants transformed into the starving migrant hitchhikers of the Depression.

If I didn't write much I got through a lot of reading, and much of it for its power and its insights was stunning to me. When I wrote I copied only the best — Tolstoy, Hamsun, Hemingway, James Cain.

Four years of college studying creative writing had not made me into a particularly desirable piece of military property. It was hard for personnel — though they weren't operating at full efficiency either — to fit me into a slot where I might function with a certain flair. I was like an ex-used-car salesman made colonel by some grotesque fuck-up in the department of records. I operated at about 20% efficiency. It was possible that in time I might learn to pull the string on a 155 mm rifle and make a big boom; they put me in a gun crew. Standing in the back row with my peers at the early morning roll calls, I had never felt so alone, so useless, so almost despairing.

What I did best was peel potatoes and scour pots; standing before a sink of steaming, almost boiling water and fishing out plates, my mind dulled into torpid animal bliss. Pulling an imaginary string on an imaginary gun was kid stuff, the war play of the cub scout set. Humiliating. I analyzed my military aspirations and the paralyzing depression of devoting one's days to idiot activities, the main activity being inactivity, and I went to the top sergeant with a proposition. He remembered me as the fool who had tried to dry a shirt on the flues in the furnace room and had almost burned down B barracks. "Give me a permanent weekend pass," I said, "and I'll be a steady KP for the rest of the week." He must have seen me as a low-grade menace — the player on the football team who will eventually run the wrong way, the musician in the orchestra who will come in two beats early on the tam-tam, the priest who will giggle at the funeral. He jumped at the chance.

KP, kitchen police. It was the most hated job in the army, worse than standing guard, and vaguely degrading for the overtones that connected it with women's work, with mother in her kitchen. KP, though I believe it wasn't supposed to be, was assigned in some outfits as a punishment and on the rotating lists the names of misfits, near-morons, and fuck-ups would appear more often than the names of their more eager, more beady-eyed companions. It lasted from five in the morning until about seven at night and could be defined as cruel and unusual punishment. Not for me, who from reading the Russians had found moral grandeur in submission, humility, and noninvolvement. In an instant I transformed myself into Prince Myshkin, into Alyosha Karamazov. Smelling faintly of onions, pork grease, and potato peels, suddenly totally isolated from the idiot rhythms of the soldier's day, dressed in stained and sagging fatigues like a cartoon figure, crouched over a twenty-gallon pot or half hidden inside it, peeling spuds until my bleeding fingers stained their water, I sank into a placid and unthinking stupor that lasted for about nine months. Thinking about this paragraph and that lost time, in my sleep last night trying to define myself either as a fool or more charitably as a naive young man making a first semi-demi-heroic attempt to live by philosophical postulates that mocked my society, I dreamed myself as two superimposed Botticelli figures, vaguely androgynous, half Primavera, half Venus rising up out of the sea of my own inconsequentiality, dressed in jungle camouflage and with, instead of spring flowers falling around me, festoons of coleslaw, spaghetti, orange and potato peels, and at my feet squares of strawberry Jell-O, banana peels, and slices of watermelon rind. Okay, then, half fool, half hero. By refusing to play at soldiering, by deciding to retire from the competition, I asserted my own authenticity. For nine months I lived in the garbage disguised as offal, as happy as I had ever been while I contemplated the drama of voluntary withdrawal, and as much at peace as anyone might have expected to be in 1941, waiting for the world to explode. Where had I read that even a dog turd is a piece of God?

All of us, of course, solved our personal problems at being drafted into this citizen's army in our own ways. Some solutions were neurotic and destructive, some imaginative, some sad. A good percentage of those first men should never have been accepted. Too much malnutrition, too many untreated sicknesses, too much rage in those ten years of Depression before the war. Millions of young men had ended up damaged. One of the jokes of the time, as old as the history of war, was that the doctors told you to bend over and open your mouth; they looked up your ass and if they couldn't see light — congratulations, you have been accepted. A generation of men with rotting teeth, bad eyes, anemia, a chronic cough; they were undersized and underweight, but no matter. Look what the CCC camps had done for the national health. Big helpings of army chow would straighten them out. And in many cases it did, for there is nothing like food to cure hunger. But what the medics couldn't see, didn't exist — and where they couldn't see was into the minds of a group of men much more radical and discontented, much more psychologically disoriented than the doctors, conservative sons of middle-class families, could easily imagine. Moving from a breadline to a chow line was for many a happy step in the right direction. For others being hungry but free was better than fighting for a heartless economic system that had failed them, that had robbed them of their farms, their jobs, their self-respect. For all of us those first months in the army were a time of crisis.

Gerroad couldn't live without his wife. For three weeks he sat on his bunk and stared at his new GI shoes with their bulldog toes, and then one day he simply walked away and disappeared. If he was caught, and he probably was (though we never heard), he would have been sentenced to years in some army stockade. A few days later Hopkins, another recruit, went over the hill along with a couple of others in the next barracks. A middle-aged fellow from New Jersey who looked as mousy as a bank clerk, he went into the latrine at three o'clock one morning and began jumping from the top of the barrier that separated the showers from the toilets, time after time, until he had successfully broken his arches. I remember how he cried when the MPs came and made him walk to the jeep that would take him away.

And there was Moore, the bravest of the lot. He began to appear each morning at 5:30 holding an aluminum coffee cup out to those of us lined up at the urinal. "Please," he said in a dead voice, his face pale and mad, "please." Shocked into a paralysis that dried up our own streams, we refused to slake his thirst. Then an army captain from the hospital observed this eccentric behavior from the doorway and ordered Lugo to pee into the cup. "Your health, young fellow," the captain said, his eyes shining like blackberries. "Go ahead; bottoms up. Your prayers have been answered." Moore drank and followed docilely behind the doctor to the psycho ward where for another sixty days, observed finally by hundreds, he drank a cup of someone's urine every morning until he got that Section Eight that he was looking for. If he wasn't mad when he began that caper, God knows he was probably mad by the time it was all over.

A dozen dazed recruits were delivered from Reno like something out of the fattening pens: cowboys, horse-breakers, shills and gamblers; a charming pimp the coolest of the lot. He ended up, I believe, as a master sergeant, for he had a lovely way of making people do what he wanted. All of them were charming, witty, and strong, except for one, the oldest, who went AWOL immediately after basic training and shot himself through the head in a cheap Tacoma hotel room. It was usually the men over thirty who in their rigidity shattered like glass.

Until I moved into the cook's room where I could be roused at four-thirty without disturbing the troops, I lay at night with all these potential gunners in that long double-rowed room and listened to their bizarre music. It resembled vaguely a Cage sonata for piano: lights out at ten, the long, pure, exquisitely nostalgic sound of taps flooding the night, very near, very far away, with its little hint of death; and then after a tense silence — muffled weeping, groans, imprecations, the squeaking of bed-springs as phantom wives and sweethearts crept beneath the blankets, and the whispered desperation of one buddy bitching to another.

We waited resentfully for the war that we knew was coming and that would dignify and justify our humiliation. In midsummer all over the United States a secret and spontaneous revolt began to grow. The months were passing, our lives were passing, we existed in a limbo of last chances, we would come out of this old and punch-drunk like unused and rusted machines. In August on all the walls in all the latrines, on scraps of paper dropped on the ground, on barracks walls and fences, in the theaters and PXs, an identical message began to appear — Over the Hill in October, soon abbreviated to OHIO. We waited, half believing that together we would end this purgatory, pleasantly caught up in the fantasies of a general mutiny. If I had found fulfillment in the kitchen, still it required a tremendous effort of the imagination. I would not be among the first of the deserters — but I would not be the last rat either to flee that aimless ship, adrift and witlessly rocking through the interminable months. Hell, they couldn't shoot us all; we were millions.

But October came and passed. Nothing happened. November; nothing except new graffiti appeared: Over the Hill in April. Between November and April we had first to pass through December.

By the middle of the 1930s, in Seattle at least, bad music had pretty well driven out good music from every radio station. Looking back I find it hard to believe that when I was born and for some years afterwards there was not a single radio station in the world and that less than fifteen years after I had heard my first broadcast at the age of six (the "Washington Post March," music that almost made me faint with joy) the airways had been taken over by the Bings, Bobs, Russes, and Skinnies. Not that I didn't like them, too, but I longed to hear Beethoven from time to time. Good second-rate music like *Scheherazade* by, the radio announcer informed us, "those two famous Russians," had gradually been replaced by half-hour programs sponsored by fellows trying to maintain high standards and come on classy, music that featured sweet stuff like "In a Monastery Garden," "In a Persian Market," "Ave Maria" or the other joint effort of that talented team, "The Flight of the Bumblebee," soon to be turned into camp by Jack Benny and his lagging fingers. This was all music that I pretended to detest — and finally truly did. As for recorded music, Victor's Red Seal catalogue of classical music was still skimpy. For those of us who longed to hear good music then, the high points of each week were the Saturday morning opera from the Metropolitan (a low-grade high point) and the live broadcast on Sunday morning of the New York Philharmonic.

And so on that Sunday morning I was doing what I always tried to be doing on those Sunday mornings of my youth: tuning in to Carnegie Hall. I had come home from Fort Lewis and was lying on my bed as the music began. My father is in a room down the hall; being sick he has moved into his daughter's room, is lying in bed surrounded by bottles of painkiller and hospital smells. My stepmother is in the house but she has been swept out of my memory by the day's events.

The music is a pleasant surprise, Shostakovich's First Symphony — music of the times, brassy, brilliant, and best of all, new. I lay in the room enjoying martial rhythms and crazy Soviet discords. Fuck Stalin if he didn't like it. Great red flags billowed slowly like heavy curtains in the crisp air; their nostrils steaming, Russian horses pawed the icy ground; smiling peasants hammered and sickled.

There is a lively clashing, are we to the second movement yet? And suddenly a switch is thrown, the music is cut off, the radio goes dead. And a moment later a strange, frightened, agitated voice announces, "We interrupt this program with an unconfirmed notice that has just been received. An unidentified shortwave station in the Hawaiian Islands reports that hundreds of Japanese planes are bombing and strafing the military facilities at Pearl Harbor." There is another silence, I guess. It's true, of course; you know immediately that it's true, you've been waiting for years, waiting for them to break in through the front door, and you're a little surprised that it has come like this, through the kitchen and with an insolence that will silence every pacifist. The music comes back, but now it is unheard, as irrelevant as the chittering of birds. What had been important and beautiful a minute before has become irritating and hateful. I lay there raging at the music, thinking, "How can the bastards keep sawing away as though nothing has happened?" I wanted the microphones in Carnegie Hall to swing out over the audience where they would pick up the screams and curses that would mirror my own rage.

It is impossible to reconstruct at this late date the complications of the next couple of minutes. But I remember a couple of things, one of which I confess with a certain degree of reluctance since it seems to contradict my earlier theory that we are changed by world catastrophes into larger-than-life actors in history. My first thought at the realization that we were at war brought me to a state of mild panic. I had made plans to engage that Sunday afternoon in some serious lovemaking, plans that included, exciting and paralyzing thought, doing it for the first time with the lights on. At the same time, like listening to two different pieces of music simultaneously, the terrible grandeur of the moment brought tears to my eyes. I wept with the same impersonal and almost reluctant emotion that overpowers one upon hearing certain final apocalyptic chords in a Mahler symphony. This time I was weeping, almost joyfully it seems, for the magnificence, for the immensity of the coming horror, a whole world engaged and convulsed. Embracing the whole world, I was still panicked at the possibility of missing out on a good screw.

And in a room down the hall my sick father, dizzy with the news, is having similar thoughts of a general and personal nature. At fifty-two, too old and battered to fight, he is about to be rejected by history unless he can figure out a way, through me, to get involved. His wheels and gears have already begun to whir. After a time, my eyes still teary, I walked down and stood in the doorway to his room. "Well," I asked, "have you heard the news?"

"Jesus Christ," my father said, dumbfounded.

He lay propped up on pillows with his arms cruciform, trying to breathe deeply. During times of emotion he was often attacked by asthmatic seizures and now he was wheezing and gasping and trying to suck air into his lungs. From a small radio by his head, nested among bottles of different colored pills, a syrupy voice of suspicious gender went tip-toe-ing through the tulips. His dog, Missy (Missy number two?), lay at the foot of his bed contemplating, cross-eyed, a design in the bedspread. She was ostentatiously purebred, all the brains had been bred out of her, and she was nothing but fifty pounds of long hair with legs. Big for a dog, hairy as an Amazon sloth, she was smaller than she looked once you had checked her out, plunging your hands in up to the elbows. Her eyes were about a half-inch apart; looking at her head-on was like being stabbed by her appallingly long, sharp nose, at the base of which she carried about a teaspoonful of brains — level, not heaped. I have suggested here that she was the second of the five identical Missys who gradually took over my father's house and in whose memory an obscenely extravagant portion of his money would be left to the Humane Society upon his death. But Missy two, three, four, what difference could it have made; they were all identical, identically crazy.

I walked up and down the hallway, hesitating at each turning by a radio, his or mine, for some further bulletin, some crushing detail that would make the morning real. The music continued, I suppose; Mr. Metropolis or whoever it was that year kept beating it out. I can't remember now, but after an hour I went back to my room and lay on my bed. The radio had begun to come up with hard news: an unidentified American battleship had been slightly damaged; Jap planes continued to come diving out of the sun and Hickam Field was being strafed with machine-gun fire; a little toy-like two-man submarine had been sighted skulking in the harbor; the secretary of state, Cordell Hull, had issued a furious statement about shameless treachery; President Roosevelt will address Congress in the morning when war will be declared. All leaves have been canceled; return, soldiers and sailors, return to your bases. It is expected that Seattle, San Francisco, and Long Beach will come under attack at any moment. Panic in that district south of San Francisco where the rows of ticky-tacky houses run in lines to the desperate horizons. Panic in Golden Gate Park where bands of Japanese soldiers have been seen hiding in the Japanese Tea Garden. A middle-aged woman fearing Oriental rape jumps to her death from a bridge. All soldiers on leave or weekend passes will immediately report to their units.

What a lot of problems the attack on Pearl Harbor solved. In the army a common rage made brothers of us all. The future, once more clear, let us make sense of our own lives. Heroism became a possibility.

9

FLINGING MYSELF OFF A CLIFF and riding down a mountain face on skis once, I had conquered my fear and almost wept with joy. I had stood on the cliff edge for twenty minutes, sick and trembling to the point of vomiting until, unable to live with my cowardice, I had dropped into space, offering up my life to be free of the coward's taint. When caught in the ocean's undertow, let go. "Don't fight it," my instructor had said. "Let yourself go; become a part of the ocean and you'll survive." A couple of times I had had the chance to test his words. How comforting to throw yourself (or to be thrown) into the hands of some overpowering force and give yourself over to the inevitable; losing yourself, you are released to a new freedom.

Pearl Harbor, in catching us all up in a monumental catastrophe, had instantaneously obliterated millions of egos; now we were all part of a holy brotherhood. In one blinding flash, like the born-again Christian who, for a time at least, feels that the very organization of his atoms has been rearranged, or like the ecstatically howling young wolf who at last has been invited to hunt with the pack, we were joined and transfigured.

All that year waiting for the war I had stood (until I moved into the kitchen) at attention every evening while the flag was lowered and the national anthem blared out through a loudspeaker. How I had hated the long minutes of the brainwashing ritual, not because it was obligatory or boring but because I was so vulnerable, so moved by the sound of the music. How I hated the emotion that threatened to overpower me and how I fought against the seductions of patriotism. Tolstoy had taught me that governments could only exist with an army, a police force, and a subservient church backing them up. Stuart Chase and Swanberg had taught me that America was a country owned and being ravaged by a few rich families. I had seen the grandeur of the world, stood on national borders, and found that Canadian or Mexican or Philippine or German mountains were no less beautiful than mine, the people no less human. I wanted to detest the chauvinistic rantings of small minds that insisted we were a unique and superior people and that we could prove it by waving flags or putting Indians on reservations.

Now, in a moment's time, I was undone. From the first instant of that first announcement on the radio, deeper than any thought that might be articulated, I knew that I must change my life. Underneath everything that I thought I had learned, I was as patriotic as the draft board's General Hershey. No more fool's idealism; no more individualistic stances. The time had come to offer one's life to the nation. But suddenly the idea of being bombed while cleaning a pot had become obscene, unthinkable, a real Bugs Bunny finale. I was ready to die, but I wanted to go out in a noble way that would exactly define and mirror the burning urgings of my soul. Ah, those purple-mountained majesties, those waving, waving fields of grain; and damn those bucktoothed Nips with their tennis shoes, their raw fish salads, and their two-inch-thick eyeglasses.

I walked up and down the hallway for an hour until my thoughts could be put into words. Everything was clear: I must get out of the kitchen, out of that artillery outfit. Once more it was time to push off and give oneself up to the drama of total involvement with its reward of a noble death. The joy was in losing oneself and becoming a member of the pack. Tomorrow at the latest I would have to volunteer for hazardous duty; by military law this was something that could not be denied me. Geronimo. Bombs away. Etc. Etc.

About three o'clock I got up and went into my father's room again. My own emotions were too private, too intense to share with him, but I had to say good-bye. I hoped that by keeping my face carefully blank, as though a Japanese sneak attack were an everyday event, I could give him that kiss on the cheek that he expected and make an ordinary withdrawal. Knowing him, I knew he would with time figure out a way to use the war to his own purpose, and I dreaded the possibility that he would use it to construct some father–son relationship that would tend to bind us together in some excruciatingly sentimental way. In the passion of the moment it would be a father-and-son-go-marching-off-to-war fantasy that he would regret having invented as soon as his emotions had cooled.

"All leaves are canceled, all leaves are canceled, all soldiers and sailors will report to their units," the radio repeated for the tenth time.

"Well," I said, "I'd better get back to the kitchen."

My father nodded. Sometime during that long afternoon he had taken two five-dollar bills from his wallet by the radio, and now he clutched them in one hand. As soon as he saw me he held out his hand with the money in it; his eyes were unnaturally large and there was a mistiness swimming in them. This as much as anything was a proof that he saw the moment as historic; he was not normally so generous. But what was he paying for? Those two little tears that he had seen running down my cheeks, the first ones of mine that he had seen since I was ten years old?

"What's this for?" I asked, needing it, of course, but not wanting to give him the pleasure of buying whatever he thought ten dollars could buy.

"Take it," he said. "Spend it."

"Recklessly?" I asked, recklessly. Ten dollars, while it would buy three tanks of gas or a dozen decent meals, was not as impressive a sum to me as it was to him. One of my father's certainties about me was that I had no sense of money and that without constant surveillance I would immediately spend myself into that same bankruptcy that he had come so close to achieving in 1932. But he didn't challenge my sarcasm now with his usual comments about money not growing on trees or the fact that the only reason I had never lost my head was because it was tied on. Instead he gave me a mild look, one that was more alarming than anger. If he were going to be patient and friendly he would be treating me in a unique way which would leave me defenseless; I could always stand up to his anger and give him anger back, but what could I give him back should he now begin to offer me love? I took the money and walked across the room to the window, and turning saw Missy standing before a full-length mirror in the bathroom. She was immobile, staring at herself with a terrible concentrated fascination, a thing she often did for hours at a time.

"Well, I don't know when I'll be getting another pass," I said. "This is going to change things. I'll probably get off KP."

"No, you just stay where you are," my father said. "I know how you feel, but don't go jumping into any heroics. That job you've got is a good job, don't go doing something foolish. Soldiers have to eat, that's good honorable work, nothing to be ashamed of."

"I don't know. Another year of KP. That's an awful lot of dirty dishes."

"You just stay with your outfit. With your education there's no reason why you shouldn't advance, make sergeant, move up to be head cook."

"Oh, boy," I said.

"Don't be sarcastic," my father said mildly. "Head cook is a fine position. They do a lot of buying. You could come out in a very strong position."

"Yeah," I said, understanding him completely, "with a ten-year jail sentence."

"I'm not talking about anything downright dishonest," my father said. "But business is business. Some people have a head for it, some don't."

"Speaking of business," I said, "don't you think I'd better sell the cows and close down the farm? God knows how long this is going to last." About a year before being drafted, with the idea of escaping the draft by being engaged in a vital industry, I had purchased eighteen cows. They were the first cows I had ever owned; in fact they were almost the first cows I had ever looked at closely. The criminally innocent way I had bought them certainly tended to prove my father's thesis that I had no business sense. I had gone to the auction yard in Spokane where old animals were sent to be slaughtered and there, stunned with shock at their sad faces and the death that awaited them, I had bought every black cow in the yard. The amazed seller was honest, I think, and would stop me from time to time when I tried to make him offers for black steers. I referred to this senile and broken-down band of creatures as my little herd of Angus, though the truth was they were mostly Holsteins. Whatever they were, I loved them, and looking at their black hides against green pasture my eyes spun with delight.

When I was finally called before the draft board I went with a gloating heart. "You can't draft me," I said. "I'm a cattleman." "Well, yes and no," the draft board said. "We'll give you a four-month deferment to sell your cows." I had refused their deferment and refused to sell my shiny black beauties who had begun to grow sleek and young under my loving hands and had even begun to drop calves. Two weeks later I had found an ancient married couple; I paid them forty dollars a month to live on the farm and take care of the cows, and a few days later reported to the Tacoma induction center.

"Sell your little herd of cows?" my father asked in surprise. He looked at me and I think for the first time realized that the war would be bringing enormous changes and that nothing would ever be the same again. "No, no, no. You just hang on. No, don't sell your little herd of cows. This trouble will be over in six months. Those little people, what are they thinking of, for God's sake? Listen, mark my words, within two weeks the fleet will be anchored in Yokohama harbor, and then I feel sorry for Tokyo."

I tended to agree and said nothing, and my father was silent for a moment, staring at his hands. Then looking at him, I noticed his face begin to darken and his throat thicken with pounding blood. Suddenly he burst out, "Oh, that son of a bitch. He finally did it, that dirty little commie Jew. He's got the whole world dancing to his tune at last. Well, I hope he's satisfied. It makes you want to weep, yes, it makes you want to weep for this great nation of ours sold down the river by that traitor to his class, that Jew king who wants to rule forever. King Rosenfeld, that . . . ."

"Listen, Father, I've really got to get back. And it's not as though I hadn't heard your spiel."

"George Washington didn't run three times. No one has ever wanted it three times. King for life, that's what he's planning. Oh God, how it makes you want to weep. If you hadn't had your brains scrambled by those commie college professors you'd understand what he's cooked up with Churchill — to get us in this war, to get American boys into Europe again to die for their rotten schemes. Dirty, rotten, old Europe, like a vampire bat that can't live without American blood."

"Are you trying to say that Roosevelt ordered the Japanese to bomb Hawaii so we'd go to war in Europe?"

"That's just a ruse," my father cried. "My God, can't you understand? Roosevelt forced the Japanese to attack. He's absolutely anti-business. Wasn't cutting off the scrap iron a declaration of war? You wait and see, we're not at war with Japan; the war is in Europe and tomorrow we'll be at war with Germany, picking Churchill's chestnuts out of the fire for him. Japan? Those little people? War? All they want to do is take baths and make flower arrangements. No, my boy, screw your head on straight, and you keep out of this one. Don't go volunteering for any foolishness. I give it four months, six months at the most."

"All right," I said. "Six months for Japan, but what about Hitler?"

"If we're smart we'll let the Russians take care of Hitler, and if we're lucky they'll kill each other off. My God, now we're shoulder to shoulder with those godless atheistic Mongolians, Stalin and Roosevelt holding hands. My God, can you believe it? Am I losing my mind?"

I went back to the window and looked down lovingly at my little red pickup parked in the gravel drive. I imagined it driving up to Helen's house, imagined it parked under the shade of the street trees, imagined with a growing excitement what we would do inside the house. Would we show ourselves in all our nakedness? Would the first shame go away? Would my father stop talking so I could leave? Because it was really time to leave, and I didn't want to run out of time, war or no war.

Sometime in that year before I was drafted I had become involved with Helen. From the very first, without romance and without sentiment, we had been wildly involved, an affair clearly sinful, without love — pure lust and pleasure. Helen was married, and though I admired her husband who was an airline pilot, I felt little guilt, since from the day we met their marriage was already dissolving, a publicly acknowledged failure. Our first furtive meetings were models of teenage incompetence. We parked the car on dark streets in strange neighborhoods, blurring the windows with our hot steamy breathing. Later, driven and desperate, I learned how to rent rooms in hotels without stuttering, and later still, after I was drafted, moving symbolically from adolescence to maturity, the affair became less dangerous, less blatantly wicked, (less interesting), for she left her husband, sued for divorce, and rented a house in Tacoma not far from Fort Lewis.

Helen's marital problem had been of a purely sexual nature. The world was slipping into crisis and the airline where her husband worked, short of pilots, had put him on an impossible flying schedule that in a year had left him impotent. "Not that he was ever that great," Helen said. When I first met her at a party, in the first moment of looking into her face, I had recognized a fully sexed and desperate woman who was being pushed past her limits.

Her black eyes darted, her hands were quick and irrational, her laugh was pitched at the edge of hysteria. She seemed unable to compose her face, and her expression would switch for no apparent reason from a smile to a frown. When we danced she began to tremble violently and between dances recklessly tossed down double measures of scotch. I had never met a woman like her and was terrified, but at the same time I had dreamed of exactly such a woman who would be all lust and passion and who would strip me of my shame, my reticences.

At twenty-two, though I thought quite the contrary at the time, I was hopelessly ignorant about sexual matters; my few adventures had been quick and dirty — awful and incredible bone-snapping contortions in the rumble seats of roadsters, so athletic and surreal that we would both become hysterical with laughter at the wrong moment; badly stung in the nettle patches of vacant lots; or on sandy beaches in California where, having badly judged the tides, our enthusiasms were suddenly dampened by the froth of a dying breaker. I had never made serious love to a girl whom I really liked, for it was clearly understood in the bourgeois ambience of the late thirties that one did not take advantage of nice girls of one's own class. In the company of classmates, and made brave by their protecting presence, I had visited and fled from a few whorehouses in Tijuana, Tacoma, Shanghai, and Vancouver, B.C. We timidly hunted nurses, waitresses, and the daughters of poor farmers in the little hick towns of eastern Washington, and at the University of Oregon I had had some weird experiences with a couple of girls: a stutterer and a lesbian. I had never slept naked in a bed with a naked woman, but I felt that much of my life was spent dreaming of lying in a dim light with a bare-assed girl where everything would be slow, slow and endlessly prolonged. At twenty-two "endlessly prolonged" probably meant about fifteen minutes.

At the party I felt instantly that she was the one I had been evoking from the depths of my masturbatory fantasies. I was much too cowardly to pursue her immediately and to confront her naked sexuality with my own. It wasn't necessary: she had courage for both of us. Pressing against me as we danced and without speaking, she learned everything she needed to know. Late in the evening she came back from the bathroom, hiding in her closed hand a paper with her address and telephone number. I was to meet her the next night on a certain street two blocks from her house. Helen lived in Seattle; I lived on a dry land ranch in eastern Washington, so that our first half dozen meetings were spread over several months. If it was October of 1940 when we met, it was perhaps not until February of the following year that things finally calmed down a little, and instead of grabbing convulsively at one another we began to trade kisses and talk.

On Friday evening of December fifth, when I had scrubbed the last pot and picked up my weekend pass, I drove in to Tacoma and spent most of the night at Helen's house. I was still somewhat shy, still convinced that sexual intercourse was evil. Helen mocked me for being reticent and laughed at me when I insisted upon turning off the lights to hide my aroused condition. We had talked it over; on Sunday I would come back in the afternoon and we would make love without lowering the shades and darkening the room. The idea must have excited me, for as I was leaving, calm and spent, and as she walked with me to the pickup, I said with the most narrow-minded and unthinking candor, "Jesus, Helen, you remind me of Molly Bloom."

"Okay, who's Molly Bloom?" Helen asked in a suspicious voice. "Another of your babes, I suppose."

"No, no. She's a woman in a book." I told her about Joyce, showing off, I suppose, and told her that his book had been banned for years for obscenity but that it was considered a great masterpiece.

"Do you have a copy?" she asked.

"Yes, but it's at the farm."

How long ago that conversation seemed; how long ago even the memory of the symphony and the sudden silence and the voice breaking in to tell us that the world had changed. Standing at the window and thinking about Helen and beginning to get excited about what we would be doing in the next hour or so, I half-listened to my father's complaining voice behind me. The world had changed, and he didn't seem to know it yet. He was preaching the same old stuff, and I heard him with a kind of pity; an irrelevance. I was seeing him through this new war that would take me away to distant combat zones where his power would evaporate and where he would appear in my thoughts only when his frequent and irritating letters would arrive to harass me.

Once more from the radio at my father's bed: "All military personnel will immediately report to their units." I used the voice to break away.

"No kidding," I said, turning to him and approaching his bed. "I've really got to go. And right now." I leaned over, kissed my father on his cheek, and quickly left the room.

"You keep in touch now, you hear?" my father called after me weakly. He sounded disappointed, as though unhappy that this convulsive moment in our lives, which had promised to climax in some vivid and operatic way, was ending with such banality.

I walked down the back stairs and went outside through the kitchen. As I was about to climb into my pickup my father did a curious thing. He was just back from the hospital after an operation on his back and I don't know how much pain getting out of bed and walking across the room had caused him. But there he was, standing at the opened window and calling down to me. His face was agitated with fear and excitement as though he were experiencing panic. "Where's El Vera?" he called down, trying to keep his voice low.

"I don't know. She's not down here."

"She's not in the kitchen?"

"No. She's probably in her room."

"Look," my father called down to me, muffling his voice as though he were terrified that his wife might hear, "don't worry about anything; everything is going to be okay, you understand? I think you're right about selling your cows, and I'll do that for you as soon as I'm up and around. Shut down the farm, and you take that money and enjoy yourself. And look, when this is over I'll help you buy a good farm, pastures, barns, a nice little house. Three hundred cows."

I stood by the truck door with my mouth open, staring up at him, unable to believe my ears. A couple of years earlier, and only a short time before being drafted, I had found six hundred acres of mountain pasture in the Okanogan. It was for sale for three thousand dollars, and after bitter argument my father had offered to pay for half of it. It would be my inheritance, he said, and for the next year he never stopped mentioning his generosity or, since that poor land was incapable of keeping me, what an impractical move I had made. (Actually, the farm was making ten percent; considerably more than my father's investments at the time.) I had wanted land in that wonderful dry country of pines and apple orchards, of mountain streams and clear skies. To live in paradise, avoid the draft, write and fish and camp out and drink whiskey by hidden lakes — it was that short and perfect year when, deliriously happy, I almost froze to death and where, living on elk meat and baked potatoes, I had written thirty thousand incredibly awful words of a second novel that was even worse than the first one that I had started and abandoned in New York.

My father's promise was the most stunning he would ever make. It made me nervously happy, but it was so unreal, so unlike anything that had ever come before that I immediately questioned his motives. Five minutes before I had begun to project a new degree of freedom from his domination; now I felt as though I were about to lose something of great value. Perhaps it would be the right time to confront him with my own truths. Considered realistically, he would loan me the money; I was sure it wouldn't be a gift. But even at that, a loan of one hundred thousand dollars would tie us together in ways that later might prove to be almost unbearable. It is never easy to be the victim of overwhelming generosity, but maybe I wanted to believe that he felt guilty and wanted to make right those years which he had described in his memoirs as that time "when I guess I was a little hard to get along with." At the same time I figured he had suddenly realized that with the war he could only continue to control me by offering me the kind of future that he knew I dreamed of. It was only years later when it occurred to me that his offer had been a kind of testing, that he had wanted to know if I were man enough to resist this benign castration. In truth, he could have bought my soul that afternoon for — oh, say one hundred and fifty cows. Perhaps a hundred. I was smart enough to question his motives, stupid for not questioning his intentions.

After a long moment I called up to him. "Hey, Father, I don't think I heard you. You don't mean it."

"Of course, I'd like it if you were somewhere close, but if you want to live in eastern Washington, I'll go along with that."

"But three hundred cows? You're talking lots of money, big money, ninety, a hundred thousand dollars."

"You've got forty thousand dollars that your grandfather left you. I'll put up the rest. I mean it, this is a promise."

"I'm just speechless," I said, and I looked up at him, smiling, and he smiled back. And I believed him.

"We'll talk about it later," my father called down to me. He looked over his shoulder nervously, as though his wife had just come into the room and caught him at the window. "You get back to camp now, and no foolishness, understand?"

"That's not a string?"

"No, no. No strings. Just get back alive, that's the only string."

"Yeah," I said. "There's no sense in coming back dead now."

As I got into the truck and slammed the door my father's dog appeared at the window and my father put one arm around her neck, bent, and nuzzled her coat. When I stepped on the starter she began to bark insanely, and fifty feet down the drive I could still hear her yapping.

My father lived a few miles north of Seattle at the end of Lake Washington, and I had to drive through a curiously deserted city to reach the Tacoma highway — out through the industrial section past the lithograph company that used to make candy labels, calendars, and signboards for my grandfather's cracker business, the old candy factory now owned by National Biscuit, the wholesale grocers where my father bought cases of tinned vegetables for the house, the old Rainier brewery that was starting up again. Out past the Boeing plant, enormous now, where dozens of bombers, lightly camouflaged under netting, stretched along the road in a long row. They were B-17s, and with their bubble turrets top and bottom, their long wings and slim, graceful fuselages, they looked swift, powerful, and deadly.

The highway was empty of traffic, and this as much as anything gave to this Sunday afternoon an ominous quality, as though the war had already started and had devastated the population or frightened them into caves. It was only years later that I understood the menacing quality of that late afternoon. It had about it an awful sense of a slumbering portentousness that emptied the air of life and continuity. It was like a gigantic stutter, an awful stopping of time, a hiatus that promised horrific changes. In a very real sense that day in December of 1941 was the true beginning of the twentieth century. That day the Depression was officially over, the ownership of America changed hands, bankrupt American farmers, the last symbols of an agricultural America built on the principles of Jeffersonian democracy, could now desert the land for five-dollar-a-day jobs in the war factories. Doctors and dentists began to buy up the abandoned farms. The small farmer and the honest work-man, who were the glory and strength of the nation, disappeared into the urban slums. December seventh was the last day that the country represented an ideal for which one might with dignity offer to fight and die. Ten years later it was no longer worth fighting for. Twenty years later, when three million farmers a year were going bankrupt and the Bank of America owned most of the farmland in California and you couldn't raise tomatoes without a $150,000 harvesting machine, it was not even a country fit to live in. Unless, of course, you enjoyed working in a factory.

Halfway between Seattle and Tacoma there was a roadhouse and a dark coffee shop paneled in blackening knotty pine. I stopped there to drink coffee and to call Helen. The idea of the war had heightened my percep-tions, and though I wouldn't be able to stay long with her, I felt the strongest necessity to test my new feelings. She answered almost imme-diately, as though she had been sitting by the phone and waiting for my call.

"Helen?"

"Yes," she said, "this is Helen. What the hell do you want?" Her voice was cold and furious.

"Hey," I said. "Is this Helen?"

"You son of a bitch," Helen said.

I stood in the booth for almost a minute with the hum and crackle of distance between us, my mind searching for an explanation of an anger that seemed to be completely irrational. It had been only slightly more than twenty-four hours since we had parted on what I had thought were the tenderest of terms.

"Listen," I said finally, "let's start all over again, okay? This is M., that army fellow you've been going around with. You know, that guy with the red pickup? . . . Are you Helen? Are you Helen — ?" saying her full name.

"That's right, kiddo," she said. "That's right, you bastard."

"Oh, come on," I said. "What's eating you? What the hell's wrong? I haven't done anything to get you mad."

"Not much." There was another long silence and then she said, "I think I'll hang up now."

"Go ahead," I said. I listened for the click of the receiver, but she hung on and I could hear her breathing. "I've got one dime in change," I said. "You better tell me what's wrong before we run out of time."

"All right, I will," she said. She hesitated and took a deep breath. "What's wrong is that you think I'm a slut, that's what's wrong."

"Helen, for Christ's sake, what are you talking about? I don't think you're a slut."

"I'm talking about what we do together, you know what I mean."

"No, I don't know what you mean."

"I've got the book here. *Ulysses*. I'm reading it now, that last part about Molly Bloom."

"You didn't waste much time."

"No," she said. "I had to drive all the way to Seattle, to Harry Hartman's. And I don't think I ever want to see you again."

"Helen, for heaven's sake, Molly Bloom is the heroine; she's absolutely great. Look at the last sentence. 'And yes, I said, yes, yes,' or some goddamn thing. She's a very affirmative woman."

"She certainly is," Helen said dryly.

"Look, she's the greatest woman in literature." I hesitated, trying to recall what the critics had said or what Judge Woolsey had written in his court decision. The truth was that Molly Bloom was to me a highly intimidating character and had she existed and glanced into my eyes I would no more have thoughts of climbing into bed with her than I would have entertained the fantasy of accepting an invitation from Ernest Hemingway to go lion hunting. "Look, Helen, she's an earth goddess with all the healthy passions of a normal woman. She's that perfect woman who says Yes to life."

"Really?" Helen asked in a conciliatory way. "Do you really think so?"

"Yes, of course. She's a wonderful, healthy, normal woman. She's sort of an ideal. Don't you think so?"

"We're talking about what you think," Helen said.

"Molly Bloom is no slut," I said.

"It's lovely to do those things," Helen said. "But it's ugly to read about them written down in a book."

"Yes, it's like standing apart and watching yourself. It must look funny to watch someone." I started to giggle and over the phone I could hear Helen chuckling. "The two-backed beast," I said.

"What was that last crack?" Helen asked. "What's that about the beast?"

"Nothing," I said. "Maybe John Donne. Poetry."

"Then you don't think it's bad? You don't think I'm bad?"

"Christ, Helen, no. You're not bad, and I'm coming over right now. I'll show you who's bad."

"Yes," Helen said. "Yes. And hurry."

"You see, you talk just like her."

"Yes," Helen said, beginning to laugh. "I'm a very affirmative women, too. And you're sure you don't think it's bad?" But she didn't wait for my answer. "Hurry up," she said.

"I'm at the halfway house. Give me thirty minutes. . . . Have you heard the radio? We're at war, you know."

"Yes," Helen said. "I know. But the war can wait. We can talk about that later. There's more important things than wars."

The whole conversation excited me and made me proud; it had sounded like something right out of Hemingway. The rest of that day has disappeared from my memory. I suspect that if I had actually been changed by the war into a super-demon lover that I would now remember it, and would feel impelled to describe my newly exploding passion in great detail. But I guess nothing of great moment occurred. We tend to remember the truly important things, but it is strange, a weird dichotomy, what the mind finds worth forgetting. And what the mind holds fast to. And it is strange that when we go digging into the past we often fail to find what we expect; in our most vivid memories we are seldom wrapped in someone's arms but are almost always alone, and perhaps doing nothing more important than standing in a window as a full moon rises above the trees or, in a kind of grace, staring into the clear waters of a mountain lake.

10

WHILE THE GERMANS SWEPT ACROSS RUSSIA and laid siege to Leningrad, while the Japanese drove MacArthur out of the Philippines and began their march on Singapore, I scrubbed pots on the Pacific beaches of Washington, waiting for the invasion of the West Coast and waiting to be transferred into the Air Corps. We were bivouacked in a small town from which all the civilians had been driven and we set up the 155 mm rifles in the back yards of summer cottages on the bluffs overlooking a permanent bank of winter fog that hung over the ocean. But nothing we could ever do would make that innocent resort look like a battleground. The air and the trees and the winding dirt roads and the little cottages were impregnated with our own childhoods — memories of girls in bathing suits, beach picnics, kids with tin pails, men digging for clams. We could imagine everything but the sun. It rained perpetually, day after day, month after month. We were never dry, seldom warm, and our shoes, balled in mud, were almost too heavy to lift; our uniforms smelled of mildew.

No more drills, no more barracks life; no more taps at night or beer drinking in the PX; no more twenty-cent movies. We crouched in the backs of trucks or in garages or underneath canvas tarps trying to keep dry — and waiting. As a KP I now had very few responsibilities. The soldiers ate out of mess kits that they had to wash themselves; the food we cooked was canned combat rations. We cooked in the back of trucks and dished out incredibly vile food from twenty-gallon pots to small groups of soldiers who walked in from their gun positions along roads that the army trucks had almost destroyed. The little summer cottages with their sweetly landscaped yards turned into lakes of mud and the roads simply melted away. I had never seen such a fragile landscape, one that so quickly disintegrated under the boots of men and the wheels of trucks. Still it never became ugly; drifting fog softened everything.

We waited for the Japanese battleships that would blast the bluffs and the landing barges that would vomit out their countless yellow hordes, and after a couple of months of waiting — wet, cold, and depressed by a style of life that began to turn stone-age, we almost wished that they would come. When we thought of them trying to start fires to cook their rations of rice in this soggy, fog-shrouded land of firs and cedars we had to laugh; the poor bastards would starve to death. It never occurred to us that we might be beaten. In fact, all through the war I never talked to anyone who thought we were in a war that might be lost. Americans did not lose wars. The stupidity of the attack on Pearl Harbor was something we could never understand; it was as insane as Hitler's belief that he had created a Third Reich that would last for a thousand years.

We stood guard on the bluffs above the beach where miles of rolled barbed wire had now been strung in long and wandering looping lines, standing for hours above the muffled boom of the breakers and peering into the fog, standing underneath dripping pine trees, shivering in the mist, watching seagulls in the fog turn into fighter planes and drifting logs into battleships. How long did this go on? Before starting to write this chapter, I listed all the months between December of 1941 and October of 1945 and tried to put myself in each month where I belonged, but there is almost a year missing someplace, plus a couple of extra Novembers and some Januarys, and those months of rain and shrieking winds that slip from the mind, thank God, like the pain of a rotten tooth. Those years must have been much more boring than I now remember them to have so completely faded away. . . . Ah yes, a lost January suddenly comes back: a surreal January lying in a Quonset hut in Goose Bay, Labrador waiting for a break in the weather or a change in the jet stream so that we could fly the Atlantic with reasonable expectations of arrival. What a nasty little outpost that was in which to have invested a month of one's life, and how completely irrelevant it now seems — like a stolen memory that more truly belongs to someone else, or like the memory of someone who had been deep-frozen for some possible later resurrection.

One curious moment comes back now from those forgotten months as we guarded the Pacific Coast. It reveals as much as anything the lack of self-confidence that poisoned this period of my life, but it is curious that in forty years I have seldom remembered something so pleasant, so intoxicating and dangerous.

It is early evening and the gun crews are coming in to eat. A light rain falls and around us a circle of pine and cedar encloses us in a quiet intimacy, a family setting comfortable and small, a kind of protecting isolation from everything outside. It is a calm and tranquil evening with pale light lingering in the sky behind the clouds with its hint of days that have begun to lengthen. The monotony has taken on an enchanted quality, as though we are living days that will not be added on to our life spans; worthless dividends, but ones from which, with imagination, one might salvage a few mildly joyous moments. Pots of chow are set out under a long tarp, and there are two barrels of scalding water at the end of the line, one orange with GI soap, one clear and steaming.

For over a year now I have honored that contract I made to take the worst job in the battery and do it with humility. It is a contract that strikes me this evening as having been juvenile and self-destructive. It no longer gives me pleasure, for I hunger for nobler work and am beginning to feel that, unlike Cinderella crouched in the kitchen ashes but discovered at last and raised to glory, the war will pass me by and I will lose my chance to be raised up to general admiration. This shameful work has poisoned my self-respect. Out of loneliness and a sense of being excluded, I feel that I am regarded by my comrades as unworthy to be included within the tight brotherhood that has begun to form in the battery since the war began. Choosing to be a KP had perhaps been an act of cowardice, or some deep need to play the part of a fool that would truly reflect my father's opinion of me.

Was what now happened something that I imagined, an hallucination produced by some extreme of loneliness? No, it was real, profound, and mysterious. Suddenly, for no reason and completely undeserved, I am aware of a wave of love that is being directed upon my person; I stand at the center of about ninety men as though under a strong, outside illumination, like an actor playing the disguised prince in some second-rate musical comedy.

Damp in my stinking fatigues, I stand behind large pots of canned tomatoes, string beans, and stew, ladling out generous portions into the mess kits of each soldier in the line — speaking to each one by name, smiling at each one, making jokes. For over a year we have lived in the enforced intimacy of army life and a loyalty that overrides our flaws has produced a closeness that is certainly more profound and moving than anything I ever experienced in my own family. All of those snobbish things that at first tended to separate me from them — my college education, the still vivid memory of my grandfather's wealth and the private schooling it bought me, the pickup I drove (not even our captain had a car and he often bummed rides with me on weekends), the strong, earthy, proletarian climate that had been strange to me and somehow threatening, the absolute nonintellectual quality of bivouac life where every adjective had been transformed into the word "fucking" and "Oh, my aching back" described every degree of frustration, pain, and sorrow — all of these things that had made me uncertain and apt to feel slightly superior to the pimps, the cowboys, the farm kids, the Reno shills, the guitar-plunking Okies, and the New Jersey Italians straight from the CCC camps, all of these had faded away. I think we had begun to see each other as perhaps God saw us: essences, with our class differences and all the differences that in other circumstances would have made friendships between us unlikely, rubbed away or disguised behind our identical clothing, our identical situation. I have grown to like them all, even Staff Sergeant Matthews who much of the time, out of an awful insecurity, pulled his weight on us and acted the asshole.

Now suddenly this affection which I feel for each of them is violently twisted around, magnified, and turned back upon me, and I am overwhelmed by their love. When I become aware of what is happening I begin to blush and tremble, for I feel like someone in a crowd who has just been singled out and told that he is the winner of some fabulous lottery. In some strange abrupt way a bunch of vague and ungeneralized emotions have become focused into a single group emotion as sharp as a piercing blade. It is a group judgment suddenly made manifest, as though an election has been held and I have been unanimously elected — what? not their leader surely, but their mascot, perhaps, a symbolic figure suddenly revealed in the soft evening light and in my damp stinking clothes and hopeless position as some true Charlie Chaplin aspect of themselves.

I had never in my life been wildly popular, never made a touchdown in the last sixty seconds, saved a child from drowning, broken the school record for the one-hundred-yard dash, been elected president of something; on the contrary, accepting my father's appraisal that essentially I was unlovable and that the only friendships I would ever have would be friendships that I had bought with money, I had affected a private stance that scorned popularity and that made me unable to handle the intense and passionate friendships of my adolescence. Not much respecting myself, I didn't much respect anyone who had the bad taste to like me.

Just as this deeply buried but consuming hunger to be loved and admired had helped me in my decision to die gloriously as a combat pilot, in the same way and out of the same need perhaps, my desire to be a writer had grown from the same contaminated soil. Well, let me end this memory as quickly as I can. We are entering territory where I have seldom ventured. And if, as I begin to write about it, I don't understand why I have so seldom brought this memory up to be prized and fondled, I am beginning to understand the reasons now.

Final scene: I am standing at the center of everyone's affection, drunk with joy and amazement and made foolish as a puppy. Someone calls out, "Hey, Tommy, make a speech," and others echo him, "A speech, Tommy. Come on, make a speech." And God help me, for a few seconds, like a plain girl deciding to allow herself to be seduced because for the first time in her life someone has said she has lovely ear lobes, making a speech seems like something that I should do. I have nothing to say except what, of course, can't be said, "My buddies, oh, my buddies, how could I have ever thought to leave you for the Air Corps," but it seems appropriate that I fulfill their expectations and acknowledge my new status by saying something. And God help me, I put one foot up on the back of the truck and prepare to leap upon the stage. And just before I did, just a split second before I did, the full forbidden nature of this vicious and superficial pleasure hit me with all its implications. I went back to the pots, my cheeks glowing, and continued to ladle out slop, my face lowered in a kind of shame.

Soon after this, since the army somehow knows when transferring you to another unit will cause the maximum of anguish, I was relieved of my duties in the field artillery and sent to the Fort Lewis headquarters to stand permanent guard duty — four hours on, eight hours off, four hours on, eight hours off. As permanent guards, most of us unassigned, we lived in the old brick building that had been built at about the time of the Revolutionary War and whose design must have been inspired by that prison where the Count of Monte Cristo had once hung out. Off duty we lay in our bunks unable to sleep, staring off into the distance toward cracks in the walls that let in a minimum of light. These apertures were cunningly referred to as windows; in my memory, rain is continually slanting down across them.

I guarded a water tower at the top of a hill with a good view of the road that the officer of the guard would have to use to catch me doing unmilitary things. I did a lot of serious reading during the day and at night with a flashlight memorized long lyrical passages from Walt Whitman. From time to time I dozed. I could never take guard duty seriously, feeling that the Fort Lewis water tank was probably the least likely enemy target in the western states to be sabotaged, but I went through the motions, shrieking, "Halt, who goes there?" whenever the lieutenant, hoping to catch me napping, sneaked up the road with his lights off and then came pussyfooting through the tangle of sodden brush beside the road. He stood before me almost every night identifying himself, his pants wet and muddy and covered with the hooked seeds of weeds.

He was a vile little man, that second lieutenant, and had probably been booted out of a combat outfit for the pompous, ignorant, pig-eyed, pot-bellied ass he was. Booted out to save his life, for ten minutes into a combat situation and his own troops would have shot him in the back. Like the rest of us he was unassigned, and he must have felt that he was on trial and that he could only redeem himself by catching one of his guards asleep on duty.

And so one morning at three o'clock when I heard him skulking out in the bushes it made me nervous, for there was a new soldier standing guard just around the hill who had come on duty with me complaining of an awful hangover and I was afraid that he was probably not standing guard in a very military manner. So "Halt, who goes there?" I screamed in a terrible voice, and "Advance, sir, to be recognized." I shrieked, certain that every guard within a mile would be alerted. The lieutenant passed me and walked on around the hill; five minutes later he was back, his hands and face smeared with mud and panting with excitement. "Quick," he said. "Come with me, soldier, and make it quiet, you hear?" Making as much noise as I could, in danger of being placed under arrest for blatant disobedience, I followed him back to the next post.

There was the soldier, the poor bugger, sitting on a box and leaning back against a brick wall, his rifle between his sprawling legs and tilted back against him, his mouth open, his head back. His helmet lay on the ground, and his uncombed hair lay plastered against his forehead. He looked like one of Breughel's drunken peasants, and strangely, his face in sleep had taken on a loutish expression that exactly mirrored the lieutenant's. I have never in my life seen a more profoundly sleeping man. "Okay, soldier, you see that?" the officer whispered. "You're a witness that this soldier is asleep on duty. You got that?" I nodded my head. "Okay, soldier," the lieutenant said to the man, standing just in front of him and speaking in a very loud, serious, military voice. "You're under arrest." The soldier slept on. "Okay, there, private," the lieutenant shouted. "Stand at attention when you're addressed by an officer. Come on, come on, look alive." No reaction except a small groan, a small smile; the poor GI was miles away in the waving wheat fields of home, unaware that in another moment he would be changed into a criminal, his life wrecked for years. "Well, Jesus Christ," the lieutenant shouted grabbing his shoulders and beginning to shake him, "don't you know there's a war on? By God, they can shoot you for this." And now the soldier, still half asleep, opened his eyes and, only half aware, struggled to his feet. He began to smile foolishly, a dumb little farm kid, pure cannon fodder.

Ten minutes later, when they left me at the Jeep — the lieutenant have driven with one hand, holding a .45 pistol in the other, the soldier sitting beside him still dazed and uncomprehending and almost, it seemed, ready to go back to sleep again — I went back to my post, sick with disgust. How I hated the army and the power it gave to neurotics. The fact that with luck in six more months I would be an officer myself, with the power to dominate poor slobs with my own slobbishness, did not confuse me. In my fantasies I had begun to practice my role more or less in the Russian manner. I would be a lieutenant but a comrade, and so hot a pilot that the enlisted men under me would fight to serve me.

A week after the caper at the water tank my name appeared on two separate lists on the guard room bulletin board. On Friday I would proceed to the Air Force Selection Center at Santa Ana, California. On Thursday I would report to such and such a place to give evidence in a court-martial. My time had finally come; on the Wednesday before leaving Fort Lewis forever, I drove home to say good-bye.

Though at first my father had been opposed to my transferring out of my kitchen job in the Field Artillery to a place in the army where most likely I would face the terror of combat, within a few months he had become reconciled to the change. He never admitted it in so many words on those infrequent weekends when I saw him, and in fact kept insisting that I had applied for pilot training for the simple pleasure of going against his wishes. But he was caught up in the general war fever and there were aspects of grandeur in having a son who was fearlessly confronting the enemy that gave him deep satisfactions. I was becoming a conversation piece and for the first time in my life was doing something that he could boast about.

I had phoned the house that I was coming and that I could stay no more than an hour. My father had arranged a ceremony. He filled his movie camera with a new roll of film, he bought a new shovel and an expensive tree, and he proposed to take pictures of me planting it. "If you don't come back," he said, "though I pray every night to almighty God that nothing happens, we'll have a bronze plaque made, and we'll call this the Moritz Thomsen memorial tree." "Oh boy," I said, "you can't begin to imagine how happy that makes me. Jesus, somehow that makes it all worthwhile, doesn't it?" My father, who missed most of my ironic comments, looked at me with a budding and then dying look of confusion. The tree was a flowering Japanese plum, and years later it grew to a real magnificence, in spring darkly aflame with red leaves and deep blood-red blossoms. That day it was just a stick, its balled roots wrapped in burlap. In my father's mind the stick had already come to represent me alive, and the beauty of the tree that the stick would grow would represent me transformed by death. My death would sanctify those blossoms that in the springtime exploded out of the dead wood.

The camera was screwed onto its tripod and set up to record this memorable scene. My father marked off the spot where I was to dig. Behind him — first to watch and then, at the conclusion of this holy ritual, to walk on camera and shake my hand — my father's two black employees, cook and gardener (both of them, though no one knew it yet, affected with second-degree syphilis). Straining to remember, I resurrect the sound of Missy's insane barking. And my stepmother? Where was she? Probably there beside my father, her pretty face cold and sour — and probably because she gardened, smudged. I look for her in my memory, but she remains an unseen presence as though her hatred for her husband's children had been strong enough to erase her from our minds.

"Okay, lights, action, camera," my father called and began cranking his machine. "Go on, now, hurry, pick up the shovel and start digging." I started to dig, making idiot faces into the camera and ostentatiously wiping away the sweat, mocking the phony solemnity of this phony moment — Sonny Boy giving his last screen performance. The turf was very thick and the shovel scarcely made a dent in the grass. "Dig faster," my father yelled, "we'll run out of film. And stop that clowning. Don't you realize this just may be the last time we'll ever see you?" "Okay," I called back, "you want something solemn? How's this?" I knelt on the lawn, rolled my eyes back until only the whites showed and made the sign of the cross to the four points of the compass; I held the shovel in the air like the pope's staff and blessed the populace. "Well, shit," my father said, "just leave it to you." He stopped cranking, turned his back to me, and folded his arms across his chest. I could hear him mumbling to himself. I was leaving for combat, for death perhaps, and I had him in a kind of trap, for if this were the last time he would ever see me how could he bear to destroy this moment with one of his bursts of anger? I decided to be nice.

I unwrapped the burlap from the tree's roots and worked at the hole for about ten minutes, cutting out a square piece of sod and loosening the dirt beneath it with my hands. When the hole was big enough I walked over to my father who was watching me with dramatic sadness. "Okay," I said, "take two." "Now be a sport," my father said. "This means a lot to me." He started to crank the camera again; I put the tree into the hole and shoveled dirt around it. The entire drama lasted about ten seconds and what it lacked in tension it made up for in conciseness. "Wilberson, Edie," my father yelled. "Quick. Go on in there and shake hands." These two twenty-year-old black innocents had been plucked out of the deep South where my father had spied them standing on a highway. After a ten-minute conversation he had given them the money to travel across the continent to Seattle, and two weeks later they had appeared, half out of their minds from moving too suddenly into the western, all-white world. Now they trotted onto the scene. Wildly grinning, Edie — in and out of an apron that she kept throwing over her head — was giggling like Butterfly McQueen in *Gone with the Wind*. "All right, shake hands," my father yelled. "Oh, Jesus, not with each other. Shake hands with Moritz." They moved up to me and Wilberson offered his hand without looking at me, staring at the camera with a kind of terror as though it were stealing his soul.

I remember this ceremony, just one more of the home productions that my father manufactured to create eternity. I remember it without the aid of the developed scenario, for it was one of the few of my father's home movies that I never saw. Its meaning would have appeared only in the event that I had become a combat casualty; then, watching it, people might have politely broken into moans and cries of grief.

Like my father, I was aware that this day had a certain symbolic importance, but I hid my feelings; they were private, very much my own. Out of the pickup that I drove I took the sack of GI clothes, the portable phonograph, a long box that held my bows and arrows, a .22 target pistol and carried them up to my room — and then, saying farewell, stood staring into the closet that held my civilian clothes: sports jackets, flannel trousers, dinner jacket and tails, the expensive, heavy, plaid English trousers that Mr. Littler had sold me in the fall two years ago when I had gone elk hunting. Here in this closet was piled that large part of my life that had ended with the letter from the draft board: ice skates, skis and poles, ski boots, woolen shirts and parkas, tennis racquets and golf clubs, fly rods and hunting guns, rubber boots, hiking boots, six-inch caulked logger's boots; and the sweater I was still proud of, my high school sweater with two yellow stripes on one sleeve and a golden football letter shining below the heart. How unreal and abandoned they looked, these things from which I had been torn and, though I suspected that even if I did return I might never use them, how precious still. Good-bye, good-bye, youth, good-bye, mountains and streams, the powder snow of Paradise, the frozen ponds of Winthrop. In one corner my pack leaned against the wall, sweat-stained and torn but ready, made pregnant and serious by a rolled sleeping bag and a clever set of camper's pots, one inside the other and blackened by the smoke of a hundred campfires.

In a small bookshelf by the bed a ratty collection of dog-eared books, most of them the Scribner's editions of Defoe and Stevenson with the magical illustrations of Wyeth. On the desk a marble bust of Apollo, a gift from Grandmother which I had permanently defaced by painting in with oils a pair of red spectacles and a bright blue mustache. The bed, heavy with shameful erotic memories of solitary and forbidden voyages. Below the window the swimming pool lay in a dead calm; slow clouds moved across its surface. The bed and the pool were connected in my mind, for I had spent whole summers swimming end to end, back and forth, hour after hour, seventy, eighty, ninety laps, trying to exhaust myself in a way that would make it possible to fall quickly asleep with my hands in saintly innocence lying at my sides and outside the blankets.

My father was sitting in his big chair when I went downstairs to say good-bye. He had mixed a drink for himself — bourbon, sugar, angostura bitters, almost the only thing he ever drank now; he was hooked on the sudden jolt and lift it gave him, a jolt as sweet as courage. One drink made him sentimental, two drinks made him belligerent and accusing. But he scarcely ever drank anything before six o'clock and it was surprising to see him now, so early in the afternoon, giving in to the non-scheduled emotion of my early departure. He stirred the drink with one finger and then licked it. "Can I fix you one?"

"No, no thanks, I have to leave now, and driving and drinking...."

"Do you have to go so soon? You just got here."

"I'm a witness tomorrow in a court-martial, have to help send this poor bastard to the firing squad or the rock pile. For twenty years, probably."

"Yeah," my father said, "but sleeping on duty, you know. Where would the army be...." He looked at me sadly. "Sit down for a minute. I have a surprise for you."

I sat and he began to talk, and at first I only half listened or listened resentfully to these words from outside that clashed against the swell of my own emotions. Even this little parlor where my father sat, a room I hated for the years of ugliness it held, now dimly glowed with a bit of nostalgia. Through the leaded windows, diamond-shaped as the windows of an English country manor, the sun shone brightly on a spread of lawn, the clumped rhododendrons, a little six-tree clump of baby redwoods, and the dead wand that stood alone now in its little square of bare earth, the stick of sleeping plum that was me.

My father was talking about a drinking fountain, a big one, five thousand dollars it would cost, shaped like a shell with garlands of grape leaves and paired dolphins with their tails entwined, all of it very big, monumental, in cast aluminum, and burnished to a soft brightness like old silver. One of his former salesmen from the biscuit company at the factory in Los Angeles — "You couldn't remember, it was before your time when I was the sales manager and we lived in Hollywood." — well, now he was working for this company that cast drinking fountains, a crackerjack of a salesman, one of the best, and he had come out to the farm and left a brochure. And had suggested that one of these drinking fountains was a tasteful gift to an institution, a perfect memorial to a loved one. I found myself listening in a kind of horror. Maybe I even began to tremble a little. There was a faint tingling at the back of my head as though my hair were standing on end. It was the dread a kid has listening to a ghost story or the dread identical to the scalp-tingling terror produced by confronting a snarling dog who seems about to leap at your throat. My scrotum tightened, my balls fled into hiding.

"Now God forbid that anything should happen to you, and though you probably don't believe it, I pray every night for your safe return. . . ."

"Yeah," I said, "you told me that about a half an hour ago, out there under the branches of the spreading memorial plum tree."

"Why are you so impatient always, so sarcastic? I just want to tell you that we love you, that you won't be forgotten."

"Oh Christ," I said. "Let me guess what you're coming to. Hey, I've got it. The Moritz Thomsen memorial drinking fountain underneath the Moritz Thomsen memorial plum tree. Boy, play your cards right you've got the makings of a nice little business, a goddamn shrine — miracle water."

"You're not happy, are you, unless you're mocking something?" my father said peevishly. He pushed the ice cubes around and around in his glass with his little finger. "All I wanted was to leave you something to hang on to."

"Listen, Father, when you promised to help me buy a cattle ranch after the war, well, that is something to hang on to. But a plum tree I'll never see, a drinking fountain I'll never drink out off — what the hell kind of a consolation is that?"

"I was thinking of Lakeside, your old high school."

"Lakeside has a drinking fountain — several in fact."

"But not like this one, son. Porcelain's one thing; cast aluminum, that's something else. Imperishable. And with your name engraved in the metal. Cut deep."

"Oh man," I said, "you're talking me into it. Keep going, sounds better by the second."

But no sarcasm would have stopped my father now that he was under the spell of his imagination. "Cut deep," he said again, and then in a suddenly loud, portentous, but breaking voice he declaimed, "Moritz Thomsen, War Hero . . . with dates."

"Ah," I said, "sure. With dates Sounds absolutely marvelous."

Shoes shined, hair plastered down, trembling, I stood before the court "as directed." The panel who judged the case were aging men with the dissolving faces that come with boredom and lost illusions. They were men too old for combat who had, out of patriotic fervor, offered their subtle talents to the army. For me they were terrifying figures of power, fanatic in their determination to protect the local water tanks. But they were condescending toward me and insisted that I stand at ease. And finally, "Will you describe what you saw when you accompanied Lt. Thorndike to post six."

"Yes, sir. (Gulp.) Private Jones was sitting at this post with a distracted look on his face. The lieutenant placed him under arrest, took out his .45, and marched the private down to the Jeep. I walked behind and then returned to my post."

"What do you mean, 'distracted look'? Was the soldier asleep?"

"Oh, I don't know if he was asleep, sir."

"What's a 'distracted look,' private?" one of the majors asked me.

"Well, sir, sort of a meditative look, you know, deep in thought."

"Are you trying to say that Private Jones was not asleep?"

"Oh, no, sir. Simply that I don't know."

"Just answer yes or no. Was the soldier asleep?"

"I don't know, sir. I don't think anyone but the soldier himself knows if he was asleep or not."

"Well, tell us, Private, were his eyes closed?"

"It was three o'clock in the morning, sir. I couldn't see his eyes."

"But you could see that he had a distracted look on his face. There was enough light for that, eh?"

"Yes, sir, there was enough light for that."

The officers all stared at me for a full minute with various degrees of distaste. On either side of me sat the victim and his persecutor, both with identical surly looks, staring at the floor.

"Is Private Jones a particular friend of yours?" the president of the court asked me, finally.

"No, sir, I've hardly ever spoken to him, sir."

The colonel sighed deeply, gave me an ironic look, told me I was excused, and I gave him a snappy salute, put my right toe three inches behind the left heel, swiveled sharply in a super-military manner, and, without lurching or stumbling for a change, marched out of the room. It was my first combat experience and though I had won nothing and the poor private would doubtless be condemned to three years in the stockade, and though no medals were given for this kind of heroic confrontation, still, I felt exalted, as though I had stood up to the forces of evil.

Eighteen hours later, with a generous pile of gas coupons and ample per diem, I dusted Fort Lewis from my heels forever and headed south to the glorious destiny that finally seemed just within my grasp. The huge bulk of Mt. Rainier, mysterious and golden, emerged out of the clouds as I left the fort. What a wonderful mountain; it was the only thing I would miss.

11

BY THE TIME PILOT TRAINING BEGAN my fantasies about combat had changed drastically. I no longer saw myself diving out of the sky, guns blazing, in a single-engine fighter. We were all of us subtly educated by the media to want to be what the army wanted us to be. It had become apparent that the "big" war would be fought in Europe and that the Japanese would have to wait until Hitler's Germany had been bombed to rubble. The Air Corps needed bomber pilots and so little by little I discovered that I wanted to be a bomber pilot; I began to feel that fighter pilots were hotshot prima donnas or wild-eyed teenagers nakedly seeking cheap glory. Bomber pilots, on the other hand, were mature, unflappable, steady. Hour after hour they would fly straight and level through the worst, never swerving, solid as mountains, faithful as your favorite dog. In a sense fighter pilots were defensive, flying escort on the bombers, scaring off the German fighters as they swarmed in to scatter a bombing party. It was the bombers laying waste to the factories that would win the war.

This public relations effort to make you think that you had chosen your own way to die was usually successful, but not always. John Steinbeck, for instance, offered his talents to the War Department and promised to turn bombardiers into glamorous devil-may-cares; he wrote a foolish book called *Bombs Away* so obviously the work of a prostitute that only mentally damaged teenyboppers could have been seduced into wanting to drop bombs. A couple of weeks after publication, copies began to show up on bookstore tables with signs above them reading "Specials: Five for a dollar." Steinbeck, maddened and made rash by antifascist passions, seriously damaged his reputation as an artist when, instead of offering his body, he offered up his soul to the war effort. Perhaps he felt he was competing with Hemingway who, in the preface to a book of short stories, suggested that all Germans be castrated. Almost every artist who worked for a government during the war came out of it diminished, none more so, of course, than Ezra Pound, who ranted for the losers and ended up in an insane asylum.

It was an April of some unidentifiable year that I began to fly army planes; nothing could have been less warlike, less military. Released to drift alone above the vineyards and prune orchards of Visalia, swooping around or through the puffy clouds of spring, was like living the essence of some extraordinary dream. The Primary trainers were all fitted with open cockpits, the wind washed against your face, everything was visual and sensual. The plane so immediately responded to your intentions that you had the powerful illusion of being completely in control, or better yet that this feisty and joyous mechanism was nothing but an extension of your own unlimited potential. It was only later, in Basic training and in another, more sluggish plane, that the instruments were stuck into our faces to be dominated, and the romance began to fade. We had to fly with hooded canopies that isolated us from that horizon that made sense of everything else, and those whirling dials that all looked identical but each of which had a different story to tell, would, if you believed them, indicate that instead of steadily climbing toward the north at three-hun-dred-feet-a-minute as your instructor had ordered you to do, you were by some miracle of confusion diving in a slightly southerly direction to-ward the business section of Chico, California.

But that came a few months later; Primary was magical. Beneath my fear of flying and the very slowly growing awareness that my flying skills verged on the brink of incompetence, was the absolute delight of being alone in the immense sky. Being alone in the spring sky was like being alone with a beautiful and loving girl and being told to study nothing but the articulation of her limbs. Instead of practicing maneuvers, I chased clouds, dove on bands of sheep, or simply dreamed away an hour gazing down in rapture at the greening hills and the blossoming or-chards. From above, the earth had never seemed so pure, beautiful, and childlike. Studying the innocence of the winding dirt roads and the white farm houses, and the small Ford tractors turning up rich dark fields of buried sod, the earth seemed so vulnerable. Impossible to be-lieve in the reality of war and that men were gross enough to bomb and churn this holy stuff into mud and dust.

One afternoon I saw something hanging from a power pole that from three thousand feet glowed with a strange warm light; it was a something that seemed to be illuminated from within. Curious, I circled down to identify this mysterious object that had caught my eye with its burning glow. It was simply a lineman, naked to the waist, his skin red with the year's first sunburn. It wasn't just the earth, I realized, that was vulnerable; it was man, too, hidden beneath that glowing skin so easily torn and shredded, so quickly and easily smeared with his own blood. Well, it is easier to love the earth than the men who pollute it, and I wondered, confused, if the yellow skin of a Japanese would shine so brightly and so clearly speak of man's beauty, man's nobility.

What a lovely plane that little PT was, and how it stood up against the indignities we inflicted upon it. Here I am one afternoon on my first solo flight, terrified but wildly happy, and singing at the top of my lungs the music from the last movement of Beethoven's Ninth Symphony. I stall out about one hundred feet above the runway, fall, bounce back into the air, and, giving the plane full throttle, continue my flight and circle the field again. The second time around I feel a little too foolish to be singing such triumphant music. Here comes Russell on the following day; he is making his first solo, and as he comes in for a perfect landing we notice that he is trailing one hundred and fifty yards of telephone wire behind him. Manson follows Russell on another day and climbs out of his plane looking combat-tested; he has run a goose through his propeller and his face is covered with blood and feathers.

An instructor with his cadet is flying at five thousand feet a few miles north of the airfield. They have been practicing stalls, lazy eights, and Immelmanns. The instructor gazing down sees someone falling through the sky at the end of an opened parachute. "Hey," he calls back to his student, "look at that crazy bastard." When he receives no answer he turns to discover that his student, forgetting to fasten his safety-belt, has fallen out of the plane. Not a really funny story; doing grotesque things like falling out of airplanes was regarded as eccentric behavior and was almost certain to get you sent before an elimination board. Unless you were passionately defended by your instructor you might end up transferred to bombardier school. Cadet pilots felt that being washed out and sent to bombardier school was like standing at the gates of heaven and being told to go to hell.

Well, somehow I got through Primary and went, along with a hundred of my comrades, a hundred miles up the road to Chico. Basic training was a big change; we had been flying with civilian instructors; now the army would take over. Suddenly it wasn't fun anymore.

With about a hundred hours of flying behind us — just scarcely enough time in my case to fool myself into thinking I could do a few sensible things like takeoff, fly in a reasonably straight line, and land, sometimes in bizarre attitudes but more or less safely — our instruction became ridiculously confusing. We were like children with a dozen music lessons behind us suddenly given the score of a Prokofiev concerto and told that in six months we would be appearing with the London Philharmonic. I had come without realizing it to almost the end of my flying talents, and instead of letting me endlessly polish my simple skills, I was now expected to fly on instruments, or fly in formation six inches off the wing of my terrified instructor, or take off in the dead of night and run a triangular course. I had difficulty finding Sacramento, let alone some pip-squeak grass-covered landing strip in the heart of darkness. Hell, let's face it: in that tangle of instruments I could hardly find the radio. Memorizing East is Least and West is Best to help me figure out compass variation simply befuddled me more. East is less than what? West is better than what?

Nor was I the only one. Randolph was one of those young handsome dashing types who flew like an angel. He was a sweet combination of trigger-quick reflexes and physical perfection. He always beat everyone through the obstacle course, always recovered first from those two-mile runs that nearly killed the rest of us. He had been the first to solo in Primary. (For murky psychological reasons — to give me needed self-confidence, the instructor said — I had been the second.) If any of us would end up flying fighters it would be that brilliant son of a bitch; he did everything so well, so easily. But on our night cross-country flight Randolph got lost. Trying to reconstruct his weird journey with those of us who were pledged to secrecy, Randolph figured he had passed well to the west of Sacramento as he searched desperately for the lights of a city that never showed up, and he only turned around when he realized with horror that he was flying over San Francisco's Golden Gate Bridge. Trying to fly back, hopelessly confused, he came to some strange mountains and he panicked. "Mayday, Mayday," he called in on his radio. "I'm lost; I don't know where I am; I'm all fucked up." The calm voice of a WAC radio operator answered him, and he was chilled to hear a woman's voice. "Okay, give me your name and your plane number," and Randolph, preferring death, called back, "Ma'am, I may be fucked up, but I'm not that fucked up." He snapped off his radio was and roaming around looking for a nice place to crash-land when he spotted the lights of a plane. And luckily it was a plane from Chico and he followed it home. (Younger readers who may not get the point of this story should understand that in the 1940s there were certain words one did not use in the presence of women.)

Randolph's goof-up helped to enforce my wavering confidence; if he who was so superior in every way could do something so silly, maybe there was hope for me. I blundered on, a dull work horse behind this brilliant prancer. And didn't even lose my confidence in him two weeks later when he collided with another plane at four thousand feet. Both planes crashed in flames; both cadets parachuted safely down. An hour later (to give him needed self-confidence, his instructor said) Randolph had been rushed into another plane and was burning up the airways with brilliantly intricate maneuvers. He had a twenty-nine-inch waist, black curly hair, black quick eyes, a jaunty walk. God, he was impressive, climbing into a plane and giving that thumbs up signal to the mechanic who stood below him in clouds of gasoline fumes. The Ronnie Reagan of A Squadron. No one with that manner and with that face could ever be anything but the idealized pilot who lived in the back of our heads, that secret self we dreamed of being. Cadets and instructors alike were enchanted with him; he could have crashed ten planes in ten days and no one would have thought to suggest that perhaps some other line of work would better suit him. (Six or nine months later I flew with his twin brother for a few minutes from a British airfield where my crew had crash-landed after taking flak. I had never been so terrified or come so close to being killed by one of our own men.)

It is the last day of Basic and those of us who have passed the course — about 70 percent of the 70 percent who have survived Primary — are lined up in ranks on the runway to watch an exhibition of flying. Most of us when asked our preference have said we would like to be bomber pilots, and for some strange reason, since this was the right answer, our squadron commander, Captain Muldoon, is disgusted with us. He says that flying bombers is like driving a truck, and to humiliate us a little he has asked a couple of pilots from a single-engine advanced training field to fly over and show us how nifty the little advanced trainers are and what we will be missing by going to Texas to fly sluggish twin-engine trainers. We wait for a long time in the sun (ah, but haven't many of us been doing this for years), and finally the little trainers appear. The captain was right; the planes are slim, fast, beautiful, and maneuverable as swallows. Pure delight, if that's the sort of thing that turns you on. They swoop and dance above us for a while and then come in to land — fast, like bullets, stalling out at about ninety miles an hour.

Captain Muldoon calls us to attention and says with sarcasm, "Okay, hotshots, as you'll see in a minute, you still have lots to learn. Now watch some real flying." And a second later the first pilot, having forgotten to lower his wheels, hits the runway with a hideous scraping sound and, sending out sparks like a Carborundum wheel in a blacksmith's shop, passes in front of us. Bits of plane from the undercarriage go wheeling and whirling through the air. All of us at attention, mouths gaping, watch this exhibition; we are confused at first, not quite sure what we are being taught, for it seems criminally extravagant to destroy a plane and endanger the life of the pilot simply to teach us that wheels should be lowered before landing. But our meditations are interrupted. "About face," screams Captain Muldoon, as though by forbidding us the sight of this horrible thing it was actually not happening. Back in the barracks we lay on our cots howling, howling with laughter. It could only have been funnier if the plane had exploded.

These comic book memories are truer to the realities of air force training than one supposes. We lived a communal life, a barracks life, and were joined together by the meanest of details. It was, from our level, a real communism with all the pleasures and aggravations of democracy. We lived on rumors, the unjudging observation of one another's foibles, and the stultifying discipline that taught us to accept the unnatural nature of our situation. A single loud fart in the flight line, if it came at a suitably unsuitable time (as one hundred and twenty of us stood at attention listening to banal marches or some idiotic pep talk), could unite us all into the strongest kind of brotherhood; that sound, if properly vulgar and juicy, expressed with wonderful precision our deepest group feelings of victimization, and if we had been able to select our own cadet commander, it would have been Jimmy Brooks; his machine-gun farts were monumental.

It was the rare cadet who washed out of Advanced training. Captain Muldoon was right again; flying the fat, lethargic twin-engine trainer was exactly like driving a truck. Among ourselves and out of hearing of our instructors we talked about "driving" the plane. We had been sent to a training base in Texas, just where I blessedly no longer remember, though the terrain over which we flew was unforgettable — brown, blasted desert with small black mountains erupting senselessly from its surface like boils on sick flesh. A single highway (almost empty of traffic) cut across this waste. A single moribund town — its storefront windows shining through the dusty air and one or two trucks ambling aimlessly up its wide, empty street — looked as abandoned as an old movie set. From the ground — on our infrequent visits to its dance halls where we sat at incredibly long bars drinking beer — the town was just as depressing. It was a town that repudiated the sixty thousand years of history since man moved out of the caves. To make it worse the faces of the people were as empty as the parched land where they had chosen to live. The slack faces, the pointy heads, the droolers, the chinless wonders, the broken-hipped limpers in their hundred-dollar boots, the crimson-faced winos, the old, hunched coughers and spitters — they were not exactly typical of that eastern Texas of the forties. They were what was left after the draft's winnowing: everyone else in Texas with an IQ of ninety or better had volunteered for the army the day after Pearl Harbor.

Since we had acquired all the basics in Basic, in Advanced training we were expected simply to polish the skills it was assumed we had already learned. We were scheduled for night, instrument, and formation flying. No more loops and dives, no more exuberant antics; now it was going to be precision work, wing tip to wing tip, moving across the sky in bunches of six as solemn as bishops. We began to discover that by choosing bombers we had cut ourselves off from the individualistic and romantic aspects of flying; bombing was a group exercise, pure technological expertise. Dropping bombs on Germany was going to be as romantic as picking up a load of brussels sprouts in Salinas and dropping it off in Little Rock.

On the first morning as I was waiting to fly, my new instructor set me in a parked plane and told me to memorize the instrument panel and a checklist of about eighty items, the last one being to my mind the only one that made real sense: takeoff when the tower flashes the green light. Was he kidding? I sat there for three hours before this doubled up chaos of manifold pressure gauges, magnetic and gyrocompasses, temperature, altimeter, flight attitude, rate of descent gauges (these are just a few of the hundreds that come to mind now), and I began to feel paralyzed with great confusion. It had been bad enough in a single-engine plane, but this memorization of dials, switches, valves, handles, wheels, and flaps was like trying to become just another part of an incredibly complicated and inhuman machine; they were trying to turn me into a robot.

Sitting in the parked plane that morning I had my first premonition that not only would I be a stupid pilot, but that I would be a public menace and that on my first combat mission, if I hadn't crashed before then, I would probably do something that would kill my whole crew. It was a real moment of truth, but one I immediately buried. Reality and my own romantic idea of myself were too far apart; the intensive training and the traumatic news of enemy victories had exhausted my capacity to think my own thoughts. Now it occurs to me that if I had been less of a coward and under less pressure, I would have gone to my instructor and admitted that I was hopelessly confused. But who would have believed that it was not fear but courage that had driven me to eliminate myself? And how could I have faced the embarrassed but half-gloating and hurried solace of my friends? Over half of my group had already washed out, and for those of us who remained (and for those who didn't) their failure was a kind of death. We would have lingered and wept for them as they lay as inert as corpses on their cots, speechless with misery and staring at the ceiling as they waited to be transferred to bombardier or gunnery school, but there was no time, no time. We rushed to classes or the flight line on an impossible schedule and left them alone in the barracks to contemplate their flaws now made public. One by one they would be gone, an empty cot left to remember them by. But we couldn't bear to remember them; the army, by bringing us together and then tearing us apart, put such emotional pressure on us that finally we couldn't feel much of anything. In an awful sense their failures fed our romantic illusions about ourselves; in an awful sense we were like vampires who needed their blood to keep going. They were gone; we were still here.

We now come to the last of the funny stories about pilot training.

One of the characteristics of the twin-engine trainer we flew was its appalling sluggishness at low speeds. It was so unresponsive on takeoff, for instance, that for the first three-quarters of that slow, endless trip down the runway, as the plane shuddered and shimmied trying to pick up flying speed, the rudders could not be used to control its direction. One used the engines to keep lined up with the runway until, at about forty miles an hour, the rudders would suddenly respond to the rush of air and begin to function. How, after six hours of instruction in these lumbering kites, this simple fact had never become apparent to me is incomprehensible. Probably to cadets more in tune with the laws of aerodynamics this aberrant behavior was immediately obvious. Well, not to this particular hot pilot who taxies out one afternoon with his instructor, lines up with the runway, shoves the two throttles forward to full power on the green light, and begins to move with immense slow dignity down the strip which now shimmers like water in the Texas heat.

Let me exaggerate a little, for I will live through the next minutes a thousand times in my imagination as I lie on my cot, staring at the ceiling and waiting to be reassigned. We advance down the runway for about fifteen minutes, imperceptibly picking up speed. After an interminable time, when we have reached a breathtaking velocity of about twenty miles an hour, the plane drifts a few degrees to the right. I apply a little left rudder. Nothing happens. I apply a little more left rudder. Nothing, nothing. "Well," I think, "this is an extremely strange situation," and I jam my foot down hard — full left rudder. A few seconds later the rudder functions in a violent and emphatic way and the plane makes a ninety degree turn to the left, leaves the runway in the blink of an eye, and begins to bounce over the cactus plains. "Okay," my instructor says in a conversational way, "I've got it." And I give him the plane. Still at full throttle we lumber off across the desert, sometimes, but rarely, in the air. We hop over all but the last cactus, a big mother, fifteen feet of dull green fluted column with stupid little spiked arms sticking out near its top. We ram into this monstrous obstacle that has been sitting there for thirty years waiting to destroy my life, and I sit watching it chew a great hole in the leading edge of the right wing. We have stopped finally, and the swirling dust behind us begins to settle. The instructor takes off his cap, wipes his forehead, and gives me a long, bemused look. "Are you okay?"

"Sure, are you? . . . Sir?"

"What the hell happened?" he asked me.

"The rudder, sir. There was something wrong with the rudder."

"Well, if there wasn't, there probably is now," he said.

We climbed out of the plane as the ambulance and a fire truck, sirens shrieking, drove up. A Jeep with the squadron commander at the wheel followed behind. All of this happened with unbelievable rapidity. My instructor and I climbed into the Jeep with the captain, and as we drove back to the flight line the captain and the lieutenant spoke quietly together. "Well, do you still want to fly?" the captain said, turning to me.

"Oh, yes, sir, of course."

"I mean right now."

"Yes, sir," I lied. "You know, sir, I swear to God there was something wrong with the rudder. I know I can drive one of these things."

"What did you say?" the captain asked incredulously. "Did you say *drive?*"

I like to feel that using that unfortunate word had as much to do with my being washed out of pilot training as my somewhat heavy-handed way with aircraft. At any rate, I did not fly again that day and a week later, having forgotten everything, flew a final disastrous check ride with the captain. A couple of weeks after that, while my ex-comrades were trying on their new officers' uniforms in the next room, I went before the elimination board where my request for another chance was denied. I was to be sent back to Santa Ana for reassignment. Looking back forty years later, washing out of pilot training seems to have been one of the most inconsequential of my wartime disappointments. At the time, however, it was a shattering tragedy, a public humiliation that poisoned my life for months. When it was time for the others to fly, trying to save my friends their embarrassment as much as to hide my own shame, I would creep into the latrine and lock myself into one of the toilets and sit there listening to the planes taking off.

I was reading Conrad's *Lord Jim* for the first time while I waited for my travel orders, and I so identified my failure with Jim's that certain passages in that book were almost too painful to read. I could feel my insides burning with grief for the two of us; we had thrown away our chance at greatness. Phony tragedies are, of course, just as painful as real ones.

12

Perhaps it is premature to begin introducing characters who will so quickly disappear, but I awoke this morning with a bright clear memory; it was an amazing thing to come bursting up from the depths of the past — a little nine-year-old girl in a Texas hotel, a smart-alecky pre-Lolita who flirted shamelessly with the cadets who used to spend their desperate weekends there trying to get as drunk as possible. She was about the only female in the hotel who didn't have a mustache, or a red face blasted by the Panhandle winds, or the loud intimidating voice of a mule skinner, and we all courted her for her freckles, her sassy charm, and her cute, outrageous disdain. To every question that we put to her she would answer in a singsong voice, "Ah ain't a gonna tell ya," pouting out her lips and tossing her blonde, bobbed hair, turning us for a few seconds into Humbert Humberts, not with sexual lust but almost its opposite — the wild impulse to lay her over our laps and civilize her with sharp slaps on her bottom.

Awakening now forty years later, repeating to myself, "Ah ain't a gonna tell ya," I immediately think of Murdock, who was my best friend for a time; remembering a weekend when Murdock and I and a couple of other cadets had gone to that awful little Texas hotel with its slanting wooden porch, its small, airtight rooms, and its oil-clothed, fly-specked dining room tables. At this time I was still flying and like everyone else was under unrelenting pressure to survive the course, and we had gone there, all of us, because there wasn't any other place to go. We'd gone there with the single idea of getting blind, stinking, stupid, staggering drunk. And I'm sure we did; but that memory is obliterated.

I had become friendly with Murdock in an unlikely way. Cadets whose names began with T usually had friends with names like Turner, Thomas, Tunney, Todd, Trumbell. Normally we should never have met, since we were assigned to flights in alphabetical order, and in Basic training Murdock flew with another squadron and lived in another barracks. For some reason I had come back an hour early from a weekend pass on a Sunday evening and, alone in the barracks and free to be myself for a time, had put some wild modern music on my phonograph. I think it was either a Shostakovitch piano concerto or *The Planets* by Holst, both of which in the 1940s were regarded as being pretty far-out. Murdock had come back early, too. He was probably the only other cadet on the base who liked good music, heard it from his room, and came upstairs to listen. He stood in the doorway for a few minutes and then moved in and sat on one of the cots, head down, absorbed.

He was from Boston, and he had all the cool reserve of an easterner that, until then, I had always thought indicated an inbred pride of place that was undeserved. But if he was from an aristocratic eastern family, and he probably was, he never mentioned it. And if he felt a faint disdain for my westernness, which he probably did, he translated it into a quiet question of my preference for modern music over the classical music of the eighteenth century. This confrontation was at first the basis of our friendship — Stravinsky versus Bach; Mozart versus Bartok. On a level far below the passions of war we were both solaced by music; it was almost the only thing in that ambience of patriotism, bombs, airplanes, and invasion that wasn't completely insane. We became friends when, after the next weekend pass, he brought me a Brahms trio as a present (I found it dull and academic) and after that we began spending our weekends together in San Francisco — or part of them.

Helen, like a faithful camp follower, had moved to Santa Ana only two weeks after I had been sent there, and when I went north she took an apartment in San Francisco. I would take Murdock with me when I went to visit her, the three of us would have dinner, and then Murdock, who was engaged to marry a Boston girl, would excuse himself and wander off to some bar. Late the next morning, spent from wild love, I would float into the hotel lobby on uncertain legs where Murdock, cool and suave, would be sitting waiting for me, a cigarette hanging from his mouth and his eyes red with hangover. There was something about this Sunday morning situation that made me feel sophisticated. I think it was more Murdock's presence, and the somewhat pretentious gentility of the hotel where he stayed, than the fact that I was having my first prolonged affair with a woman older than myself, but I felt like a man of the world.

We scarcely ever mentioned the war or flying to each other. I think
he had no romantic illusions about flying and his coolness about being a
pilot encouraged me to conceal my own diminishing romanticism. He
was a serious and gentle man with old-fashioned, civilized values, and we
talked about serious things. The war was a rotten interruption in the
main business of life, and when it was over he would go back to the university. I forget now what he planned to be: a lawyer or a teacher, but
whatever, it would be less important to him than his passion for the
woods and streams of Maine. What he liked more than music was the
wilderness. His family had a summer camp in Maine and I would have
to come there after the war and spend a month, he told me. Perhaps in
late August, when the nights grew cold and the salmon began to lie off
the river mouths. All right, I told him, but only if he'd promise to come
to Washington where I'd take him into the primitive area around Cathedral Peak, forty, fifty miles away from the nearest human being. Well, here
or there, he said, whichever. I think we'll keep in touch when this shit
blows over, don't you?

It was Murdock who loaned me his copy of *Lord Jim*, and it was Murdock who had been sitting with me a month before drinking coffee and
groaning in that decrepit hotel in Texas after the most serious drinking
either of us had ever done....And the little girl is sitting at the table with
us, this future Daisy Mae with her mouth full of chewing gum and her
lap piled with comic books, and as usual she is being haughty and capricious and sort of delightful in an incredible and menacing Texas hillbilly
sort of way. I ask her a question, and before she has time to answer it I
answer it for her, mimicking her Texas drawl. "Ah ain't a gonna tell ya."
And she looks at me with her mouth hung open, absolutely amazed,
dazed with amazement, and says, "Now Mister Man, how did you all
know I was going to say that?" Murdock, bursting into laughter, tips too
far in his chair and goes over on his back.

He had a pitted skin and a ruddy complexion like a black Irishman,
and his hair was dark brown and as tightly curled as a Negro's. I think his
first name was John. He died over Ploesti, bombing the Romanian oil
fields in a suicide raid that got a lot of publicity and was probably one of
those spectaculars that the air force dreamed up from time to time when
they felt they weren't getting a square deal in the matter of headlines.
And if I haven't remembered Murdock (not once in forty years) it is

because when I heard that he was dead I was already some months into combat myself, and I had learned to close my mind to news that I couldn't bear to hear, to thrust it away from me as though it were something that I hadn't quite heard, or had heard in a dream.

Five or six of those missing months I can't account for must have been a part of that time between washing out of pilot training and an early March morning in another year when, lowering through clouds, our brand new B-17 broke into the open and we saw, like the great chords of a monumental and menacing symphony, green Ireland ablaze below us and a green sea dashing against it. After a thousand months of winter — in Utah with its naked cottonwoods, dead brown mountains, and frozen streams; through a dozen blizzards in Texas; in snowbound Maine with its Christmas card fir trees; and in the utter white desolation of Labrador — the hills and pastures of Ireland, just beginning to come awake to spring, were miraculous and as joltingly beautiful as the memory of a dream out of childhood. We dove low and rushed over it, and it was like coming back to life again, like approaching a brilliantly lit stage which for months has been dark and empty and upon which, now, you will play a leading role — a role you have been practicing for three years. We were in the war zone at last, or a reasonable facsimile; for the first time I could contemplate without shame this thing branded upon my breast like an adulterous A that characterized my incompetence: the silver wings that flapped off into space with a bomb between them.

We had just flown across the Atlantic, over a thousand miles of grey seas furious with breaking water and spotted with great chunks of ice against which the waves boiled and shattered. Northern lights glowed in the sky; it was sixty degrees below zero. We flew, I think, at about six thousand feet, trying to stay below what for the first few hours had been solid cloud cover, and we couldn't stop gazing at that awful immensity of sea beneath us where, if our wings had picked up ice and we had gone down, they had told us in Goose Bay not to worry because the water was so cold that we would be dead in forty seconds. Having always detested cold showers, I was not consoled.

About halfway across, about midnight, purely for practice since we were flying on a radio beam, our navigator stood beneath the astral

dome in the nose of the plane and did fancy celestial navigation with
certain stars he claimed to know intimately — and announced after an
hour of frenzied figuring and in a stunned voice that, believe it or not,
we were just sixty miles off the African coast and flying approximately
two degrees north of and parallel with the equator. It was the first and
last time I ever saw celestial navigation practiced during the war — if
that's what it was.

But we have arrived in Ireland ahead of time, and I have skipped over
some momentous things that happened during that almost forgotten period. Let me go back and subject you for a few pages to the mixed
delights of bombardier training, and a windswept field in Utah, and a
wartime marriage that didn't take. A little patience and we will get to
England and to a certain cabbage patch some miles out of Berlin that I
so brilliantly bombed one day.

After months back in Santa Ana again, waiting to be reassigned, I am on
my way at last to the bombardier school in Victorville. Still grieving for
my changed status and wanting to relive a moment out of a more vibrant
past, I have stopped at a hotel in Santa Monica. It is the same hotel
where, six months before, Helen and I had spent our last night together.
Since it is wartime and the hotel is almost deserted, I have been given
the same room, or one very much like it. At midnight I stand naked at a
tenth floor window. It is opened wide and looks out over the Pacific
Ocean; a light breeze as faint as breathing scarcely moves the curtains.
Everything is blacked out, the beach is deserted, the parks with their Fer-
ris wheels and fun houses are closed. A calm sea, the long lines of
breakers white with phosphorescence, spills and hisses on the sand. Helen has gone back to Seattle. I peer into the night where the Japanese
submarines are prowling and using the lights of Long Beach to occasionally sink the silhouetted freighters. Tonight there is nothing out there but
a sense of wasted time and a dimly felt menace, the distant war toward
which I am once more moving. It is a vague danger, softened by the
calmness of the sea but made immediate by my nakedness. Probably it is
both the menace and the nakedness that together suddenly define me to
myself as a man utterly alone, defenseless, and vulnerable. And while a
moment before I was excited to lust by the memory of Helen, she is

abruptly removed from my imagination as a figure of passionate nostalgia and replaced by an unrecognized figure — the woman I have created out of my own fear of death, the woman I must marry and impregnate before I am blown to pieces by the war. She has no shape, no face, no identity, but she looms before me like a concept as formless and overpowering as a sunrise; she is an idea toward which I strain — the mother of my children. This is nothing but the furious shrieking of my genes who are ordering me to seek, not my immortality, but theirs; against all common sense and my own self-interest they have taken over and dominated my will and my imagination. There is no time to lose; I must get married.

The Norden bombsight was a small twenty- to thirty-pound instrument. filled with whirling gyroscopes and so connected to the plane's controls that when a few switches were activated the bombardier was, to a limited degree, flying the plane. But it was small consolation for me to know that for about three minutes over an enemy target I would be the master of the ship. It struck me as being similar to putting a six-year-old in your lap and letting him steer your car for a couple of blocks. The bombsight was supposed to be almost magically accurate, but this was pure propaganda —though it wasn't until many months after the war had ended that an army* study revealed that only about 5 percent of the bombs dropped had come anywhere near what they had been aimed at.

It was probably John Steinbeck who had popularized the belief that bombing with the Norden, one could drop a bomb into a picklebarrel from eighteen thousand feet. Perhaps our disillusion with Mr. Steinbeck began when, sweating out perfect bomb runs, our practice bombs, landing in little flashes of flame a thousand feet from the center of the target, proved to us that not only could we miss a picklebarrel but the factory that made them. Plus the parking area around the picklebarrel factory and the special railroad spur that hauled off the picklebarrels and the town where ten thousand employees slaved for the war effort making picklebarrels. (Among ourselves we discussed what kind of a postwar monument might be erected in honor of bombardiers and decided that the most appropriate construction would be an enormous pickle-barrel with a diameter of seven hundred feet. To be called the Steinbeck Memorial.)

Of course, the officers in charge of bombardier training knew what a capricious little animal we were expected to tame, and their standards were not unreasonable. If I remember correctly, we were expected to average, in the fifty or sixty official practice bombs that were counted against our record, a somewhat sloppy three hundred and fifty feet. The few statistically probable bulls-eyes that we scored by chance helped tremendously to bring our averages down, though these pinprick flashes at the center of the target gave us little pleasure; they were as senseless as those rumored bombs that were said to have fallen fifty miles from the target range, one of which supposedly killed a sheep.

Even though bombing was about as scientific as rolling dice, we were drilled for months in this idiot skill, and we learned by rote a ritual as mystic and arcane as that of some exotic Eastern cult. At first, across the cement floor of a hangar, we sat ten feet up on a moving tower that crawled across the floor and responded to the corrections that we twirled into that whirling black box; at the proper moment a little inked needle would plop down onto a sheet of ringed paper, and the instructor would announce, straining to make this jukebox activity at least minimally dramatic, "Good boy, you have just knocked out the ball-bearing plant at Essen." Or, and more likely, "Congratulations, you missed the Ruhr, but it looks like you still hit Germany." Except for learning how to blow up bridges with wads of powder or how to strangle an enemy with a piece of piano wire, I don't think there was any other skill in the army that would prove to be so useless in civilian life. But if we were ashamed to be used in a way that was unworthy of our aspirations and that ultimately involved no more than the memorization and perfection of certain actions which our hands were trained to do automatically, still the procedure was as intricate as Javanese temple dancing and when done well was beautiful to watch. The two or three minutes on the bomb run with the bombardier taking the burden of the mission on his shoulders was a time of exquisite concentration. If the releasing of the bombs might be compared in the sexual act to the moment of ejaculation then, let's face it, the bombardier was no more, really, than the plane's sexual organs. I don't remember that we ever thought of bombing in sexual terms, however. Now I wonder why.

When by act of Congress one is changed instantly from buck-ass private to officer and gentleman, the foundations of one's military philosophy tend to tremble. I had never much liked or trusted officers; now I found myself one of them, and almost immediately I became aware from the other side of what an abyss had opened up between the enlisted men with whom I still identified, and who would never trust me now, and my new legislated peers, those pink-cheeked postadolescents with their silver wings, their tailored uniforms, and the weird caps, from which, to make us look rakish and devil-may-care, the inside metal band that kept the cap as flat and formal as an apple pie had been removed. Now the caps hung down on each side of our faces like the long, drooping ears of a dachshund.

It was the custom that immediately after being commissioned you would give a dollar to the first soldier who saluted you. It was the hundreds of soldiers who hung around outside the hall where we received our wings that helped me to accept the gap that now separated us. What a mob of men ready to humiliate themselves for a buck; what a shameless rabble.

I got my salute and paid for it. I was already packed and ready to leave for the next post — Salt Lake City. From there we would be shipped out for bomber training with our crews. I climbed into my pickup and headed north. But first a night in Los Angeles. At a bar I drank a couple of whiskies, changed a five-dollar bill into ones, and, feeling guilty and apart, walked down a street by a USO club waiting to be saluted. For some reason I needed more salutes to make me feel real; they were gratuitous recognitions that I wanted to pay for. It took an hour, I got five salutes, paid out five dollars, and had the solace of explaining five times that if I was an officer, I had only been one for an hour, whereas I had been a buck private for three years.

Then one of those smart-asses strolled up the street, a soldier who looks you in the eye, begins to salute, and instead scratches at the side of his head while you have returned a salute which you've never been given. Feeling foolish and misjudged, I mastered the impulse to have him arrested for impertinence. And then I got out of town.

Having already mentioned its stripped cottonwoods, its brown mountains, and its frozen streams, I have almost exhausted my memories of Utah in the late fall of 1943. But not quite. Something long forgotten has come bubbling up.

Salt Lake had a staging area, whatever that means, just at the city limits on the west-bound highway. It was not an army camp so much as a large, frozen parade ground with a few barracks at one end and a small headquarters building near the entrance gate. Here, thousands of newly commissioned airmen were herded together in a sad, unassigned limbo. It was here that we waited to be assigned to a combat crew and to a theater of operations. We had no duties and only one obligation — to be present at an eight o'clock roll call and afterward to study the lists of names tacked to a large bulletin board that would tell us when and where we were headed next. Being there was absolutely forgettable, except for the half hour we spent each morning with the camp commander.

He was a cavalry major from the First World War, and he had probably volunteered to serve again out of patriotism and that fanatic desire to be involved in the wartime ambience of noble American emotions. He was the kind of man who had never quite made it as a civilian, the adventures of his youth lived in his mind again, and now another war had come along that would give him a second chance. At the threshold of old age he was coming back to life again.

The Major was a man in his middle fifties with hair that was still black and with a large English-style mustache that was as fierce and shining as though he polished it each morning with a well-blacked shoe brush. He wore a cavalry hat, riding breeches, carried a swagger stick, and he was fiercely correct and military. There were a thousand of us there, and to the man we detested him. We detested him because he was old and of another war which all of us knew had been corrupt and criminally political, a war in which millions of men had been sacrificed for the glory of military incompetents. We detested him because the medals he so proudly wore were of another dead time that had nothing to do with us, and because imagining his past we saw him waving a sword and riding a horse into battle, screaming idiotic slogans: Don't Tread On Me;

Tippecanoe and Tyler, Too. Here in the purest way the two wars — two worlds — confronted each other with rage and contempt. But of course the main reason we detested him was because he detested us.

He remembered that old war of spit and shine, decent order, crisp salutes, manly bearing. Out of chance, and perhaps because he wasn't good for anything else, they had put him in charge of a phantom air base out in the deserts of Utah — an air base without planes. And in charge of officers who were louts. As air force officers we were proud of being louts and of lacking all the qualities that gave meaning to the old major's life. We gave sloppy salutes, we slouched in a loose way with our hands in our pockets and cigarettes hanging from our lips. Our clothes were unpressed, and our shoes unshined. We had set ourselves apart from all the other branches of the service by a cultivated raunchiness that mocked all military pretensions.

Every morning after roll call we would gather in a mob in front of the headquarters building and wait to be addressed by our commanding officer. Sometimes our names would be read out, directing us to pack and leave. It was like a scene from a gulag movie where the POWs are huddled in the wind before the platform of some Nazi sadist. Presently, the major would step from the open door and smartly slapping his swagger stick against his leg, would stand at the edge of the porch studying us with aversion and disgust. Then he would begin to speak, his dark eyes blazing, his too-black mustache looking as if it had been glued on, moving up and down in funny jerks. He gave us fundamental talks on what being an officer and a gentleman meant, about respect and discipline, about the impossibility of winning the war if we couldn't drill like robots. He talked about the way we stood, the way we saluted, the unbuttoned shirts, the unshined shoes. He talked about democracy and the flag and how our uniforms were symbols of American might and right. God, he said, probably wore a uniform very much like ours. Would God go around with his pants half zipped? The whole performance was incredibly unreal, childish, and interminable.

And finally some second lieutenant hidden in the middle of that mob who perhaps had listened for a week to this desperate madness would say aloud, "Oh, bullshit, Major," or "Why don't you blow it out your ass, sir?" or "Major, for Christ's sake, dismiss, dismiss." And the major, glaring into our faces, his cheeks turning crimson, would bark with outrage and contempt, "All right, who said that? I want the man who said that to step forward and identify himself." He would wait, and of course no one was stupid enough to step forward, and the major, slapping his swagger stick against his leg, one hand on his hip, would shake his head with disgust. "Who is the knave? Isn't he man enough to step forward? . . . No, I imagine not." He would stare into our faces, while here and there in the crowd low boos and scattered catcalls grew. "What a mob of scum," he would yell finally in a loud, fearless voice. "Don't you realize what it means to wear the uniform, what it means to be an officer?" And then turning to his sergeant, "Dismiss this lawless rabble," and he would salute sharply, spin around with incredible precision, and disappear into his office.

Upon being dismissed we would crowd to the different bulletin boards checking our names against travel orders and, finding nothing, head for town. Almost all of us had rooms in hotels, and by late afternoon almost all of us had begun to drink seriously. At eight o'clock the next morning we would line up for roll call and then gather before the major's office in the thin November light with a chill wind driving in incessantly from across the salt flats. The major would appear, his face cold, rigid, and contemptuous, and begin to talk; his voice unchanged from yesterday, still angry but no angrier; talking to us about the Stars and Stripes, about the way we slouched, about our holy duty to preserve freedom, about the honor of wearing the uniform, until finally that most impatient and outraged of us would once again yell some insult out of that faceless mob and others would begin to growl and boo. He hated what we represented; it hinted at social chaos and the breakdown of the old imperialist values; we were the future with its awful changes: disrespectful, slovenly, undisciplined, cynical.

He confronted us each morning unchanged, convinced that he was right and that he was doing his duty and that to do less would be cowardice. He was like a man who, knowing that freezing temperatures are fatal, commands the falling snow to lose its coldness. He was absolutely sure of himself, proud and rigid in his isolation, as calm and furious as a Baptist preacher who has stumbled into a dance hall. Now, thinking about this deluded man and thinking about him facing our loathing every day, day after day, it strikes me that he was probably the bravest soldier that I met in the war. Who else but a true hero could have stood up to that solid wall of contemptuous men, glared back into our faces and tried without ceasing to plant in our hearts the old glory, the honor, the manliness, the shattering magnificence of 1914, when a million men from time to time would march across the muddy fields, faces smiling, to die in piled heaps for flag and country?

13

A FTER UTAH it was back to Texas. A period that may have lasted for months is represented in my mind by a tremendously impressive blankness, as though hundreds of feet of badly developed film, whole reels, had been ripped from the film strip of my army life. Texas could do that to a non-Texan, especially in December, and the combination of Texas and army training could drive more sensitive souls to madness, suicide, or violent crime.

It was in Texas on some grotesque Panhandle base that our combat crew assembled and began to train together. Staff sergeant gunners from Michigan, South Carolina, and Missouri; a radio operator from Pennsylvania; a navigator from Illinois; a pilot from California. Aside from combat itself there should be no more unforgettable day in the war than this moment when we first met — the ten men who, if we died, would probably die together; who, if we lived, would perhaps owe our lives to one another. I am trying to look at that moment and pick it out of that Texas blankness, but there is an awful sepia-tinted haze in the air, everything is in slow motion, invented, and that figure who is advancing and the smiling group behind him could just as well be a memory of some religious spectacle where Christ, bathed in a glowing light, moves across a temple floor open-armed and radiant, with his disciples behind him. Christ, of course, was our pilot. But then who am I, standing apart and watching? Judas?

And what right have I, a secret masturbator, lazy, incompetent, a dreamer, undoubtedly a coward — what right have I to claim membership in this group of perfect men? Through luck as much as anything else, I was spared the role of Judas. But Judas, unrecognized, is there in that group of smiling men; he is the one who will prefer life to glory, the one with the courage to proclaim his cowardice.

If I cannot remember how we met, it is probably the intensity of the moment that has obliterated the scene form my memory, and if it was staged to bind us together psychologically, the air force should have provided us with smoked glasses against its blinding power. What I can remember now is that from the first minute we were joined in an absolutely uncritical brotherhood; each of us was like an Indian bridegroom standing before an altar and about to be married to a girl he has never seen; our hearts opened up to one another in a simultaneous burst of love as we walked, perhaps through different doors, into that room, if it was a room, strangely lit by a late afternoon sun (lies, lies) that turned the faces of the enlisted men, the pilot, and the navigator into bronzed Homeric heroes. What a badly imagined fantasy. No, let me strip it of its religious patina; it is like a scene from some third-rate war movie with Buddy Rogers, Richard Arlen, or Jack Oakie. Is it possible we saw ourselves in such simpleminded terms? Ask it another way: if we had been incapable of imagining a romantic ambience that would allow us to play out an heroic melodrama, would any of us have volunteered to climb into those aluminum constructions and fly into the heart of Germany?

But what had awakened us to this nobility of feeling? Why were we so immediately disposed to find strength and comfort in being a member of that group? The answer is simple: we were all scared shitless. When you are put into a combat crew, then combat is not far behind. We had all begun to realize that we were surrounded by enemies — the Nazi war machine, of course; but just as ominous, the Air Corps brass, who for one brilliant headline would be willing to schedule us for a glorious death; and worst of all that secret cowardice that made us unsure of who we were, that made us wonder when the moment came would our nerves crack and would we panic like schoolgirls. We loved each other with all the directness of terrified rats huddling together in the hold of a sinking ship.

The golden mist is beginning to lift, but when I begin to remember definite moments we have been flying a B-17 as a crew almost daily for over a month — over a frozen land so wind-blasted that even the snow has been swept up and piled in inconsequential drifts. These high altitude flights, so against nature (for, as we pointed out to each other, if God had wanted us to fly at 25,000 feet we would have been born with wings and oxygen tanks), were exhausting, bone-chilling, and incredibly boring. It was the pilot who was being tested and checked out; the rest of us were just along for the ride. Though I dropped a few practice bombs at night, and the navigator incessantly navigated, and the gunners fired at towed targets a couple of times, it was Bob Wylie, our pilot, who was under the most intense pressure. We had not yet been assigned a copilot, and his seat was occupied by a series of captains, majors, and lieutenant colonels. They rode beside Wylie with clipboards on their laps writing down judgments that kept us all uncertain and nervous.

It was the pilot who now held our lives in his hands; we also watched him with an intense curiosity, not in a critical way, but to enforce the desperate conviction we all held, and which we probably all had held from the moment he first stood before us — that he was competent to get us through thirty bombing missions over Europe. Like two-year-olds who insist that their mommy is the prettiest and best mommy in the world, we decided immediately that Wylie was probably the best pilot in the U.S. Army Air Corps.

About six weeks before flying overseas we were assigned our own copilot, Jack Oates. We found it difficult to accept him into our tight group; he had a few things going against him. First and most important, he was a copilot, and though we knew we had to have one, we didn't like the word. If he were truly a first class flier, surely he would have been given his own crew. Now here he was, sitting at Wylie's right side with almost equal power and responsibility. He was tense and very serious, and in his face in repose there was a kind of uncertain frown, as though he were no happier to find himself thrust into our crew than we were to have him. I think he sensed for a couple of weeks that we treated him with a certain reserve. He was like a stranger, the last guest to arrive at an intimate party where everyone else is already drunk, dancing in corners, exchanging confidences in the linen closet, feeling up the hostess, kissing on the staircase.

We didn't like at all what he had told us about himself: that he had flunked his pilot's physical because his eyes were bad and because he was underweight. He had spent a month at home eating bunches of bananas and a hundred pounds of carrots before he finally passed a second physical in another recruiting office. How we watched him after that information. My God, was he squinting against the sun? Were his eyes watering? Was the poor bastard going to go blind on us? And how slim and frail he looked beside Wylie. It seemed highly improbable that he would have the strength to manhandle a bomber for ten or twelve hours and wrestle it back to a safe landing.

The other thing that we didn't like about Oates: he was a Texan. All the rest of us had been raised in more or less civilized parts of the United States, and to a man we found the rural simplemindedness of the Panhandle unbelievable. We took out our rage against Texas on Oates (*Oates*, for Christ's sake — what a cornpone name. From, for Christ's sake, *Waco*). We kidded him savagely, but he only gave us back a mild smile and said over and over, "But ah cain't hep it, ah cain't hep it."

I think we recognized soon enough that Oates was a better flier than Wylie, but we were loyal to our pilot and suppressed this knowledge even from ourselves. We clung to Wylie as our real leader; in those days just before combat we liked his tranquilizing style. Oates was nervous and intense. He flew with fierce concentration, as though what he might lack in brawn he would make up for with pure nerve, and after long flights he would stagger from the plane, his face grey, his eyes sunken, his hands beginning to develop the first signs of a tremor.

Wylie on the other hand was always cool, always steady and unruffled. He flew in a smooth, nonaggressive way — relaxed, smiling, unhurried. Even when the check pilots were trying to rattle him with emergency procedures — the trim tabs secretly rolled back or one of the engines suddenly made inoperative — Wylie would calmly and slowly think things over before deciding what to do. He was solidly upper middle-class and had been educated to feel secure and unthreatened by anything that he might encounter in the outside world, and he handled a plane with some of the same courtesy and grace with which he handled the enlisted gunners or the mechanics or the barmen who served us beer in the officers' club.

I don't know how he felt about the war; the war was something that we scarcely ever discussed, but perhaps I may safely give him some of my own feelings: if the war was being fought to preserve the system under which we lived, then it was more his war than it was some bankrupt farmer's ruined by the Depression. And what of that almost invisible figure in the wartime America of the 1940s, the black soldier drafted out of the ghettos or the rural slums of the South? He was kept apart and hidden from the rest of us. Out of all the millions of soldiers who wandered lost and dazed through the sleazier parts of American towns on weekend passes, I don't remember seeing many blacks. But I don't think I ever saw one without feeling guilty; there was something shameful about drafting shoeshine boys to fight and die in a war that would only institutionalize their impossible position in America. It was like drafting Jews to fight for Hitler. By the mid-1930s there were twelve million unemployed; they rode on boxcars and hitchhiked through the dying American towns. Was this their war? Was it as much their war as mine, who at its conclusion would be handed a hundred thousand dollars to buy land and cattle?

Wylie, I'm sure, felt the same way; he had a kind of aristocratic vision of himself, a kind of guilt for the privileges he had inherited. He was like the sons of Kennedy who, having benefited and been enriched by American democracy, immediately when war was declared volunteered to fight in the most exposed positions.

This, then, was the difference between Wylie and Oates: Wylie had nothing to gain from the war except the chance to demonstrate his nobility and to find out for himself the limits of his courage. For Oates becoming a pilot was upward mobility, a chance to get out of Texas. After the war maybe he could fly for an airline or with luck run a little crop dusting company, and he could fly forever, swooping low over the cotton fields of Arizona or the bean fields of California or the long rolling rows of Iowa's corn. Wylie flew like a gentleman; Oates, like a man who would fly for the rest of his life, sought incessantly to perfect his skill and to become a true professional. How strange that we preferred Wylie's style. I suppose it was because he more truly acted out the role that our romantic natures demanded of him. The war had placed us at the disposal of society, and it was Wylie's coolness and grace, this unstated attitude that the war was simply an episode to be endured with no more than the proper degree of dedication that helped us to see ourselves as something more than a faceless group, that helped us see that man, even in a war that would kill millions, was still the central measure of value.

Another blizzard comes sweeping across Texas; outside the wind howls and shrieks, and from the endless rows of Quonset huts lined up on a hundred acres of hardscrabble, smoke in hundreds of thin lines pours into the freezing air and is immediately beaten to the ground. Dirty piles of snow are banked against barracks, and the American flag outside headquarters snaps and pops in the wind like pistol shots. All planes are grounded. Since it seems likely that we may not fly for weeks, we are doing what we usually do to dull the desperate boredom of unscheduled days — we are getting drunk. Wylie, Oates, the navigator Moburg, and I are sitting at a table in the officers' club with a second bottle of whiskey. Though it is not much more than eleven o'clock, we are all pretty stupidly close to the limits of what we can safely handle.

There is nothing in my mind to draw on for an account of the next thirty minutes; alcohol and time have done their job, but here is a possible scenario: Oates and Moburg are both married, and it occurs to Wylie that it would be cute if all four of us had faithful little war brides waiting for us while we plow through enemy skies. Combat is only about six weeks away, and it looms in the near distance like some strange planet where everything will be radically different, hostile, and disorienting. A wife would be something to anchor us to the world, something wonderful to come home to. And it will save us from the whores, Wylie points out. If you're married here then you can't get married there; you know damn well it's going to be confusing in England where you can screw any girl on the island for a chocolate bar or a bar of soap. It was a strange philosophy, coming from Wylie, who in the two months that I had known him had fallen in love with at least three nurses on the base, all of whom he had seduced. But it struck hard at my own growing obsession with being married, and as we sat there drinking it seemed more and more like a good idea. By eleven-thirty it seems like a brilliant idea, because suddenly I have even thought of the girl who would probably be willing to marry me. Why had I never thought of her before?

Moburg has been married for about six months and is carried away with enthusiasm: he begins listing the wonders of married life. Oates, who has been married for less than six months and whose marriage is already disintegrating, says nothing. It would be months before he could talk about his wife and the goddamn civilian she had fallen for and the divorce she was demanding, without tears standing in his eyes. From eleven-thirty until midnight Wylie and I are strangely silent but drinking strongly. We are the only two actors on the stage now and the scene is tense with interior monologues.

Through the cigarette smoke and the whiskey fumes, one of us finally speaks. "Okay, I will if you will."

Another blank spot in my memory, a blank as portentous as the elapsed time between the pressed trigger and the bullet that smashes at your temple. When the mists clear, Wylie and I are out in a long, cold hallway standing side by side at one end of a row of telephones. We have each placed long-distance calls to the West Coast and as we wait we have only to glance at each other's faces to break into wild hoots of laughter. We pass the bottle back and forth and keep our exuberance aflame with great gulps of whiskey. And the walls of the officers' club are slanting, and the floor rises and falls like a ship at sea, and five minutes after the connections have been made we are both engaged to be married. Immediately.

I don't know how well Wylie knows the girl he is about to marry. In my case, however, I have proposed to someone I scarcely know. Once more the genes have taken over, not only directing me to marry but selecting the perfect mother of my children.

I had met Dorothy through a friendship with her brother, and I had met him one summer on top of a mountain peak while I was hiking through an enormous primitive area near the Canadian border and miles from the end of the Forest Service road. He was a forest lookout; when he came out at the end of the fire season I had met his immediate family, and a little later all of his uncles, aunts, and cousins. They owned apple orchards in the Okanogan, and they were the best people I had ever met — hardworking farmers, their hardworking wives, and their suntanned children, young men about my age who had extraordinary skills and pure uncomplicated emotions. They lived to hunt and fish, to ski and ice skate on the frozen winter ponds. These families lived off the land, their lockers were full of frozen elk roasts and packaged venison steaks. Everything they did was connected with the streams and the pine-covered hills, and it was impossible to imagine any of them living in a city. They were in the truest sense the real aristocrats of America, strong, true pioneers who had never lost their awe of the land, who had never been seduced, like my own semi-pioneer grandfather, into sacrificing their delight in natural things to the soul-deadening insanity of accumulating wealth.

That eastern Washington of the middle thirties, poverty-stricken and virile, seemed to me, who had hiked into it over the Cascade Mountains one spring, like a land that had escaped all of the evils of progress. It was pure and beautiful, the America of Mark Twain, Wallace Stegner, Sherwood Anderson. Winthrop, a one-street town almost at the end of a dirt road that twisted north through a valley of dry pastureland, sagebrush, and small orchards, was like some magic place that hadn't changed since the Civil War. In the evenings herds of deer browsed in the alfalfa fields; five hundred farms in that valley and not one tractor. Ah, Winthrop, you were perfect then, and if I haven't walked your street for forty-five years, I still dream of you and mourn the circumstances that made it impossible to go back. Winthrop: a seedy little bank; a seedy hotel that leaned over a mountain stream; a seedy little cafe that served almost nothing but roast pork or hot beef sandwiches drowned in gravy; a seedy equipment store that sold sacks of cement or pieces of corrugated iron and on certain days, when the truck arrived from Wenatchee, displayed a few crates of green vegetables; a dark seedy beer joint with a row of antlers above the bar; a cement box called a creamery, another cement box that rented freeze lockers for ten dollars a year — there wasn't much more. It was a town reduced to an essence.

The town was dominated by a Forest Service headquarters building just across a log bridge where two streams came together. In those years when a hundred starving men survived by selling apples on the streets of American cities for a nickel, the growing of apples was almost as unprofitable as growing pigs, those too-prolific creatures which the government was paying farmers to destroy. Forest Service money kept the town alive. Twenty miles up the road toward Canada there was a CCC camp full of kids from the eastern cities who were sent out during the summer months to clean forest trails, build small bridges, or haul blocks of salt to the wild mountain goats who lived on the black shale slides below Dollar Watch Peak. It was a town of forest rangers, cattlemen, sheepherders, half-goofy prospectors who worked the abandoned gold, silver, and tungsten claims. In July and August a small bunch of unemployed high school kids camped in the cottonwoods just outside of town, waiting for the good luck of a forest fire that would give them jobs. To the west and to the north and starting at the town's limits, the largest and most magnificent primitive area in the United States rolled away in rowed mountains — to the west, to the coastal plains; to the north, to the Yukon, to the North Pole.

What made the whole area absolutely authentic and historic to me was a small log cabin on a back street where the old timers claimed

Owen Wister had written *The Virginian* — or, for the story was confused, the log cabin which had once been a bar where one of Winthrop's most notorious whores had danced on a tabletop one night for Owen Wister. Was it on that night and in this cabin that Gary Cooper had spoken the most famous words in American literature? "When you call me that, smile." Perhaps not; still, as I got to know the people of Winthrop it was obvious that it was here that Wister had met the soft-speaking and noble cowboys who would be his heroes, the little blue-eyed school-teachers who had come from a more corrupt outside and fallen under the spell of the pure men and the mountains around which their lives were centered.

It was almost the first time in my life I had met decent families, and to finally observe families that worked was like seeing some intricate dance being perfectly performed by the Ballet Russe — everyone in his proper place, everyone doing the proper steps with ease and grace. Or rather, it was like seeing the Ballet Russe after twenty-two years of having seen nothing more aesthetically moving than endless dance marathons, those grisly exercises in sadism that so aptly delineated certain desperations of the Depression years. Now I was meeting whole extended groups of people who loved one another. It was the most staggering spectacle, and its implications were more profound than that other knowledge that had hit me a few years before when I had read a one-sentence description of Darwinian theory: we are all descended from monkeys.

That bitter definition of a family — a group of related individuals dominated by its most neurotic member — had always seemed like a perfect definition. Now in a matter of days my loathing of family hypocrisy melted away; I realized with a terrible sense of my own deprivation that the family unit lay at the foundation of American greatness and that, like Darwin's theory, it gave profound coherence to certain fundamental aspects of the world. And the most stunning revelation of all: the coherence of the world is grounded in morality. Deeply shaken by these perceptions, I staggered around for a time redefining my prejudices. How could this new awareness not completely change my life? (I am sitting here now, an old man looking for meanings in old actions, and another question grows out my remembrance: isn't it possible that all the insights that come out of experience — or philosophy, psychology, religion, and art — don't all these man-constructed concepts, when they are true, have the identical message: you must change your life; you must change the way you live?)

I had fallen in love with a whole family and immediately struggled desperately to be accepted into its heart. After a time, finding a strength and solace I had never found in my own family, I decided that I could never live away from that valley and those great-hearted people. It was here in Winthrop that I bought those six hundred acres of mountain pasture and where, for almost a whole year before being drafted, I had hunted and skied and drunk hot rum with the people who had so generously adopted me. It was a man's world perfectly constructed to mirror my youthful ideas of how life should be, a man's world of guns, hiking boots, happy wives sweating their asses off in the kitchen, trout streams and Chinese pheasants, the five-point buck lined up in the gun sights, cold clear nights under the stars when we ice-skated on the frozen ponds and the girls we went with huddled around bonfires and admired us. They were almost irrelevant in that perfect world except for the final few minutes when we drove them home and they fought nicely and sometimes unsuccessfully to preserve their virginity.

Certainly the most irrelevant girl during that time was Dorothy, one of the cousins, seventeen years old, self-effacing, and almost invisible in that landscape of timbered hillsides and mountain glaciers, in all the activity of packhorses, forest fires, and elk hunts. She was going to high school in another town and appeared in Winthrop infrequently. I was five years out of high school and the difference in our ages made it difficult for me to take her seriously. Still, she was a member of that perfect family; her blood was noble; she breathed the same pure mountain air and shared in an unconscious way the qualities that out of my infatuation I had found in her grandmother, her mother, and her aunts.

Sometime during pilot training she had begun to write to me or I had begun to write to her. A kind of fabricated wartime flirtation developed, made intense and idealistic by separation and the convulsions of history. Knitting mittens or scarves in olive drab, baking batches of chocolate chip cookies, she, too, saw herself as a romantic figure in the drama.

Now it is eight o'clock on the morning after I have become engaged to be married, and I sit across the table from Wylie, who is in the same boat. We are drinking coffee in the officers' mess, heads throbbing, stomachs heaving, contemplating the fruits of our drunkenness. Nothing seems to be very funny this morning.

"Well," Wylie said finally, "there's only one thing to do. Call up the girls and tell them we were drunk, that we were kidding."

"You can't do that tb a girl," I said. "That's too shitty a trick."

"Not as shitty as getting married and then going out and getting killed," Wylie said.

"Yeah, and maybe we'll have bad luck and won't get killed," I said.

"Exactly," Wylie said, trying to laugh. "And you come back married to some babe that's been screwing the troops for the war effort. Or you get one of those Dear Johns. No, M., we've got to call them up. What time is it in Los Angeles?"

"You're going to call her up at 5 A.M. and tell her you were kidding? Jesus, Bob, you can't do that. She's probably already half packed. And besides, goddammit, you made a deal with me."

"I'm sorry, I really am, but I can't go through with it. Shit, man, last night I was drunk out of my mind." I sat there desolate and frightened, half angry at being deserted. Wylie said, "Look, just call her up, talk sweet, tell her you've thought it over; you're not breaking it off, you just want to wait until after the war. Well, until after combat anyway."

"I can't do that," I said. "Shit, I don't know her well enough."

"Exactly," Wylie said. "We were both ready to marry babes we don't know well enough to be honest with."

"The trouble is I'd sort of like to get married," I said. "Sort of, you know? Not as much as last night, God knows, but sort of. I am being tossed, as they say, hither and thither by conflicting emotions."

"Not this little fucker," Wylie said, getting up from the table and turning toward the hall and the row of telephones. "Come on, come with me. Is it really 5 A.M. in L.A.? Oh, shit."

"Oh, you bastard," I called after him as he moved away. "You fucking traitor." But I didn't follow him and I knew I didn't have the strength of character to walk behind him, to call up Dorothy and postpone things. I think I felt in my decision to go ahead with the promise I had made not only a depressing resignation but a strange release in allowing myself to make some tremendous error. It was probably going to be a horrible mistake, but at least it would be all mine. It was an act of will as wild as that decision to throw myself off a cliff and ski down the face of a mountain; it was a kind of affirmation of life and free will set against the hero's death that was being planned for me.

About two seconds later, if my memory can be trusted, I was driving down to the train station to pick up Dorothy and her mother and take them to the hotel room I had reserved for them. Standing in the wind and peeking through a rime-coated window I saw them sitting on one of the curved benches in the little station; their faces were desolate and frightened, and looking at them I had the impression that they hadn't spoken to each other for hours. Dorothy was dressed in a light blue suit that exaggerated her monumental lines — this earth mother that my genes had chosen for me. She seemed to have gained another ten pounds. When I walked into the station she smiled dimly, greeted me in a voice that was less than a whisper, and gave me the look of a lamb about to be led to slaughter. My God, she was still a child. We looked at each other in the full knowledge that we were engaged in a ridiculous business. Those big dewy eyes, those trembling fingers tearing a piece of paper to shreds, the guilty face on the mother, whose eyes acknowledged that she was allowing something questionable to take place.

Another two seconds pass; we are standing before the altar in the base chapel; some Pfc. is playing wedding music; a fundamentalist Baptist minister with a narrow, severe Baptist face, and wearing granny glasses, is preaching a premarital sermon about the fires of hell; Wylie, the best man, stands at my side, and as I place the ring on Dorothy's finger, I notice that all the skin has begun to peel off my hands, as though I were in the grip of a consuming fever.

The skin had begun to peel off my hands the night before when Dorothy's mother, after a few too many belts of scotch, had shooed her daughter off to bed and set me down in a corner of the hotel lobby for a serious talk. Until then my fantasies about being married to Dorothy had made her more or less interchangeable with Helen; I had dared to anticipate something sort of wild and abandoned.

"Now listen, boy, you go slow, you understand? That girl's absolutely innocent; you've got yourself a virgin. You just take it easy, you understand?" She looked at me with an awful smile that held distrust and a mild repugnance — the mother's look at the man who is scheduled to violate her daughter and bloody the wedding sheets.

"God, it took me years to get over my wedding night," she said, gulping down a half glass of whiskey, shaking her head, and accusing me with a look of being identical to that monster who, slobbering and moaning, had crushed her beneath him, forced her legs apart, raped her, and shattered her romantic illusions forever. As I listened to the details and was instructed in the intricacies of honeymoon foreplay, I could feel my testicles withdrawing into the deepest recesses of my body. The same thing had happened three years before in basic training when I had watched the army's thirty-minute movie on venereal disease, and I wondered then, as I was wondering now, if those poor old shuddering nuts would ever come out of hiding. I realized with terror that Dorothy wasn't Helen and that the mother had spent years passing on to the daughter a fear and loathing of the sexual act that was going to make the next few days as delicate and difficult as any I had ever had to endure. In about ten days we were scheduled to fly overseas. Combat seemed, having suddenly lost its terrors, very far away.

After the wedding party, the two of us escaped to a sordid motel room on the outskirts of town, and all my forebodings were realized. Lying beside Dorothy, who rested beside me waiting for the worst in a state of terror that was close to catatonia, my shriveled machinery made one heroic effort at resurrection that filled me for a minute or two with overconfidence. And then somebody cut off the power. I suspected, but very dimly, that between my father and my wife's mother I had been successfully castrated; this suspicion did little to console my humiliation, but I was very slightly comforted by the possibility that Dorothy, out of an innocence that was almost criminal, was too ignorant to know that the marriage had not been consummated.

We spent a week of nights like this. During the day I flew high altitude practice missions and came back to use my exhaustion as a poor excuse. There we lay, brother and sister, mildly interested in one another's bodies, as chaste as angels, Dorothy softly moaning when I touched something that wasn't supposed to be touched, the eunuch bridegroom devastated with the knowledge that he couldn't fuck any better than he could fly.

14

In england, April may be the cruelest month but spring came early that year, and March held its own special kind of cruelty, too. We had a memory of a country we had never seen — in a strange, disquieting sense, we felt that we had come home. How green and familiar everything was under those fleecy puffs of clouds that drifted across the spring sky. Every day gentle showers filled with light fell on groves of ancient trees, winding roads, pastures filling with lambs, black, shining, new-plowed earth. Chaucer and Shakespeare were just around the corner taking notes. How green the grass was in that spring air which still held faintly the biting memory of winter. How quiet the days; England at first was a sleeping, breathing island. It was only at night and for short, intense hours that in the near distance the war howled and boomed; that was another kind of cruelty, crueler but less troubling.

We had been sent to our last temporary posting, a great staging area just outside London. It was from this field that all the combat groups in England were serviced, where new crews waited to replace old crews who had completed their missions and gone home, or who had been shot down. We were spare parts; essential, but no more essential than tires or propellers. While this camp had an airfield, it handled personnel rather than planes; the greenness of England in the absence of the roaring engines was made greener by a rural ambience, and we felt ourselves dropping through time into old fairy tales.

While we waited to fill some final gap in the lines, we went to classes and listened to combat veterans who reviewed techniques for the hundredth time. Outside the gates of the air base England lay, tranquil and sleepy, growing heavier each day, like a pregnant woman under its bursting weight of new leaves and the blooming of hawthorn, lilacs, daffodils. How could so small an island support this furious proliferation? After months of Texas, Utah, and the California desert, England was as exotic as a Brazilian rain forest. At every opportunity we walked away from the asphalted camp into the countryside. Oates, who had never before seen much of anything but mesquite and sagebrush, was stunned; he leaped and danced at the side of the road like a calf put out to pasture for the first time. Birds by the thousands peeped and squeaked and warbled. In the distance, always in the distance, old farmers in shapeless work tweeds did things with hoes or shovels; old women carrying heavy baskets disappeared in the gaps of hedgerows. No one ever spoke to us. English soldiers on bicycles, or people from the suburbs in shabby dark suits and carrying briefcases, averted their eyes if they passed us on the road. Our delight in England embarrassed them, and they preferred to consider us invisible. It was not hostility, just a terrible reserve. Beginning to doubt our own existence, we felt as though we were walking through the pages of a rural novel by Hardy or drifting, without speaking parts, between the lines of a Wordsworth ode.

Ten miles away to the south in an enormous curve, barrage balloons encircled London; strings of cables hung from the balloons like broken strands of spider webs. It was a spectacle, and it had a festive look at first, like a distant view of a world's fair; below those grey floating forms you knew that exciting things were happening.

Almost every night, into a black sky suddenly turned as gaudy as a Hollywood premier by lancing searchlights, a half dozen German bombers, separate and incredibly lonesome looking, would slowly move across the sky like pin-pierced insects. From far away the flak guns would begin to stutter, at first just one, then more and more, like a single howling dog in a sleeping city who rouses every cur until the city from every street across the horizon is nothing but howling dogs. Below the sound of the guns and filling every inch of English space, the air raid sirens moaned and wailed like wounded ghosts; it was an awful sound, passive and psychotic, symbolic of an insane and dying civilization. If the planes moved closer, the sounds of the flak guns following their flight below came closer and more intense until — my God, there was a gun crew just behind our Quonset hut, hidden in trees. Suddenly the walls, the ground, and the air heaved and vibrated. We stared at each other with vacant, stunned smiles or if, as was more likely, we were standing outside in the darkness watching the show, we flinched and ducked as the guns deafened us. We had the feeling that we stood now, finally, almost at the center of man's intentions, but like to children who watch their parents screaming at each other with rage and hatred, it was all incomprehensible.

In a classroom one morning twenty or thirty of us sit in hopeless boredom while a young bombardier instructor who has completed his missions lectures us on — something I had heard too often to be able to remember now what he was trying to tell us. The officers in the back rows tilted back in their chairs are sleeping. A couple of officers in my row are reading novels — one of which, to prove something about the mysterious nature of memory, was *The Last Days of Pompeii*. I have chosen a seat by a window, and the better part of me has slipped away to walk in the grass. No one is listening to the instructor or bothers to glance at the trajectories he has drawn on the blackboard. Suddenly we hear a sound like a pistol, and we look up in amazement. The instructor has slammed a book down on his desk and has begun to scream at us. "Listen to me, for Christ's sake," he cries. His eyes have filled with tears, his hands tremble, and he clutches at his throat. He fights for a long moment to get control and then says in a calmer voice, "Please. Please listen to me. I am telling you something that you should know; this is important. Don't you realize that in four months half of you will be dead?"

I think we are more embarrassed at first by this emotional outburst than shocked by the somewhat incredible information he has let slip out. It is the first time we have seen what we immediately recognize as a war casualty, a man whose self-control has been undermined by something terrible that we can't quite imagine. It is the first time we have heard the statistics. The numbers are a little more brutal than we had imagined. As a matter of fact, it was a kind of statistic so unspeakable and with such intensely personal implications that during the time that it took us to handle it (it was about now that we began having serious trouble getting to sleep) we couldn't bring ourselves to mention it to each other. So. We had a fifty-fifty chance. Each of us absorbed this information in his own way. To the optimist the glass is half full; to the pessimist. . . .

Outside the classroom building was a long, narrow shed; it contained nothing but a row of half-a-dozen toilets, individual cubicles with doors that opened up into the yard. In Palo Alto someone had pointed out a house that Frank Lloyd Wright had designed for a rich student who had wanted her own place for the four years she planned on spending at

Stanford; according to the story the architect had forgotten to include a kitchen, and I had never really believed this tale until I ran across this building in England to which had been appended, like an afterthought, this row of finely built toilets. After a time, though, what had seemed like bad planning began to take on aspects of metaphysical subtlety. Of the thousands of American airman who had used these cubicles during the past couple of years, a good percentage of them had felt compelled to write something upon these shit–house walls. There was scarcely a blank space on the walls or on the doors where one of us might have added another sentiment. The intensity of the private emotions written on the walls made of the place and of its separation from the main building a kind of individual chapel. There was nothing there that mentioned sex, but man's other equally engrossing preoccupation, death, was here spread out for us in all its anguish.

"Bud Turner, November 10, 1942. If I am alive in six months I will come back and erase this."

"J. L. Hoskins. Born 1920, Died 1942."

"Sunset and evening star and all that there bullshit. Lt. Thomas 'Sparky' Muldoon. 23 April 1942."

"Mama, mama, I'm too young and pretty to die. T. Y. L., 2nd Lt., Air Force."

It was here in the toilets that we received the first direct messages from the dead, and we began to find in the stink of our own excrement that overwhelming connection between shit and earth. It was here in the toilets, isolated and private, that, though not quite real yet, the awareness of death came to us as a physical knowledge deeper than words which was manifested in the disintegrating quality of our turds. We now began to see ourselves as delicate and mortal, standing just barely hidden in the wings of history, where at any moment we could expect to be flung onto the stage. Our bodies more than our minds shrank in terror from the approaching annihilation. Our bowels turned to water. In our minds we still tended to see death as that outrageous thing that happened to others, or a condition which could be softened by treating it as one of art's preoccupations, like unrequited love. Death was something you wrote poems about.

Soon after we arrived in England, and while we were sitting in another classroom late one afternoon, we heard the strange, heavy sound of a new kind of plane. In a gap between the buildings for just a second a monstrously large bomber, obliterating the trees behind it, rolled past our vision. In was a Boeing B-29 with the same sleek deadly lines as its baby brother, our B-17. It had been designed for those very long flights that still had to be made from the islands of the southern sea in order to bomb Japan. Later, at the far end of the airfield we saw this gigantic plane parked in front of a hangar which was much too small to receive it. We resented this plane; it dwarfed our own bomber, make it look puny and just a little bit old-fashioned; it diminished our pretensions that of all the action going on in the world just then, the actions of the Eighth Air Force were the most glamorous, most deadly, and the most central to the war. But what was a B-29 doing in England?

It seemed that Winston Churchill had been curious to see the new super-fortress. After a short telephone chat with President Roosevelt, as a gracious gesture it had been flown over for his quick inspection. Winnie would drive out one morning on his way to work, stroll around the plane, give a few brave V-for-victory signs to the assembled troops, and an hour later the plane would be on its way back to America. The B-29 was still a highly secret weapon, and it was heavily guarded by military police. During the daylight hours a half dozen English fighters patrolled the sky ready to scare off snooping Krauts. The plane was scheduled to remain in England for no more than two days. When it was still parked outside the hangar ten days after it arrived, the secret story of what had happened leaked out. While it was not especially funny, it delighted the combat crews.

The two pilots who had flown to England in this conversation piece of a bomber had thought it would be fun to fly on a mission over Germany. It was arranged that each of them would take a copilot's seat on a comfortable milk run to the French coast, one of those missions that we would grow to love because they didn't last much more than four or five hours. Take off at six and back to the base for lunch. But of course there was the possibility of death on even the easiest of missions. The planes carrying the two pilots were both shot down, and the two crews of ten men each were drowned in the English Channel. I suppose this unanticipated disaster turned into a humiliating situation for the colonels who had arranged for the pilots to fly that day. Especially because in all of England there wasn't one man who had ever been checked out in a B-29 and so was authorized to fly one. Day after day, while a couple of new pilots in America waited for decent weather to fly the Atlantic, the secret bomber sat on the tarmac. It was no longer of much interest to anyone, and more than anything had become a symbol of incompetence at some high level.

What we as potential combat crews found more diminishing than the great size of the plane was the fact that two pilots, who had been under no obligation to do so, had decided that it would be amusing to fly over a Europe at war. They wanted to soar over places where steel projectiles aimed at them would be flung into the sky. They had done it for kicks, and we couldn't forgive them that. It was the kind of bravado that, as our apprehensions grew, we found unbelievable, obscene, and false to life's first demand — to live.

Wylie walked into our hut one evening after dinner as the rest of us sat on cots next to a foul-smelling, coal-burning stove that produced lots of gases but little heat. "Just get up very casually," he said in a low voice. "Very casually put on your overcoats and drift outside. Walk behind me at a distance. I've got a cab waiting in that lane of trees by the flak guns. We're going to London."

Going into London had been forbidden to us, and our casualness as we sneaked off the base may have been slightly overdone, but an hour later we were all drinking glasses of straight scotch in a very crowded pub not far from Piccadilly Circus. Everything was straight out of the movies — the blacked-out London streets, the taxis driving without lights, the ruins of buildings dimly seen in that long English evening hesitating between dusk and darkness, the blackout curtains in the doorway of the pub, the mob of soldiers standing three deep at the bar and wearing the uniforms of England, Canada, Poland, France. Above all of this, a full moon, a bomber's moon, drifted through a sky of scattered clouds. The streets in the center of the city were full of marching armies.

Before going to the pub we had stopped for a few minutes at the Red Cross and at the information desk had asked if it were possible that they could find us a hotel room for the night. One of the women at the desk was the most beautiful Englishwoman I would ever see — and the most overwhelmingly captivating. The bloom of her skin, the fine-textured bones, the intelligent eyes, the smile, the beautifully managed distance-closeness that she immediately established between us — all of this literally more Hollywood at its best than anything that had ever happened to me in life since a rather digressive incident in my fifteenth year when I had very, very softly patted Joan Crawford on the ass in a crowded elevator in a Beverly-Wilshire department store. But this ravishing young woman had qualities which were so obviously aristocratic that it has taken me almost forty years to make that unlikely connection between some heroine out of a Meredith novel and the showbiz ambience of Beverly Hills.

It was only Wylie who spoke to her (Wylie was in charge of everything that night), and her answer was immediate and warming. "But, of course, Lieutenant, I'm sure we can find you a place." She called what may have been the most expensive hotel in London and in a lovely voice, to which probably no one had ever said no, said, "This is Lady Ashley. Four friends of mine will be dropping by later, and they will need a room."

For twenty years I wondered who Lady Ashley was, half wondering if she were not, perhaps, the sister of Fred Astaire and deciding that she couldn't be because of the dichotomy between time's ravages and the luminous bloom of Lady Ashley's cheeks. And then for twenty years I didn't think much about it and only now, remembering back, trying to fit everything together or at least the little that still remains in my memory, finally realized in a little pea-sized burst of pleasure just who had gotten us the room that night. But, of course. It was the woman who would soon become Mrs. Clark Gable, who would marry a tail-gunner sergeant from a heavy bomber outfit. If at that time she had deep connections with Hollywood, it was only to repudiate with the slightest movement of a hand or an eyebrow, a toss of her hair, all of Hollywood's pretentious vulgarities. Lady Ashley made a floozy out of Joan Crawford and just about everyone else who had ever flounced, panted, and pouted upon the silver screens of my youth.

We had time for little more than a single glass of booze in that pub crowded with the armies of the allied nations when we were caught up in history. My single insight from that bar, where I stood for the first time within touching distance of English soldiers, was that bunched together they smelled like a band of sheep. It was the lanolin in their thick, woolen uniforms, uniforms that seemed to have been cut from rugs, and that in the warmth of the bar released their perfume of raw wool, pine tar, and heather; they were uniforms so thick and bulky that they also held the dampness of the English fog, and so monumental that it seemed impossible a bullet could penetrate through to English flesh.

We stood in this smoke-filled room caught up in the pleasant drama of a comradeship that we hoped to be worthy of, if only the testing were not too severe — that man's world of whiskey, obscenities, and warmth. Together it said Tobruk, Singapore, Dunkirk, and we were very aware of standing with heroes. Suddenly, from every compass point the air-raid sirens began to wail and a moment later, still far away but coming closer from every side, the ack-ack guns, and after that, much too close it seemed, the terrible air-ripping sound of exploding bombs. We had arrived just in time for the last great German air raid on London, though of course we didn't know it at the time. The soldiers went on drinking.

Too ignorant to be afraid (much) and more interested in destruction than in whiskey, I slipped outside and walked alone through the blacked-out streets, streets that had suddenly emptied. In the next year I would walk these streets a hundred times, but I always moved under the spell of that first night. The sounds of war, the immensity of the desolation, the dust from collapsing buildings, the distant flare of flames, the distant shrieking of ambulances, air-raid sirens, antiaircraft guns, terrified people — all of it was too grand, too terrible. That couple of hours was so intense that my own reactions to it were permanently imprinted on my mind, and later I would never see London except through the distorting mirror of my own experiences. Even today to think of London is to think of smoke, sirens, the smash of buildings as they fall into the street and the fine dust of powdered glass and plaster rushing in a wave just ahead of the collapsing walls. In youth you hear the opening chords of some powerful and romantic concerto and for the rest of your life are captive to the echo of some identical emotion that through each rehearsing the music resurrects. War as a symbol of man's failure turns experience into a kind of art, and walking through London that night was like walking directly into the middle distances of a Bosch painting of hell where, being human, I tried in a panic to impose my own order. It was a time that held not only terrible despair but an aesthetic grandeur as well. Certainly the part of me that demands and responds to rage, chaos, destruction, filth, and obscenity was filled with a kind of joy, and even the other part that seeks order, truth, and meaning was moved.

More than consolation man seeks meaning; Calvin's conviction that we are all damned to hell, that we are all putrid, stinking sinners, delights us. Walking through the deserted London streets, the cosmic message was wonderfully clear and exhilarating. It answered Hamlet's question in a way that could never be refuted. It must certainly be far better not to have to live in such a world. It is easier for the mind than the body to accept this truth, especially the body of a twenty-eight-year-old who is still strongly oriented toward the few sensuous pleasures that life offers. The sudden conviction that pound for pound life is not worth enduring, that it cannot be lived in anything but a shameful way, for all its portentous and windy grandeur, charms the young mind with that bitter shriek of despair that nourishes youth and helps him define himself in dramatic terms.

What an overblown and pompous way to say that all in all war is sort of neat, and that it answers certain youthful needs. I have been trying to write the last couple of pages as I might have written them forty years ago. If I remember correctly, the half dozen or so stories that I wrote about this time and submitted to *The New Yorker* sounded pretty much like this, and I am beginning to understand why they were rejected, those that passed the censor.

I walked below the lights that swept the night sky searching for enemy planes; probably humming something from Wagner. Everyone else in London, knowing better, stayed indoors. I seem to remember being the only person on the street. Thousands of pieces of steel had begun to fall from the sky, spent flak that at times sounded like metallic gusts of rain. A small ringing chunk fell at my feet, but when I picked it up, I dropped it immediately with all the fingers of one hand spouting blood. A little later an air-raid warden standing in a doorway spotted me and cursing me for my stupidity, calling me a Yank, yanked me under the projecting protection of a cornice.

Later still, when the planes had gone and the city lay quiet, except for the occasional ambulance siren or the bell-clanging of a fire truck, I walked again in streets that once more had begun to fill with whores and soldiers. Behind the faint smell of blasted plaster and cordite, the sour smell of wartime London — semen, urine, sweat.

At two o'clock I staggered into Lady Ashley's hotel. An old man by the desk greeted me. "Bit of a dustup in the streets tonight, sir, if you'll pardon the expression." He was dressed in the black sateen clothes of a hotel lackey; he led me down long wide halls paneled in mahogany. Under a dim green light another old man, grey-faced as death, sat at a desk in an alcove guarding rows of keys; freshly shined shoes stood at attention beside doorways; the hall was as wide as a two-lane highway. It would take a direct bomb hit to disturb the funereal ambience of this place where all sounds were muffled by blackout curtains and thick rugs and hardwood timbering and what seemed to be a heavy kind of dust that lingered in the air dulling the lights — ancient dust from the nineteenth century. (I could imagine one of these old men rising up out of the ruins of this place, his hair singed, his face bloody, and saying, "Well, sir, that was a bit of a dustup, if you'll allow me an opinion.") The shameful class-ridden past, now shabby, threadbare, wasteful of space and smelling faintly of another century, suddenly seemed as unreal as the shattered buildings that were the symbol of the times. One felt with mixed emotions that out there on the rubble of gutted tenements the future would be constructed, and that these pretentiously noble and imperial establishments would disappear or remain as curious and irrelevant monuments to that old, pompous, mercantile England that was being swept away.

At the door of my room the old man, with a great key chained to a slab of bronze, unlocked the door and bowed me in. Wylie, Moburg, Oates slept their drunken sleep beneath satin coverlets. The ceiling of the room disappeared in the dusky heights.

It is 6 A.M. the next day; the four of us are walking down a wide avenue lined with government buildings and looking for a cab that will take us back to the base for the seven o'clock roll call. London, faintly illuminated by dawn, lies quiet like an exhausted patient the morning after some frightful operation. A few blocks to the north a pillar of smoke slowly rises, hiding the barrage balloons. The streets are empty. On our left is something famous — a carved lion or Hyde Park or a fancy shop that caters to the king. And now turning a corner and walking toward us with a quick manly step, dressed impeccably in a dark, pinstripe suit and a stiff, black homburg that half conceals his fantastically white and waving hair — Edward R. Stettinius, the secretary of state. Two young men in dark clothes and carrying double burdens of thick black leather briefcases walk slightly behind him, slightly panting. Beside the grandeur of Stettinius the two men are as inconsequential as summer leaves blowing in the street. I immediately reject my first reactions of guilt — that the four of us have been found out in some fiendishly clever and unscheduled roll call and that the secretary of state has been sent out to run us down.

How ruddy the cheeks of Stettinius, how well his clothes hang on him, how beautiful his hair. He is the perfect handsome diplomat whom only God, Choate, and Harvard could have produced. Christ, in less than ten hours we have been subjected to an amount of aristocracy that is almost unbearable. What is most dazzling about famous people whom you have seen only in newspaper pictures is to confront them and confront the red blood coloring their cheeks that suddenly makes them heartbreakingly human and vulnerable. Stettinius, of course, was impressive in black and white but to meet him in technicolor was almost too stunning. (Once I had been allowed to sit directly in front of the Roosevelt family at the Sunday services of the National Cathedral in Washington. I turned for just a glimpse of the president as his son, Eliot, wheeled him down the aisle and his aide, Admiral Leahy, lifting his dead and heavily braced legs, helped him into a pew. It was his high pink coloring that had amazed me and that had given beauty to his face. Franklin was a beautiful man; his wife, Eleanor, beautiful too in her lively flesh tones and in the modest goodness of her plain, disciplined face.)

What made our meeting with Stettinius unforgettable was the fact that not only did we have a chance to look closely into his face, but he was forced to look closely into ours. No, it was not that he was forced to, I realize now. I think he was as impressed by us, four young combat officers walking down a deserted street like something off a poster for *Beau Geste,* just as we were impressed to run into the secretary of state in this most private moment. From thirty feet away he gave us a naked look of comradeship and admiration; he wanted desperately to be recognized. His eyes moved across our faces like a question, he smiled a shy uncertain smile. How vulnerable and human he seemed for those few seconds as we approached him.

But ten thousand hours of training instruction had never touched on the proper etiquette of this awesome moment. We knew immediately that he wished to be acknowledged, but we didn't know how to do it. Should we give him a military salute? Do officers salute civilians? Should we remove our sloppy, raunchy caps? Bow? Make a snappy V-for-victory sign? Nothing seemed appropriate. So just before we passed each other we gave back that same shy smile and lowered our eyes like timid children. Is it possible that I remember Oates saying in a low strangled voice as raw as a Waco cow pasture, "Well, hi there, Mr. Secretary"? Stettinius, with obvious relief, smiled broadly and touched his homburg in a snappy greeting. For perhaps four seconds we had totally occupied the thoughts of the secretary of state; for perhaps four seconds, bright and glamorous, we had come between and obliterated his strategic preoccupations.

On what may have been the afternoon of that same day, we heard a little later, Stettinius had toured the air base to which within a week we would be assigned. One of the myths about his visit, which probably isn't true but could be, is that the pilot who had been assigned to accompany him and to answer any of his questions had, while illustrating the proper technique for inflating the large rubber life rafts which the bombers carried, pulled too hard on the inflating ring and had almost blown Stettinius out of the small room where these lifesaving devices were stored. Hissing, writhing, swelling, the raft had grown to tremendous size, pushed a couple of generals hard up against the wall, and shoved the secretary of state out into the hallway. It was said that Stettinius found this highly amusing.

15

THE 91ST HEAVY BOMBARDMENT GROUP must have been one of the first American flying units to arrive in England. It had the best air base in the country, with permanent brick buildings, a long, cement runway, big solid hangars for airplane maintenance, an impressive high-ceilinged officers' club that looked like an enormous cement crypt. Before the war, the base had been a kind of English West Point, a showplace installation less than an hour from London where visiting dignitaries like Stettinius or Eisenhower could be received. Looking for it now on a map I am unable to find it. Or the small village beside it, or the railway line that could get us to London, or the winding highway to Cambridge, six or seven miles to the north. If the countryside has faded from the maps, it has faded even more from my memory. Like a man being marched to be shot before a wall who will fail to have taken note of what kind of wall it was, I must have been noticing other things besides the rural, rolling beauty of the place.

We arrived late one afternoon, one of three replacement crews, delivered like sacks of flour or dazed steers in a small converted school bus whose rows of seats designed for smaller limbs had left us aching. We drove through a guarded gate and the bus stopped in front of a large brick building. I remember it now, and I'm sure falsely, as a building without windows. A light rain was falling. The immediate area was deserted, and I remember this moment which I had inflated into something dramatic as being frozen in silence. How can one's memory be so false? Just visible behind rows of buildings, hangars, and Quonset huts, from the glassed top of the control tower red and green flares arced into the air at thirty-second intervals; above the field a couple of dozen bombers circled low, a couple of them signaling with red flares that because of engine damage, or because there were wounded aboard, they wished to land immediately. The 91st was returning from a combat mission over Europe. But silence, in memory at any rate, could absorb the roaring of four-engine planes circling above us at a thousand feet, a rumbling, tearing sound that had now become part of our lives, unnoticed background.

We received our luggage: flight bags and blue denim barracks bags; then we stood together in an indecisive group wondering what we should do next; we watched the circling planes; they were flying much too low and in a way that could only be described as sloppy and reckless. It looked like things were out of control and we were filled with the unease that comes from seeing something slightly obscene and not meant for your eyes. A sergeant gunner appeared and led the enlisted men away, and a moment later — so, we were not to be welcomed — a very small, yellow-faced officer, a second lieutenant with bombardier's wings pinned to his shirt, hurried out of the officers' club and approached us. He was talking to himself and from time to time would make weird and uncoordinated gestures with his arms, as though he were arguing with an invisible companion. His clothes were stained and unpressed, his hair uncombed. When he came closer and shook hands with us we couldn't help but fight the impulse to draw back. His nails were caked with dirt and he stank with that particular sweat that dogs supposedly immediately recognize as terror and that makes them want to jump at your throat. And he was very drunk. Oh my God, I thought, am I looking at some aspect of myself a month from now?

"Come on, I'll show you where you'll sleep." As we followed behind him he began to babble. "Oh shit, oh my God, it's terrible, terrible. Now they say Morgan's shot down. No chutes, no chutes. Christ, five in a week. Incredible. A fucking death camp." We followed him toward the large brick wall from above which a bomber with two of its engines feathered back rushed low over the field, spouting red flares. "Oh my God," the little bombardier cried, "they're going to kill us all, I swear to God. We're all doomed men, man, I swear to God."

Panting, we packed our bags across the cement parking area and entered the building through a hall toward one wing of the club.

It was a long row of small rooms, and it reminded me of the Molino Rojo in Tijuana where I had gone once when I was fifteen years old, a place that was advertised as the largest whorehouse in the world, a great block-square labyrinth of identical bare halls and small rooms, in the doorways of which sat women in kimonos who jeered me out of the place for my youth and the minimal pleasure, both economic and sexual, which I seemed to promise. On the way we passed the entrance of the crypt-like club room. It was long and narrow with a fireplace at one end and a small bar at the other. In front of the fireplace were a half dozen flying officers silently playing poker or blackjack. The middle of the hall held three pool tables; they were all in use; at the bar a group of officers stood drinking beer. No one looked up or greeted us as we struggled past the doorway with our bags, but the sergeant gunner who was working behind the bar came over to us and said something to the little bombardier who was guiding us. The gunner was wearing a white apron over his uniform and he had pinned his combat wings to the apron; this pride somehow pierced me to the heart and made me feel like crying. Behind the pool tables a large window opened out toward the inner workings of the air base: the ready rooms, the squadron offices, and the maintenance hangars. Between the hangars was an open space, and in that second as my eyes perceived it, a landing bomber flashed across this space, its tires smoking, its brakes squealing. The little bombardier saw it too; he turned and faced us, his eyes wide and crazy. "When they blow up it's like a flower blooming," he said. "A big red blossom of flame and out of it falling chunks of aluminum and your buddies." He looked at us accusingly and began to shake his head. Or rather, his head began to shake.

We were scattered two to a room along the length of the hall; pilots with copilots, navigators with bombardiers. "This ain't much," the little bombardier said standing in the door, "but don't worry, you won't be here long. I mean there's better quarters, and you'll be moving up." He turned to leave, staring down the hallway, and said before he closed the door. "As space becomes available." And he began to giggle.

I stared at Moburg in disbelief when we were alone. "Listen, that little creep is *weird*."

"He's a Jew," Moburg said. "Maybe Jews are under special pressures these days."

"Yeah, well, I am too. I don't care if he's Jewish or Mongolian. He shouldn't have been sent out to herd us in. That is *bad* PR."

"The thing about Jews," Moburg said, "they deny the divinity of Jesus. They're cut off from Salvation; they're just out there on their own, aren't they?"

"Wise up, Moburg — don't kid yourself. We're all out there on our own."

It made me nervous when Moburg talked about God. Ever since we had flown the Atlantic he had become increasingly preoccupied with religious thoughts; it was as though that ten hours as we soared through the ice clouds and above a green, frozen infinity of ocean sprinkled with inhuman icebergs had opened him up to the awareness of his own mortality. I was suspicious of the motives of men who only prayed out of terror, who only thought of God during times of despair. They reminded me of boars who live tranquil and unthinking lives sunk in the pleasant depths of mudholes and who, at the whiff of a sow in heat, end up with their brains addled and directed toward the most ridiculous behavior. They reminded me of my father. He could go years without once thinking about God, but when life began to cut him down, how quickly and automatically he would dig his Mary Baker Eddy out of the bottom drawer where he hid his condoms and begin pondering her *Key to Scriptures*. While he was losing all his money or when his second wife divorced him, he was as conscious of God as a redneck country preacher. When he had his money and his wife back, God went sailing out the window like a buzzing alarm clock that clatters for a while in the downstairs bushes and then goes silent.

Moburg had turned and was staring out the window. There was a knock and the little bombardier stuck his head through the door again. "Hey, I almost forgot, who's the bombardier here? You guys are B Squadron, right? Captain Hudson wants to see the bombardier in the bar." As I followed him back down the hall, and just before we entered the officers' lounge, he turned and said in a low voice, "You don't have to say yes, you know."

We entered the big room and headed for the bar, but before we reached it there was a terrible sound of scraping metal, and I looked out the big window to see a bomber sliding very fast down the runway, its undercarriage hidden in sparks. From the waist door a figure bulky in flying clothes jumped or fell from the plane. Just before the bomber disappeared behind the hangars, another figure leaped and rolled. I stood

frozen in stupefaction in an assessment that was like insanity, clearly seeing something that couldn't be happening. More unbelievable than the
seconds-long view of this wounded bomber rushing and scraping across
my vision was the fact that no one else in the room had even turned toward the window. The card players played cards; the pool players made
their shots or leaned languidly over the tables staring into the green felt
like statues; the beer drinkers, some with their backs to the windows,
gazed into their glasses in mild and abstracted ways. As I started across
the floor again there was a tremendously loud explosion at the end of
the runway, and above the buildings a pillar of black smoke boiled up. A
couple of the pool players closest to the window now turned and gazed
for a moment with expressionless faces toward the smoke; then they returned to the game. And now, as though unbelievable action were
nothing but staged drama (apparently for my eyes alone, and apparently
now concluded), someone snapped on the lights in the officers' club and
two enlisted men drew shut the blackout curtains. They came together
slowly like the slow, final curtain of the kind of play that is supposed to
leave you in a thoughtful frame of mind. Yes, indeed, the technique was
very effective. My mood was so thoughtful that I couldn't move.

A large-faced combat captain left his friends at the bar and came over
to me. His face was open, naive, and complicated, an Oklahoma face
made secret and deep with Indian blood. He carried two glasses of beer
and offered me one. "Hudson," he said. "You're — ?" I told him, and he
raised his glass. "Welcome to cuckoo country." A cap set far back on his
head made him look like a raunchy mechanic; he wore a dirty GI shirt.

Later, I would know that he was almost exactly my age, twenty-eight,
but today he struck me as a man in his late forties, that menopausal age
in men when disillusion collapses their faces and leaves them grey, slack,
and lined. Though he was only about four years older than most of the
flying officers, four years in the middle twenties and in the stress of combat is often that difference between youth and middle age. (In another
three months some of those snot-nosed bombardiers would be calling
me Pop.) The captain had a rare look that almost no one else had who
flew: he looked as though he had had a past. He had run a garage or
maybe he had owned a little herd of white-faced cows or maybe he had
run the only beer parlor in some little town of ten thousand, some god-

forsaken dump in the heartland of America. The others had faces that mainly held only the blank innocent beauty of kids who hadn't yet begun to live, who hadn't decided who they were, whose voices, being puppyish, had not yet marred their faces. Perfect sacrificial victims to the gods of war.

The captain and I drank and observed one another without speaking. After a time, when the silence had stretched out long enough, I felt like saying something like, "Well, having a bit of a dustup, aren't you?" but decided against it. How could I mock his despair or fear or confusion or whatever it was that he was feeling when I was still such an outsider? And wouldn't it be gauche as shit to make something out of this ambience of weirdness, which for all I knew was simply the way things were on a combat base? Jumping out of planes as they came in to land had looked pretty insane, but when the plane blew up ten seconds later this eccentric behavior took on a certain logic. The English beer was only slightly chilled; it had a salty, bitter, watered down taste, but it was good if you tasted it with an open mind. Perhaps with my dry throat and taut nerves, a glass of horse piss would have struck me as refreshing at that moment. Come to think of it, and trying to recapture the taste of that first glass of English bitters, perhaps it was something that had been poured through a horse.

Finally the captain spoke. "What I'd like to ask you is would you like to fly tomorrow perchance?"

Perchance? It seemed odd that so soon after arriving on the base I would be sent out to drop practice bombs. But maybe everything that was happening was SOP. "Sure," I shrugged and nodded. "Do you have to check me out?"

"It's a little late for that. No, I'm not checking you out. We're short of bombardiers. The bastards are all either on leave, dead, or dead drunk. I'm short a bombardier."

"You mean combat?" I said appalled. "Tomorrow? Over Germany? You mean I won't fly with my crew?"

"You'll fly with an experienced crew, probably with Guyens. And I doubt if we'll hit Germany. We've had a rough week and we've got some milk runs coming. But I can't guarantee that. That's up to Wing and God knows where those bastards will send us."

We stood staring at each other, each of us smiling dimly. I could feel my stomach churning out acids and fought the impulse to burst into tears. I felt betrayed and helpless, like a kid standing on the thirty-foot high dive above a pool and who is being pushed over the edge instead of given the time he needs to gather his courage for an act of free will. "What do you say?" Captain Hudson asked me. "You don't have to say yes, but I'd take it as a favor."

"All right. Okay. What do I have to do?"

"Just don't get drunk; that's all you have to do. I need five bombardiers tomorrow who can climb into those planes under their own power."

I stopped in the door of my pilots' room. Wylie and Oates were both sitting on their cots looking toward the window and the column of smoke. The sirens and bells of the fire trucks and the ambulances had finally stopped, and the smoke was thinning out and looked like the smoke from a pile of smoldering leaves, floating up languid and spent behind the hangars.

"Bit of a bad show, that," Wylie said, trying to smile.

"Bloody fucking incredible," I said. "Pip-pip, and keep your pecker up."

Oates said for the hundredth time, "It appears to me that a body could get hurt in one of those things."

"Oh, chappie," Wylie said, "you ain't just woofin'. That thing came in without brakes. Them dreaded Krauts, they shot out the brakes."

"Maybe it had brakes," I said, "but it sure as hell didn't have wheels. They came in on their belly. I could see it from the window in the club. You never saw such sparks. And the guys jumping out, listen, there were guys jumping out, and listen, for Christ's sake, nobody in that room even looked up. That's what scares the shit out of me — it wasn't *noteworthy.*"

"My aching back," Oates said. "Like they've seen this movie about ten times."

"Exactly," I said. "My opinion is that things are not exactly ticketyboo around here."

"This is obviously not a good show," Wylie said. "I suggest we transfer back to square one. Why did they want to see you? Something pleasant no doubt."

"Hudson, the squadron bombardier. You won't believe it; he wants me to fly combat tomorrow."

"I trust you pointed out that you're on my crew," Wylie said. He looked at his watch. "I mean, shit oh dear, we've only been here for twenty-seven minutes."

"Flying with your crew is no longer a big thing," I said. "Oh shit, tomorrow it's off into the dreaded wild blue yonder."

"You mean you said yes?" Wylie asked. "You didn't say yes; I don't believe it."

"Bob, I wasn't brave enough to say no. B Squadron is going through a crisis; all the bombardiers are drunk, like that weird character that met us outside."

"Yeah," Oates said, "imagine flying in the same plane with him."

"Besides, I think I'd better check combat out for you guys. It might be something you'd prefer not to get involved with."

"Are you kidding?" Wylie said. "I'm all for transferring to gliders right now. I admit it, I'm a coward. Get out the old LMF stamp."

We were trying to be clever and funny, trying to say flippant things that Spencer Tracy or Noel Coward would be saying if they were placed in a similar situation. But it was too much work. Finally we simply stood there smiling at each other. Someone walked down the hall and as he passed the door said, "Chow." We decided to eat, and I went into the next room to tell Moburg.

He was still standing by the window. It was getting dark outside and the rain was coming down harder and the pools of water on the asphalt caught the light so that the ground still held a radiance that the sky had begun to lose. The last of the bombers was landing. "Come on, Moburg, we're going to eat." I snapped on the light and Moburg sighed and pulled the heavy blackout curtains across the window. I put my hands up on my shoulders and flapped them like little angel wings. "The sons of bitches want me to fly tomorrow," I said. "Like over Germany, for instance."

I had the normal self-loathing of a bombardier and that knowledge that all bombardiers had — that we were the most useless component of the combat crew. Behind my fears for tomorrow I felt a certain proud agitation at being the first of the crew who was being sought out. It gave me a certain undeserved value, a certain status. Like the first kid in school who can come back and tell his stunned classmates how you work a girl around to letting you unsnap her brassiere.

Moburg looked startled. "Are they splitting up the crew? They shouldn't do that. We should fly together."

"I don't think it's permanent. All the bombardiers are having nervous breakdowns."

"So are the navigators," Moburg said. He giggled and held his arms out in front of him to show me his trembling fingers. His pale cheeks suddenly flushed with color. "Look, M. It's time we got serious. Tell me that you believe in Jesus Christ as your personal savior."

"Jerry, for shit sake, not now."

"It's not too late, M. Accept him. Face it, tomorrow could be too late."

"We're going to go eat, Moburg. Come on, let's go." I flicked the light off and on a couple of times.

"M., you're my friend. I want to help you. Take Him into your heart." He stared at me with his distracted face flaming with color, and his fingers trembled with a life of their own like little animals. "Look, M., kneel down with me. Right now. Let's pray together. I know you don't want to go to hell."

"Go to hell?" I yelled, caving in from a dozen pressures that suddenly turned to anger and left me shaking. "Go to hell? Why you dumb fucker, we've been there for thirty minutes."

Wylie and Oates appeared in the doorway behind me. "Hey, hey, hey," Wylie said. He put a hand on my shoulder and, feeling the tightness below his fingers, began to knead the muscles that I hadn't realized were aching. "Come on, let's check out this dump. Get a beer, some chow."

Feeling ashamed of myself, I walked beside Moburg and threw an arm around him. I said in a low voice, "Jerry, listen, do you know what soldiers yell when they're dying? They don't yell to God or to Jesus. You know what they yell with their last breath?" And now, carried away and in a breaking voice — in a voice so loud that Oates turned around pale and smiling — I cried, "Mommy, mommy, mommy, mommy."

16

THE FIRST COMBAT MISSION was to an airfield on the outskirts of Toulouse. I remember little about it except that it completely contradicted my idea, after that first half hour on a combat base, of what combat was going to be like. Everything went with a marvelous precision that made me feel mildly impregnable. We assembled on the lead plane as it slowly circled the base in a ten mile circle, rising through clouds from an English night into a flaming dawn. When we were all gathered in loose formation (eighteen bombers? twenty-four bombers? I can't remember), we headed south. How calm and businesslike it all was. Like a whore, I immediately repudiated my crew of innocents and rejoiced that I was flying with veterans. Not that I didn't love my crew, I was just separated from them by a vast experience. I hoped I wouldn't have to fly with them until they were worthy of me.

We left England with Bournemouth green and cold beneath us showing through clouds. Thousands of boats filled all the harbors and river mouths in southern England. They floated in black lines like rows of frog eggs in spring ponds given over to amphibious passions. Gaining altitude we flew south over water. France, blue, immobile, mysterious, and captive, lay to the port side as we left cool spring and flew into summer. A cloudless day, finally. The green water turned tropical — deep blue with the sun gold-plating the troughs of the waves. It was an empty ocean which for years now no one had used except with terror. Hours later at eighteen thousand feet we turned and invaded France. Below us the red earth, the pure light of Van Gogh, the red, Spanish tiled roofs of Toulouse; and over there Spain was dry, dark mountains the color of cinnabar. Five or six miles away lay an airfield, and as we approached it we could see black German fighters scattered within revetments or lined up carelessly in front of hangars. There was no flak and we took a long bomb run and dropped small incendiaries, multi-clustered, hundreds to a

plane. I leaned over the bombsight, pressing my head against the Plexiglas nose, and watched them tumbling and dwindling directly below the
plane. After a time they flashed in patterns among the rows of barracks.
Beautiful. Some of those bombs were mine, though it was difficult to
make the connection between the meeting of the indices on the bombsight's face and after an incredible amount of time those strung-out puffs
of flame. Still, it filled one with a sense of power and satisfaction. After
four years in the army I was finally killing Germans. If this didn't bring
me great delight, I didn't feel an instant's guilt either.

It occurred to none of us, neither then nor back at the base, that we
had bombed the soldiers' barracks rather than the hangars at which we
had been aiming.

I seem to remember something now. Did I dream it or really see it? —
a German fighter crawling down the runway ahead of a long line of exploding bombs, and just before it takes off a hundred incendiaries
blossom at the end of the runway and the plane disappears in a burst of
flame. I think I truly remember this, disentangling it from dreams and
war movies, for it is made authentic by its inconsequentiality, a little
something that caught the eye for a few seconds before it searched for
more interesting things.

A dark steel flak tower floated a mile or so off the French coast, and as
we turned and headed north we passed with what seemed like insolence
just out of range of its guns. A thousand feet below us bursts of black flak
followed us for a few yards. It was clown stuff to be shot at so ineptly, and
I imagined that these Wehrmacht gunners were the scum of the German
population, old men picked up on the streets of Berlin and sent to this
improbable spot where we were undoubtedly the first enemy planes
they had ever seen. Just before the flak tower disappeared behind our
wings, two prowling P-38s coming in low and fast from over the land
made a sweeping pass at the flak guns and disappeared ahead of us. They
had been sent to protect us from German fighters, but the fighters had
remained hidden; the P-38s roamed the land like hungry predators free
to attack targets of choice, targets of opportunity.

We came home in the early afternoon, descending to six thousand
feet over the ocean and flying in loose formation over an England
that sparkled green as a jewel — hills and park lands clearly defined like
crisp, detailed drawings; winding hedgerows, towns and rivers precise

and pure. To come home. What terrible connotations these words had always held for me. But now they offered something snug and safe, a consolation that choked up the throat.

Wylie and Oates drove out in the Jeep that would take the crew to its debriefing; they were standing beneath the plane waiting as I climbed out and felt the ground steady and welcoming through the heavy fleece-lined flying boots. Their eyes searched my face; they wanted the low-down from a voice they could trust. They must have seen something reassuring before I spoke; their smiles were wide and full of relief.

Okay, tell us, what was it *really* like?

Here's the truth, it's a no-sweat operation. It was — well, it was *fun*. It was exciting — *beautiful*. A cruise down the coast right into summer and not a single German fighter in the sky. We absolutely dominated the air. Yes, there was flak, maybe ten bursts, incredibly bad shooting, panic shooting almost, without aiming. What it was like more than anything was a color travelogue, a little jaunt into the orange landscapes of Cezanne; the hot flaming yellows, the tender greens of Van Gogh; the deep blues of seascapes — Monet, Derain, Matisse. Flying to Toulouse was like taking a short course in the Impressionists, an intense course in which everything is made clear. "And now," I said, mimicking the phony English accent of Fitzgerald, a dull producer of dull travel shorts, "and now as the flaming sun falls toward the west — or is it east? — in molten radiance we say good-bye to Toulouse and a ta-ta to the nearby Dordogne, fatherland of ancient races and the immortal painters of the nineteenth century."

"Well la-de-da and pip-pip," Wylie said.

"It's lucky you're mad about combat because Hudson wants you to fly again tomorrow," Oates said.

"You're kidding," I said, my heart beginning to pound. "Did he really say that? What about you guys?"

"They're saving us for the big ones," Oates said. "Rembrandt, don't you know. Berlin. Etc."

Second mission: Metz. Another airfield a few miles from the town's center. I remember the name and flying across northern France and the long, narrow French fields packed together like rows of matches and the airfield and the long lines of curving smoke from smoke bombs that someone coming in earlier had dropped as markers, and which the high altitude winds were beginning to tear apart. The name Metz has a high metallic ring to it in my memory; I don't remember why, though the day may have been intensely clear, and maybe it was that day when, looking down, I was fascinated by the silver shimmer of curving French rivers, so much more civilized than the rivers of home, and by the intimate nature of the land where man had absolutely dominated and tamed the landscape and where the fields were as intricately fitted together as the parts of some beautifully crafted machine. It was a land that had replaced God with the sacred precepts of the French bourgeoisie: there is nothing so holy and inviolable as the rights of landowners.

The next day we bombed the Orly airfield. Paris lay frozen in the near distance, half smudged by smoke. Scattered flak at the coast, a bit of flak as we prepared to start the bomb run, discouraged the impulse to sightsee, though I seem to remember contemplating for a second or two the Eiffel tower, a dim, black silhouette standing up through the haze far away; it was serenely lonely and noble, as tragic as a raped woman.

We came back to an England that had clouded over in the few hours that we had been gone. Flying blind we waited our turn to land; the tips of our wings were lost in cloud, and water smashed against the plane's nose; it was as dark as night. Some kind of a message finally reached the pilot and we dropped down through the clouds as cautiously as a blind man tapping his way through traffic. Breaking out, we skimmed through a narrow zone of visibility between the bases of the clouds and the green fields just below us, now ominously dark and menacing. It was not fun to be in one of those hundreds of planes flying blind through clouds lit up from time to time by flashes of lightning, blue bursts of terrible light that looked as much as anything like the explosions of colliding planes. Everything seemed out of control and obscenely hazardous, and when we finally landed I was exhausted, tense, and trembling with the kind of depressed foreboding that doesn't go away for days. Sitting up in the nose, useless and helpless, time had stretched out like some awful, formless thing that defined life; I could feel everything that I had defined to myself as courage leaking away. Without knowing it yet, I had exhausted my own small surplus of recuperative energy. From now on out I would be spending little parts of myself.

How we grew to love the storms that swept down out of the North Sea or out of Russia. Heavy cloud cover over either England or continental Europe would ground all planes, and a sweet silence that we had almost forgotten would bathe England in the illusion of peace. Wonderful to stand inside and watch the rain pouring down and the low clouds, thick and heavy, moving across the sky. We hoped that it would storm forever so that we could lie on our cots all day listening to incredibly high-flown cultural programs on the BBC or wander into the officers' lounge to watch from a distance the perpetual poker game that went on month after month. (Thinking back now it is almost impossible to imagine that the same yellow-faced combat officers, brooding and sullen, aren't still slouched at the same tables, gulping scotch each from his own bottle and throwing away money that they were convinced that they would never live to spend. As much as the old trees, the thatched roofed cottages, the country churches, they are a permanent part of the England that I remember.)

During that icy month in Labrador, Moburg and I had taught Wylie and Oates how to play chess, and until I began to fly combat I could usually beat them. Now, grounded, we played for whole afternoons, but there was a terrible connection between chess and combat, and I took less and less pleasure in the game. Unless we played for money, which was a kind of symbolic substitute for the symbolic death of losing my king, I seldom won. I hated to be forced into making bad trades, and my style, which was not aggressive but sneaky, could not stand up against the brutal attacks of my pilots. Chess kept reminding me of the passive function of the bombardier who simply sat in the nose, trapped in a plastic bubble, waiting for something unspeakable to be done to him. Chess depressed me and made my stomach heave and mutter. Besides, I was a veteran now and playing with kids who hadn't yet been out there, getting shot at; I tended to hurl the pieces to the floor when trapped.

We were grounded for a week, and on the third day Wylie asked me to go into London with him. He had been given the address of a first-class English tailor who made uniforms for American officers. Wylie wanted an Eisenhower combat jacket with a red satin lining — and so did I until I found out how much one cost. Forty pounds if I remember correctly; a hundred and sixty dollars. It wasn't that I didn't have the money; for months I had been collecting officer's pay without being able to spend it and my wallet bulged with a thousand dollars in pound notes. What made me decide to hold off then was what makes me hold off now. As much as I would love to own a nicely made Harris tweed jacket, being sixty-six makes investing three hundred dollars in a coat that will outlive me by twenty years the most presumptuous kind of conspicuous consumption. Life, I'm convinced, imitates art and needs trick O. Henry endings to stories. How could I then or now call attention to myself and dare whoever it is who decides such things to strike me dead for arrogance? "I'll be back later," I told the tailor. "If things turn out well." "I'm looking forward to fitting you whenever you should find it convenient," he told me. He smiled.

He was a big, portly man, as impressive as Prime Minister Baldwin, and he treated us with a wonderful delicacy that perhaps only an English tailor (or Lady Ashley) could show toward brash Yankee second lieutenants. He made us feel comfortable in his very smart shop, and he honored us as few Englishmen ever succeeded in doing: by completely concealing his natural English contempt for the colonial and uncivilized underclasses.

After an impressively lengthy time with the tailor and his two assistants, Wylie left a ten-pound deposit on his jacket, and we walked out into the street. He was to come back in a month for the first of many fittings; it was an appointment that he did not keep.

We went back to the base together on the six o'clock train to Cambridge, but we had separated on Bond Street outside the tailor's establishment, Wylie to prowl the Red Cross club looking for girls (at 11 A.M.?); I, to walk through the rain-lashed streets looking for the desolation that would mirror an inner emptiness that had begun to grow with combat. There was nothing more isolating than the growing awareness that one's imminent death had become a logical alternative to the long writer's life that I had planned. I needed to be alone now almost all the time; the earlier passion that had put me in the heart of a combat crew, a closed brotherhood of heroic comrades, seemed to me now to be blatant chauvinistic hogwash. Apparently we wouldn't even fly together; and if we did, so what? The consolation of dying among friends seemed suddenly, now that the possibility was more than fantasy, like no consolation at all. We were living very closely together, but the pressures of combat, pressures of which I was hardly aware, were beginning to tear us apart. Secretly, and hating myself, I would observe my crew. It was unrealistic to think that all of us would survive the next few months. I would study each face, looking for some barely perceptible sign of death's intentions. "Just let it not be me," I prayed.

I walked in the rain and a short story grew out of that day. It was sad and hopeless and soaked in torrents of cold cloudbursts, bombed-out buildings, and the sour smell of urine, blood, and semen. Back on the base I wrote it down and sent it to *The New Yorker*. Years later I found it and read it with shame; the last sentence was the last sentence of Joyce's "The Dead" — except that I had changed the snow that fell upon the living and the dead to rain.

During the week that we were grounded I had my first chance to examine the air base and the nearby countryside. If there were two thousand American soldiers on that base (and I am only guessing) then there were two thousand bicycles leaning against walls, rowed into bicycle stands, or lying in piles outside the buildings. All of us immediately bought bicycles and for a short while used them every time we left one building for another, no matter if it was only fifty feet away. It was the thing to do. Between showers of rain, that rain we hoped would never stop, we enjoyed the last days of our disintegrating closeness, and together we cycled down roads that glistened black as coal. The bombers dispersed in fields glistened dully and deadly within their revetments like resting predators peering above the grassy mounds. Humble weeds beside the road, thick-leafed and hairy, lost their self-effacing qualities by being English. Half-drowned birds sat on dripping branches and peeped pathetically; the fields and the trees were greener every day. Everything had the same message: you'd better enjoy this while you can. Every sparrow began to carry its burden of anguish; circling rooks took on crushing symbolic significance. The world became unbearably beautiful, unbearably fragile. How could we have stumbled through life so blindly, missing so much? Still, as much as we yearned to take this new awareness into ourselves on life's terms, we were prevented by our preoccupations. Life, as usual, glistened and throbbed out there just beyond our grasp.

In the rain we packed our bags to another building; we were moving up the ladder, away from the small concrete cubicles to a fine brick dormitory with leaded windows and surprising alcoves. We were assigned an enlisted man to take care of us — gather our clothes for the laundry, make our beds, shine our shoes, buy us black-market eggs and the bottle of whiskey that we drank each evening. Strange when I bought so many that I can't remember now if we paid one or four pounds for a bottle. If in May we were each buying a couple of quarts a week, by September we would each be drinking a bottle on every night that we weren't scheduled to fly the next day. It was about the only thing finally that put us to sleep. We moved into the new building behind a Lt. Hall who went into a small house where the lead crews lived. Hall was going to be our new squadron commander. During those few days when nothing happened, how fast everything happened. The day he moved he was a lieutenant; the next morning he wore captain's bars. That night in his new cottage he dreamed a dream. Those in the upstairs rooms awoke to hear him yelling, "Bail out, bail out, bail out" — and the crashing of broken glass. He burst out of the second-story window, bounced off the roof of the little downstairs room where the enlisted soldier shined shoes, and still shouting, still asleep, landed on the cement entranceway with a grotesquely broken leg. The flight surgeon sent him home — or sent him someplace.

The weather cleared. Wylie and Oates were scheduled to fly in separate planes as copilots on a mission to somewhere. Moburg, in a third plane, took the place of a navigator who for some reason was indisposed. I was told that I would fly but was not awakened for the 4 A.M. briefing. I lay in bed pretending sleep as my crew dressed for their first mission. None of them spoke. But what is there to say at 4 A.M.? Not going was almost as bad as going, I discovered as I lay there with closed eyes sharing their apprehensions. To wish them luck would have implied that luck was something they needed, so I let them go and, unable to sleep, waited for the sun and at six o'clock the growling of the bombers as they took off. Something strange that would continue to grow as the months passed began that morning: I felt guilty for not flying with them. It was a kind of double guilt: for not having to do something that I desperately wanted not to do, and for being unneeded. I was beginning to be terrified of flying but at the same time was wretched to find myself uninvolved in a madness where others might be destroyed. The guilt would grow until in the end it had become a secret and poisonous longing to die. How I hated myself at the end of the tour when I found myself still living.

After breakfast I wandered down to the squadron office on the flight line. The offices were three small rooms with large windows that looked out over the strip and a couple of B-17s that were parked in front of hangars. Mechanics on iron platforms bent half-hidden into engine cowlings; they looked like the newly arrived swallows peering into holes and looking for a place to nest. Lt. Davis sat behind a desk, and Captain Hudson stood just behind him. He was removing Davis' lieutenant bars and replacing them with the double bars of a captain. "Congratulations," I said, not exactly meaning it. I had flown two of my three missions with Davis and half regretted his promotion, for it meant that I would no longer fly with him. "But how come? I heard it was Hall's turn."

"Yeah. Well, Hall had a little accident so now it's my turn, and don't think I'm pleased about it 'cause I ain't."

"What do you call a little accident around here anyway?" I asked. "Blowing up on the runway, getting hit by German fighters?"

"No, no," Captain Davis said, "a little accident is a little accident. He fell out the window Thursday morning; broke a leg."

"Commonly known as the million-dollar leg break," Hudson said.

"What I wanted to ask about. I was put down to fly this morning, and then all of a sudden I'm scratched."

"Don't worry if that's what you're doing," Hudson said. "You'll get your turn. I took you off because just by coincidence we found a couple of sober bombardiers hanging around; I decided to use them while I had the chance; something like that may never happen again."

"Do you like the new quarters?" Davis asked.

"Sure. It's a lot quieter than the club. In fact right now it's too quiet with everybody gone."

"They'll be back by five," Davis said. "Nobody goes down on their first mission. But nobody."

"Yeah, John, well, hardly nobody," Hudson said glumly.

Davis called into the other room, "Hey, Hamilton, who's on tomorrow? Bring out the lists, will you?"

Hamilton came into the room with a clipboard, and Davis took it. Hamilton was a second lieutenant and unlike almost everyone on the base was dressed in full uniform. Below his pilot's wings he wore a modest couple of ribbons — a theater ribbon and an air medal with a bronze oak leaf. This meant that he had flown more than ten and less than fifteen combat missions. He had a soft, gentle face and soft eyes, and because it was Hamilton who had always come into my room to shake me awake for the missions and because he did it with great care and gentleness, I had the impression that it was a job he hated. I had watched him this morning as he called my crew out of their black sleep and had thought that he had done it like a loving mother, full of pain, reluctance, and apology.

Davis said, "You're down for tomorrow, and you'll fly with your crew. Okay?"

"Good; it's about time," I said, not knowing if it was good or if it was really what I wanted.

Davis handed the clipboard back to Hamilton, who stood by the desk studying the list.

"Don't get in a sweat and all hopeful about flying with your crew," Davis said. "We'd all like to fly with our crews, and then things come up. You know."

"What are you standing here for?" Hudson asked Hamilton. "We just asked for the list, not to have a goddamn conference."

Hamilton, who had looked at no one, flushed scarlet and with downcast eyes turned and went back into the inner office.

"Don't, Frank," Davis said in a low voice.

"Ach," Hudson said. "Just looking at him." His face was flushed and disgusted.

"Come on, just let him do his job, okay?"

"Well, I'm off," I said. "Pip-pip." I was reluctant to be witness to something that I didn't understand. "Oh, listen, can I come down here in the evenings and use one of the typewriters?"

"Sure," Davis said. "This place is always open."

I was halfway through the door when Hudson called out, "Hey, wait a minute, Thomsen." He put a hand on Davis's shoulder and said, "Why not tell him, what the hell." He pointed to the old first lieutenant's bars on the desk.

Davis nodded and smiled; he picked up the silver bars and held them out to me. "Here," he said. "You're down for a promotion, but for Christ's sake don't put these on until they cut the orders."

"No shit," I said. "Do things really happen that fast?"

"Oh, we've got plans for you, kid," Hudson said, smiling wickedly.

Whatever had happened to the squadron during that disastrous week just before we arrived was something no one ever talked about. Or if I did hear something, my passionate need to repudiate the implications immediately wiped all of this information from my mind. If five or six planes with their crews had been lost, the survivors were as reluctant to discuss it as we were to hear about it; *death* had become an unspeakably dirty word.

We were also becoming increasingly sensitive about the word *cowardice*. When we had to confront what could be regarded as cowardice in others, we blushed and stared at the floor. Each of us, looking inward, could hardly sneer or mock at someone's collapse under the pressures of combat when we recognized our own capacity to behave in the same way. We began to realize after a few missions that enduring a tour of combat duty did not test us and prove once and for all our courage. Each mission, no matter how uneventful, rather than enforcing our idea of ourselves as potentially noble and heroic, gnawed at the cores of our self-control and left us weaker. We were being bled dry of confidence; we were like bricks under hammer blows that could shatter into dust at some final touch.

No one ever talked about Lt. Hamilton in any detail; he was like a member of the family who had turned out badly and whose vices were overlooked. What we knew was simply this: after a dozen missions he had refused to fly. He had been threatened with every kind of punishment; reduction to the ranks, court-martial, the public humiliation of having his wings ripped from his uniform on the parade ground. And he had stood firm. "Take me out and shoot me if you want," he had said. "Do whatever you want, but I will never climb into another plane as long as I live." To avoid scandal which would have reflected on the squadron, he was kept on flying status and had been turned into the squadron flunky. He kept all the flying lists, assigned the combat crews their living quarters, shipped off bodies, and, hardest of all, he woke the combat crews at those terrible hours between midnight and dawn, tramping down dark halls through the different barracks and shaking each of us awake with that soft, shamed, reluctance.

I think Captain Hudson was the only man in the squadron who treated Lt. Hamilton with contempt. Perhaps Hudson was the only one of us who was absolutely sure that under any circumstances he would find the resources to act like a man. It is just as likely, of course, that Hudson's contempt camouflaged darker secrets and that he may have been much closer to cracking up than any of us realized. (I saw him once when he came back from a mission in which he had led the group, and while over the target, because the bombsight had been badly installed, he found himself sitting in the nose of the plane with the sight in his lap. His rage at the enlisted sergeant who had failed to secure the bombsight against Hudson's passionate embrace was as wild and irrational as any rage I had ever seen outside my father's house. It was the only time I ever saw an officer break into tears.) The truth is we were all constrained by an awareness of our inner frailty, and our emotions were locked up tight; we were drawn to display an insouciance that in many respects turned us into almost identical comic book characters, closed shells who acted out a bravado that was false to our quivering natures. In a way this was a kind of courage; there is nothing more infectious than fear, and we knew that it was pure self-indulgence to lay our own terror on someone else. Remembering that little yellow-faced bombardier who had greeted us the day we arrived, I was filled with anger for the way he had used us. He had been too weak to keep his own fears to himself; he had vomited everything out on us. If my first three missions had not turned into Disney travelogues, I wonder now if the gift of his terror might not have turned me into another Lt. Hamilton.

On those days when we were grounded, if the weather allowed, we took our bicycles and pedaled up the road toward Cambridge or entered, feeling gawky and intrusive, one of the great eighteenth-century estates. A mile-long lane, straight as an arrow and bordered by enormous oaks, prepared one for the glory of the place like some pretentious overture full of blatting trumpets. There it reared up at the end of the road, exactly centered on it, a huge and ugly castle of at least a hundred rooms and around it rolling lawns, weeping willows, and Greek temples bordering swan-spattered lakes, stables and kennels, hedged labyrinths, formal gardens, and straight graveled paths — a square mile of the essential things a decent Englishman needs to salve his spirit, a square pile of pure horseshit. At the rear of the castle, and concealed by high brick walls, were vegetable gardens planted to cabbages, artichokes, and brussels sprouts, empty greenhouses, and bricked alcoves where long rows of sheets slowly dried in the thin spring air. One day, alone, I cycled through the heavy domesticity of that great back yard and at a turning between walls and boxwood hedges was confronted by a hideously angry woman dressed in thick tweeds the color of shit. She was short and dumpy and a cigarette hung from her mouth. Her cheeks, weird scarlet with broken veins. Wind and whiskey and riding to hounds had turned her as flaming red as a house afire. "Get out of here, you son of a bitch," she screamed. Later, someone at the base told me that I had made contact with Rudyard Kipling's daughter, but I could never quite, as much as I wanted to, believe it. That shrieking fury with all the charm of a drunken whorehouse madam must have been a duchess at least. There were endless generations of high and gentle breeding behind that cry which so precisely delineated the abyss between royalty and rabble.

"This arrogant old Europe which so little befriends us." Has there ever been an American in England who hasn't echoed these words of Henry James? Bicycling through the duchess's brussels sprouts, indeed.

17

FOR A MONTH I FLEW with my own crew at last. The weather over Europe was still largely overcast well into May and we went out not more than four times. But if we didn't fly much we were on constant call and always tremendously relieved when Lt. Hamilton, wanting to console us, would gently shake us awake at six to tell us that the mission had been scrubbed. Wanting to be a good crew we took our combat seriously, and the worst feature of being constantly on call was being unable to get drunk on the night before a mission. We considered it rough duty to go to bed cold sober and lie for hours in the darkness, a victim of hopeless thoughts, and then to sink finally into a half sleep that was slightly hallucinatory and menacing. That beating heart of mine that I hadn't thought about for years — I could feel it again thumping and jumping in my chest with a new kind of intensity, a kind of alienation. A repudiation was taking place that separated me from my heart; it seemed to pump the blood through my body with a kind of rage, as though I had put my body, through some insane weakness, into a situation of mortal peril. Listen to me, my heart seemed to be saying, listen to what a fine strong instrument you've got. How dare you treat me with such contempt?

In the bar one night the captain had complimented Moburg and me on the nice way we handled our liquor; he hinted that we were being watched by our commanding colonel and were being considered as squadron leaders when the time came. Someone was watching Oates, too. He flew too well and deserved his own crew — when the time came.

So, if aside from simply surviving, knowing how to handle your liquor was the final criterion for determining your combat future, Wylie was destined to end up as a general in Wing. After a few drinks he became as suave and gracious as an old-time southern politician. Smooth and charming, staggering like a gentleman, he set us a fine example which we tried to copy. One evening, boasting slightly, he confessed that he had been an actor in the movies and that his Hollywood connections had taught him sophistication. Remember the climactic scene in *It Happened One Night* when Clark Gable picks up Claudette Colbert and carries her away from that wedding where she is about to marry the wrong man? Well, Wylie had been in it, a little singer in a church choir of boys' voices — ten years old, pink-cheeked, angel-faced. He had gone to a Hollywood high school and in the back seats of roadsters had engaged in delightful and unspeakable activities with starlets whose pictures were now pasted in army Quonset huts all over the world.

On those four missions that we flew together, where did we fly to, my crew and I? Late spring was opening up the German skies, and if I can't remember the targets I can remember that they were German, and I have an absolutely clear memory of one golden day when we crossed the channel and invaded Europe over Holland. But like trying to recapture the reality of some particular sexual engagement where chronology and detail are obliterated by the egoism of passion, those German targets are, if we hit them, have disappeared, torn and bloody, from the chronology of combat, obliterated in my memory by fear, or the pure intensity of the bomb run when for a few minutes the bombardier becomes no more than an extension of the bombsight. What I remember is the foreplay — the long, slow, sliding entrance into Germany.

It is the fourth mission, this last mission we flew as a crew, that rose out of the past and laid itself over an Ecuadorian valley as I drove up from the coastal plain with the Stegners a few years ago. To describe that Ecuadorian afternoon is to describe that certain morning over Holland, though perhaps nothing was identical except the quality of the light, golden light as rich as honey that thickened the air and through which, flashing dully, the windows in the towns burned and sparkled. Holland. We came in from the sea and the roads were empty; the sirens must have been shrieking all across that land below us as the bombers came over in formation, a hundred, two hundred, three hundred of us. Out ahead a single flashing reflection on the road, and I sight through the bombsight to the distant and tranquil figure of a boy pedaling his bicycle. Is he blind to the menace above him or is he the only one wise enough to know that we are out for bigger game? Or does he know what we know, that closely guarded secret, that we probably couldn't hit him if we tried?

In Ecuador the fields were green with barley and alfalfa, yellow with mustard, the unplanted fields black with turned earth. In Holland the fields stretched away tableflat and solid-colored — white, scarlet, yellow, and purple, thousands of acres of blooming tulips, their strong primitive colors dimmed by distance to pastel in the golden air. Amazing and unbelievable to see tulips growing in such profusion in 1944. Amazing to think of the Dutch going about a business so completely irrelevant to the war.

Watching the boy as he moved without fear along the road, I made him Dutch in my imagination and it occurred to me that the lines of bombers flying over and past him were filling him with joy instead of fear and that our presence was giving him a feeling of invulnerability. The road he traveled was built along the top of a wide embankment; parallel with the road lay a canal lined with old trees heavy with new leaves, and past the trees the fields of tulips, their colors as muted and subtle as Rembrandt might have painted them.

Now here is a ridiculous confession that could throw doubt on all this narrative, all these precisely rendered conversations: this couple of minutes over Holland at twenty thousand feet, and a couple of minutes that will take place about an hour later, is almost all that I truly remember vividly enough to capture again and hold in my hand of all that forty-year-old war. It is as impossible to recapture the pain and terror of war as it is to truly remember the agony of an infected tooth.

Moburg, just behind me in the navigator's seat, is working with his usual wild intensity to pinpoint our constantly advancing position on his charts. His hands, quick and nervous as the wings of birds, flutter and swoop over the maps; his fingers tremble with their own life, their own awareness of mortality. To Moburg the maps are more real than anything that lies below us. Needing to share with someone an almost ecstatic flooding up of emotion, I turn, grab Moburg's arm, and pull him into the nose of the plane. We kneel together (as close as we ever got to communal prayer) and stare down into this golden abyss, down through amber-colored air as thick as honey, as rich as beer. In the near distance on our right a great city lies like a resting animal; thin smoke rises from thousands of chimneys; windows flash secret but intensely personal messages; here and there the spires of cathedrals soar above the layer of smoke. Quite close now, almost below us, the figure of the boy continues to pedal stolidly, and all around him the flat Dutch countryside burns with the flaming flowers of spring.

That moving figure was the only human being I ever saw in all my combat missions over Europe; and this, I imagine, is what gave him his power and opened me up to the knowledge that our tight, incestuous, self-absorbed world of combat was only one way of responding to the pressures of war.

Total wars where unconditional surrender is demanded and where total destruction is used to force the issue make those of us who are deeply involved hold a hundred contradictory opinions. Usually without breaking down into madness we can believe that white is black — or green — or any color that we are asked to see; as patriots we are the madmen who lay the foundations for the next war. Being able to hold contradictory opinions is part of war's madness. Taught all our lives, for instance, to loathe a murderer, we find that those of us who murder best are looked up to as heroes, and we discover with a guilty amazement as mild as boredom that we are not kept awake at night, filled with remorse for those we have killed. It is only being killed that bothers us. We wear our morals like marked-down, ready-made clothes, following the style of any chauvinistic propagandist.

One of my convictions (and one that I knew was absolutely false) held that it was immoral to be involved in anything that wasn't specifically aimed at winning the war. I had constructed my own personal hierarchy for Americans, and like a fanatic I admired only those who had put themselves into a mortal peril that was equal to my own. I would never completely free myself from this prejudice, but as I watched the boy on his bicycle moving across that peaceful landscape, for that minute all of my perceptions reversed themselves. It was the free boy and the fields of tulips, it was that Dutch order laid so nicely over the earth — the resting city, the carefully constructed dikes, the rows of great trees, it was all this that made sense of life and gave it grandeur. And it was these bombers heading into Germany with their loads of high explosives that represented the most idiotic of solutions to the failures of mankind. In an instant I saw myself not as a hero but as a knave. An honorable alternative flashed in my head; that thing I should have done, that act against society that might have kept me whole: I should have refused to become involved.

I am making much of this solitary Dutch kid, and I'm not through yet. I've got to hang as much as I can on this single authentic recollection, which even as I write about it has begun to change into dream, into something mythic that is perhaps half invented. But I will make it this day and this moment when the power of that lonely child moving slowly under the shadow of bombers somehow told me that below us in a Europe which we were trying to destroy were multitudes of people who by honoring continuity were keeping the future alive for all of us. Among them — like the Jewish legend of the thirty-six men who keep the world from being destroyed by God's wrath — were those brave few whose names I would not know for years yet, but whose presence I could now feel in the subzero air of high altitude. For just a few instants I was shaken by an awareness of their presences, those hidden artists whom we need to interpret the transcendental nature of reality, or the dark thinkers who in the absence of God can only show us how to move toward our own extinction with grace and courage.

Who heard the sound of the invading bombers in those months? Anne Frank, walled into a garret and still unmurdered? Nolde, the degenerate painter, forbidden by Hitler to paint, and living (and painting) on the secret northern beaches? Who else was down there carrying the burden of the world, holding the world together, recreating a world out of the bits and pieces of his own experience and his own unique vision? Stockhausen, perhaps? Böll, Ensor, Beckmann? And down to the south, who of those still unknown men whom years later I would honor listened to the bombers or the crashing of our bombs? Camus, Honegger, Poulenc, Sartre, Giacometti? Was I on their side?

I had written half of the preceding pages about the Dutch tulip fields before I realized that the day I was remembering included more than flowers, bicycles, and the echoes of still unwritten symphonies. It was also the day of our first flight over Berlin. And Berlin on that day was simply this: a field of black smoke lying in the sky at twenty-four thousand feet, a tremendous layer of smoke, thick and filthy, a one-thousand-acre lake of smoke that held the memory of exploded antiaircraft shells. We flew directly toward and through this dark cloud, this ugly fog that roughly delineated the borders of the city beneath. As we advanced across it at a pace that was obscenely slow, new bursts of flak exploded around us like the magical blooming of flowers, thick poppy-like bursts of black with flame at their centers. We gazed at the near misses, those orange flashes that instantly turned black and soft as puffs of cumulus, as evil as the boiling out of bursting chancres; we gazed with the same vacant eyes of a child coming across a Breughel for the first time and recognizing that the artist has precisely visualized the hell of the child's imagination. I remember being surprised that the city was visible through that dark, man-made cloud on which, from a distance, it seemed one might have walked. Certainly that first flight over Berlin held a horror that numbed response and that engendered a kind of amnesia. But through the months there were other, more terrible visits to that city which was turning into a pile of rubble, missions so much more terrifying as we grew to realize the dangers, that those first fears on that first day have been buried and forgotten below more monumental and hopeless terrors. On that first day, incapable of understanding much, I felt almost nothing, anesthetized with the same terror that makes a lamb, about to have its throat cut, faint.

And perhaps I was still dazed by things that had happened about an hour before, about an hour after we had left Holland.

Trying to conceal our intentions and confuse the German fighters, we move toward Berlin in a sly, sideways manner. Still over Holland, we turn in a wide sweep and head toward Denmark, and after half an hour change course again, still bearing north but with a hint of easternness. We are as tricky as dogs preparing to fight and advancing toward the enemy ass first. We feint toward the submarine pens, then head toward Peenemünde, then toward Stuttgart, Posen, Manheim. We fly over forests and farmland, avoiding cities and industrial centers. Almost by accident we find ourselves over a small, nearly hidden, grass-sodded airfield. American intelligence has plotted all but the most moveable of the German antiaircraft batteries and we swerve around them and discover below us this little forgotten field spread over with little German trainers. It is one of the places where almost the last of the Germans who will fly against us are learning to be pilots, German children in their middle teens. It is a warm day, and thin vertical columns of cumulus clouds have begun to form over the pastureland so that we advance through a sky that is filling with straight pillars of upward-rushing clouds; they frame the ground, make scenery of the earth, and give us, who are above their tops, a vague feeling of majesty and godlike uninvolvement as we watch flights of P-38s as small as toys rushing low over the tops of the trees to attack the German trainers. I watch without emotion as the trainers burst into flames or, trying to takeoff, stall and crash into the trees just past the end of the runway. It is like watching some childishly conceived construction of Tinkertoys as it disintegrates.

Five hundred feet below our group, another wing of B-17s on a slightly different heading, crosses below us. They are flying in a ragged, undisciplined way that fills me with something that I only later recognize was apprehension. As I watch the planes, wondering why they aren't flying in the tight formation that combat requires, I notice below them a single bomber doing acrobatics. For a few seconds it dives straight for the earth, then it pulls up, curves and climbs, and begins to loop. It is a maneuver right out of Primary training, a great free swooping that is like the joyful cry of a young man. How wonderful to climb straight into the sky and, weightless and upside down, hang suspended and confused, and then slowly turning, dive again, picking up speed through those enormous spaces. Still, while it is extremely beautiful to see, watching this transformation of plodding duckling into soaring swan, this wild impossible maneuver that no bomber has ever made before, I am filled with disgust for this pilot. For Christ's sake, we are over hostile territory; this is no time for some hotshot to be entertaining his crew with adolescent foolishness. It is an insolence that mocks our grim and deadly work. Doesn't he know there's a war on?

At twenty-eight I am one of the oldest members of a combat crew. Though I am not really tottering on the edges of senility, still I am of a ripeness that makes me tend to judge unkindly the puppyish antics of the twenty-year-old pilots who sometimes give in to the impulse to be children again. Their little prankish foolishnesses, when they turn out badly, kill people. Like this stupid asshole doing loops.

I want the crew to see this maniac who justifies my conservative feelings about flying; holding the throat-mike against my neck, filled with incredulity and disgust, I push the intercom button that will connect me with the crew. And as I do so the wings of the diving plane below fold back and break away from the fuselage, the fuselage breaks at the middle into two pieces, and flashing bits of aluminum, like leaves shaken off a tree by a gust of wind, flutter and swoop in the air; hundreds of sheets of paper — flight plans and navigational charts — twinkle in the air like lights going off and on as the sun hits them. Out of the split shell of the plane and falling through the dancing litter, a half dozen bodies with unopened chutes spill out and down, falling with incredible slowness. Their last gift will be that interminable minute as they fall, a whole minute to make some final peace. It is more than some of us will get.

I am still tightly squeezing the intercom button, but at this point am speechless, and even now, staring down at the fluttering debris (the wings of the bomber, instead of falling, are swinging back and forth like pendulums, held in the air by their surfaces), I have still not connected the broken plane with the ragged formation above it from which it must have come. Nor even now, as a second plane suddenly and violently dives up out of the formation, climbs steeply — almost vertically — and with two of its engines now beginning to flame and trail long lines of smoke, disappears in one tremendous scarlet burst.

Burning bodies or bodies wrapped and trapped in burning parachutes begin to spill out of the smoke and fall like flaring matches through the glittering debris. There is not a trace of flak in the sky; it slowly occurs to me, though I have seen no signs, that the group below us has been attacked by German fighters, but even with this realization I am still not impelled to warn my crew; in fact, quite the contrary. If I have any obligation at all to them, it is to shield them from the terrible knowledge of something that will only diminish their ability to function. These flaming bodies are superfluous information.

Moburg, behind me, has seen nothing. I feel him tapping on my shoulder and with an effort turn to face him. He is pointing to my frozen hand that is still depressing the intercom button and he shouts in my ear, "You're fucking up the system; nobody can talk." I nod, smile, and turn back to watch the spectacle of exploding bombers and to say into the intercom, in probably the calmest voice I have ever used, "Okay, men, the dreaded oxygen check."

"Tail gunner," Dugas calls back immediately. "Oxygen okay, and fuck you, sir."

"Earl here, sir, and fuck you, sir."

"Radio okay, sir . . . Fuck you, sir." Savasuk, in the radio room, hesitates. He uses the obscenity with uncertainty, a little shocked. He is the only holdout, besides Sullivan, who would never use this vulgarity, and who, while open and friendly, prefers to respect the differences in rank. For a couple of months we have been trying to break down Savasuk's resistance, seducing him with a comradeship that will make him forget that he is a staff sergeant under, for better or worse, our domination. I am waiting for the day when Savasuk will tell me to go fuck myself; that will be the day when he declares his love, or if not love, the day when he will have risen above all of the bullshit about rank and understand that we are all together in a common peril. Sullivan, the flight engineer, stands just behind Wylie and Oates in the cockpit; he is not a part of the oxygen ritual, and so I wait for the last of the sergeants, Johnson, the belly gunner, to check in.

Johnson is silent in his ball turret, and after a second I call in, "Hey, Johnson, what's wrong? Oxygen check."

"Sir, I'm okay," Johnson calls back. "But listen, there's about fifty German fighters just down below us, and they're raising hell. . . . Oh, and excuse me. Fuck you, sir."

"Yeah, I see them," I said. "But they're not after us. Okay, okay, everybody, watch for fighters and call them in."

During this crew exchange, which couldn't have lasted more than half a minute, a third bomber has exploded and another has fallen away from the formation and dropped into a long, straight dive. Just before this last plane, beginning to disintegrate, disappears in clouds, four parachutes open above the plane and hang in the air. I watch — or I imagine now that I remember watching — a German plane circling and rushing and shooting at the four crewmen as they hang defenseless in their harnesses, drifting down to be welcomed with the pitchforks and the axe handles wielded by the wives of German farmers. Wylie and Oates, who haven't spoken, are powerful presences. The sour metallic taste of oxygen dries the throat.

We fly over new clouds into new scenery; the group below us has disappeared. Though silence is not the right word to describe what I hear sitting between the four engines as they grind away at 1600 rpm, I have a memory of a great stillness that fills the plane. We are floating away untouched from a bloody battleground, and I am overwhelmed with an exhaustion as profound as the *post coitum triste* that follows some great storm of passion. I am overcome with fits of yawning and, though I gulp in oxygen through the face mask, am so dazed that I can hardly keep my eyes open. Even when Earl calls in and cries with astonishment, "Hey, the dreaded Hun out there low at nine o'clock," my fear is swallowed up in a great drowsiness; and a minute later when Sullivan calls in that the dreaded Hun is only the distant glittering of the first of the P-38s climbing to an altitude to herd us over Berlin, I give in to my exhaustion and, sitting on the stool with the bombsight between my knees, fall into a profound sleep that perhaps lasts no more than four or five minutes but that erases everything, everything.

After that, flying through that field of black flak over the target and watching the bombs flowering in the center of the city among blocks of building that were already rubble, I felt nothing but a dim sense of relief in getting rid of the bombs. What I was proudest of was simply that I had remembered at the proper moment to tighten my sphincter and deny my body its profound urge to void itself.

18

D URING THAT FIRST COUPLE OF MONTHS the events that had
happened before continued to happen: crews were shot down, or
completed their thirty missions and went back to America for reassignment; certain crew members wounded physically or mentally were
shipped off to hospitals; certain outstanding types born to lead moved
up into the castles of Wing, and at almost the speed of light captains
turned into majors, colonels, and generals. Our commanding officer, a
colonel, rose almost instantaneously into the upper echelons, and a
twenty-five-year-old pilot with the pink cheeks of a baby and the blond
curls of a teenage movie star took over. He was a colonel for almost two
months before he was shot down. There was a constant juggling of crew
members as empty slots in other crews were filled by those of us who
had lately arrived. Oates was taken away from Wylie and became pilot of
his own plane. Moburg was assigned to an older crew and told to prepare himself to lead. I was made squadron bombardier and once more
began to fly with Captain Davis. Captain Hudson, whose job I took,
turned into a major with a new title. I think they called him a Wing
bombardier; this probably meant that he didn't have to fly at all. As a
squadron bombardier, as a member of a lead crew, I was to fly only on
those days when our squadron led the group, or more rarely, when our
group with my squadron in the lead position led the Wing. In one letter
home, written with an enthusiasm which I'm sure I didn't feel about a
mission which I have completely forgotten, I mentioned that as our
plane crossed the beaches of Europe I was, for the split second that it
took the crew to join me, the only American soldier in Germany. Remembering back now, I find it hard to believe that I was ever allowed to
lead the Eighth Air Force into combat. The bright side: now, since I
would fly only one out of four missions, no more perhaps than three or

four times a month, my circle of friends began to change and I could get drunk almost every night with a clear conscience.

Davis drew me aside one day and told me that I could expect my captain's bars within a week. "As soon as they cut the orders you're to move into the lead house," he told me.

"Where the only happy ending is to jump out the window," I said.

"Maybe we'll put bars on the windows in your room," Davis told me, smiling.

"Oh John, I've got bars on my windows already. HALP."

With fewer than ten missions, and with more than twenty yet to go, I had become an old combat veteran and was beginning to be treated with a certain deference by the new replacements who began to appear in the bar when it opened at five o'clock, or who moved into the vacant beds in the officers' quarters. They were impressed by my aging face and a kind of disorientation that made it appear (and rightly) that I wasn't fully in tune with what was going on around me. Their faces were irritatingly innocent. My God, some of them had scarcely begun to shave. They were bright, enthusiastic, and optimistic, qualities that we found almost inexcusable in their inappropriateness. They were "eager beavers," and we felt a dim pity for them which we hid. No sense in panicking these sacrificial lambs as they leaped and bleated in the spring sunshine. Jesus, had we, only a few months before, been so naive?

I remember only two of the new replacements from that period; they are memorable because they were killed so quickly — one of them, I believe, on his first mission. The other, lively and curious, brought the squadron to life for a few days with his bursting enthusiasms. He was so young that the skin on his face still boiled with the hormonal changes of adolescence; he had a humorous face — horsey, bucktoothed, big-nosed, and the hair that fell down over his eyes was as stiff as a horse's mane. He hadn't been two days in the squadron before he knew everyone, and well enough so that when he walked into a room we wanted to begin smiling, anticipating that little bit of joy that he would bring us.

He had one joke and he told it constantly. In the few days he spent with us I must have heard it fifty times. He would tell us the joke, study us gravely, and if we groaned instead of laughed, he would begin again in the same voice and with the same expression. "This man was riding his horse through the street, see, and he came to a little fair with a little booth and a sign outside, 'Twenty-five cents to see the talking dog.' So the man and his horse went inside and sure enough, in the tent was a little stage with a dog on it, and the dog could talk. The man was absolutely amazed and he turned to his horse — the horse said, 'Well, what do you know, a talking dog.'" It was a cute story but truly not the kind to make one dissolve into hoots of laughter; but he worked on us, telling it over and over again in the most solemn and patient way until finally it turned into the funniest story we had ever heard. Now he would walk into a room and someone would grab the young pilot by the shoulders and say, "Listen, here's a good one. This man was riding his horse through the street, see. . . ."

How little I remember now about that boy and his bad complexion and his big white teeth and his thirst to live and to make human contacts. He had the kind of radiance about him that you don't recognize, but after he is dead you realize it was the purity of one who is destined to die young. And after talking to him a little, in love with his simplicity and innocence, you knew that he had grown up in a family who adored him and had given him a tremendous glad strength to confront life with courage and on noble terms.

He trotted out of a building one day to stop me as I was bicycling past in the rain. "Hey," he cried, "listen. I'm just beginning to realize how wonderful it is to hear Englishmen talk. They really have imagination, precision, that wonderful understatement. Their expressions are absolutely wonderful."

"Like what, for instance?"

"Well, like 'to take a dim view,' God, that is just great. I take a dim view of something — classic understatement, what? Or, you know, a bomb drops in the middle of an airfield, all the planes are destroyed, the buildings are all on fire, the fire hoses don't work, and the Englishman says, 'Well, this is rathah a bit of a muck-up, don't you know, a bit of a flap.'"

"Yes, you're probably right, but we have a certain style ourselves, you know. 'Oh, my fucking, aching back'; that's not bad; that says a lot."

"Now really, old chap, don't you take a dim view of my aching back? Oh, before I forget; this man was riding his horse down the street, stop me if you've heard this one. . . ."

"Stop. Not in the main, please. I'll see you later, and keep your pecker up."

"Yes, isn't that a wonderful expression? Keeping your pecker up isn't what you think it is, you know. . . . Something's 'a piece of cake.' Isn't that great? Or 'browned off'— I'm browned off. Isn't that great?"

"Yeah, not bad. Well, keep it up and ta-ta."

"Pip, old chappie, pip-pip."

I went to London for three or four days. The theaters around Piccadilly were full of Rita Hayworth movies and I saw them all, sitting through the air-raid warnings with that 95 percent of the audience who refused to climb down into the shelters. At times, and usually in the distance, the heavy earth-moving crunch of bombs. Behind the music, the singing and the dancing, and the unearthly sexuality of Hayworth, a goddess beautiful beyond desire, the throbbing moan of the sirens turned that softest and most anguishing of porn into a profound drama that one couldn't quite understand. Sex and death mingled in my soul.

Down two or three streets from the officers' Red Cross club where I slept, I used to pass a small art gallery. It had a single small painting in its single small window, a country scene all blacks and greys, a dark village street below black storm clouds, a winter tree blasted and leafless, and a single furious figure in a bright yellow slicker striding through slush. I wanted to buy that painting that spoke in some way of England's sad destiny and of the rural past, a rural greatness that England had repudiated, or at least let slip through her fingers. The painting looked so much like a Vlaminck that I was afraid to ask the price, but I wandered through the gallery and though I knew nothing about art was thunderstruck to find its walls hung with Picassos, Klees, Kandinskys, Derains. There was even a small Breughel, the head of a burgher with a bright red cap, painted on a wood panel. The quality of the paintings in this little gallery seemed to illuminate the still almost secret changes that the war was bringing to a shattered nation; the treasures of the once-rich were being dumped on the market.

At the end of a little hallway, a large cubist Picasso picked up all the light in that second-story landing and blazed with a passionate heat. It was for sale for a thousand guineas; even I in all my innocence knew that this must represent about 5 percent of its real value.

The owner of the gallery, a fatly soft, enormous, bearded man, a colonel in the Spanish Civil War he told me, was kind in a rough Bo-hemian way. He wore a beret, black turtleneck sweater, and corduroy pants; I don't believe he bathed very often. I began to spend my after-noons with him and began to be introduced to his friends as "the only modest American soldier in England." I was too stupid to take this as an insult, this judgment that was like an American's, "Some of my best friends are niggers," and upon being presented to some old threadbare music teacher dressed in plumes and robes and heavy turquoise chains like a bargain basement Edith Sitwell, I would smile modestly and stare at the floor, shuffling my feet like a midwestern hayseed. I wanted to do what was expected of me.

My friend, the ex-colonel, was an artist too, but not a very good one, I'm afraid. An upstairs room in his gallery was full of his own paintings. The colors were dirty, the forms, ectoplasmic: he was painting trees with the shapes of women, pale rocks with breasts, leaves that were unmistak-ably phallic. He was a kind of genial charlatan who, it seemed to me, was doomed never to never sell a picture (though I finally bought one) and would never achieve fame (though years after the war *Time* magazine ran a picture of one of his sculptures with some mocking comments; he had built a gigantic statue in cement of a grotesque woman with monu-mental pointed breasts and a tremendous inflated ass, and if I remember correctly, this statue when exhibited resulted in a series of bloody riots). In a short time I got to know about his obsession with women's asses. Nice, big, spreading ones were so beautiful to him that he was unable to leave them untouched. Over the months, I watched him lose sale after sale by standing beside some potential customer as she was studying a Henry Moore drawing or a Graham Sutherland watercolor, caressing her ass saying, "Madame, you must forgive me, but I cannot control myself; you have the most magnificent ass I've ever seen." He told me once, and knowing him I tended to believe it, that he had even run his hands down the royal backside of the refugee, Queen Wilhelmina, as she wandered through his galleries — and was told in a no-nonsense way, "For heaven's sake, young man, now stop that foolishness."

Back at the base, after a few days I missed the lovely clownish pilot. "Ah, yes," Davis told me, "he was shot down at the coast coming back from Essen." I think that was the last time I ever heard his name men-tioned. He had been like some wildly lively bird who had flown through the open window of our lives, dived and swooped and sung, filling the room with music and color for a minute or two, only to fly away and disappear forever.

The other pilot I remember as little more than a combat-suited child who came up to the room where we slept and introduced himself to Oates with whom he was scheduled to fly the next day. I watched him carefully as I watched all the men who were scheduled to fly with my crew, and decided that he was competent. He was very young and beautiful in the way that people who have still not lived and been marked by life are beautiful: there is nothing written on their faces but the decent future they have planned for themselves. Yes, Oates would be safe with him.

Late the next afternoon when their plane had landed, an ambulance hauled away the body of Oates' copilot. A burst of flak had taken off both legs above the knees, and with Oates beside him in the pilot's seat he had died on the way back to England. I remember no details; they were details that if you were not there yourself, you would never hear from anyone else's mouth. I remember talking with Oates that same evening about other things. His face was grey as death, terrible tremors shook his body, and his hands had developed a violent trembling that never quite left him. Fifteen years later when he was a major on an air base in Alaska his hands still shook, and among the enlisted men of his squadron he had earned the nickname Shakey Jakey.

The very next day, I think, Oates was shipped off to some magical castle by the sea where combat officers driven to the point of breakdown were sent to recover what was left of their unraveling nervous systems. Wonderful meals — thick steaks, wine, waffles with little pork sausages. Long quiet walks along the edges of the white chalk cliffs. Tea parties and afternoon dances. Pretty English girls in long, flowing dresses. Everyone kind and loving and ready to listen and ready to hold your hand when, talking, you broke down and began to weep. It was a real life version, or as close as they could make it, to the Rita Hayworth movies — everything dreamy, misty, and romantically unreal, a silk veil hung over the lens, Rita Hayworth in a Swan Lake setting. After a week or ten days Oates came back. He still trembled, he still flew. But on those nights when he was not scheduled to fly the next day, he tended to become curiously maudlin and sentimental in the last few minutes before he passed out and we hauled him off to bed. Watching him, I sometimes wondered if he weren't trying to regress back to babyhood.

When you are flying in a tight combat formation and sitting in the nose of the lead plane, everything that happens behind you is invisible. All the planes you are leading could be blown out of the sky and you would never know it. The lead bombardier, isolated in the nose of the plane, was like some drummer boy with a stiff neck unable to look back and drumming, drumming out ahead, perhaps, of nothing. In a way it was reassuring not to know what was happening behind you; on the other hand, according to the mythology of combat, it was the lead plane that the Krauts were after.

I came back one afternoon from a mission to someplace; I had been a little more terrified than usual. Three or four fighters had made a single pass through our formation; I hadn't seen them but there had been a lot of wild screaming back and forth on the intercom. At the coast and over the target, flak had been heavy, and I was half aware in the most foreboding way that behind me over the target something terrible had taken place. I had absolutely no curiosity, however, about what might have happened. I crawled out of the plane so exhausted I could hardly move and was driven into the headquarters area. I went into the Quonset hut on the flight line where each of us had a locker and began to take off my paraphernalia. We kept certain of our gear there — throat-mikes, headphones, oxygen masks, parachutes — and a squad of enlisted men had the job of receiving, checking, and cleaning these things for the next mission. It was a dark place with benches lined up in front of the lockers, like the locker room of a football team, and with the same funky stink of sweat-stained clothes. But this was sweat more sour, more fetid — unhealthy sweat, squeezed out of us by fear. Wylie was flying that day but with a new crew; Oates, after his ten days in cloud-cuckoo-land, was still not flying.

Now he came into the Quonset hut and stood before me as I was taking off my gear, and on his face was such an expression of shock and grief that I was instantly filled with resentment; it was an anger against the messenger who arrives with the bad news that will prove to be unbearable. And coming just now, when I was least prepared to handle any-thing but my own emotions. I had just returned from a devastating experience and I was alive and unwounded, and against this miracle there was no bad news in the world that could rob me of my selfish tri-umph or diminish those feelings of relief and joy that lay buried beneath the body's exhaustion. And it occurs to me now, as I try to understand this little minute when I came off so badly, that my resentment against Oates — a feeling that was almost contempt for the sadness in his face that refused to acknowledge the slightest degree of satisfaction in my safe return — was built in part around the simplicity and incongruity of his Texas expression which was incapable of nobly reflecting the terrible thing he was about to tell me. No, his face was screwed up, as shriveled as a prune, his eyes lugubrious. He was a country singer about to use all the wrong gestures and sing me a cheap fucking song in a nasal voice about the death of Wylie. I stood there and stared at him with hatred, waiting.

"Wylie's shot down," he said.

I knew absolutely that it was true, I had known it was true before he had said it, but what appalled me now more than the confirmation of Wylie's death was a smile that spread over my face and which I tried, horrified and without success, to control. Grinning and terrified of this grin that lit up my face, fighting with a terrible embarrassment to wipe it away, I tried to cover up what must have seemed like the most brutal cal-lousness by pretending to deny this news that Oates had brought me. I said, almost yelling, "No, no, you're wrong. I don't believe it. I was there, goddammit, I was there; it's not true."

With the greatest effort I took control of my body and almost succeeded in matching Oates' tragic expression, though I could feel something triumphantly elemental trying to burst out of its depths. It was a swelling rush of triumph straight from the body's core made of blood and organs, flesh and glands, bones and tissue, a physical thing that had nothing to do with my feelings for Wylie — my love for him and my grief at his death. It was that something as inhuman as the DNA mole-cule that would gladly have sacrificed the entire universe to keep on living and that must have seen in Wylie's death the sacrifice that would save me; or the end of some game, like a game of chess that he had lost and that in winning I had, and almost for the last time, been brought violently to life. And so this part of me that had nothing to do with me was exultantly proclaiming, "Wylie is dead, but you're alive, you're alive, you're alive."

Later over Berlin, pissing in my pants with terror, I would experience this same dichotomy between me and my body. And later still over Berlin, on other days of sitting on piles of flak vests, aghast while the shells burst around the plane and my penis shriveled and my testicles, trying to hide, crawled into the deepest recesses of my silently shrieking body, I would experience it again.

It is not strictly true to write that I felt grief when Wylie died; it would be more honest to say that, like someone who has just been clubbed, I felt nothing — or rather that in those few minutes after the mission when, in debriefing, the intelligence officers interrogating us to put together what had happened, my body, still going its own way, began constructing impregnable defenses around my heart. I could feel this happening. I could feel myself being cut off from experience as though some benign power were pumping me full of the opiates that would dull whatever pain should come when the shock had worn off. Growing up under the shadow of my father's rage had already tended to isolate me from emotion; yet if I were more or less insulated against real anguish there were a few windows still open in the fortress I had constructed for myself. Now, as we discussed in the debriefing the destruction of Wylie and his crew, I could feel the last of the open windows closing and the lights behind the windows going out. I had the feeling, and it was not particularly distressing, that from now on I would never feel much of anything. And I am probably not giving away too much of this book's ending if I mention now, flouting chronology, that for sixteen years Wylie's death and the deaths of many others and the whole combat experience was locked up and forgotten in some unused closet of my mind. Until I stood alone in a California alfalfa field where I had gone to change the irrigating water one midnight. I was middle-aged now, and probably hadn't wept since that morning when the Japanese attacked Pearl Harbor and I had squeezed out those three or four skimpy little tears that had so impressed my father. Out of nowhere, under a still bright sky and up to my knees in black, quick-flowing water, suddenly I was shaken with oceanic emotions and released to feel the reality of Wylie's death. Everything that had been locked up and guarded came flooding out, and I stood there in the night, the tears gushing from my eyes, shrieking out that long accumulation of grief. How proud I was after this hurricane of emotion had subsided and I found myself on my hands and knees in the mud, proud to find that I could weep again, and that in a sense I was finally cured.

Oates was waiting for me outside the debriefing hut; we went to our quarters together and found Lt. Hamilton packing up the last of Wylie's personal property for shipment home. If we had thought to save his family some final confusion we might have removed the dozen boxes of silk stockings that he had brought with him from a Maine PX to aid him in his seductions. In ten minutes every trace of Wylie had been removed, but by coincidence that very afternoon he had received a box from home. A sergeant in the mail room, not knowing that Wylie was dead, came by with the information. I went back to the mail room with him, opened up the package that was already split wide from a hard journey, and removed two rolls of 35 mm color film that were tucked in among the woolen hand-knit scarves, the packages of cookies, and the special undergarments that Wylie liked to wear — or that his mother thought he liked to wear.

The next morning I went to London on the early train and walked across that town as it came to life for another day. I headed directly for Wylie's tailor on Bond Street. Wylie's dead, I said. Would it be possible for me to become the new owner of his combat jacket? I would pay the balance on what was owed. The tailor's eyes filled with tears, and he agreed instantly. While the tailor, his eyes damp and stunned, draped Wylie's jacket over my shoulders and made certain alterations, I stood before him in a dead calm. "Can you finish it in a hurry?" I asked. "Otherwise you might have to make new changes for a guy named Oates." I never felt an instant's guilt for these thefts until a year later while I was having dinner with Wylie's parents in Los Angeles. His mother, admiring my jacket, said, "Bob wrote us that he had bought a jacket just like yours. Does yours have the red satin lining, too?" It did, but it was not half so red as my flaming cheeks as I stared into her face, feeling like a grave-robber and trying not to blink.

Pondering Wylie's death, I had trouble sleeping, even in London where I usually walked the streets until early morning and climbed up into the Red Cross dormitory only after I was too exhausted to keep going. London had become menacing again; the German buzz bombs had begun to come in about this time, and at terribly short intervals you could hear their brutal growling as they flew in very swift and low from across the Channel. They were small, black, and evil-looking — snake-headed. A blast of red flame gushed from their tails, a furnace that made a cold hot sound both low and high, as ugly and raw as a promise of damnation.

During the day you could watch them as they came in just above the tops of the building; at night the hot flames, as furious as the blasts from a blowtorch, moved across the sky like comets. But in their squat black ugliness and their terrible roaring they were a little like the dragons out of folklore — wind and flame and noise. These first jets to be used in war were weapons of terror more than anything else; there was no way to aim them accurately. The launching ramps on the Dutch coast were built pointing toward London, and the projectiles were fueled with what the Germans figured was just enough kerosene to get them there. They were not dangerous while they screamed above us, rattling the fillings in our teeth, but when the fuel was gone they stuttered a time or two and then dropped in a quick steep dive. It was the silence that lasted for a few seconds between the exhaustion of the fuel and the explosion of the warhead that was momentarily terrifying. What an exquisite pleasure it was to hear, finally, the bursting of the bomb; hearing it meant that you were still alive. It was a sound as satisfying as the final chord of some symphony that at its end resolves the mounting tensions of its constructions. Or the relief of the empty click of a revolver held against your temple when you are playing Russian roulette. The Londoners, with their usual flair for understatement, called them doodlebugs, but in spite of the contempt that this term implied, once more the city began to empty of people.

I could handle the buzz bombs in the daytime, but to be awakened at three or four in the morning and to hear one of those Nazi bombs coming right at me as I lay naked and vulnerable and alone in some strange bed in the center of a city that was turning to ruins. . . .

Here is one night that hasn't faded away.

For some reason, instead of sleeping in the Red Cross club I have taken a room in a hotel. It is a couple weeks after Wylie's death, and on this particular night I have been lying in bed for an hour or so watching with interest as some part of me slowly feeds the new reality of Wylie's destruction into my mind. Getting through combat was as much luck as anything, but I hated to acknowledge this. Turning your life over to luck at such a time was to lose control of it. I needed to find good solid reason behind the random explosions of flak that brought planes down.

Denying luck didn't mean, of course, that there were not irrational ways of hamstringing destiny. For instance, one reason I was not killed (perhaps the only reason): I had received some special and esoteric knowledge from a drunken navigator in the combat officers' bar. He had only two more missions to fly. "Don't ever change your shirt," he told me. "On every mission you wear the same shirt that got you through the first one, the second one, the third one." It was certainly worth a try. The shirt that I wore in combat for almost a year was a GI shirt that I had neglected to turn in when I was commissioned. It was already slightly worn when I began to fly, and by the time I had completed my tour it was as caked with filth, as black, tattered, and stinking as the carefully dirtied clothes of a professional beggar.

Out of loyalty and an inability to coolly analyze the man upon whom depended my own hopes of surviving, I had never dared think that Wylie was anything but a first-rate flier and that I had been lucky to have been assigned to his crew. Tonight as I lie in bed listening to the almost perpetual wailing of the air-raid sirens and the faraway growling of the V-1s, I begin to fly that last mission over again — again and again flying it, trying to understand it, and gradually moving out of the lead plane into the wing positions.

I watch the fighters coming in, one swift and deadly pass that takes the squadron by surprise; I watch Wylie's plane as it abruptly leaves the formation, wavers out there alone, stalls, and begins to fall. There are no chutes, no smoking engines, just this dive that becomes steeper until the plane is rushing toward earth, diving down into a green German field. Drifting toward sleep I watch Wylie as he falls out of the sky — from a pilot's window, from the waist, locked into the belly gunner's bubble. And now one more time I fly the mission, standing just behind Wylie as he struggles with the controls. The rudder and aileron cables have been shot away, and the plane does not respond. Wylie has fifteen seconds to save his crew, fifteen seconds to analyze the situation and then yell "Bail out!" And then unstrap himself from the pilot's seat and rush toward an escape hatch. Or open the bomb bay doors, jettison the bombs and throw himself out into the slipstream. He is a big man, let's face it, he has a kind of flabby ass; he is not a man who moves quickly. That crooked smile of his now seems to hint at a lack of basic coordination; he has a funny little lurch when he walks, a subtle clumsiness. Oh, Wylie, you were too secure ever to feel threatened, weren't you? All those graceful manners, that California coolness, that kind of aristocratic disdain and disassociation from a moment like this, when to live you must scream and punch and claw your way out of this plane that has now begun to dive straight down and as it accelerates pins you back into your seat. Wylie, Wylie, you weren't tough enough, you weren't quite good enough at survival. Move, for Christ's sake, stop smiling and, goddamn it, move.

If this was a brutal repudiation of Wylie, it was a denial of his competence that was forced out of me by my own passion to live and the necessity to try and make sense of the gratuitousness of all these sudden deaths that in a sense were not deaths at all, but absences — empty places at a table, empty beds that were almost immediately filled with strangers. There was a mysterious incompleteness about these deaths that was like the endings of badly written stories whose heroic characters had not been sufficiently pondered. To disappear in aerial combat was too clean, bloodless, and sudden, and we missed (and were spared) the solemn ritual of the church — the solid message of the casket, that overwhelming hole cut into the turf above which one might stand, listening perhaps in mild disgust to the banal Christian words which, if they did not solace, at least helped to make death real. Without bodies for certain identification these comrades were listed as Missing in Action; they lay in us, poisonous and rotting, like indigestible food. Out there over Europe the planes with their crews simply disappeared in orange bursts of flame or, diving through clouds, faded away into an ambiguous oblivion. No blood, no last grey-faced gaspings, no screams of pain or outrage.

I lie there in the darkness, washed in confusion as Wylie's plane dives down and down; and just before it crashes I fall into an obliterating sleep.

Later, a few minutes or an hour later, I come fully awake. I am not in bed. The air-raid sirens are weeping obscenely, and the growl of a buzz bomb fills the room. The window frames and the dresser drawers are dancing, rattling like dead bones, like the first warning spasms of an earthquake. The floor shakes. But most disturbing, I have the impression that I am not alone in the room. Someone is choking to fill his lungs with air, someone is squealing, moaning, panting. In my sleep I have heard the bomb coming toward me, know absolutely that it is going to explode in this room, and as I awake I am already in the grip of a terror that is stronger than anything I have ever experienced before or since. It is absolute. Asleep, I have climbed from the bed, rushed to the window, and wrapped myself in the heavy blackout curtains. I am whispering and panting like an animal; I claw at my face and make little pig-like shrieks. Awake now, I realize that the curtains will protect me from nothing. I can see the shards of glass as sharp as daggers as they burst from the window and pin me into this shroud. Squealing with pain, on hands and knees, but at full speed, I crawl back to the bed and try to climb under it. No good; the bedframe is too low. A second later as the bomb passes over the hotel and its sound diminishes toward Hyde Park, I find myself pressed into one corner of the clothes closet, with both hands, in a gesture of monumental redundancy, cupping my genitals.

In fifteen seconds the whole extent of my cowardice has been revealed, but like most things that we do alone behind locked doors, this shameful exhibition of unmanly panic did not much bother me. The explosion of the bomb in the distance was as cleansing to my psyche as a wet dream. Lying in bed and trying to sleep again, knowing that in some way I was being paid back for my uncharitable thoughts about Wylie, I could only think, "Thank God nobody saw me; thank God nobody knows."

A month later when the German V-2s, those enormous bombs that arced sixty miles into the air, began dropping at random over the English countryside, I watched a new major who slept for a time in my room as he went through an identical performance. A tremendous explosion about a mile away had blasted the night, and the major had leaped from the bed with a wild scream. Watching him, I had the feeling at first that he was mocking the dance steps that I had perfected that night in London. But since I had told no one, and haven't to this day, how could he have known? He wrapped the bedclothes around him, tore at his hair, circled the room whimpering, ripped all his uniforms out of a closet and threw them into the center of the room. Untouched by panic this time, I

lay on my cot smoking a cigarette and watching him with a contemptuous smile. The major was fresh from a Texas training center and was new
to combat, and like many of my friends I resented his rank, which he had
earned instructing cadets. Like picking your nose, pissing in the wash-
basin, or masturbating, his uninhibited exhibition, I felt, should not be
performed in public. How much easier to be calm and suave under the
watchful eyes of your peers.

What he kept crying over and over again as he ran distractedly a-
round the room, I found at the time to be ridiculous, almost insane: "My
babies, oh, my babies." But now, looking back from the tremendous distance of forty years, it strikes me that this cry that was torn from him,
and which perhaps not even he could understand, grew from that same
primal sense of panic and outrage that had made me grab my balls as I
cowered in a London clothes closet. It occurs to me that this terror that
strips you of your identity, of dignity, of humanity, this terror that leaves
you helpless and moaning, has little to do with your own individual destruction. It is some deep revolt in the genes, some insatiable greediness
that hungers for immortality through the reproduction of the human
species. When I write that we had a passion to live, it is the gene's passion
to live that I am describing; when I find myself mocking Wylie because
he seemed to have died so passively, it is Wylie's failure to let himself instantly be called to violent personal combat with the death that claimed
him that makes me see him as flawed. The truth is that on a rational level
— exhausted by combat, stretched for months in a tension which for
those of us who were cursed with imagination was almost unbearable,
and facing at too young an age man's essential capacity to act in bestial
and despicable ways — life was not something that any longer had much
value.

To those of us who survived combat, who flew time after time and
returned to the ordinary routines, routines that at first struck us as
being miraculous — eating, sleeping, bicycling along the summer roads,
drinking whiskey in that absolutely exclusive group of combat airmen
(pleasures that gave us less and less pleasure) — a slowly growing boredom with life began to be apparent in our conscious thoughts. We were
touched with shame to be still living, to be doing the same banal things
in the center of that encircling and invisible and growing pile of bodies.
Why had we been unchosen? There seemed to be no way to be worthy

of the dead without joining them; we were in competition with the dead who had left us, and left us filled with guilt. A passion to live. A passion to die. How could we reconcile these two emotions that kept rising in us, except in the way we did, by sinking into a kind of catatonia, an emotional hibernation that was like insanity.

19

O VER EUROPE THE AMERICAN BOMBERS almost always flew at the extreme limits of their altitude range. On missions where it seemed unlikely that we would encounter either enemy fighters or anti-aircraft fire, we sometimes cruised in and out of Germany at altitudes as low as eighteen thousand feet; on missions of deep penetration or when the target was heavily protected, we climbed as high as thirty thousand feet. At the higher altitudes the B-17 mushed and strained, responding sluggishly to the controls, and moved through the sky at speeds that even in those days we regarded as insolent and provocative. It was bad enough passing over Germany at a hundred and twenty miles an hour like fleets of fully loaded beer trucks; worse over the target when, seeking a steadier bombing platform, flying speed was reduced to a hundred and ten miles an hour. Sometimes then, coming into the target and beating against a high altitude wind of sixty or seventy miles an hours, our passage across the sky was so slow that it seemed like suicide, and we felt vulnerable enough to be brought down with .22 rifles or the flung pitchfork of a German farmer.

One day we came back from one of those missions where we had fought strong head winds and had lingered over the target for an interminable time. I am unable to place this mission in its proper chronology, remembering only that Wylie was not the pilot but I was flying with all the other members of my crew. When we reached the coast finally, and made out England floating blue and solid across the Channel, we were filled with immense relief. In another half hour we would have dropped to six thousand feet and be circling over English woods; in another two hours we would be taking hot showers or gulping straight shots of scotch. And so just as we passed the coast, beginning to feel safe, I turned around in the bombardier's seat to give Moburg a triumphant smile and to point out England in the near distance. In that instant, as we looked at each other, smiling, the plane was hit by an exploding shell. Immediately afterward, so quickly that we were both instantly aware that in all probability we were about to spin out of control into the Channel, another shell exploded. And another. We were still smiling at each other like idiots, for there had been no time to rearrange our faces in a suitable way.

The hits had been direct; the plane lurched, rose in the air, staggered, and, wheeling over, dropped steeply from the formation. The sounds of the exploding shells had been as unequivocal and straightforward as a sentence of death translated into abstract music. It was a message made portentous and otherworldly by the quality of the sound traveling through a space from which the air had been violently driven; a sound which echoed and boomed in a completely new way. Remember the echo chambers and the electronic devices De Mille used to bring us God's growling voice as he gave Moses the Ten Commandments? It was like that; we were hearing reality for the first time. It was as though at the moment of death you were illuminated by some great secret truth — God's own lowdown. Of course, being allowed to hold forbidden knowledge meant we would never be allowed back to life. It was like the last page of a murder mystery with a sad ending. The murderer goes free and with a gun pointed at your head says, "Yes, you figured it out; since you will be dead in another ten seconds I confess that I am the one who dropped the ice pick into Throckwaite's tea bag." Bang.

Since so few of the airmen who heard the particular sound of flak exploding against their planes lived to tell about it, let me linger here for just a moment and wax lyrical. I am plowing new ground. The timbres of this new sound were so intense that I can still, with a minimum of effort, manufacture certain of its resonances from my failing memory.

First: a great metallic grunting thunk as the plane staggers, lifts, and drops; it is a completely solid confrontation like a head-on collision between two trucks, a great whop. At the same time a smacking sound, as sharp and cruel as your very own face being slapped by your very own wicked stepmother — hard, hateful, neurotic. Then a hollowness as you move into the vacuum, an echoing, stretched-out confusion, a chord made up of every tone — the metallic whistling of a falling guillotine blade, the awful smacking of scissors slicing through the very threads of your destiny. And then, into what at first seems like an overpowering silence, the high-pitched whistling of a new sound — death's scythe whooshing through dried weeds, the screaming rush of air through new holes torn in the plane's skin, hundreds of ragged holes in the aluminum, pitting the Plexiglas. The sound is like the high plains winds in winter shrieking through telephone lines. And all it says is "Dead, dead."

It occurs to me now that perhaps for a few seconds we heard these minatory shrieks and whistles, these shrill ghostly hissings, with some special part of the brain that was reserved for life's most profound and ultimate messages. For up in front of the mind all our attention was focused on the sounds of the engines. What we wanted without hope was to continue to hear the same monotonous roaring, the same pitch, the same solid sounds of healthy motors — holding us up, taking us home. It was only the sound of good strong engines that could cancel out the strongly held conviction that we were living out our last few minutes and that at any second the plane would heel over and drop, or a wing would crumple, or an engine would begin to blaze, or this flimsy contraption in which we rode would simply disintegrate in a blast of flame. More out of custom than evasive action I sat in the nose, tightly holding my balls and staring out ahead and down, down into the North Sea where rows of white breaking water suddenly took on a cold, hard, bronzed look.

Little Sullivan, the flight engineer, stuck his head down into the bubble where Moburg and I sat. He yelled something that I couldn't hear and disappeared. I clicked on the intercom, but it was dead. I crawled back past Moburg and squeezed into the pilot's area. As I passed Moburg he dropped to his knees and, with pressed hands before his face, began to pray. Oates and a copilot I can't remember were flying — intensely; there was a godlike beauty in their concentration. Sullivan, white-faced, stood behind them studying the dials. "What did you say?" I yelled. "Nothing, sir," Sullivan yelled back. "I was just checking. The intercom's gone." At this instant Savasuk, the radio man, tapped me on the shoulder. I turned to see a face which had never held much of anything now transfigured into a kind of beautiful wildness. Terror had cracked open his impassivity. "You better come back to the waist, sir. Please. Look, my foot. Earl. Earl, sir. He says he can't see. And Jones. Jones, sir."

I looked at Savasuk's foot, clumsy in flying boots, but could see nothing beyond a small tear in the sole. "You're okay," I said. I pushed past him and crawled through the plane's belly into the bomb bays where the bombs had lain in rows — that place of shrieking winds and darkness that had always filled me with irrational horror — and past it, past the radio room, into the open waist of the plane where the unmanned guns now swung untended and where, through a hundred torn holes, the air shrieked and whistled. Earl stood, one hand cupping an eye, above Jones, who lay stretched out where he had fallen on a pile of flak vests. "Can you look at this eye, sir?" Earl cried, grabbing me. I pulled his hand away, glanced into his eyes, saw nothing out of the way, and ignoring his cries, knelt beside Jones. He lay below his machine gun, eyes closed and with hands lying carefully at his sides; he looked unbearably fragile and vulnerable. The oxygen mask he had been wearing had been ripped from his face, and across his neck a thin line of blood like a razor's slash, a red line as thin as a thread, showed just above his fleece-lined jacket. I opened his jacket an inch and closed it quickly, my mind trying to pretend that I had seen nothing. A piece of flak had torn across his throat and exposed and ripped open all of that subtle machinery that took air and food into the lungs, the stomach. "Can you look at this eye, sir, please?" Earl cried, shaking me where I knelt just above Jones. "Your fucking eye's okay," I yelled, glancing into his face again. "Go get me the first-aid kit; bring me the morphine, the morphine." I turned the oxygen on full and pressed the mask over Jones's face. "Can you hear me?" I yelled into Jones's ear. "You're okay, you hear; you're going to be okay. Are you in pain?" Just barely, just barely Jones nodded. Earl brought me the first-aid packet, and I broke open a tube of morphine and plunged its needle into Jones's arm. I knew that what I was doing was probably wrong, but how could I simply kneel there, doing nothing, letting him die? The thought of Jones's possible suffering filled me with a terrible anguish. I opened his jacket again, shielding the sight from Earl with my body; I stared at the slashed throat and at the thick bubbles of blood that were oozing out from the lungs, and I realized that I was the only one in the plane who knew what was happening and that in order to save Jones I would have to take charge of everything. "Keep the mask on his face," I yelled at Earl and started back into the pilot's compartment. Savasuk was sitting in the radio room as I pushed past him. He was staring at his foot. "What shall I do, sir, take off my boot?" "No, leave it alone," I yelled after him. "Don't worry, we're going to land now." Now I was bending over the seats between Oates and the copilot and yelling at both of them.

"Land this fucker, land it right now. Jones is hit bad; there's no time to get back to the base." Oates nodded and pushed the nose of the plane down and we rushed, dropping, toward the English coast.

And now, beginning to pant, I crawled back through the plane again and knelt beside Jones. The plane was losing altitude fast and I could begin to breathe again, and with oxygen to pull into my lungs I was losing that high altitude euphoria that is like drunkenness dulling anxieties. "Please sir, goddammit, sir," Earl said, squatting beside me. "Look at my eye again; tell me the truth. I felt steel rip through it, I swear to Christ." I looked very carefully into Earl's eye, spreading the lids open and concentrating all my force on this eye which he was convinced — and rightly — had been sliced open with flak. It was like looking into his soul. He had black hair and very deep blue eyes; all I could see was the beauty of his eyes, misted with tears, and the fear in them. He was the son of a steelworker, I think. He had thick straight eyebrows which had always made me think, feeling that outward strength reflected inner reserves, that in some crisis he would prove to be the strongest of us all. Unwounded, I had suddenly become his father, and I had the impulse to take him in my arms and rock him back and forth. "Your eye's okay," I said. "Listen, the intercom is out, so pound on the belly bubble and get Johnson out of there. And then lie down. I'm sure your eye is okay but go lie down. And don't touch your eyes, don't rub them, and listen, I swear to God, your eye looks okay." Jones, with the last of his strength, tore at the mask that was covering his face. I took it off him, checked it, and discovered, appalled, that the oxygen tank was empty, and if there was still any connection between his mouth and his lungs, he had been suffocating behind that rubber construction all choked now with spit and blood.

Outside the waist window as the plane turned and dropped, the English coast appeared from time to time — waves beating against a high bluff, patches of trees, stretches of pasture. I put my mouth close to Jones's ear and began to talk to him. "We're almost back. I can see the field where we're going to land. You're going to be okay. I looked and you're not hurt bad. In twenty minutes there'll be a doctor and he'll fix you up. Don't worry, don't worry, you're going to be okay." Jones, eyes closed and his face the color of ivory, slowly and with a tremendous effort nodded his head. And now just before we landed, once more, and given strength by my own words which I wanted desperately to believe, I opened his flying jacket, down past his throat where his wool shirt lay before my eyes shredded and torn, and beneath it to a great area of meat and blood, the lungs exposed and bubbling and something pulsing wildly in the center of all that mangled flesh, something terrified and outraged that was beating insanely.

Clarence Jones. He was a country kid from South Carolina and he spoke an English that was so drawling and Southern that it was months before any of us had even begun to understand him. Everything he said (I think) was meant to make you laugh; his jokes were cynical, irreverent, vulgar, absolutely down-to-earth, and they concealed his passionate love of America. He was tense and cocky, with long stringy muscles and the special alertness of a hunter, and I was always awed by his savvy, for he was as streetwise and pragmatic as a New York urchin. He was as spare and tough as an old plucked rooster, with pale Southern washed-out eyes and straight pale hair that sprang tensely from his head. He reminded me of a fighting and feisty kid who was purely molded in the image of those Southern rebels with their hawk faces and their noble dedication to a lost cause. He was nineteen. Before I saw him half naked and dying, I had thought of him as being as large as his presence and his cockiness, but there in the plane, stripped to expose his chest which had been blown away, I saw him as he was — small, excruciatingly vulnerable, tender as a child. Lost.

We landed on an English airfield, a short turfed field pointing out to the Channel, onto which we had to dive, and then brake violently to keep from dropping off the cliff's edge into the sea. It was a Spitfire base, manned by those men about whom Churchill had said "never has so much been owed to so few," and even in our extreme state of fear and confusion we were awed to be received by these surviving heroes who had saved England from the German invasion. Almost before we stopped taxiing an ambulance appeared, and at the waist door as we opened it medics and airmen were waiting to rush Jones away.

And now my memory breaks down. Did Earl, who had been blinded in one eye, get into the ambulance with Jones? Did Savasuk, whose boot had now filled with blood, join them? And what of Dugas, the tail gunner who, though unwounded, was the most wounded one of all? I can't remember. There are about two hours that has been ripped from my life, the two hours when we climbed from one bomber and waited for another plane that had been sent from the base to pick us up and bring us home. I vaguely remember eating lunch at the commanding officers' table (where no one spoke, as though we had no common language) and I vaguely remember being driven to another airfield with a longer runway. I remember that there was blood on my hands and that for some reason I was reluctant to wash it away.

The pilot who had flown in to get us was the twin brother to that madman who kept crashing planes in Basic training — a hot little pilot with specially tailored clothes, a squashed-down cap, and with half a tube of Vaseline rubbed into his black curling locks. This fancy little show-off should have been flying kites or fighters instead of bombers. He takes off wildly, climbing so steeply that he almost stalls, then circles back and dives for the field, putting on a little show for the British. There's not much you can do with a four-engine bomber, but he does what he can. Dipping and climbing, dipping and climbing, we lurch homeward. Those of us in the waist can't believe it. Climbing, we are smashed to the floor, our limbs as heavy as lead. Dipping, we become weightless and float like men in space. Everything loose in the plane begins to float; machine guns smash and tear at the aluminum skin, flak vests and ammo boxes sail through the air. It is a time as terrifying as combat — and yes, now I remember looking into Dugas' face. Naked terror. He has just barely escaped with his life over Germany and is now being subjected to this. Did I see in his face what indeed he was feeling — that if he ever got out of this alive, he would never fly again? Perhaps it was his naked look that turned my own fear into rage. Floating and crawling down the catwalk in the darkened bomb bays where the empty bomb racks rattled and shook with menace, I fought my way up into the pilot's compartment and, pounding on the pilot's shoulder, began screaming. "Listen, you dumb, ignorant, stupid son of a bitch, level out. You're wrecking the plane; do you want to kill us all?" What a hurt look of surprise he gave me — but he stopped his clowning. When we landed, Lt. Hamilton was waiting for us with the news that Jones was dead.

In the group debriefing it was reported that our plane had last been seen diving toward the sea; it was generally presumed by those who tended to jump to pessimistic conclusions that we had all been killed. The rumor that we had been shot down set the combat officers to prowling through our personal effects. An ill wind had blown us away; an ill wind brought us back. All through that afternoon things I hadn't even missed yet were brought back to me — the radio, the typewriter, Wylie's fine combat jacket. They had been taken by friends, and I can't remember that there was any resentment on my part or on theirs.

And then, of course, after death, if there is a body to go with it, there is a funeral. Jones was buried in an American cemetery somewhere south of London. The five of us who were still unwounded and still flying were provided with a command car and a driver. In my memory I have made him into a middle-aged semi-alcoholic who had been plucked at random from the car pool. He pressed pub stops upon us and we arrived for the service very late and half drunk. After walking an enormous distance across lawns and through clumps of trees — through row after row of white crosses, through thousands of rows of white crosses, we arrived at a long trench with a dozen flag-draped coffins lying along one side. An army chaplain was just completing the burial service; a squad of armed soldiers in brilliantly polished helmets and white canvas puttees waited in the background like an operatic chorus. We moved in unobtrusively and stood at the end of a double row of soldiers who had come to honor and to mourn their friends. It all went smoothly, without a hitch — the chaplain was eloquent, the guard of honor as well drilled as robots. The American flags were removed from the coffins and folded into cute triangular diapers, dirt was sprinkled, the guns popped, the chaplain and his squad of soldiers hurried off. They were scheduled for another service in that part of the cemetery reserved for officers. As we wandered back to our car, a bulldozer concealed in trees started up its engine.

A day or two later Dugas came to my room and began to babble. At first I couldn't understand what he was saying, but what he wanted, I finally gathered, was that I should talk to the flight surgeon about him; I was to explain that he had not refused to fly again, but had only insisted that he needed a few weeks off. Dugas at thirty-five was by far the oldest man on the crew; he had a wife and children. Whether or not Dugas would ever fly again was of little concern to me. If he could find the strength to keep offering himself to German guns he would continue to fly. I saw his choice as somehow lying outside anything he could do about it with his conscious mind. But whatever he felt, or whatever he decided to do — and I remember this conversation as having been extremely embarrassing — surely my duty was to defend him. The flight surgeon was about to publicly brand him as a coward and stamp an LMF on his record; we had been programmed to feel that Lack of Moral Fiber was somehow worse than being killed. Later, I would learn that the flight surgeon had flown several combat missions, but at the time I thought of him as a ground officer, and it seemed obscene to me that those of us who flew might be judged and humiliated by men who had no knowledge of the tensions that were destroying the tattered remnants of our fucking moral fiber.

At the flight surgeon's, when I told him why I had come, he very pointedly did not invite me into his inner office. We stood outside in the hall with all the doors open and with a line of combat sergeants standing before a couple of corporals typing out forms. "Listen, Doc, Dugas doesn't want an LMF, he just wants a little time. He was scared shitless on that flight back with Miller. I don't blame him; I was scared shitless myself." "Yes," the doctor said, "you went through the same thing, and did you request that you be taken off flying status?" "He didn't ask to be taken off, he just wants time. That dizzy Miller, he's the one you ought to ground. He's a fucking menace." "Oh Captain, competence at the controls is not within my jurisdiction. I'm just supposed to be an expert on states of mind." "Well, you've got Dugas's state of mind all wrong, Doc, and I think you could be a little more understanding." "Oh, Captain, Captain, don't you think I know my job? Don't you think I know an LMF when I see one? Look, I've seen a hundred like him. Dugas, whatever he told you, will never as long as he lives climb into another plane." "Shit fire, how can he if you ground him?" "No, by his own choice, Captain, by his own choice." He moved away from me, stood in the door to his office with his back to me, studying some sheets of paper that a corporal handed him, and angry at being dismissed in such a way, I yelled after him, "Who's going to stick up for Dugas, who's going to stick up for Dugas, Captain?" The flight surgeon turned, shrugging, looked at me very hard, as though he were appraising my mental condition, and said in a kind, sad voice, "Dugas."

This scene, which was observed by a dozen gunners, gained me a little degree of fame. Apparently it was not often that an officer had a chance to defend an enlisted man. Even months later a mechanic on the lead plane or a sergeant gunner flying for the first time with our crew, would give me a smile that I knew I didn't deserve, and perhaps say something like, "Hey, you're the one who told off the doc. Glad to fly with you, sir."

Of course, the flight surgeon had been right; he knew his job. Dugas had never seriously entertained the possibility that he might fly again. I used to see him pushing a big broom across hangar floors or, covered with grease, staggering across the tarmac with buckets of old oil. He was dressed in filthy fatigues and a floppy hat and he looked exactly like what the air force wanted him to look like, a derelict, that half amusing, half repugnant sad sack. I don't remember that we ever spoke to each other again except in the most casual way and under circumstances when a greeting could not be avoided. "How you doing, Dugas?" "Okay, Captain, can't complain. How you doing, Captain?" These were very painful confrontations and we could hardly bear to look into one another's faces for what lay between us, that thing that we couldn't talk about, our own secret awareness of the cowardices that directed our actions. Dugas wanted to live more than he wanted to be respected by his peers; I had to conform and do what was expected of me. The difference between us was that my cowardice was defined as courage, and his decision to walk away from the war was something that I didn't have the courage even to imagine.

A year after combat I was sitting in the office of a desk-bound colonel in Texas as he tried to fit me into a non-combat slot. The war in Europe was over now and within a month the bombs of Hiroshima and Nagasaki would end that other war that kept us all in uniform and saved us from having to consider a civilian future that promised few of the delights we had imagined years before. We had gone into the army as young men and would be getting out middle-aged. My army record lay before the colonel, that secret record which evaluated my five years in the army and which I had never been allowed to see. But now the colonel was called out of the office, and I quickly got up and stood before this folder that he had forgotten to close. I don't remember what qualities I had been granted by my commanding officers, except that leadership was not among them. There it was, a long row of neatly checked off appraisals by the twenty or so men who had commanded me since 1940. Some I had never seen and most of them had never seen me, and yet they had all checked off the same thing: I had no qualities of leadership. I went back to my chair and sat down and, until I thought about it, felt a kind of outrage.

Considering my career realistically, the truth was that I had only had two chances to exercise my qualities of leadership. When I yelled at Miller to "fly straight and level you stupid son of a bitch" I had shone at my brightest, a true Napoleon. That other moment — two hours earlier when, whispering to myself, "I'm in charge here," I had crawled back toward the nose and ordered the pilot of our flak-sieved plane to land on the nearest airfield — had ended a little less brilliantly. Yelling at Miller had been inspired by pure rage, and I had always been a little proud, even though I outranked him, of the contemptuous way I had dominated that silly bastard. But that other little foray into leadership had turned out to have consequences. By ordering our B-17 onto an English fighter field hundreds of miles from our own base I had made it necessary to send whole squads of mechanics there to repair the plane. It had over three hundred holes in it, without counting that piece of steel that flashed between the bombardier's seat and the bombardier's ass, neatly slicing through all the combat clothing but somehow missing flesh. And finally, the most awkward development of all: when the plane had finally been repaired someone pointed out that the runway was too short for a safe takeoff. It was a million-dollar fuckup. I would like to feel that our old bomber is still sitting in the high grass up there on the south English coast someplace, high up on a bluff with its poor old battered nose proudly facing across the Channel toward the flak guns that brought it down. In my imagination I can see that trusting hulk, a nesting place for birds and field mice, a playground for children and lovers, a monument to my genius, that ability to make quick, whip-like decisions that might have, had I been given the opportunity, lost us the war.

20

D<small>AVIS, WHO WAS NOW A MAJOR,</small> came to my room one night and asked me if I would walk outside with him. We stood in the darkness on the sidewalk and, in a low voice, he broke the rules of secrecy and told me that the next few missions would probably be milk runs. High-flying photographic planes had cruised the European coast and pinpointed the V-1 launching sites. "Nothing official, you understand, pure scuttlebutt, but I think the next few missions are going to be short and sweet. The coastal rocket sites, in and out, wham bam, thank you ma'am. I suspect we'll miss them but get an A for effort. I know you've got some leave coming and that you'd probably prefer not to fly for a time, so I'll leave it up to you. If you want, I'll put down for leave; if you want, I'll keep you on call."

What I wanted more than anything in life was simply not to have to fly for a while. I had completed fifteen missions, I was halfway through, and I was convinced that my luck was running out. If I had any long range plans they did not involve much more than the next couple of weeks. All I wanted was to be alone, to be away from soldiers and the sounds of revving engines. I thought of the big, half empty London theaters that opened at noon, and I dreamed of spending whole days in their womb-like darknesses staring at Rita Hayworth and the way her hair swirled when she tossed her head — the wide, brilliant, beautiful smile that almost flooded her face with intelligence. And so I hesitated a long time until Davis said, "Well, if you could let me know — soon. In the morning?"

"Keep me on status," I said. "I'd be delighted to fly a few four-hour missions for a change — though maybe delighted isn't exactly the right word. But listen, John, that major with the little blond mustache, the one who sleeps in my room, I don't want to fly with him."

"Why not?"

"He's no good for pinpoint bombing, John. He goes ape-shit over the target. Last time he refused to connect the automatic pilot and there we were, floundering around from the IP while he was making manual corrections off the bombsight."

"Oh, shit, why didn't you tell me?"

"Well, I'm telling you. That bastard has no business in the lead plane."

"And how would you like him flying off your wing?" Davis asked, shaking his head. "Well, okay, I'll try to keep him off these subtle little pinpoint flights that I think are coming up. But look, M., I can't guarantee nothin', so don't blame me if the next ten missions head for Berlin."

"Okay, John, I understand. And thanks."

"And for Christ's sake, not a word, you understand; I have not talked to you."

The next day we bombed a rocket site. The target was small, hard to find, and almost impossible to hit — a short, gleaming white launching ramp that began in a cave carved from a French cliff. From eighteen thousand feet the ramps looked like strips of paper laid out in radii whose center when extended was London. It was like one of my first missions with its overtones of tourism — sparkling sunlight on the sea and the resort towns spread along the sandy beaches that held the great hotels I had read about in Proust. England was never far out of sight and hundreds of American fighters went in and out with us to protect us from the German fighters (who failed to show). But today, as though I had lost some vital resistance, the cold of high altitude, forty or fifty below zero, chilled me to the bone. My hands shook, and I sat through the flight in a kind of terrified apprehension, dead to the grandeur of altitude and the immense views. What terrified me more than anything, a terror that had grown steadily since the first mission, was my real horror of crawling alone into the darkness of the bomb bay and arming the bombs. This was my job once we had left England, doing that little something to the nose of each bomb that I can no longer remember, but that brought those thousand-pound lumps of steel and gunpowder to life. Back in the nose I could feel the pulsing behind me in the plane's belly, feel the menace of those black squat presences, ready, I was sure, to detonate at any moment.

On another day, another thirty-mile cruise across the Channel to the coast: these short, jabbing missions were like an interlude between the fear that so far I had handled and the big horrors ahead that would crack me open. I saw these flights in musical terms when I was half asleep; they were like little pastoral themes that I knew would develop later into a great discordant apocalyptic howling; these missions came too late to give me much pleasure except for their shortness and the exhausted relief that came at night as I mentally crossed off missions. The sixteenth mission, fourteen more to go; the seventeenth mission, thirteen more to go. Trying to sleep, I counted missions instead of sheep.

Out of habit I still watched the bombs as they fell below the plane, but it had been some time since their point of impact had been of intense interest. Peering miles down through summer haze until red flashes flared at the centers of blossoming smoke, I studied the pattern that the bombs made. I was a craftsman appraising the quality of my work. A tight round pattern meant that all the bombardiers behind me had toggled out their bombs in the same instant when they had seen my bombs leave the plane. Sometimes we hit targets, more often we missed; it didn't matter much what happened to the target if the pattern was good.

Sometimes the bomb patterns were as strung out and irrational as the yellow stains in snow made by a man who dances wildly while pissing. The air force, though they never told us except indirectly in newspaper headlines, had realized that pinpoint bombing was an illusion. Tonnage was the big word now, so many thousands of tons of bombs dropped on a raid over the Ruhr or Berlin. So many thousands of planes pounding at Germany. Well, yes, if you were an hour into Germany it was hard to miss. It was even hard to miss Berlin, though I am one of the few who managed it. Leading a couple of hundred bombers one day in heavy overcast, I overshot the city by seven miles and we dropped our bombs in what looked like — from four miles up and through a hole in the clouds — a great field of cabbages. I had wasted another million dollars of the taxpayers' money and perhaps thirty or forty lives, but no one ever said a word.

Did we hit the rocket launching sites? I don't remember. My lack of memory on this point probably has dismal connotations.

Up until now I have been trying to write as though the months in England had a certain flow — or at least as though I might impose a kind of order onto combat. I have never really understood what happened to me during that time, but I have wanted to believe that connecting the re-membered episodes — like connecting the numbers on a child's cartoon with a pencil — will reveal some hidden figure; I would finally discover some secret meaning. But now I have come to a point where my mem-ory of combat is full of blanks and resistances, and trying to remember its continuity is like trying to remember the precise order of fireworks blaz-ing and dying in a night sky. I sit here peering into the emptiness of forgotten time, thinking, "If you look deeply enough it will all come back," but what comes back is only a great confusion of disconnected and irrelevant images — a bang here, a bang there, the view from a win-dow at evening of lines of large black birds flying across the sky, a stretch of road on the way to Cambridge where I am bicycling up to see a uni-versity production of *Medea*, Oates coming back from Cambridge one day to tell me he had met a Texas historian turned into a visiting Cam-bridge professor, the smell of an English graveyard, the sight of a half dozen Italian POWs weeding strawberries on a local farm. And all of this is seen through a remembrance of depression. (Was I thinking of suicide as I watched those dismal birds flapping toward the belfry of some church?) How sad I am now at sixty-seven when I try to return and am infected with that deep mood of futility, walking through a fog that twists and obliterates the details that I need.

And I am beginning to catch myself in lies. A few nights after I wrote about Jones's funeral, lying in bed, trying to sleep, and trying to think of nothing, suddenly, stretched across my mind like a snapshot in true color, I see our crew sitting in the command car that is taking us south for the burial service. In the background at a crossroads, half obliterated by a fig-ure in the front seat, we pass in brilliant sunshine one of those pretentious English country pubs, white-fronted and crisscrossed with exposed and blackened beams. The figure in the front seat turns, smiling, and I am jolted fully awake. It is Wylie, it is unmistakably Wylie, who has turned to say something funny or to ask, What do you think? Shall we have another glass of bitter? It is startling to realize that I have been be-trayed in something that was so plainly chronological, that I am not remembering truly. If Wylie died after Jones, then Wylie must have been flying that day when the flak exploded against our plane, and if we were flying as a crew this can only mean that I was not in the lead plane; we were flying off someone's wing. Why had Wylie disappeared from the memory of that day, a day so intense and awful that I had always thought that every detail might be dragged up from out of the past whenever I should need it?

I am lying, too, about the rocket launching sites. Until almost today I had remembered those vaguely lyrical missions as having taken place immediately before the June sixth invasion of Europe. It suddenly occurs to me that this was impossible, that it was French bridges that we bombed in the last days of May and the first days of June. The point of this effort was, of course, to isolate the German armies and make it impossible for them to concentrate in Normandy before an Allied bridgehead could be secured.

All of this account has been aiming toward D day. The month of June was symbolically and realistically that month when all of us who flew began to reappraise our combat roles. The rest of the war belonged to the foot soldiers, and D day seems to me to mark that point when all the glamor leaked out of the combat flier's job. For several reasons.

A war correspondent named Ernie Pyle, who lived with the ground troops and was filled with pity and admiration for the infantryman, had spent a few days before the invasion with the air force. The strong brick houses, our warm beds, hot showers, and good food disgusted him; he couldn't help but compare the way we lived and the few hours each month when we were shot at with the brutal living conditions of the ground troops who slept in hayricks or slit trenches half full of water, who ate canned C rations, went weeks without bathing, and who endured appalling boredom month after month. In his newspaper column he publicly denigrated the air force, suggesting we were all fops and knaves; he went back to the ground troops and left us to our degenerate way of life. Ernie Pyle was an immensely popular and powerful shaper of opinion, though many of us had not needed his needling voice to make us uncertain and half ashamed of the way we lived. When he was killed in combat, we mourned him even though he didn't like us.

I had always been uncomfortable having an enlisted man to stoke the furnace in the lead house, to shine my shoes, buy my whiskey or wander the countryside looking for the black market eggs that each of us carried each morning, precious as gold, to the mess hall to be fried or scrambled. Our orderly was a middle-aged man who slept in a broom closet on the first floor next to an unused kitchen, and I saw him as a kind of aging Cinderella, completely isolated from the enlisted men, sleeping in the ashes, enduring that drab's life, and whose coach, if it ever came, would be pure pumpkin. In reality, I suppose, being sensible and down-to-earth, he longed for glory about as passionately as Dugas. He used to weep uncontrollably when one of us was shot down.

I had also been uncomfortable receiving the starry-eyed admiration of the cooks and waiters who, it seemed, considered themselves blessed in being able to serve us. We could make a messboy's day by throwing him a smile or addressing to him a few banal but friendly words. To meet a dogface private in a London bar and have him begin to express awe and admiration for the air force made me squirm with self-loathing. I knew my peril, but it seemed like nothing beside the plodding endurance and the patient suffering of the infantryman. Our mouths loosened with whiskey, we admired each other extravagantly, but I felt like a fake, a man loved for the wrong reasons.

By D day it was apparent to all of us who flew that our pinpoint bombing was a failure. Like the British with their massive night raids aimed at whole cities, our work was only effective on immense targets, but for those of us who were sent out to bomb cities already three-quarters reduced to rubble, it was only our violent hatred of Germans that kept us from judging our actions and admitting that they were as mean, brutal, wicked, and basically non-strategic as the Nazi Luftwaffe's horror raids. If we could blow up a railroad yard or a factory, fine, but our main job now was simply to spread terror.

Early in the morning of June sixth, a date as famous in the war as Pearl Harbor or Hiroshima, a light wind was blowing from east to west across Normandy; it was this wind and what it did that put a final end to our glamorous pretentions. It slowly moved the line of smoke, which had been laid down by the first planes and into which we had been directed to aim our bombs, across that fiercely contested territory where the Allied troops had advanced from the beaches. Paratroops were setting up positions in the orchards and in the hedgerows. By noon the Eighth Air Force, going in again in waves of thousands of bombers, was dropping bombs into the American lines. For months after that those of us with our wings and ribbons and our fancy squashed-down caps walked in shame and trepidation through the streets of London. All through the warmest days of summer we wore the overcoats that concealed our flying status. MPs now began to hassle me, handing out chits that I ignored, but that damned me for being out of uniform. (I had lost the belt to my overcoat.) Combat infantrymen and paratroopers spending a few days on furlough, their faces exhausted and drained, gave me cold looks in the street. Some of them would turn away when we passed on the sidewalk, depriving my uniform of the salute that it deserved; others, more full of resentments, would pretend to salute and instead, while I saluted them, would scratch their ears and shoot me a look of insolence, daring me to make something of it.

So. Via the rocket launching sites, I have come by the wrong road to D day. At least we're there, or almost. If I can't remember much about that day, at least my memory has been reinforced by the innumerable movies about it. But in the months that follow everything is vague and confused. I have thought of the past as a brightly lit building through which I might wander, but someone in the upper stories has begun turning off the lights. When I peer back, searching for a glimpse of something typical, more often than not I see myself lying on an army cot in the fetal position with the blinds drawn. In a drawer all to itself the combat shirt, now black and stinking, is an overpowering presence in that quiet room. Perhaps if I write of combat in the disconnected way that I remember it, I will be more honestly describing my own growing desperation and the dull insane quality of my war's last months.

Out of dozens of letters that I wrote my mother as a soldier, let me test your patience with a single one. It is the least boring of that whole bunch, which she saved like holy relics and sent me a few months ago to help me with my failing memory. This letter would seem to indicate that I was at the apex of my Ernest Hemingway phase and that I took a certain satisfaction in trying to scare the home folks. It was written just a few days before the invasion and just a few days after Jones was killed. I can think of no other occasion when I might have gone back into the waist without my parachute. And so it seems to me now that far from being a callous letter written to terrify, it was, on the contrary, news from the front that spared my mother as much as I could spare her while still trying to prepare her for the certain death that I expected.

May 20th

Dear Maw:

Your letter number five has just arrived, a little behind number six, if I remember correctly; thank you for writing so often, but I am feeling guilty from hearing from you so often when I realize how much you hate writing letters; so don't knock yourself out doing it, just when you are in the mood.

Anne wrote me giving me hell for writing letters that make you worry. I am sorry; she didn't say which letter it was so I don't know what I said; whatever it was, well, whatever it was don't worry about it; that won't do anybody any good, etc. I guess I wrote you that I was squadron bombardier; I am still sweating out my first ride, as such. Thought last night that I was to lead and spent a sleepless night, only to discover at briefing time that our group was leading the wing and didn't need me; what a relief; I went to sleep then, all my worries gone, as though tomorrow or the next day I wouldn't be up there looking for the target, trying to remember switches, bubbles, knobs and gears. Doors, etc. I haven't noticed but they tell me that when the bombardier looks through the telescope at the target, it magnifies the flak and makes it look twice as big and close. About that time your brave son will probably bail out of the ship, screaming. On missions we are torn between our love of flak vests and our parachutes; since we can't wear them together it takes a subtle perception to know when to ungird your armor and get ready to jump. I am not too subtle yet but I have made the change — though when things were really rough I was so worried about the crew that I didn't remember to even take my chute back when there was someone with a piece of flak in him. . . . I wish I had your warrior blood; it would make it much easier to go out. But what we are doing is not pretty. The only battle any of us is fighting is the battle with common sense that says, "Get out while you can." And each mission is harder to face. The ones with a few missions in are all neurasthenic; the raids actually are no harder, they are simply harder to accept, and the greatest courage one can have here is to accept it when it seems impossible; there are many who do and many who don't, and there is no question in anyone's mind that those who don't are simply suffering more than they can bear; what a bunch of neurotics we will all be from this hash; can't you hear us screaming when a door slams; I have been at that stage for some time, and take an intense literary interest in watching myself slowly go to pieces. It is really fascinating, and I am serious. I guess I have written you this before, but you mustn't worry or feel sorry for me, because (wanting to be a writer) I am getting what I want, and what I want is to go through everything, every bit of hell there is; don't you see how lucky you are to have such a screwy son? What happens to the mind, the body, how do you face death and the death of others, and what are the compensations; no one will ever know who doesn't go through it, and no one can honestly hate war until he has bloodied his hands with it. . . . etc., etc., etc. I don't know why my letters get in such a rut; you asked me to tell you everything, and since I can't and evade the censors (they are getting very strict) about all I can do is generalize. Well, gotta drop some practice bombs.

Love, *M.*

Yesterday, as I sat copying this letter into the manuscript and came to that line, "I wish I had your warrior blood" (what did I mean when I wrote that almost fifty years ago?), a light suddenly flashed on and I was confronted with the long forgotten feelings that I had had for my mother during the war. They were complicated — full of awe and re-sentment. No wonder I had buried them so deep, amazing that I have resurrected them now so easily, without trying, without wanting to. I read the letter again almost remembering exactly how I had felt when I wrote it, and my mother springs to life as she was in 1942 when she was forty-five and I was twenty-six. (No, that letter I defended yesterday as having been written to spare — between the lines it was cold and mean.)

In the years before the war my mother had settled down to a decently plodding life. Her second divorce was behind her and she lived in her own home with my half sister in Sausalito and worked in San Francisco as a kind of non-technical dental technician. (She took color pho-tographs of people's teeth and had studied photography for a time with

Ansel Adams.) I admired her liveliness, her independence, and her open mind. She pretended to be fed up with men, but men were always falling in love with her, and I admired the way she handled them. I saw her seldom, no more than a week or two each year, since I lived with my father in Seattle and part of his meanness was to keep us apart. I could never remember her as having fulfilled motherly duties, and I thought with some part of my mind that her divorce, scandalous and bitter, had in a good sense freed both of us from those family complications, those squalid family hypocrisies that I had learned to detest; she had always been more friend than mother, and on my yearly visits she planned wonderful trips to Yosemite, or the Russian River, or the Geysers.

The war came and inflamed her passions; she was at that certain age, I guess, when the future rolled out ahead of her endlessly dull. She thirsted to be involved in the pulsing history of those times. It was her last chance to live. She quit her job, put her daughter in a nursing school, and signed up as a waitress for the captain's table on a Norwegian freighter that hauled ammunition and airplane parts to some of the still unconquered islands in the South Pacific. In those days only the strongest, only the most fiercely independent of women would have dared move into that man's world of danger.

By the time of her return, the war in the Pacific had become much more hazardous and the ship's captain, who I suspect had fallen in love with my mother, refused to sign her on again. She got a job as a nurse in an army hospital that hung on the cliffs underneath the Golden Gate Bridge and put in twelve-hour days all through the war caring for the wounded of Guadalcanal, Saipan, all those bloody islands. I was a cadet in pilot training by this time and stationed within a few miles of San Francisco, and so I saw her almost every month. That trip to the South Pacific had left her fifteen pounds lighter, ten years younger. Her eyes flashed, her step was quick and light, she began to wear red dresses again, and it seemed to me that I couldn't remember that she had ever laughed so much. The war had aroused her deepest emotions, had brought her to the same pitch of involvement that she had displayed as a Red Cross ambulance driver in the First World War. Her flashing eyes and her laughter bothered me. Had she so easily forgotten those friends in 1917 who came back from France with their lungs destroyed by gas, the ones who came back as drunkards, the ones who committed suicide? The few times I met my mother after her work and she suggested that we have a drink in some bar before going home or out for dinner, like as not she would end up buying rounds of drinks for the soldiers at the next table. It was bad enough sitting in a bar with my mother while she tossed down a couple of straight shots of bourbon, but almost unsupportable when she began to play housemother to the troops. She had a terrible way with soldiers; in that barroom ambience and on a superficial level she was irresistible.

There is a vague unseemliness in this almost sexual arousal that captures women in wartime — that puts color in the cheeks, a sparkle in the eyes, this latent chauvinism that infects the soul and awakens an impulse to make wild sacrifices. Of course, my mother was proud of me, she was proud of everyone in uniform. What more than her pride of me did I need from her? In the deepest, most secret part of that still living and frustrated child, I still at times almost hated her for having left my father when I was six years old. I suppose what I needed from my mother was some undeniable proof that she loved me, something grander and more shameless than her pride. I suppose what I really wanted was my mother on her knees before me, grabbing at my legs with the tears streaming out of her eyes, shrieking, "Don't go. I can't bear to have you go." I would have gone, of course, but purged by the knowledge that she loved me more than her honor or even mine. It would be another twenty years and in another war before women would be strong and angry enough to deny their sons to the military, before they would empty their savings accounts and send their sons off to Canada or England.

It is there still, that little separateness between us, that mean little disappointment that my mother, her face dazed with patriotic ardor, could so bravely have let me go. The light in this room is dim and poisonous; let us wander through the halls looking for a place more decently illuminated.

D day, that billion-dollar spectacle. We flew across the Channel, passing over Bournemouth in an endless line of bombers; there were thousands of us in the air. What a miracle of planning just to get us in, get us over a target, and get us back. Wave after wave of bombers. There was no way to stop us when we began to bomb our own troops. Below us the sea was thick with every kind of boat, and off Omaha beach thousands of craft were drifting a mile or two offshore, waiting. Flash of guns, puffs of drifting smoke. From three miles up waves broke on a beach that looked deserted; from three miles up there were no sounds of war above the roaring of the engines. . . . John Wayne, his jaws clenching and unclenching as though he were chewing bubble gum, studies the shore, the spouting geysers, the flashes of flame from the German bunkers, and plunges into the surf. Lee Marvin, a cigarette dangling from his mouth, stands up, contemptuous of the bullets, and with a sardonic smile drawls, "Okay, you guys, this is it." Just behind him the good nigger, Jim Brown, miraculously translated from the Liverpool docks where he unloads cargo to a sergeant in an all white outfit, adjusts his helmet, smiles with teeth as bright as God's own, and joins his white buddy.

Whoops, wrong room. How did I get in here without a ticket?

I truly remember only three things about that day:

As we leave England I switch my radio from intercom to Armed Forces. It is carrying Eisenhower's announcement to Europe that the invasion has begun. It is a good speech, being short, but it is played over and over at ten minute intervals. In the spaces between the speech Harry James's recording of "Sleepy Lagoon" makes a bizarre accompaniment to the waves and the curving white wakes of the boats below. The purity of those trumpet solos lives in my memory much more clearly than anything Eisenhower said. On another wavelength the BBC has come out of the closet and without code is sending instructions to units of the French Resistance.

Coming in across the countryside, I remember that tremendously long line of smoke into which we bombed, not knowing at the time, of course, that we were bombing our own men. The smoke was so thick that the bombs fell into it and disappeared. That day of all days I wanted to see the flash of my own bombs killing Germans, and then to have them vanish without a trace — it gave me the disquieting feeling that the bombs were duds or that I had failed to properly arm them. Everything that day was too big, too monumental, and I think many of us in the air looking down at the action began to realize that we were more or less irrelevant and that the war now belonged to the ground troops.

A few miles into France, and before we began that slow wide circle that would take us back, we flew over a small town. I think it was Saint-

Lô. I remembered it from another day when we had bombed bridges —
a spired church, small stone cottages with orchards behind them, narrow
streets, clumps of great trees. Now it was gone; everything had been
blown up. In the center of the place where the town had stood, where
the church had stood, there was nothing but a glistening white pile of
something that shone in the sun like sugar.

21

A HOT, CLEAR DAY IN JUNE; deep pools of shade under the double line of oaks that leads to the castle. Burt, one of my new friends, has come to my room and begged me to come with him out into the sun. The bicycles we bought in April have long since been stolen and so we steal a couple that are lying in the grass outside the lead house and cycle up the road toward Cambridge. In front of a farm house, Italian POWs are laying down straw between rows of strawberries, and we stop and buy a dozen boxes from them. It can't be true, but I remember the Italians as having been dressed in a loose material that looked like flour sacks; their shirts had big black identifying letters stenciled across their backs. They were reluctant to look into our faces. Well, we were reluctant to look into theirs. We bike a little further, to the oaks, sit in the sun, eat strawberries, and talk earnestly of the war. The memory of this afternoon is clear and intense — probably because a little later Burt wrote a book about it.

Burt was a copilot replacement, one member of a new bunch of combat crews who had arrived toward the end of May. He was a writer of short stories, and we had become acquainted almost immediately. Poor Burt; there was probably no one in all the air forces of the world less fit to be a combat flier. He was a very young man with intense ambition, the strongest will, and the fanatic drive to accomplish every one of his unrealistic fantasies. Burt was small and his cheeks blazed with a high unnatural color; he had a high voice and a laugh that was a kind of high nervous shriek. He had wide hips and small hands that fluttered effeminately when he spoke of things that interested him. And here is what was probably most impressive about him — that God had constructed him to be a woman and at some point in his life he had stared down God. He had denied his destiny. It may have been as straightforward as that: Burt one day facing his own impulses and the rather grotesque body that enclosed him, and shouting into the sky, "Screw you, God, I am going to be a man."

Burt surely was a man, though not even he, willing with everything, could turn himself into a good flier. It was as though when he had been given his three wishes, he'd wished to be a combat pilot and had forgotten to mention that he wanted to be a good one. It was not that he was afraid or timid on the controls; it was simply a question of coordination. His hands and feet did not make contact with the soul of the plane. At one level he had learned everything that the air force could teach him; on another level his youth, his appalling enthusiasm, and his romantic tendencies had opened him up to the drama of the bombers — the roar of the engines, those dawn takeoffs, the boiling cumulus through which he flew. But at his core something was missing that he could not manufacture out of his determination.

He flew bravely but so badly that finally no one wanted to fly with him, and toward the end of his tour in bombers he would be assigned to the tail gunner's position in the lead plane and asked to take notes on the quality of the pilot's formation flying.

It was unbelievable that he had made it through pilot training and had been sent into combat, but no more unbelievable than his adolescent dream to become a famous writer. If that had been his second wish he had screwed up again: he had asked to be a famous writer instead of a good one.

He had grown up on a cattle ranch in the Colorado mountains, an English teacher in a sixth grade class had praised one of his essays, and he had got it into his head that he was going to write. Before he was seventeen he left home and hitchhiked to Boston. Let us imagine him there and ringing the doorbell of a house whose address he has somehow gotten hold of — grimy with travel, his cowboy boots worn and dusty, his red cheeks blazing, and his limbs, as they tended to do when he was overcome with emotion, beginning to jerk in an almost spastic way. He has come with not much more than a briefcase of short stories, and he is ringing the doorbell of J. P. Marquand, no less, a man who at that time was perhaps the most highly paid writer in America. Let me imagine Marquand in a dark silk dressing gown standing there in the morning sun and contemplating this somewhat weird figure who has come to him out of the western sage. "I am going to be a writer, sir, and I want to learn from you. I can help you — cut lawns, do your typing, help out in the kitchen. I will do anything if you will teach me." "I don't teach," Marquand said. "You're barking up the wrong tree, son." "You're the greatest writer in America," Burt said. "You are the only teacher I want." "Well, as long as you're here, come in for a cup of coffee, but then, young man, you're going to have to leave." I am making up this conversation, though not its essential thrust; but how can one invent such an improbable scenario — and its incredible conclusion. I read some of those first stories, and they were pretty bad, and since they showed such a minimum amount of talent it must have been Burt himself with his absolutely unswerving and fanatic determination that impressed Marquand. Before that morning was over Burt had moved into the Marquand garage, and he stayed there, I think, with not much more than a bed and a table, until he was drafted into the army. I don't know how long that was, perhaps it was more than a year, but now what a happy ending to this tale. Before he went into pilot training he had been taken on by Marquand's literary agent and had sold two stories to the *Saturday Evening Post*. I believe his agent's name was Max Brand, though it seems to me now, looking back to the forties, that all the best agents in New York at that time were named Max Brand, or some slight variation on the name.

It was June when we sat in the tall summer grass eating strawberries. How can I ever forget this only time in my life when I ate strawberries until they were coming out my ears? If it had not been for the book I would probably have forgotten everything but the buggy sounds of June and the sun shining through the leaves and the taste of childhood summers bursting in my mouth as we ate box after box of strawberries. Our bicycles were hidden, and we lay in the shade of a great oak, half concealed from that duchess who might at any moment have toured by in her Rolls Royce and, seeing us, demanded of God himself that we be struck dead for insolence.

It was late in October when Burt brought me the manuscript of the book that he had written. The autumn storms had come, and rain beat against the windows, and no matter how many lights were turned on, my room in the lead house was dark and full of shadows. It was the kind of darkness that made you wonder if you were not beginning to lose the sharpness of your vision. The manuscript was not very long, and I sat through an afternoon reading it. A few days later, looking for comments, Burt came back, and we had a conversation that I can still almost remember.

Part of it may have gone something like this (though since Burt gave himself all the good lines in his book, I fully intend to give myself the good lines in this one):

"Oh, you bastard, Burt; you set me up. You planned that whole day, didn't you?"

Burt laughed and shook his head. "Not true, not true."

"You had this cornball title, 'Salute to the Big Bird.' And, of course, you had to be the hero, so I get to wear the black hat and the black gloves. You get me out there and make me talk anti-America."

"No, M., I knew what I wanted to say. Putting you in, that idea came later. You were something perfect that fit in, a kind of tension I could push against. Making it a dialogue, putting it out under the trees, that all came later."

"Yeah, this cranky old bastard who keeps cutting you down, makes fun of glory and patriotism and the great aims of the war. How many times do you have me say that the war will solve nothing?"

"Just enough times to show you're wrong, M."

"And Jesus, Burt, you didn't even spell my name right; I got no P."

"Well, if it's not you, you can't sue, can you?" Burt said, smiling.

" 'Salute to the Big Bird' my ass. You're pimping for the air force, Burt. How the big birds won the war, fearless and dashing through flak and shit, straight for the target, unswerving. And everybody lives happily ever after."

"You think it won't sell? It's a book for the war effort, a book that people will want to read. The public deserves to feel pride. Why shouldn't people feel justified in the sacrifices they're making?"

"Sacrifices? What fucking sacrifices? This war is making everybody rich."

"Unless you're dead."

"Yeah, unless you're dead. But you know my theory: it takes an awful lot of blood to keep the system going, an awful lot of slavery, an awful lot of guys working for two bits an hour."

"We're going to change all that; isn't that what the war's all about?"

"Well, that's what your book's all about anyway. Win this war that's going to be the last one; win the war and save democracy. We'll change the school system and everybody's going to go to college. No more world hunger when we win the war, no more starving billions 'cause good old democracy's going to see that everybody gets his loaf of bread and a swell job in a factory with piped-in music. Democracy cares. No more radical discrimination, right, Burt? No more Ku Klux Klan, no more pogroms; never no more. Russia and America, they're good buddies now. We're all going to get together and change the system and peace will reign over all the earth. Praise God and the Eighth Air Force. Drunk dads won't beat up on their kids no more, will they, Burt? The rich boys will stop trying to screw the poor boys. Hot water in the jails and the whores come in on Sundays, hey, Burt? No more jerking off in the jails, no more buggery. Hooray for the Eighth Air Force; hooray for the big bird."

"Oh my God," Burt said. "Just because I spelled you name wrong."

We looked at each other and began to laugh. After a while Burt said, "You know, at times you sound like an anarchist. Don't you believe in democracy?"

"My father's got a bumper sticker on his car, Burt. It says, 'This is a republic, not a democracy, thank God!' Ten years ago in the Depression he lost his only million, but only four years of war and he's got it all back. How can we believe in democracy? It hasn't been tried for twenty-five hundred years. Look, I hate fascism, I hate communism, but to tell you the truth I sure got my doubts about American democracy. That sweet sweat-stained America that Whitman saw — what happened? That wonderful Jeffersonian yeomanry — where did it go? Listen, Burt, we're going to come out of this war as the most powerful nation in the world, and we're going to call it an empire not a democracy."

"No," Burt said, "I can't believe that this war is all for nothing."

"Well, you better start believing it, kiddo. World War One, World War Two, World War Three, World War Four. Oh man, Burt, number four is going to be a dandy."

"You're a fanatic," Burt said. "You're in love with despair. Those stories of yours, M. — sad second lieutenants walking around in the rain while the buildings crash down. Why do you write something like that when you know there's not a publisher in the United States would touch it with a ten-foot pole?"

"I though maybe *The New Yorker* . . ."

"*The New Yorker* doesn't want mobs of people carrying American flags to throw rocks through their windows, M. That stuff is subversive; it's against the war effort."

"It's not against the war effort, it's against war and the big lie that war solves problems. Burt, think hard. Don't send this stuff in to be published, because in ten years, kid, it will make you very ashamed."

"Let's be realistic," Burt said. "Let's be honest. You and I, we want to be writers, and for my part, at least, I'm damn well going to be. I'm going to be as good as the best: Zane Grey, Robert Ormond Case, Edison Marshall, Irvin Cobb. Look, we're not to blame for this fucking war. The war isn't your fault, it isn't my fault. But we're in it up to our asses, and if we can use it, why not? What extraordinary material, and who knows more about it than us? Nobody blames Hemingway because he's getting his nuts off on the war and because he's got a great thing going for him. . . . Oh, listen, M., do you want to meet him? I have a friend in London, a major in Public Information. Those two are very close. Did I tell you I sat just two tables over from him the other day? Big man, very impressive, hunched over his table, eats with real gusto. They say he's screwing some little blonde from *Time*. Martha Gellhorn's at another table with some correspondents very dramatically not seeing him. I was with this gal from the *London Times* and Gellhorn waved to her. You should think of your career, M.; you should get around and meet people."

Etc., etc., etc.

Burt finished up his bomber missions, and instead of going home he volunteered to fly a tour of duty in single-engine fighters. This kind of enthusiasm was unheard of; worrying about his career and chasing after fame had addled his brains. He must have used all his influence to get transferred to a P-51 squadron, but he was gathering combat material, he said, and I guess the air force loved his stories. Six months after I had returned to the States (going crazy in Texas again) I ran across Burt's latest story in the *Saturday Evening Post*. It was about a fighter pilot in P-51s, and it was well written, tense and lyrical. I had to admit it, he was learning to write; maybe finally he was even learning to fly. Some of the bang-bang stuff had a chilling immediacy. At the end of the story the hero for some reason sacrifices his life and dives, guns chattering, into a chaos of boiling smoke.

A month later Mr. Brand, Burt's literary agent, wrote me a letter beg-
ging me for details, if I had any, about the manner of Burt's death. All
Mr. Brand knew was that over France one morning his flight of P-51s
had bombed a freight train. Burt, flying low and last, had flown into a
black cloud that appeared before him as the train, fifty cars of German
ammunition, suddenly erupted in one great bang. Burt had, it turned
out, described with excruciating authenticity his own death; I could
only hope that in his last few seconds he was as filled with patriotic exultation as the hero of his story. Knowing Burt and his capacity to delude
himself, he probably was.

This story about Burt doesn't end until about fifteen years later; for
dramatic purposes it would be nice it there were a connection between
Burt and that night in the alfalfa field when, middle-aged and going
bankrupt, I fell to my knees in the mud and wept and screamed in anguish for the war and the friends I had lost. But searching back into the
past I can find no real connection, remembering only that it was a summer day when I walked into the Vina grocery store and saw among the
paperbacks in the rack by the counter a slim volume with B-17s wheeling through a flak-filled sky printed across its cover. A critic's blurb
hailed it as "Stupendous." It was Burt's shameful book, *Salute to the Big
Bird*.

We were sent out one day to bomb Munich. Assembling over England
the sky was clear, but an hour into France heavy cumulus clouds began
to build up. Above the clouds and off on the right as we entered Germany, the Swiss Alps, bright in their mantle of summer snow, floated in
the sky, blue-cold and monumental. The ground below us began to disappear in clouds, and by the time we reached Munich we only knew we
were there because of the few wild bursts of flak that exploded in black
puffs a thousand feet below us.

My pilot that day was our commanding officer, the twenty-five-year-
old colonel (who was shot down on another mission a few days later). I
didn't much want to bomb Munich; I had spent a Christmas there ten
years before and my memories of snow and horse-drawn sleighs with
bells and handsome young skiers and medieval grog shops where the
beer was marvelous still lived in my mind. On the whole I had hated

Germany and for a time I couldn't figure out why such a beautiful country had choked me up with so much resentment. Then I realized that the
reason I hated Germany was because there were so many Germans in it.
Still, Munich in the middle thirties seemed like a little center of anti-
Fascism. I had met some Germans there who said they hated Hitler, and
some who refused to walk up a certain street past a certain monument
where they would be obliged to execute a Fascist salute. I was relieved
when the colonel called me on the intercom and told me that Eighth Air
Force headquarters had just radioed in canceling the Munich mission
because of the overcast and freeing us to bomb targets of opportunity.

We flew north for an hour looking for something nice to destroy; the
overcast began to break up and the fields and forests of central Germany
appeared in patches between the high cloud walls. Finally, as we broke
out ahead of the weather and the sky became as clear as though it had
been swept, ahead of us we saw a town all red-tiled and orange and surrounded by miles of deep green fields. Coming upon it so suddenly out
of the clouds was like breaking through some time barrier into the past,
into the fourteenth century, into the illustrated fairy tales of my childhood where darling children with blond bangs and wooden shoes
herded geese through cobbled lanes and the jolly baker stood outside his
shop, his apron dusted with flour and sugar, and the little mermaid, every
step an agony, walked slowly toward the castle.

The colonel called in on the intercom. "Okay, there she is; we'll go in
on this one. You've got all the time in the world; make it good."

To bomb that little country town which under any circumstances
could not have been regarded as a military objective was, of course, out
of the question. But colonels still tended to terrify, and I said, "Yes, sir,"
knelt over the bombsight, and locked it onto the spires of the cathedral
that stood in the town's center. Through the bombsight the town leaped
out of the landscape enormously enlarged and wrenchingly vulnerable.
Impossible, impossible. The town was as perfect, as perfectly preserved, as
some rare and ancient and intricately carved chess set locked in the
vaults of a museum.

Kneeling in the nose of the plane I began searching wildly for some
substitute target, some little spot of German earth upon which one
might drop a hundred tons of bombs with a clear conscience. I could feel
the navigator's eyes on me, and I turned to look into his face which was

drawn and troubled. He came over, stood behind me, and stared down at the town. "You can't bomb that," he said. "I know it, for Christ's sake," I yelled. "But find me a target then." We were only two or three minutes from the town now; the windows in the old houses sparkled in the sun and straight lines of smoke from dozens of chimneys rose into the still air. All around the town there was nothing but open fields, and squared fields of trees, and four roads from the four directions coming in straight and true as though they were the only connection between the present and the past.

Tracing out one of the roads, the western one, my eyes were caught on a place where the road and a stream came together at almost ninety degrees. I pointed to it and yelled to the navigator. "Look, there's got to be a bridge out there; let's bomb that." He smiled and nodded and turned to his maps. Without considering that I was being insubordinate, I called the colonel and told him that the town didn't look very interesting militarily but that we had found a good bridge out on the left. "If we could bomb that, we can cut off all the traffic coming in from Berlin."

"Tie up the Berlin traffic?" the colonel asked, beginning to laugh. "Three mules, five wagons, two motorcycles? Look Thomsen, don't bullshit your old commanding officer; I can see that town, too. And you're right, we can't bomb it. So go ahead; cut off the Berlin traffic."

"Okay, then turn about twenty degrees left, sir, and then give me the plane, and colonel, sir, you are okay?"

"Roger," the colonel said, and then, "She's all yours." And we came in dozens upon dozens of bombers and bombed at a little one-way wooden bridge about thirty feet long out in the middle of the German cow pastures. If I remember correctly, we missed it, but then all of us tended to forget the irrelevant details of combat, and certainly whether or not we hit a target was the most inconsequential thing of all.

For years I remembered the name of that town that we hadn't bombed; for years, raging like God, I would address myself to the inhabitants of that town when I awoke at 3 A.M. and found myself fighting insomnia. "But for me, you lousy krauts . . . ," I would begin, because by that time, years after it was all over, it had sunk in that what we hadn't bombed had been the people. That day over Germany none of us had given a thought to the people who lived in the town. They had been spared a good bombing, or a bombing at least, by having had the luck to live in a medieval village of historic significance. A town with a high stone wall around it and a moat and red tiled roofs and a soaring cathedral at its center, a town where a little mermaid crippled with pain and love had slowly walked along those shaded lanes past ponds full of floating, brilliantly white swans and giant goldfish with gems for eyes.

Another mission to Munich. It is the same kind of a day with the same beautiful massed clouds boiling up and completely hiding the southern area of Germany. Once again at the last minute we are released by the chair-bound high mucky-mucks in London to wander the countryside like formations of buzzards looking for something to foul. Over a hidden Munich we make about a 120 degree turn that will take us back to England through Belgium.

The colonel is dead now, and today the crazy major who refused to fly on automatic pilot is leading the group. Someone has threatened him with a court-martial if he doesn't switch the automatic pilot into the bombsight when I tell him to. Every time a burst of flak explodes above the overcast, no matter that it is miles away, the crazy major engages in violent evasive action; he wheels to the right, to the left, he dives and climbs. This cleverness, he feels, will confuse the ground crew gunners, but he is so terrified and his flying is so wild and abrupt that all the other pilots, with their prejudices about being rammed, disperse. The formation becomes loose and ragged; it is the kind of formation that German fighters love to attack. Furious messages crackle back and forth between the planes; over Germany, apparently, it is legal to say things like, "What do you think you're doing, you fucking asshole?"

In retrospect, nothing strikes me as more insane than these two missions where faulty weather predictions sent hundreds of bombers to a city that couldn't be bombed, put thousands of men and millions of dollars worth of airplanes in danger, and where suddenly, and for absolutely no reason, I find myself leading hundreds of bombers with the freedom to pick out any target that strikes my fancy. If this is work that doesn't much touch my conscience, it is work that gives me no pleasure; I am handed in the most irresponsible way a terrible power that fulfills none of my needs, and by rejecting the satisfactions that this power might have given me, I reject, too, the ethical considerations that might be expected to go along with this responsibility. Those officers who had judged my qualities and filled out my fitness report were right: I had no neurotic need to lead. I have been out about twenty times now, and bombing at cities, factories, railroad yards, airfields, and bridges no longer has any reality. So few of these targets have much military importance; aerial bombardment, or at least the way we are handling it, has begun to seem totally irrelevant to the war. These exploding flashes of light on enemy territory which I now scarcely bother to observe are less satisfying than the little, popping flash of a one-hundred-pound practice bomb filled with sand and carrying three ounces of black powder that used to explode sweetly and silently in the California desert. What is real, or what I think is real until we break through a hole in the clouds a few miles ahead, is simply this: four miles below us is a country full of millions of people who would like to kill us. And: I am sitting in a tinpot plane that is full of armed bombs, desperately anxious to get rid of them in any way that could not be described as blatantly cowardly.

The major twists and lurches through the sky in a course so erratic that not even the navigator with his radio signals, his charts and pencils and rulers, knows exactly where we are. After a time, perhaps hours, perhaps days, a hole in the clouds appears over on the left. I am about to be tempted by Satan.

"Hey, major, there's a hole out there about ten miles. Do you want to take a look?"

"Okay, but you find something down there and bomb it if it's only a shithouse. I want to get rid of these bombs."

The major wheels violently and we approach this open spot; from a distance it is just a hole dark with cloud shadows and what looks at first like bare black earth. But nearer now, and suddenly the most dangerous and horrible part of Germany comes into bloodcurdling, shattering focus. A dozen tremendously tall smokestacks from which smoke pours; below them whole concentrated units of factories, great factories that cover acres of ground, miles of ground. The earth is black with massed buildings, railroad yards, winding highways and groups of workers' houses. Out of pure chance we have stumbled upon the center of the German war industry, the steel mills of Krupp. The fucking Ruhr.

I had read some of the radical writers who had prophesied that since so much of the Ruhr is owned by American millionaires and American corporations it will never be bombed by Allied planes, and surely as we approach these gigantic installations it does seem from altitude that they have gone through the war unscathed. There are no telltale pockmarks, no rain filled craters reflecting spots of silver sky, no shattered wreckage; the roofs of the building are all standing in neat rows; lines of trains stand in the marshaling yards.

My immediate reaction to this disgusting sight is one of exultation. I have become a fictional character in an epic. The smooth way we glide over the clouds, the gradual revealing of this tremendous target as the clouds part, reminds me of an identical scene in a war movie that had agitated my fantasies when I was a cadet in pilot training. Van Johnson with his cornfed 4-F face is piloting a reconnaissance plane over the Pacific; the sky is thick with clouds; but suddenly they slide away to reveal the entire Japanese fleet cruising below him. Before he crashes to glory he alerts the navy as he fights off and destroys a couple of hundred Nip Zeros. What crescendos on the sound track, what a glorious patriotic epiphany on the drums and trumpets.

Now, like Van Johnson, I am pierced through with warlike ardor. Down there, untouched, is the great target of the war; down there waiting to be locked into the bombsight is something at last that is really worth trying to destroy. It isn't just Germany and German arms and Herr Krupp's cannon factories that I lust to blast; it is the big shareholders, the partners in all the cartels, those manipulators whom the pacifist societies that bloomed in U.S. colleges of the thirties lumped together and cursed as the Merchants of Death. J.P. Morgan and Rockefeller, Dupont and U.S. Steel, they are down there too. It is war itself that I want to bomb, war itself that excites me to make some flamboyant and magnificent gesture. Already the portentous opening measures of Brahm's First Symphony have begun to play in the back of my mind and the great curtains are parting. I am going to be a hero.

"Okay, major, we've got ourselves a target. Remember what the man said and put me on automatic pilot."

"What have you got? I can't see from up here."

"Looks like some kind of factory," I said. I was damned if I would tell him that we were over the Ruhr for fear that he might pull rank on me and forbid me my chance at immortality.

"What kind of factory?"

"I'll tell you later, Major; now goddammit, put me on automatic pilot."

I open the bomb bay doors, and a moment later the planes in my flight snuggle up into a combat formation. I flick on a dozen switches, and the bombsight begins to throb and purr in my hands. "Okay, we're on the bomb run," I call up into the pilot's compartment. "Steady as she goes." We are going to have a long, straight run and plenty of time. I begin to sweat and tremble.

I stare down at the Ruhr through the bombsight, ready to freeze the crosshairs on the largest of the steel mills — and I see little flashes of flame among the trees at the towns' edges, flashes of flame between the factory buildings, blinking flashes by the thousands at the edges of a winding river, along the railroad tracks, in the cross streets, and along the highways. For about five seconds I watch this peculiar phenomenon without understanding what it means. In a way the scene below me, enormous as it is, is miniaturized by distance and looks as simplified and logical as a child's arrangement of trees, buildings, and choochoo trains set up on a table top. The twinkling flashes are like Christmas lights; they add a touch of festiveness — and then, my heart freezing, sobered to the bone, my patriotic emotions vanishing, I understand what I am looking at. We are being shot at by about fifty percent of the ack-ack guns in the Wehrmacht and in about ten seconds, ten thousand shells are going to start exploding among us.

"Turn, turn, turn," I scream into the intercom. "Out. Now. Out. Turn. Jesus Christ."

The major, thrown into a panic, not understanding anything but ready to be dominated, tips the plane on one wing and executes an indescribable maneuver that is like gaining and losing altitude at the same time. The planes behind us, their pilots confused and terrified, spread out raggedly. I toggle the switch that closes the bomb bay doors. "What's wrong, what's wrong?" the major yells, and as he asks, out on our right into that space that we had not quite entered, a field of flak, an overwhelming black field of flak, spreads out across the sky.

I have never felt anything but pride in that burst of sanity that must surely have saved lives. It was an action that Burt would describe later with admiration as "Creative Cowardice." For a few days I was a hero to the combat crews who had flown behind me. By knowing when to squeal and run I had accurately represented them.

An hour later, flying over a Belgium that is ninety percent covered with clouds and while the major and I are discussing with a touch of hysteria the probability that we will have to jettison our bombs in the Channel, a little hole appears in the overcast. In the center of the hole a large square brick building stands alone in green fields. "Bomb it," the major yells, "we got to get rid of these fucking bombs. Bomb it, bomb it." He calls in the planes and we assemble into a reasonably tight combat formation, open the bomb bays, and drop our load, hundreds of black, squat objects made roughly in the shape of rabbit turds. But we are lost and later photographic flights never find this building. For a few days I wondered what we had bombed that day: a hospital, a soldiers' barracks, a concentration camp, a shoe factory?

And I remember:

Staggering out of the briefing room and heading for the toilets. Many of us were programmed to have violent diarrheic cramps when the intelligence officer whisked away the curtain behind which had been hidden a map of Europe with the day's mission marked across it with red tape. Sadistic theater. When the curtain had been removed, whatever the target, there were always loud groans from the assembled crews, groans of despair and terror. "Our mission today, men, is the Messerschmidt plant at Posen." Or the experimental station at Peenemünde. Or the marshaling yards in the center of Berlin. The groans and cries were directly proportional to the length of the red ribbon.

The navigators and bombardiers were handed map kits — maps of Europe with the course laid out in crayon, photographs of the target, photographs of roads, buildings, or oddly shaped patches of forest that would help us find the target. The weatherman, pretending to know (or else why would he be a major instead of a Pfc.?) talked about clouds, high altitude winds, and weather fronts. But by then we were scarcely listening; our bowels in a terrible boiling revolt, in a total repudiation, had begun to make a statement. All we wanted to do was rush for the toilets before it was too late.

It is always 3 or 4 A.M., that most impossible time to have to face life. The naked light bulbs in the hallways seemed to have lost half their voltage; they were as dull as our bodies, which found it impossible to come fully awake at this frightful hour, at this unnatural and despairing hour when life itself seemed hopeless and hardly worth hanging on to. It was a time of such total exhaustion, such total vulnerability that, contemplating the endless hours ahead compounded of fear and boredom, it seemed impossible that we could gather together enough strength to endure them. Not even the naming of the target, which I remember now as a kind of psychic pistol shot, could fully activate the sluggish blood; our pounding hearts pumped a cold and thick molasses.

Off the hallway on the way to the toilets there are three small rooms rigged up in a raunchy way as counterfeit combat chapels. When the doors are left open you can look in and see rows of kneeling men, fully dressed for combat, their faces pale and rapt. A priest or a minister or a rabbi is giving them communion or praying or hearing confessions. It is terrible to see in that bad light men who believe in a God who forbids murder as they kneel and ask for mercy just before flying off to drop bombs on cities that are already half destroyed. After briefing you can either shit or pray. Ever since that day when the bombers had begun to explode and fall below our group, I had been furiously angry with that God whom I scarcely believed in. All that death, all that death. Why are You doing this to us? Why have You made us the way we are? Why, when life is so unspeakably foul, are we so terrified of being released from it?

Walking out of the briefing room and heading for the toilets one morning at three o'clock I was stopped at the doorway by an intelligence officer who had hopped off the stage to intercept me. I knew him very slightly; he had debriefed me a few times after missions, and I almost liked him for the human way his face had crumpled when he realized that Wylie had died. He was a man who could still weep. Now he grabbed my arm and smiled and said something to me in a low intimate voice as he walked with me to the door of the latrine. What he told me was something that I didn't hear or forgot immediately or was so anxious not to hear, or not understanding, I still couldn't bring myself to ask him to repeat it. He said something like this, "We've got the pictures they took after that raid you led on ——, and we've just got some new intelligence from the underground, too. A fantastically successful raid.

They report a probable —— dead. I imagine you'll be getting an extra DFC." He squeezed my arm and left me at the door where the combat officers were crowding past us, racing to empty themselves.

Completely forgotten now the name of the target; I can never drag that name back. Nor the number of dead that he mentioned. It was a number so unbelievable, so awful, that some part of my mind erected an instantaneous barrier against his words. I could hear a ringing in my ears that began as he spoke; I was like a radio being jammed with static. He had mentioned one of two numbers — he had said either 3,000 or 30,000.

I walked on into the toilet without speaking, locked myself in the last empty cubicle, and joined that long line of groaning men. How strange that this man whose eyes had filled with tears for the death of Wylie had been so elated by the deaths of thousands. How strange that I, who had been so much more deeply involved with these two events, felt scarcely anything at all.

22

SHORTLY BEFORE HEMINGWAY LIBERATED PARIS, the group came back from a mission to central France one afternoon with some wonderful photographs of bombs falling on a long cement bridge.

We were in deep summer, the river was low; it flowed slowly between long strips of sandy beach revealed by the falling water. Deep green (almost black) trees in the climax days of August bordered the beaches, and where the bridge ended on the side nearest Paris the heavily branched trees almost hid a small town whose white stone houses were lined up on each side of the road. Bridges are very hard to hit from high altitude — a little like trying to dirty a stretched thread with a one-ounce bag of horse manure dropped from the fifteenth floor. And so when the photographs were developed that showed tall geysers of water hiding the bridge and its collapse, someone in Public Information lost his cool and called the BBC.

The next morning a crew of BBC technicians had taken over one of our rooms and had set up equipment to record on a couple of 78 rpms the details of our brilliant bombing mission that had destroyed one of the last large bridges in that part of France, where large numbers of German troops were rushing here and there in an effort to frustrate the Allied invasion. As the bombardier who had led the group that day, I was allowed the starring role. I was asked to describe the action, but no words came and I asked that instead I be allowed to write my comments down and read them. "But of course; absolutely a wizard idea," one of the technicians said.

I composed a nicely modest two-minute speech, and it was recorded. Only the first sentence still lives in my mind; saying it to myself now forty years later, it has taken on the curious power of making me want to burst into tears. "It was a perfect day for bombing," I began — insane words as appropriate as the words of a lunatic who recounts his day's adventures by "It was a perfect day to rub shit in my hair."

That afternoon a P-38 reconnaissance plane coming in low above the river took a series of new photographs. Everyone, perhaps even Churchill, wanted to see the broken span, the isolated columns. But the new photographs revealed that the bridge still crossed the river. If the bombs had come close enough in the first combat photos to look like hits, it was simply the drama of those towering geysers of water. Big splashy water effects in the near vicinity, nothing more.

Public Information was embarrassed; they asked me to come over and examine the photographs that we had taken. It was the first time I had seen them, ten or twelve beautiful shots of a bridge that hadn't been hit being hit. I leafed through the series to the last one, stared at it for a full minute and handed them back. "You'd better call the BBC," I said. The last photograph had been taken by the last plane in the group. It showed all the bombs of all the planes, plus the bombs of the last plane — four explosions a hundred yards from the bomb pattern, four explosions among the trees and the country houses of that little village at the end of the bridge.

. . . And dead drunk at midnight, staggering down the hallway past the bar in the officers' club to the cement cubicles of the officers quarters. Oates, for some reason — probably simply wanting a room of his own — had gone back there to live. And I was looking for Oates.

At nine o'clock that evening Lt. Hamilton had knocked on my door and standing in the doorway, his face glowing with relief, told me that the next day's mission had been scrubbed on account of weather. By eleven o'clock, gulping glasses of scotch and water with Major Davis and Captain Hardister, I was stupid and properly nauseated. The room where we drank was blue with smoke. I had abused the magic qualities of whiskey in the last months and it no longer released me into a careless attitude toward the combat situation. Now getting drunk turned me solemn and tragic. Awful apprehensions slowly coiled in my guts, intimations of disaster that were no longer alcohol soluble.

About midnight I became obsessed with the certainty that Hamilton had forgotten to inform Oates that he didn't have to fly in the morning. I imagined him sleepless in his room staring into the darkness and trembling with dread, and it was suddenly imperative that I give him the good news. It was senseless and vaguely masochistic to be cold sober on the night before a morning when you were not scheduled to fly — and especially after receiving the gift of a reprieve, a gift that would be for some an extra day of life. I poured the last of my whiskey (we always drank from our own bottles) into a glass and staggered outside and into a night that I was expecting to find sullen with gathering clouds. Momentarily I was sobered and left me gasping, as though the night like a cold ocean breaker had suddenly crashed over me as I stood drunken and stupid in the doorway of the lead house. It was a night of such rare and extraordinary clarity and calm that it seemed to redefine life in the pure terms with which I had defined it in my youth, not as this stinking trap into which we had been drawn, but as a stretch of time connected at both ends to eternity and boiling with noble possibilities. Not a sound from the hangars, not a single light in all that blacked-out countryside, nothing but wildly glittering stars and the dark shapes of trees and the still warm air of summer. Many of us from the West, who have spent hundreds of youthful nights sleeping in the mountains under the stars, spend the rest of our alienated lives longing to feel, if only for an instant, that only other thing beside the madness of sexual passion that gives meaning (or that we feel gives meaning) to our lives, those little unexpected moments when the landscape within which we find ourselves suddenly and for no reason opens up as though bursting and enfolds us. No longer a stranger, we become a part of everything, we belong where we are, held loosely in comradeship with the earth.

This was such a moment; I stood under the night and, forgiven, was accepted into the purity and serenity of the earth and the sky. And I remembered with a nostalgia that was pure anguish other similar nights, perhaps a dozen, camped by mountain lakes or streams or in high mountain meadows, when the perfection of the breathing earth had taken me in, had said, "See? Now you understand everything." I looked up at the sky, dazed with joy, for the certainty had burst in my head that this gift of unity with the earth could not possibly be given to someone immediately before being blasted from the sky by enemy guns. It seemed that I was being given in the clearest way the reassurance that I was not going to be killed in the war.

For perhaps a full minute I stood outside without moving, until the drunkenness came down again like a curtain, muddying my perceptions. I continued on my way through a night that, though still beautiful, no longer sent out mystical, intensely personal messages. Five minutes later I stood frozen with amazement and incredulity as I entered the officers' club, pushed through the blackout curtains and was shocked back to earth by the drunken shrieks and wild laughter of the combat officers. Apparently the postponement by one day of having to fly over Germany had created a kind of mass relief that could only be expressed by mob emotions. It was a celebration so tribal, and the relief which it offered so disproportionate to the prize (one more day of life), that walking unprepared into the action was like walking into the craziest section of an insane asylum. Like me, everyone had felt impelled to spend his reprieve in the stupidest way possible.

Across the wall behind the bar was a row of ceramic beer mugs with the names or initials of officers painted on them. Someone, some long-gone colonel months before, had tried to build tradition into the group. He suggested, in a way that was very much like an order, that each combat officer buy his own drinking mug. They would hang on the wall as though they had been there for years, like the personal mugs in some exclusive and eccentric gentlemen's club. By the time my crew arrived the custom had already about gone out of fashion. On one of my first evenings there, however, I had watched in mild disapproval, feeling like a western barbarian, as a very chic and languid pilot, a Princeton man as he was quick to point out, had brought in and left his own mug to sit with the others. It was silver, very handsome and probably at least nine thousand years old, and the young officer explained to us in a bored way that bitters, to truly savor its qualities, should never be drunk out of anything but a silver tankard. He was killed a couple of weeks later, and my only memory of him whenever I noticed his silver mug behind the bar, an abandoned aristocrat slumming with clay mugs, was a half-resentful one of this slightly decadent and foppish kid who had stopped among us for a time and tried to hone away our proletarian insensitivities. (He wore his handkerchief tucked into his sleeve in the British manner, and one evening some drunk captain — maybe it was Hudson — asked him if, wearing it there, he wasn't worried about getting snot on his arm.)

Before continuing on to look for Oates, who like me preferred to get drunk in his quarters, I pushed my way through to the bar and with eyes almost too blind to see, I studied that row of mugs. There were maybe thirty of them, every one of them, without exception, representing a dead man or an MIA. In the face of this more realistic message, that momentary conviction that I would survive the war began to take on a fictional air. Someone I can no longer can identify stood at my side. He weaved and staggered and studied the mugs with a solemn face. "Oh man," he said, "tombstones in the form of beer mugs. Now ain't that a pretty concept?"

"Profound symbolism," I said. "Didn't you know we're all 87% beer?"

"Not over Berlin, buddy, not over Berlin."

"No," I said, "that's not a beer situation. That's a 93% piss situation."

"Now ain't that the truth, buddy . . . Moburg says you pissed in his flak helmet last time over Krautland."

"Indeed I did, yes indeedy. An absolute necessity. But no harm done; he poured it out and wore it like a man. The purple flak helmet, that's what he won. At least in my book."

"Oh man, ain't it the truth, buddy. We're snafued, blued, glued, screwed and tattooed."

"Yeah, I would say that is a fairly accurate description of the present situation . . . And speaking of that, have you seen Oates? Does he know tomorrow's scrubbed?"

"Haven't seen Oatsie, and you will never guess who I just did see not two doors down from Oates' room."

"Okay, spare me the suspense. I give up; who?"

"Hey, speaking of piss; did Oates tell you he picked up this piece in Piccadilly and they walked out to the middle of the London Bridge and both peed in the river together."

"Yes," I said, "Oates told me. They pledged their troth and then crossed their streams in midair. It was a solemn and beautiful moment but the actual mechanics escapes me. I thought women had to squat."

"Oh, you fool, buddy. She just lay on her back, that's all."

"All I know is, it was solemn and beautiful. Cross-cultural in the most profound sense . . . And now, tell me. You saw *someone* near Oates's door? Do tell?"

"Without more ado, buddy, without more ado." He turned away from the contemplation of the beer mugs, noticed the glass of whiskey in my hand, took it from me, drank deeply, and then stared into my eyes. For a good thirty seconds. "I see you're ready . . . Hold your hat . . . Mr. and Mrs. Lyon."

I fell back a step in amazement and held my heart. "No *shit*," I cried. "Mr. and Mrs. Lyon from Regency Square, those dear creatures that run the little feather duster shop?"

"Oh buddy, buddy, at times I find your constant levity just a little hard to take. A joke is fine, I love a man with a sense of humor, but to make jokes about the Lyons? I think that is not strictly ticketyboo."

"My God," I said, "it's not the feather duster Lyons; well, I have come a cropper, old sport. But *who* then?"

"Never mind *who* then. I've said too much already. Walk up the hall and see for yourself. I hope you'll have the decency to blush . . . But no, you're right; I think we have been taken in by the Lyons. A confidence for you alone." He put an arm around my shoulder, grabbed my glass with his free hand and put his mouth to my ear. "The Lyons in my humble opinion are not really top-notch star material. Can you keep that to yourself?"

I nodded. "Guard it with my life."

"Well, yes, for what *that's* worth. Go now, buddy, go and sin no more. Regards to the Lyons. And remember the word."

"The word?"

"Yes. Mum. Mum's the word."

The hall was narrow and as long as eternity, two white cement walls fading away to a point like a first lesson in perspective and into which at regular intervals doors had been set. Its awful straightness spoke of the sterility of second-rate architects, technicians who were capable of any offense against the soul of man. Cold bright lights lit the whole length; walking down it, falling down into it, one could imagine the sound of rubber truncheons beating on flesh behind the closed doors. After the drunken babble in the officers' club, there was a decent silence here, if only comparative. Toward the far end of the hall in a kind of smoky mist, past the showers and the toilets and the closed doors, a group of officers came boiling out of a doorway, and as I approached them a woman dressed flamboyantly in bright, flowered silk could be seen through the men who were crowded around her. Even from a distance her face was familiar. Everything was still there in essence, aged and coarsened but instantly recognizable. All that was lacking was the familiar spit curl and the black dot of a beauty mark. My God, yes, of course; it was Mrs. Lyon, Mrs. Ben Lyon, known to her immense public as Bebe Daniels, famous film star of another era. Just inside the door, dressed in a flashy houndstooth jacket and holding a glass of whiskey, her husband. They were a part of my almost forgotten childhood, the ecstatic part where I had sneaked off from violin lessons or a swim in the YMCA pool to sit alone in some dingy movie house and walk hand in hand with these gaily glittering presences. But even then, forty years ago, my memory of them had begun to fade: Ben Lyon dressed as a World War One pilot with white silk scarf and tight-fitting leather helmet. Wasn't he the one, the hero's best friend, who was always shot down? And Bebe, dark-skinned, black-eyed, beauty-spotted, doing something Spanish on top of a table. Clicking castanets while crazed suitors drank from her slipper?

Now, as I approached them, I felt cheated, outraged by time's tricks. They were so old, so simply human. Bebe, retired one imagined, had become colossal. Her clashing theatrical dress called insistent attention to her large breasts; she had become motherly. Ben Lyon, with the crumpling face of an Orpheum circuit stand-up comic with an endless patter of dirty jokes, was standing a little apart, half ignored by these drunken lieutenants who were five years too young to have seen him swooping and diving in his open-air fighter. They lived in the neighborhood and close to Cambridge, and they had adopted the 91st Bomb Group as their contribution to the war effort. But seeing them that midnight (the only occasion I ever saw them, since they generally spent their time with the colonels), I got the impression that we were more important to their morales than they to ours. "No memory of having starred atones for later disregard."

"Good evening, Miss Daniels," I said as I squeezed past her.

"Dear boy," she answered, and a faint smile erased what had looked like a certain bitter sadness in her face. She looked into my eyes over her raised glass in what later, reliving the moment, I would interpret as an in-

timate gesture, a half-invitation to drink from the cup some magic po-
tion reserved for movie stars that would restore us to the way we wished
to see ourselves — innocent, cleansed of our terrors and our aching
sense of being deeply sunk in an evil business. Was it being dead drunk
that made me see so much in this banal, this much practiced gesture of
coquetry? It was languid, ironic, theatrical, but it had value, it stirred me
since I knew Miss Daniels had perfected and sharpened its power on the
likes of Ramon Novarro, Lew Ayres, Robert Montgomery.

"You realize, of course, that mum's the word," I said as I moved past
her.

"Well now, dear, *is* it?" she said.

I continue down the hallway, half in love now with that poor old lady
— and I walk through a time warp, and I can look back now at the very
moment when I disappeared. If I hang on to this memory and try to
slow it down into its parts, seeking by cunning and patience to dive
deeper and haul up that other drunker figure (Oates, my copilot), there
is still no way to reach the end of that hall, to reach the door of the room
where I will find him, perhaps like me, an empty bottle in his hand, an
empty expression on his face, lying fully clothed on his bed staring at the
ceiling. Or as I found him once lying there at the edge of unconscious-
ness, his eyes brimming over with tears as he composed terrible
Texas-style couplets about midair explosions.

Remembering.

Toward the end of the tour, as the number of completed missions slowly
approached the mystical thirty that would cancel out my own personal
rendezvous with eternity, I began to forget my bombing skills. Any little
step in the intricate choreography that wasn't completely automatic
might, as I aimed at a city, a factory, a bridge, or an airfield, fade from my
mind, or suddenly, like a curse, flash across my mind out of its proper order. The mistakes I made, or almost made, filled me with despair, they
were so hideous. Whatever my own personal feelings about the war, I
had no right to miss targets when the lives of hundreds of men were put
in peril. Today is the first time I have faced the extent to which my brains
were addled on the combat run to the target, the level of my basic incompetence under the pressure of terror.

On what turned out to be my last flight to Berlin there was a good chance, according to Weather, that the target might be obscured by clouds. I was in the lead plane ahead of several hundred bombers, many of which would drop their bombs at the sight of my bombs falling from the plane. With me, experimenting with the possibilities, was a radar operator; we had been briefed together for this kind of a situation: if the target was obscured by clouds I was to call the radar man who would then use the radar screen to locate the city's center. At the proper moment he would call me on the intercom and tell me to drop the bombs. In all probability, my only job that day would be as dramatic as a hotel bellhop's — to open the bomb bays and toggle out the bombs — a poorly tipped bellhop tossing suitcases out into the street. Pinpoint bombing with the Norden bombsight.

Berlin, when we arrived over it, was ninety percent hidden in clouds. I called the radar man, who sat with his equipment in an especially darkened nest in the waist of the plane like a pouty hen hatching out eggs. "Can't see a damn thing," I said. "You've got the plane."

"Listen, Captain," he called back, "I can't see much of anything either."

A mile square field of black and greasy flak lay over the clouds at twenty-five thousand feet, a whole other layer of man-made clouds between the cumulus and the ice clouds in the upper jet stream. We plunged into the filth and peered below and through holes in the overcast, contemplating whole neighborhoods of gutted buildings, empty and shattered shells of houses, the streets pouring over with white rubble, cement and powdered glass, shattered stones. Flak exploded around us, some of it obscenely close. Every trip to the damned city was more painful than the last. I sat in the nose of the plane doubly paralyzed with terror because I had nothing to do but count out the last seconds of my life. After five minutes, an interminable time, there came a view through the clouds — a suburban neighborhood of fine houses and small freeform forests of black fir. I called the radar man. "You'd better hurry up, goddammit, we're leaving Berlin."

"But you're the bombardier," he cried. "Too much chaff, too much chaff; I've lost everything."

"Why you dumb jug of shit," I yelled. "Why didn't you tell me?"

"You're the bombardier, sir," he cried again. "The fucking radar's gone blind."

In a rage, trembling hysterically, I fumbled with the bombsight, strange and swollen under my hands. Came a hole in the clouds and I aimed at a wet shining darkness set like a pool of black water in the hills of clouds . . . And down through the years telling this story, playing the fool, the only bombardier in history who missed the target by at least seven miles, I have my bombs and the bombs of another hundred planes behind me, plowing up fifty acres of rowed cabbages. "Figuring roughly," I used to tell my friends, who pretended to like stories about combat but who quite frankly preferred stories of success instead of failure, "figuring roughly, that death blow to the sauerkraut industry cost the American taxpayer about $150,000 per head of cabbage." But in truth the cabbage field was an invention; perhaps all we had bombed was a cow pasture, a golf links, or a newly plowed field asleep in the early fall sun and ready to be planted to wheat or rye.

There was another mission so full of my growing incompetence that out of a vague need for self-respect I soon managed to wipe it from my mind. Still, while it was grotesque, it is also, if viewed through the patina of time, mildly funny.

We are out there over Germany on another day heading for a now forgotten target, but one said to be lousy with flak guns. Three minutes from the target, photographs of which I have been studying for the last five hours, the pilot calls me on the intercom and says, "Okay, sport, she's all yours." Out there a half dozen miles, glistening pink and rosy in clear summer sunshine, lies whatever it is that we have come to destroy. Behind me, snuggled up now into tight bombing formation, a whole gaggle (gaggles of gaggles) of B-17s. In the first minute I catch a building in the bombsight and make those thousand quick and nervous corrections that keeps the building in the crosshairs. We are now a minute and a half away from the crossing of the indices when the bombs will automatically fall free, and it is in this moment that I suddenly realize as I glance, rechecking the photograph of the target, that I am actually aiming at a building roughly similar in size and construction and built into an identical neighborhood, but one that is nevertheless at least a thousand yards away from the target area. Groaning with self-loathing I swing the bombsight ten degrees to the right, the planes behind me heel over, and we advance in this new direction. And now again, the target caught and frozen, glancing at the indices which are moving together like fate, it occurs to me, with a knock as painful as a blow across the face or a red-hot iron branding the words "stupid asshole" across my forehead, that I have forgotten to open the bomb bay doors. Trying to bomb with the bomb bays closed is like trying to commit rape on a medieval lass tightly locked into an iron chastity belt. In horror I lean on the switch and listen as the doors swing open, peer into the bombsight for some last refining touch, and feel the little orgasmic leap of the plane as the bombs slowly fall away. I close the bomb bays, which have probably not been open for more than ten seconds, and then for the next five minutes, with my face in my hands, I rock back and forth on the bombardier's seat. Moaning and rocking out of shame. I have sat ahead of a thousand men who have followed behind me into a potentially fatal adventure, and with their lives on the line, I handled my job, for which I was paid almost a thousand dollars a month, with all the flair and grace of a spastic. Moburg, the navigator, sits just behind me scribbling wildly on his charts. After a time he notices my odd behavior, touches me on the shoulder, and asks, "Are you okay?" Maybe he noticed nothing; part of guilt is being caught. I begin to feel a little better.

About three days later we are called together one afternoon for a group meeting in the Quonset hut where normally we assemble just prior to a combat mission. This thing today is just a meeting — a discussion of our flying, some sarcastic comments by our good colonel who is dismayed by ragged, sloppy formations, and there will be some threatening words from Wing about the unacceptable number of aborted missions. Still, while this is not a gathering that will end in combat, the very sight of the room, the old stink of old terrors, triggers nausea and depression. Staring at the red cloth that hangs over a map of Europe, our bowels begin to heave and bubble; the air thickens with the stink of farts.

For a half hour I sit listening to the displeasures of the brass; it is almost impossible, half-anesthetized with gas, to stay awake. And now beginning to doze and suddenly feeling an elbow jabbing me, I come awake to the realization that someone is talking about me. I start up guiltily with the conviction that I have been discovered; my hands begin to sweat, my cheeks burn.

"...a few words about that bombing we did a couple days ago with B Squadron leading the wing. As you all know, normally we take a good four or five minutes flying in an absolutely straight line from the IP to the target. This gives every flak gun in the area a chance to plot us, altitude, ground speed, you name it. Also normally at the IP we open the bomb bays; this knocks five miles off air speed and causes a good deal of mushy flying. Now what happened Wednesday was this: a couple minutes into the bomb run Thomsen suddenly made a fifteen degree turn and only then headed for the target. The bomb bays were closed until just before the bombs dropped; I don't believe they were open for half a minute. Did you notice beaucoup flak over on the left as we high-tailed out? Well, that's where we would have been if we hadn't changed course at the last second. I think that kind of bombing saves lives, so I want to say what some of us are thinking — that that was the most brilliant bombing I've ever seen."

He sat down, and sitting across the room from him I turned my face to stone and stared at the folded hands in my lap; my cheeks were blazing now. Like that day years before when, dishing out stew, I had been petted in an orgy of love by a whole artillery battery, I felt as faint as a maiden who, expecting blows, is offered an unexpected passion. Well, undeserved admiration can be just as sweet as an affection honestly earned. Combat has taught me to turn reality ass over teakettle. The worst bombing I have ever done has suddenly become the most brilliant. All that love, those smiles, that feeling that while I wasn't as fully human as a pilot, I had begun to transcend the curse of my title. I could hardly wait to leave this meeting, return to the lead house, and masturbate.

23

B Y THE FALL OF 1944, those of us who had been in the group for any length of time had probably flown a half dozen times over Berlin; in truth it was almost the only target so large that we could consistently hit it, give or take a few. The raids kept increasing in size until they became great spectacles that looked wonderful in the newsreels. Even those of us who were participants were stunned with the grandeur, the slow apocalyptic choreography, the sweep and the growl, the implacable advance of planes across a reeling sky. Raids of three or four hundred planes grew toward the end to armadas of a thousand or more, rivers of bombers that blotted out the sun, to speak poetically (and at the back of the mind, a vision of locusts). The sky rumbled and shook from horizon to horizon.

We usually moved across Berlin at altitudes between twenty-eight and thirty thousand feet. We would have climbed higher but we had already reached the upper limits of the bombers' capability; another ten feet and we would have stalled out like Primary trainers. In the space above the city where we flew the sky was black with spent and disintegrating puffs of flak. Toward the end of the war, as the German air force was annihilated, we met almost no opposition from aircraft, though from time to time a new experimental model, a jet, would rush past us at incredible speed or dive down at us from high cloud cover. It was a sight, this technological miracle, that froze our guts with foreboding, that made us half believe in Hitler's promise of new and secret weapons that would soon appear to win a German victory.

If we had been better trained in strategic concepts we might have realized that in late 1944 the war had entered some final phase. The incessant and insane bombing of Berlin, this beating, beating, beating of a dead horse, could only be a sign that we had run out of targets and that we were now bombing dead ruins to justify our existence. Apparently even tactical targets were in short supply; more and more our raids to Berlin had become orchestrated with fighter cover. When we approached the city we could see hundreds of P-38s and P-51s flashing in the sun over the flak fields, waiting to drive away those German fighters (who no longer appeared) when we should enter that immediate zone of danger, the bomb run. Perhaps in all my combat career my terror had been most extreme the first time I saw our fighting planes circling and flashing over Berlin. For about three minutes, as the gunners called them in, screaming with outrage, we had thought they were enemy planes; there were hundreds of them circling above the flak like a swarm of bees, and it seemed inevitable that all of us would be shot down. Staring at them as they flashed and danced, the conviction crossed my mind, "Christ, within five minutes you are going down to a filthy death."

Still, in a way that none of us who now regarded ourselves as veterans of combat could manage to accept, the last Berlin raids were comparatively safe. But if they were, they didn't feel any safer.

At a briefing in November our colonels announced to hoots of ungracious and ambiguous laughter that in October the Second Air Force, U.S.-based and in charge of training, had lost more planes than the Eighth Air Force. To be told this was almost an insult; it mocked our terror and the way we wanted to see ourselves. Well, true or not, Berlin safe or not, we could not think of that dying city, now lying in ruins, without being struck with fear. We remembered an earlier time, one that still lived vividly in our dreams — the bombers exploding, the combat crews falling through the air with their chutes ablaze, the hopeless panic at confronting head-on a Kraut pilot spitting fire at you as he suddenly appeared, diving down. We had been programmed to moan and shit and grow faint with the announcement that we were about to be sent there again. One of the givens of this built-in panic, unmentioned since it was so obvious, was the understanding that we would never be asked to come in over Berlin at less than twenty-five thousand feet.

But at last in the heavy bomb groups, if our group was typical, the feeling began to grow that the war, at least as far as we were concerned, was coming to an end. The Germans had been driven from France and were fleeing in Italy. Patton's tanks were streaming into south-central Germany. The possibilities of bombing were seriously restricted; there was almost nothing left to destroy. In the war's last months, as we vanished from the headlines and were replaced by infantrymen, paratroopers, and tank commanders, the air force generals pondered what must have looked to them like a fall from grace. And so one day the combat crews in the group were approached by the almost invisible brass who were holed up in a nearby requisitioned castle they had made into a fantasy headquarters for their isolated, high-level hanky-panky.

They had come, or more precisely, their representative had come, to offer us a crack at deciding tactical policy. He was an air force general as star-spangled as a summer night or the national anthem. If we reacted ungraciously to his offer to let us help determine some details of a mildly technical and a shattering psychological nature, it was because we realized that we had been consulted out of cowardice. We were all there, combat officers and enlisted gunners, several hundred of us crowded together on our rows of benches. On the stage beside our commanding officer and his staff, glowing with splendor in his own light, the general and *his* staff. We gawked at him with open mouths, for it was not often that there was a mingling of the likes of him with the likes of us. In its awesome and hopeless unreality this meeting could be compared to Moses kneeling before that burning bush that held the living and eternal God. But if this comparison crossed my mind at the time, it was complicated and made ambiguous by the razor-creased trousers, the highly, ostentatiously polished shoes, the perfectly filled and relentless combat jacket with its rows of striped colors as set against our stains, our stinks, our yellow faces and trembling hands. I think we felt a kind of pity for him, this man who had ascended so high and into air so thin. What did he know about the war? In this confrontation who should bow down to whom?

The general was introduced, and he stepped to the podium. After a joke or two, a compliment or two, he came to the crux: "Now this is just an idea that we wanted to talk over with you gentlemen; I'm going to ask you to treat it in a top secret way. I'll tell you also in confidence that it comes from the very top, from General Arnold himself. Like most inspired ideas it's simple and dramatic. It will probably shorten the war, it may even end it." He paused, smiled, and rolled around in his mouth a cigar that was every bit as preposterous as one of Churchill's. "Gentlemen, what is your gut reaction to this proposal: that we begin bombing Berlin from six thousand feet?"

For a few seconds there was a stunned silence in the room; the silence, as much as the groans, the cries of anger, the moans of desperation that began to grow, could have warned the general to wipe the grin from his face, a complacent grin which was so out of sync with our rage at his insane suggestion. It was only for a minute or two that we lost control, that our cries of "No" and "Go to hell" were mixed with insolence; then, because we had made our point — and after all, he was a three-star general — we sank into a sullen torpor. The general was as stunned by the violence of our rejection as we were by the outrageousness of his plan. I think the air force had little history of mutinous behavior; the past had little to teach him. All in all, however, he did have common sense and he brought things to an end with a certain dignity. Still smiling, he waved his cigar over our sullen faces, blessing us like a priest with his little pot of smoking incense. He studied us, chuckling. "Well, well, I seem to detect certain reservations. I'll pass them on."

And he probably did, for that was the last of that madness.

I was ordered to report on a certain day and at a certain hour to Wing headquarters. I had been picked at random along with another dozen or so squadron bombardiers to take a test devised by a smart-ass psychologist that would reveal our competence under the pressure of fear. There was enough pressure in the orders and in the definition itself to make me nervous, and I felt as though simply in being called out of the obscurity of my darkened room where I tended to huddle when not fighting or drinking, I had already begun to flunk their test. I was coming to the end of my tour; why didn't they leave me alone with what was left of me? And anyway, how in Wing's castle, far from the rush of war, would they contrive to terrorize me? I could remember back to another time when they had tried and failed.

At the selection center in Santa Ana our tendency to come apart had been roughly measured. In groups of forty we were stood at arm's length before a row of small metallic rings welded to the top of long rods. We were each given a piece of iron as long and slim as a pencil and told to hold it inside the ring without touching it. If contact were made, the rod shorted out the ring and produced an angry buzzing sound. As we stood there trying to commit a mystical rape upon the ring (to enter it without its knowledge), the sergeant in charge of the test began to berate us: "So you want to be pilots, do you? Why don't you confess it to yourselves —

you're not sure you've got what it takes? What's bothering you, cadets? Is it those dirty little things you do in secret when you're pretending to be asleep? Your hands are beginning to tremble, aren't they, those same hands that prowl around under the covers at night?" And so on. The sound of buzzers filled the room. My God we were a good, clean Christian group, and my ring buzzed with its own music. It was not guilt or shame but suppressed laughter that had made me lose control. As the oldest candidate in that crowd I had come to realize the health-giving aspects of that universal pastime; to deny that one engaged in the only recreation that kept us from killing each other out of the desperation of barracks life was sheer hypocrisy.

At eight o'clock one morning, directly after breakfast, a chauffeured command car met me at the squadron office and drove me over winding country roads to the castle. It was late summer and the earth lay worn out and motionless in the still air; the leaves of the trees were covered with a thickness of sun, a thinness of August's dust. England had an exhausted look, a greyness like the sadness of mediocrity that had come to the population in their worn-out tweeds, their frayed shirts, and the pallor of their skins from a starchy, monotonous diet.

The castle, I believe, was just outside of Cambridge; having imagined it in some distant land, I was amazed when we arrived so quickly. And, well — so maybe it wasn't the castle that I had created in my imagination, with moats and turrets and a fairy princess with long blonde braids locked in a tower. Still, it was impressive, a large, stone Georgian house set and almost dwarfed in a formal garden and hidden from the road by clumps of great trees. Until the war, until the Yanks had come, it had certainly been the glory and the pride of old nobility. I was delivered to the front entrance and walked up a short flight of marble steps, greeted on both sides by mossy, smiling nymphs who waved me on with one hand and hid their mystery with the other. I felt coarse and unworthy; wasn't this the entranceway's objective? But I began to anticipate a modest dollop of gracious living — a thoughtful stroll through the library where, if I were unobserved, I would set the great globe of the earth to twirling, glance out through French windows to the lawns and flower beds, to a Lady Ashley drifting across the grass, her arms laden with roses; in short, my only chance to become, however grotesquely, the secret character in a Meredith novel. Wartime England had turned sad and squalid; I longed for the grandeur of the old empire that I had grown up with. Instead, I was immediately taken in hand by a staff sergeant who stood by the doorway of the entrance hall, alone and waiting for me.

He was friendly, very much at ease; he scarcely acknowledged our differences in rank. Perhaps, living in the castle, he was only impressed by silver stars and large cigars. Just to the left of the main doorway was a small room which had probably once received the hats and coats of visiting aristocrats. He led me into it. There would be no strolls through galleries lined with old ancestors and battle flags. I would be received in the cloakroom — an almost empty place with filing cabinets lined against a wall, and in a corner by the door, a single chair, a rough-looking homemade table, and on it a wooden invention, a three-foot-long hammer, fastened to and swiveling from the table. Rows of holes in the table held leather straps, and the head of the hammer was fastened to a rope which, I imagined, could be used to raise or lower it.

"Major Corbett's instant-combat construction," the sergeant said, smiling. "Actually, it's quite harmless, like the giant in the *Wizard of Oz*; do you remember him, sir, straddling the road with his big hammer?"

"Sure," I said, "you had to run past him while the hammer was going up."

"Right, sir. Don't say I didn't give you a hint."

"What are you going to do to me? I'll tell you straight, Sergeant — I'm really not in the mood."

"It won't take five minutes. What I'm going to do is give you some raw bombing data — altitude, air speed, temperature, the usual stuff, and ask you to transpose it for the bombsight. Sit down here, sir, and I'll show you. Think of it as a game; we're going to try and make you — well, let's say, nervous."

"You win, Sergeant," I said. "I feel like I'm in a dentist's office. I'm nervous, I'm nervous."

"Are you left-handed or right-handed?"

"Left."

"Then sit here and put your right arm over those straps. Put your hand palm down with your elbow against the block of wood; stretch your fingers. I'm going to restrain this arm so you can't move it." He locked me into place with my arm tightly frozen in three places by three straps. He lowered and adjusted the big wooden hammer so that it lay on the table about a quarter inch from my fingertips. "We're ready," he said. "There's all the information you need on this paper. You've got three minutes. Please don't ask me any questions. Read the directions, and don't look at the next page until I tell you to."

He raised the hammer on its long arm so that it stood perpendicular above my head, waited at my side with a watch as I read, and finally told me to begin.

I leafed through the tables of conversion as quickly as I could; this was student stuff that I hadn't done for a year and I had almost forgotten how. I came up with the first of the answers; it didn't look right, but I wrote it down; and in this instant, out of the corner of my eye, I could see the hammer falling, and as it struck the table with a crash, bouncing the books and papers, filling the room with hollow echoes, I stared at my entrapped fingertips trembling at the hammer's edge and aching as though they had been flattened. There was something so senseless in this brutal invasion of one's senses, so bad-mannered, that a half dozen of my father's furious rages flashed across my mind and I thought, "Major Corbett's crazy invention has more to do with family betrayals against decency than it has to do with combat." But that was only the first blow.

The rope tensed and the sergeant raised the hammer into the air, and once more it hung above me, and once more after a few seconds it fell with a shuddering jolt that now loosely mimicked the bursting of flak against the living flesh of a plane. I began to smell the stink of cordite, began to listen for the sound of faltering engines, and I could feel my horrified testicles shrinking and scrambling away to hide among the loops of my loosening bowels like old ladies caught in a sudden downpour. The hammer rose and fell with a crash.

Years later, watching movies about the war (how quickly our B-17 had become innocent and toy-like), I would sweat through a fictional bomb run or lower my eyes before the obscenity of a mortally wounded bomber disintegrating in its last dive. *Wylie, Wylie, you bastard, fall clear.* The anguish one felt in these artfully crafted reconstructions was as nothing, of course, compared to the reality, but it was real enough for all that — as painful as the tears we shed for those star-crossed lovers who after the last act will resurrect before our eyes and take a bow before our tears have dried. Ah, the power of art to make our hair stand on end and shrivel our flesh with the awareness of our smallness, our delicacy, our fleeting and endlessly besieged lives. Even today there is for me an echo of those old hammer blows in the awful thuds of fate in the last movement of Mahler's last symphony. And I suppose it is a glory to Major Corbett, the artist of that contrivance that did not quite smash my hand, that when I hear the Mahler and am reminded by it of something grave and deadly in the past, it is not the honest terrors of combat I think of but that sadistic little toy — falling, rising, and falling.

The three minutes were over finally, and I was unstrapped, thanked, and released. Turning in the door, my face still sweating but trying to smile, I said, "I think that should count as credit for a mission."

"It probably will in your little bag of memories," the sergeant said.

Outside in the entrance hall another bombardier was waiting. He glanced at my wings and asked, "Did you get invited to take that test?" And when I nodded, he asked, "What have the bastards got up their sleeve this time?"

"They're going to scare the shit out of you," I said, "and you're going to be amazed how easy it is."

"Oh, I never thought it was hard," he said. "I've always scared easy."

Driving back to group was like coming back from combat. Fear had always made me sleepy; fear was a physical tension between every little part of the body that didn't want to be hurt or cut away or damaged, dishonored by steel. We had barely left the gardens of Wing before I dropped into the deepest kind of sleep. I had had to fight a momentary impulse to curl up in the back seat like a fetus.

I was coming to the end of the combat tour. Using statistics, I talked myself through the final months. When I had five more missions, and if it was true that our losses were two percent per mission, then I now had a ninety percent chance of coming through. Those were good odds but nothing you wanted to get cocky about. If I any longer believed in God he was a God of pure evil, his hands, his hair, his teeth hidden in gouts of blood. And statistics were only probability; some old hag with the name of Fate might already have arranged that I would not be killed until, like Jones, our plane was lowering over the Channel on my last mission. Or funnier still, climbing out of the bomber for the last time, I might fall and break my neck. This was the kind of thing that happened to men who took tomorrow for granted. I tried not to tempt the fates; why should I challenge them to do something that was so easy — to squash me like a bug? At the same time, while I still possessed the gift of life (which each day I valued less), that future which I tried not to think about began timidly to creep into my thoughts. Looking ahead, I vaguely saw myself as a civilian but couldn't quite make out what I was doing out of uniform — the author of the drama that was my life, but unable to imagine the next act or, since death was the perfect ending, to imagine myself engaged in anything that had any meaning. Well, like it or not, the future (being an extension of the past) would hold my father. Was it that first falling hammer at Wing that had put my father with all his menace back into my thoughts? Perhaps. On the very next mission, in a hard-edged moment of surrealism, I met him again as though he had been created out of that same table-smashing blow.

We headed out in a northerly direction that day — to where I no longer remember. It may even have been one of those terrible thirteen-hour flights to Peenemünde or Posen that demanded impossible endurance from the pilots. A beautiful clear day of blue skies, blue seas and, as we came over Europe, the land rich, dark, and ordered beneath us. I have invented this day in my imagination and turned it into a painting by Dufy — a brisk day of spanking winds, flags, trees, waves, sunlight.

We came to Denmark, still climbing to altitude; green fields, sharply delineated waterways, a beautiful, rational country from which had come half of my blood. I sat in the nose with a set of maps spread across my lap calling out the names of towns to the navigator behind me.

And then suddenly out ahead of us a very small town, neat and frozen at the edge of water. Sailboats were tied up against a green bank, a fishing boat lay at a wharf, a dirt road cut ruler-straight across farmland from one shore to another. The map said Tondern, and for a moment I couldn't believe it. I had visited Tondern ten years before with the family, making a kind of pilgrimage to the old dairy farms where my grandparents had played and then worked as children, to the village church that held the records of their births, the births and deaths of a hundred and fifty years of Thomsens, to the family cousins and second cousins who still worked the land. I was nineteen then, and it was there in Tondern, reading the old church records, that I had found and immediately appropriated my grandfather's middle name. And so I stared down hungrily, trying to recognize it, looking for the little whitewashed church that my grandmother in early middle age had had a country artist paint for her, a childishly executed memory that hung on the wall of her bedroom all the rest of her life. There was nothing familiar about Tondern now; from altitude it was only land with miles of water around it. I could not remember so much water; remembering frozen fields blown almost clean of snow, the small farmhouses built against the barns for warmth, the leafless trees, the tow-headed children handsome in their blazing cheeks, their country strength. From the air it seemed to resemble, more than the recent past of my adolescence, those old photographs when Father as a six-year-old had posed with his sisters in front of some cousin's barn.

It was exciting to fly by chance over a town that held so much of my family's history; it canceled out for a time that ever-present dread that was a part of the combat mission. I called up the pilot on the intercom and cried, "Taylor, down there is the town I came from, my grandparents, anyway. That's their town, their pastures, their cows. It's unbelievable. This is where Grandfather left from seventy years ago when he was twelve to make his fortune. Tondern, Tondern."

As I finished speaking a single burst of flak exploded immediately below us. From the sound of it — its sharpness, its ugliness, its nearness — I want to call it a direct hit. The plane shuddered and fell away for a few seconds, faltering in the sky as it obeyed the shuddering hands of the pilot. We waited a decent time to burst into flames and then climbed back into the lead position. A few minutes later the pilot called me back. "Nice fucking family you've got."

"We've always been closely involved with one another," I said.

That single burst had been so sudden, violent, and rude that my unconscious took it as personal message. Which mission was it? The twenty-fourth, the twenty-fifth? And why, when a moment before my struggles had seemed to be coming to an end, did they now seem to stretch away into a distant future? I think it was this: that on the level of consciousness that judged the forces that might destroy me, my father had been transformed into a figure as deadly as German guns. It was a revelation that shamed me, a thought I couldn't hold in my head for long, but while it lasted, I realized that was the name of that relationship between us. The ranch and the cows he had promised to help me buy after the war: I knew that if this was what I still wanted he had committed himself too seriously to back away; breaking that pledge would dishonor him even in his own eyes. But now it was clear that, contrary to his word, there *would* be strings attached, perhaps almost impossible conditions that would put me in his power for the rest of my life. Giving or taking, he tended to create combat conditions; the only shameful battle for him was a battle lost, and he would do anything shameful to win it. I had been free of him for two years and I liked that freedom. Moving away from his power centers, I had grown in my own way, breathed my own air, walking a little lighter without the weight of his disapproving presence. He wrote me every ten days, each letter like the one before it. I tried to find time to read them all, but they no longer touched me. They were written to a young man whom I no longer even faintly resembled.

As we flew on and left Denmark behind, I thought of the letter I would write my father. "We flew over Tondern: the plane received a direct hit from a single burst of flak. It was a real family reunion, and I'm glad you've still got your gunnery skill. But how did you get from Seattle to Denmark with the war and all? How did you know I was flying that day?"

I decided that was a letter I'd better not write; it was too brutal a joke.

It's September now and it comes as a pleasant shock today to realize that I've finally come to the end of this segment on combat. I've arrived sooner than expected, having decided to spare the reader any further details that would have more meaning for me than for him — a memory of a rabbit hopping away from us one early morning as we taxied out to bomb and how, as it was caught in our lights, we ran it down. So this is the last page, and I sit here trying to work myself back into that time — January or February of 1945, and I guess I do because suddenly the pen is so heavy in my hand I can hardly lift it, and the words are as heavy, meaningless, and unruly as boulders. And I remember the old exhaustion, am caught up again in the exhaustion of that last day — still virulent, still contagious after forty years — that exhaustion which is a symptom of my despair, a trick to confuse and disguise my own self-hatred.

We came back from what for me was the twenty-seventh mission (three more to go), and all I remember is the heavy layer of clouds we had to work our way down through when we came back to England

and how we strained to see the green of the land as we rushed through the clouds, flying blind and paralyzed with fear. Flying blind through cumulus, tipped and battered by upward-rushing air when there are another thousand planes around you doing the same thing — turning steeply on one wing, diving through holes in the overcast, circling like hysterical birds — always made me as tightly nervous as being shot at. We had an expression that roughly fits this situation: Shot at and missed, shit at and hit. When we finally landed, taxied to our position out in the grass, and cut the engines, I was too exhausted to leave the plane immediately. I sat alone in the nose, bent down over the bombsight, while the plane emptied, and I was thinking . . . three more to go . . . I can't do it, it's too much. I didn't want to move, didn't want to test myself to see if I could move. But, of course, I had to move; there was the debriefing. I wanted to sleep, crawl into a darkness, not talk to anyone, not meet anyone I would have to greet or smile at. Behind my closed eyes, a row of bombs on a stretch of road at the end of a French bridge bloomed blood-scarlet between the trees, blasting the leaves from them, shattering the stone walls of the houses. The slate roofs tinkled like wind chimes as they blew away. It was like a movie I had seen a hundred times but each time with added details. This time there were the bodies of children hurtling through the air without arms, legs, faces; dogs, blown into ditches and split open like melons, snapped at their own intestines.

Lt. Hamilton in a Jeep full of flying officers drove under the nose of the plane and called up to me through the Plexiglas, "Wait for me here. I'm coming right back for you." I nodded and after a minute or two gathered my stuff and slowly worked my way back to the door in the waist. An empty bomber deserted in its revetment, its thin aluminum skin pitted with tiny holes made by exploding flak, is as delicate and insubstantial as a spider's web. The plane moved, sighed, and wept as my body moved through it, and the wings trembled as they caught at the breeze outside. In the waist the sour, bitter smell of metal, the bronze smell of blood, the flat smell of old spit, the salt taste of ozone, the heartless stink of the guns.

Outside I lay down on the runway, using my parachute as a pillow. Two mechanics had arrived and were walking around the plane with clipboards taking notes. One of them was the mechanic of the lead plane, my favorite mechanic because at each mission as we taxied away he would kneel in the prop-blast, make the sign of the cross, and watch us intently until we were out of sight. Lt. Hamilton came back for me; he was alone, smiling. I climbed in beside him, but before we moved off he said, "I can't wait; listen to me, Tommy. Are you awake? Wake up, wake up, I have news for you. The orders have just come in from Command. Listen, not an hour ago. They've changed the number of missions for lead crews. Lead crews do twenty-seven missions now instead of thirty. Do you understand? You're all through, man; you're through, you made it."

Slowly I began to understand, like a message come to me through a thick door with all the emotion filtered out. We came to the main run-way and waited before crossing it while the last of the bombers landed. "Say something," Lt. Hamilton said, punching me on the arm.

"The tower's giving you a green light," I said.

Where was the relief, the happiness of having made it through? I felt like a man subjected to a coitus interruptus. A heavy weight was settling in my stomach like something indigestible. I began to feel as though I were being cheated out of a proper ending — as though in the last min-utes of a symphony whose final resolutions will explain everything someone suddenly lifts the needle fr——

24

ALL THROUGH THE EARLY YEARS of the war I seldom thought of my future as a civilian except in the vaguest of terms. I thought of it as a far distant time when I would be free to walk around in dirty Levis and hog-spattered boots within a life so simple that except for the dentist and a dinner invitation from time to time I would never have to mortgage a single moment of my tomorrows. Then for about a year there was no future at all that wasn't extremely short-termed; thinking about it was a kind of science fiction. Now I began to think again in a desperate way about that future which was becoming more complicated and unreal as it came closer, when all of us who had been diminished and made more than normally mediocre would have a chance to begin our lives again. Or be forced. Those years of military service — cross them out; they would contain nothing onto which a future might be grafted.

In the first years in the army as I scrubbed pots, the future had been constructed of clouds and forests, of mountain streams, ski slopes, frozen lakes. Now I was thirty. Combat and maturity had robbed the natural things of their magic. I had raped the earth with bombs, and we no longer had an understanding; through the vagueness of high altitude the earth of Europe had become target or hidden gun-emplacement. Climbing a mountain, nursing a poetic attitude toward a wilderness sunset, fly-casting into the riffles above a pool of water, rushing down on skis through powder snow — these things were the stuff of nostalgia, fairy tales that must now be filed away with the still older pleasures, splashing through a mud puddle, catching a bee in a bottle, lying hidden in tall grass below lines of clouds sliding across the sky. This war that I had wished out of ignorance to experience for the things I might learn, and about which I might write, had turned sour, bleak, and ugly; I had been emotionally castrated. I would never write about the war; I would never write about anything. If the impulse still glowed dimly, I saw it now as a childish dream that had grown out of romantic illusions; the desire had never reflected my poor talents. I had been like a man with palsy who dreams of being a brain surgeon.

The people who add up such things now estimate that 100,000,000 people died because of the Second World War. Toward its end in 1945, perhaps because it was impossible to imagine a figure so immense, the dead were estimated to be around 30,000,000, give or take a million here, a million there. Those of us with a melancholy disposition, whose natural inclination was to see the dark side of man (but who, at thirty, can seriously think of man as having a dark and evil side that can't be fixed with education, parental love, education, or a balanced diet?), contemplated the figure thirty million and the collapse of all our preconceptions that went with it. What we had been taught, what we profoundly believed, what lay at the foundation of our lives was the idea that life was sacred, that each of us was a unique and marvelous construction built in the image of God. Man with his nobility of soul, in his tenderness and recognition, was capable of intense, loving, and joyous relations with all the living things of the earth. We had been taught by voices like dying echoes out of the eighteenth century that man was perfectible, that he was better than he had been in the past, that he was rational, and that science would shortly find solutions to the irritations that made man beastly. Aldous Huxley inspired us with a book proving that football games were going to be a substitute for the murderous rages that drove men to kill each other. What platefuls of bullshit had been rammed and tamped into our heads. Man, whose greatest, most imaginative inventions were machines for killing, was killing his brothers by the millions. Well, if it wasn't especially fun, it wasn't all that terrible either. Dropping bombs on people from twenty-five thousand feet — what could be cleaner, more purely and simply scenic, than that? From five miles up no bits of flesh or brains rebounded off your face, your limbs were not entwined in human guts, there were no dying screams, no cries for mercy; hell, you couldn't even hear your bombs. We thought at first that it was a lovely way to kill and that we would be spared remorse and the stab of conscience. But we were trapped by the lies we had been taught, for if man were sacred and a manifestation of God, how could we keep killing without going mad? No, we had to decide finally — we were as sacred, as moral, as marvelous, as necessary to earth's intentions as ants. We were red or black ants killing black or red ants. Dead, we would be as mourned, as missed as a slaughtered bug, and for just about as long. Soon, when the dead became the majority, it would be the dead mourning the living; their cries to us were already almost irresistible.

Man, we had been told, was the measure of all things, but now man had shrunk to a disreputable size. And the mountains of bodies — the rotting mountains of bodies illuminated with the green phosphorescent glow of a Bosch charnel house . . . Dead men were the measure of all things.

Combat was over for me, and now what I wanted more than anything was to die, to blot out the guilt of having survived the raids that had destroyed so many of the men around me. Their deaths had raised them up to reveal, in the new light of the myths we created to make sense of the war, their true nobility. In their deaths, starkly radiant, they revealed that inner and hidden delicacy that transformed them and laid bare their trembling vulnerabilities. To die young, to die before your time, wasn't there something magnificent in such spendthrift waste? But their nobility diminished me who, being alive, was unworthy of the sacrifices they had made, the lives they had traded for mine. I could only be worthy of them, I could only make something aesthetically significant out of my life, by being blown to pieces.

I stayed on in England for more than a month. In my mind it seemed of the utmost importance that I volunteer for those three missions that I had been robbed of and that would complete my original contract. I had to do those three missions to prove to myself that I had not been completely undermined by cowardice. I told myself that I would rest up, take a few days off, and come back to offer myself to the squadron. I went to Scotland, planning to stay a week. I felt that my uniform antagonized everyone, for no one spoke to me except one doddering old man in the hotel lobby who leaned across his wife as I poured cream into my tea and hissed, "For Christ's sake man, pour the cream in first." I walked for three days in a steady drizzle, a Scotch mist, filled with sadness and my growing sense of having become redundant. I was as irrelevant as that doddering retired colonel who had tried to teach me manners and as all the other living dead who huddled around the fireplaces of the tourist hotel where I stayed until I was driven away by seeing them all in the mirror when I gazed into it, alone in my room.

The time came for my flamboyant gesture, but each day I put it off. I would lie in bed sweating, a pressure in my head, thinking, Tomorrow. Tomorrow I will talk to Davis, I'll get those three missions in, I've got to get this decided and over with. But at the last minute I couldn't do it. It was like trying to dive at night into a pool which might be empty. I wanted to die but I didn't want people saying, the dumb bastard killed himself. But more profoundly — no, I couldn't do it, couldn't make my mouth say the words. I was terrified of airplanes now. I had lost that ability to hide my fear, my fear grown into a phobia. Listening in the early mornings as the bombers warmed up and thundered away, I shook and panted, fighting the impulse to vomit or hide my head beneath the pillow like a child. Simply imagining that conversation with Davis would send me to the toilet with diarrhea.

The war in Europe was coming to a climax as Allied troops, as we had always known they would, burst through the German defenses and overwhelmed the mini-Nazis with chewing gum and cans of chipped beef. White sheets hung from the windows in the medieval towns as Jeeps drove through the streets. "Welcome, welcome," cried the meaty, big-breasted housewives and the fat-necked, red-faced, big-assed, slightly wheezing citizen smiled and lowered his eyes as his daughter pinched a little color into her cheeks and went out into the evening streets looking for Yanks to fuck her for bars of chocolate, for bars of Lux. The hypocrisy of the defeated we could understand; one day they hated us, the next day they were lying in our arms underneath a Jeep or lying in the gutter of a darkened side street. In England we read the papers and imagined how it was, for war being war always ends the same way. And then we read what we had always pretended not to know since it had been impossible to imagine: the bodies of dead Jews piled like cordwood within the fenced-in death camps. We studied the photographs of emaciated and naked victims; their faces were always the same — jutting bones, great staring, stunned eyes, bare heads made hairless by starvation. The little glow of pity we had begun to feel for the defeated shriveled to rage. How we admired the American commander who had collected a whole town and forced them at gunpoint to march through Dachau or Buchenwald, past the ovens, the barracks, the rooms (Germans have a wonderful need for order) full of hair, clothes, teeth, watches, and bracelets, one room for each item. "We didn't know, we didn't know," the Germans cried, tears gushing from their eyes, the women fainting. For two years freight cars had passed through the town and been switched off onto new tracks; from the freight cars had come the sounds of moans, screams, the stink of shit and death. For two years from two miles away the smokestacks in the camp had belched forth a black oily smoke and the stink of burned meat. "We didn't know, we didn't know," the Germans cried, tears gushing from their eyes, the women fainting.

The war was a bad war; the war was a good war; we wanted to live; we wanted to die; we were heroes; we were cowards or monsters; we wanted to be moral, to be unafraid of being judged in less excited times; we had begun to suspect that the winners in this war would be regarded only for a time as heroes, the losers as monsters. At least these ambivalent feelings, these slowly growing confusions, were partly put to rest as the monstrous enormity of the death camps filled the papers, as the photographs of the mass burial grounds, from which we were unable to tear our eyes, froze the blood. How could we question the necessity of fighting, of wiping out if necessary, a people so ready to be seduced into slavery by a degenerate Fascist lunatic?

What confused us now were the cries of outrage from our leaders who couldn't believe what was being revealed. "We didn't know, we didn't know," they cried. Millions had been murdered, and they didn't know? Was our intelligence so incompetent, or was some new and tremendous evil being dragged out to be piled atop the accumulated horrors, aspects of which served to describe us all?

But in truth, hadn't all of us known, hadn't we always known — and been too weak to hold the knowledge in our heads? These blond Nordic gods clubbing people in the streets, that particular smell of leather that hinted at odd perversions, sweat, pain, the need to humiliate; you had only to be a little suspicious of the great Ho ho ho of German laughter, a little sickened by what so much attracted them — the goose step, the black leather boots, that group of drunken men, arms about each other's waists, singing some stupid song about conquering the world — to know that the whole society was psychotic; the bastards were crazy. Knowing the little that we knew (which was enough) we could only cultivate a loathing of Germans that was so fierce and corrosive, so all-embracing, that we could bomb their cities, their homes, their wives, children, and mothers with a minimum of remorse; on the contrary, anesthetized in the conviction that we were the agents of justice. To this day more than forty years later, I would prefer to live separate from that odious race of people (my race) among whom I feel uncomfortable and grudging. Ursulla comes to visit with her wide smile, her easy laugh, her bright dresses. How does she dare?

The winter storms came; fog and driving rains grounded the bombers; heavy clouds lay over the targets. In Germany the troops were almost immobilized by snowstorms or rolling banks of fog. Allied airborne divisions were trapped in untenable positions. I sat alone in my room listening to the BBC or studying the newspaper accounts, out of my mind, I realize now, burning to become involved, as nutty as a Nazi. On one wall I had hung a map of Europe, and each day I moved the colored thumbtacks, trying to make sense of the ebb and flow of attacks and counterattacks. One day I found myself in London where I spent two days searching for the secret headquarters of the 82nd Airborne. Finally, I walked one morning into an almost empty and totally unprepossessing office near Hyde Park. A young second lieutenant with a drained, expressionless face greeted me coolly.

"I've finished my combat missions in B-17s," I said. "I'd like to transfer to your outfit." I said it from some level that I hardly recognized, listening as though someone else were speaking. I had wanted to say it but doubted if I could, and listening to the sound of my voice asking for something that was against all reason, it occurred to me (and perhaps for the first time) that I was seriously losing my marbles. Worse than the thought of more serial combat was the horror I felt at the idea of flinging myself into space and giving myself to the wind. Nor did I feel that I was the type who as he fell would cry Geronimo! in an excess of patriotic fervor. If the lieutenant who faced me now had said, "Good, we need you, sign here," I might have dropped to the floor in a dead faint.

Instead, saving me, he said, "Since yesterday the 82nd has ceased to exist; we've been wiped out." He stared at me with a tragic face, pushed himself away from a desk that had hidden a heavy cast around one leg and cried, "I'm just out of the hospital. Christ, they left without me. I don't belong here, I belong over there with my buddies." Like me, in love with death, he was giving in to the temptation to make drama out of his despair and his human weaknesses.

And now back on the base, I was saved again when Major Davis dropped into my room one evening and very nicely pointed out that Hawkins who had replaced me as the lead squadron bombardier could not be promoted to captain until I had, dead or alive, been struck from the squadron rolls.

"Okay, John," I said. "No need for handcuffs; I'll leave quietly. Tell them to cut my travel orders."

Somewhere on the outskirts of Liverpool the army had established a center where air force personnel waiting to be sent home were herded together like cattle, sorted and classified, and assigned to the ships that would take them, not to the slaughterhouse but away from it. It was one great low building, built like an octopus — miles of narrow corridors, hundreds of small unheated rooms, each filled with four double-decker cots and skimpy English straw-filled pallets as hard and lumpy as the ground and swarming with crab lice. Outside, though it never entered our heads that we might go outside, steady rains fell week after week. Though I spent at least a month in that weird and dismal place I cannot remember, among many other things, the mess hall or the food we ate. This might serve to reinforce the observations of psychologists who feel that humans are incapable of reconstructing in their memories insupportable pain, soul-shriveling sadness. Within a few days there, I had come down with a high fever and could only keep warm by huddling in a furnace room, half hidden behind rows of drying socks and GI underwear. It was there that I wrote the last story I would write for twenty years, a sad little sketch about a flier who couldn't sleep nights for seeing that row of bombs falling down the street of a French village. After I had written it I had less trouble sleeping.

We were all officers there, I believe, and most of us had come from combat situations. Combat had made us passive, and we were too tired to bitch about this latest degradation for more than two or three hours a day. The place was damp and moldering and immense in a surreal way that made us shake our heads in wonder. Where could we go? It was impossibly difficult to figure out ways of getting into Liverpool by either bus or taxi. And not worth the trouble, we were told; wartime Liverpool was the living dregs.

And so we lay in our bunks, each of us isolated and apart in a quiet stupor, a thousand of us or more, crowded into that critical space that makes rats leap at each other's throats. But we were too tired, too preoccupied with our private neurotic symptoms to quarrel or to establish any relationship at all that wasn't blatantly superficial. I remember those rooms now, the cots filled with pallid airmen, as a kind of gigantic opium den where we lay in our vacancy, slowly healing. When we spoke it was in low voices out of a kind of delirium; we found nothing serious enough to be serious about. We dozed, we wandered from room to room looking for a book to trade for the book we carried, we leafed through old magazines, lightweight editions of *The New Yorker* printed on something like toilet paper for the troops. We smoked Camels and sat for whole afternoons on the upper bunks, lost in clouds of smoke, playing blackjack. In a large reception room where I recall we gathered each day at noon and at six waiting for the mess hall to open, a half dozen poker games went on with what looked like the same players from the day I arrived until the day I shipped out. Silent poker games in sign language.

One day we panicked and began to move. The rumor had swept through the camp that anyone with crabs would be taken off travel orders. It couldn't have been true, of course. We *all* had crabs, and who could have had the clout to keep us here through eternity while the steamers returned to America empty? But we were desperate to get out of that place and couldn't think straight. And so another memory is superimposed on the first: a picture of a thousand men, each sitting on his cot with his pants down as he dusts his balls and combs DDT through his pubic hair. I used to dream on some evenings that the center simply disappeared in a great white cloud of DDT as we dusted clothes and mattresses, blankets, toilets, our packed and waiting luggage, our heads and eyebrows, every little anything that had hair around it.

My last memory of that horrid place is watching a major at the podium in a meeting hall where we have been gathered to discuss the mechanics of our next move. As he talks to us he scratches; his forehead is wrinkled in a small private agony; he claws at his crotch . . . claws,

claws, claws. It was definitely not behavior becoming to an officer and a gentleman; but we understood.

An indecent amount of time passed as we itched and scratched, scratched and dusted. Then the day came finally when some three hundred of us, having worked our way up from the bottom of the barrel, found our names on travel orders. Our next stop would be a great collection center in New Jersey. Late one afternoon we piled off buses with our barracks bags and our B-2s onto a dripping Liverpool dock as dark as the night in a Fu Manchu mystery. We were in the hands of the Navy now, and we filed aboard the ship that would take us home. Within thirty-six hours we would begin to gather outside the harbor to be part of a convoy of fifty protected by half a dozen destroyers. The ship seemed strangely empty, strangely quiet; there were not enough of us to fill the spaces. When I asked a naval lieutenant about this he told me not to worry; several hundred enlisted men would shortly join us.

They came aboard as we slept — two hundred or so infantrymen flown to England from European centers where they had been taught new skills. At breakfast time, as we searched for a chow line in the lower guts of the ship, we met them in the inside passages and in the saloons where all the furniture had been removed so that they could more easily move around. They were all in wheelchairs, a small army of men without legs and among them a sprinkling of men who had also lost their arms. Medics pushed the ones who had to be pushed. We met the first wave of them in the semidarkness of the hallways and were too frightened, too stunned to speak, wondering crazily, guessing — and the legs? Four hundred legs, where are they? And the arms? Where are the arms?

How grandiloquent this superfluity, this secret but now rawly revealed message from the army, whose policy you had better believe had been to move these hopelessly damaged men during the dead of night to spare the sensibilities of an unimaginative population. You wouldn't sell war bonds with this kind of a display, but from us, the air crews, not much more was to be expected; they could let us in on their dirty little secret. And you could look at this spectacle in a kinder light; everything the army did was on a staggering scale: a hundred and fifty medics in their white cottons, two hundred soldiers without legs, three hundred semineurotic fliers, war heroes with all the pewter wings and the brass medals to prove it. And, locked in the basement behind bars, as we found out later that day, a hundred and fifty homosexuals stripped of whatever rank they had and being shipped home to prison and dishonor. How could we not be impressed by the simple lavishness of the army's conceptions, the grandeur of the performance. We were in no grade B Reagan horse opera, this was spectacle in living color and a cast of millions, ten million to be precise. In the kitchen below us fifty cooks were frying two thousand eggs and a thousand pounds of pork sausage. A hundred gallons of coffee as bitter as battery acid bubbled and writhed in the steam urns. Out on the water a dozen destroyers as quick and nervous as wasps, lights flashing back and forth with navy gossip, prepared to guard us home through the late winter fogs and freezing blasts and damn the torpedoes.

For ten days (dragging a figure out of the air) we zigged and zagged, held to the speed of the slowest straggler. We stood at the rails on the outside decks when the wind dropped, watching the tilting destroyers dancing through the waves, cutting white curtains out of the black water, changing course every minute; sheepdogs seeing us home safe.

And late in the mornings, but long before lunch, and in the late afternoons, we stood in the saloon filled with the legless men. We were afraid to speak, to break in upon them; afraid anything we might have said would antagonize them; they saw the world from their own angle now, strange and sacred. But watching them and made ashamed of our sadness, we began to see our disillusion in a more decent perspective. In almost every respect they were the most ordinary of men, but in the matter of joy, in their capacity to laugh and clown, they were more ready than the usual run to grab at a present moment and turn it into something that throbbed with life. From my thirty years, I saw them as children, for they were all in their late teens or early twenties, and at first, watching them, wanting to weep for them, I was horrified as they played and clowned, as happy as lunatics. They wheeled and charged each other, they raced, yelling with laughter, down the corridors, they spun like tops. When they played chicken and crashed together and the wheelchairs tipped, throwing the men to the decks where they lay helpless, their arms waving like bugs, grotesque and heroic lumps of disfigured flesh beneath the still-turning wheels, everyone who watched, and the fallen men themselves, howled with laughter.

They received enormous support from one another, an absolutely honest and pitiless support that drove them to a kind of healthy acceptance, that kept them going. They had joined the most exclusive of clubs and their only competition was the brotherhood of the dead. I envied them their closeness, one that excluded all of us who had not earned a Purple Heart. Their loyalty to one another had saved them, had laid bare their sweetness and their inner human yearnings, softly sad and without a trace of bitterness. I envied them, but without the slightest desire to join their club, not even for the smallest tip of a little finger; the price was too high, and I imagined that each year the annual dues would cost more. War had made them honest. Along with their legs they had lost their patriotic fury, that lust to kill, that hunger for short-term glory, that need to merge oneself for good or bad into the world's madness.

Sometimes they sat quietly, rows of men who had been cut in half. On their faces were the faint smiles of old men remembering back to something wonderful that had happened to them long ago when they could run.

One day we lay adrift for an afternoon off an invisible coast. In the distance foghorns wailed, garbage floated in the oily sea, a little line of grey-faced KPs with garbage cans (my brothers) threw overboard one thousand fried eggs, two hundred pounds of toast, a mountain of little pig sausages white in their cold grease. Seagulls, a shameless rabble of those beautiful working-class birds, shrieked, squabbled, dove. Our turn came and we moved slowly toward the distant humming of a great city. Below a cloud of fog that had lifted, an inch Statue of Liberty beckoned us ashore with a blacked-out torch. In the afternoon we docked and went ashore, struggling with our bags and staggering past a long row of ambulances. They were waiting for the darkness that would hide their heavy freight as they secretly paraded through the empty streets.

25

THE NEXT SEVEN MONTHS (I am guessing just a little when I write the number of months and try to identify them) — March through September of 1945? — the next seven months no longer exist in my memory as connected chunks of time that might be examined. Still, even if all the days have been forgotten, I am left with the unforgettable sour taste of old emotions. Let me try to hint at the awful, slow-paced comedy of the returned veteran.

War books are written by fools like me but only God or his deputies could make a Camp Kilmer in New Jersey that is identical in every respect to a trio of camps in Texas, Iowa, and Nebraska, and to that last sad separation center in California. Like a hockey puck I was sent bounding and rebounding to them all and, sometimes in a humorous way (humorous enough to make you smile but not enough to make you laugh), sent out of one camp and four days later sent back to it. It was like being struck by lightning for the second time while standing in the same spot. But in truth what did it matter and how could I tell, when there was no smallest scar or beauty mark to differentiate among these camps cloned out of some monstrous conception?

Army camps are army camps are army camps — the endless rows of lined-up barracks square with the world, with sad sacks wandering between them picking up cigarette butts and candy wrappers, the dusty parade ground (empty), recreation huts, the theater, the officers' club (deserted all day but crowded at five with second lieutenants and their very plain-faced women), the PX that sells cheap cigarettes and funny plastic jewelry and weak beer, the headquarters building set aside in the middle of a balding patch of dying grass and protected by a twelve-inch picket fence, the delight of the camp dogs. In each camp a dead flag hangs limply from its pole like a dish towel, and in each camp, if you are outside at five o'clock, you stop whatever you are doing, face toward the vicinity of the nearest loudspeaker and standing at attention imagine the flag being slowly lowered, folded, and put to sleep for tomorrow's reveille. And at ten o'clock, the sad, sweet, the heartbreakingly sad sweet bugle cry of taps, that song of sleep, of death, of time passing. Another, my poor aching back, wasted day.

I would awaken in a BOQ and lie waiting for the first thin light of a niggardly midwestern dawn to illuminate the outside colors (whitish dust, reddish packed earth, GI grey barracks, an overexposed sky of pale washed-out blue, a white flat spinning sun that if you glanced toward it would turn into a black disk) and gradually I would figure out where I was that week. As though it made a difference. Without any strong convictions about where you are, even who you are becomes a matter for speculation. If I had been brusquely shaken out of bed, told that I was at Camp Brilliantine, Louisiana, and that my name was Pritchard Holmsberg, the captain in charge of the whiskey in the officers' bar, I might have dressed and walked right out of my own life.

If it was young hustling Lyndon Johnson who reasoned, together with his peers, that an army camp should be built on practically every other dried-up cow pasture in Texas between the Panhandle and the Gulf of Mexico, he had reasoned well. We must credit him not only with the increase in suicides among army personnel who referred to Texas as an uninhabitable planet, but for the increase in heroic acts on the world's battlefields. Those of us with combat behind us could not be sent out to fight again, but we could volunteer for a second tour; we were encouraged to put our training, which had cost the taxpayer so much, and our experience of war, which had also had a certain price, once more at the service of the nation. If most of us scoffed at the idea of going back to be shot at, six months in Texas camps softened us up. Six months in places like Marfa, Big Springs, or Midland, and any normally sensitive man was eager for the alternative — war, capture, torture, death at sunrise.

The Seventh Air Force in the Pacific needed crews for the B-29s that were moving closer and preparing to bomb Japan back into prehistory. Okay, put my name down. I surrender, dear. Better to spend a hazardous year ducking kamikazes over the endless wastes of a southern ocean than to go catatonic in the incessant, high, nasally whining prairie wind, watching tumbleweeds pile up against the cars in the parking lots, watching a blood-red sun almost extinguish in dust as it rolled down and hid behind an excruciatingly level horizon.

They didn't come right out and say so, but yes, it was the OSS. They needed volunteers for a secret and hazardous mission. (The rumor had it that those accepted and trained would be dropped in the mountains of China, all fancy drybrush work — leaping cliffs, bamboo, a bird, a plum blossom. There we would administer a democratic government in the Chiang Kai-shek style and in the vacuum of a Japanese withdrawal. Well, which shall it be? To spend another six months in Texas or go into training again, to learn impeccable Chinese in three weeks and get flung into a Chinese watercolor with a hundred commie rats with pitchforks grouping in the foreground. Which shall it be? Foolish question. Put me down, teach me how to say, I am your leader, follow me. No tickee, no washee. But get me out of Texas.)

I exaggerate? Well, yes, perhaps a little. But to the still-living old folks who remember the insularity, the bleak grandeur, the small town plainness of that poor state almost swept away in the Great Depression — they will know how little. Texas was mean and gritty. That chunk of time that still lies across those months at the middle of my life was for the most part heavy and formless but a few small chisel marks can still be made out on its flat, soaring surface.

And so I remember:

I am one of five thousand unassigned combat officers who have been organized, in an effort to keep us from going mad, into refresher courses. We attend lectures on — How to Wear Your Officer's Cap, How to Draw Flight Plans Taking into Account Wind, The Importance of Soap and Water on the Parts After Sexual Congress with Whores, etc. Now, moving between two buildings, going from one fascinating class to another, I find and pick up a wallet lying in the dust. In its pockets a number of cards that identify a certain corporal; in its heart, almost seven hundred dollars in bills.

In a free hour a day or two later I check with headquarters and discover where the soldier bunks. That afternoon when I appear at the top of the steps on the second floor of his barracks, my presence terrorizes the sack-hounds; someone screams Attention! in a voice as hysterical as though God himself had appeared. They are mocking me for invading their space, and their exaggerated respect in turn terrorizes me. I ask for the corporal, he comes forward, and I give him his wallet; the joy and disbelief on his face is so beautiful, the happy ending to his tragedy so improbable, his gratitude so extreme, that I remember that little minute, that miraculous moment when an enlisted man loved an officer, as my best moment in months — and surely the best in Texas. The corporal worked in the base photo section and for a week he came to my barracks every afternoon to take pictures of me. He blew them up to great size and presented them to me with apologies for being unable to repay me properly for returning to him what was his. I still have one of the photographs, and this has helped me to remember. I have been snapped sitting on the floor and mixing some oil paints on a palette; behind me on the door I have painted a series of pictures — the faces of screaming men with wide staring eyes, skulls, piles of bones. What had been in my mind was not the war but the feel of Texas grinding up my soul.

Thinking of money helps me remember the tremendous amounts of it that I carried around in my own wallet. For over a year I had been unable to spend the almost $1,000 a month I earned, and I could hardly sit down for the piles of five-hundred-dollar bills folded into a back pocket. And so another memory of a meeting with a friend on that same base suddenly blooms in my mind:

Leaving the mess hall, we met outside in the open prairie wind, almost deliriously delighted to run into each other since we had come from different combat groups and hadn't seen each other for over a year. We talked about the dead and the still-living, or at any rate about the dead and still-living bombardiers whose names had begun with T in our training class at Victorville. But combat was impossible to talk about except in that soldier's shorthand which reduced the most profound experience into expressions like, "Oh, my fuckin' achin' back." Just as we parted, having arranged to meet again later in the officers' club, he mentioned that he had a '39 Buick coupe that he wanted to sell.

"Is it in good shape?" I asked.

"Not bad," he said. (His name, I suddenly remember, was Jerry Twomey.) "She burns a little oil but aside from that . . . "

"How much do you want?"

"A thousand dollars?" Jerry said, blushing slightly. In 1945 a thousand dollars was a lot of money, six months wages for a laboring man. Since the age of fifteen I had seldom been without a car; back from the war, I pined for one now and dreamed of being free to leave the horrors of the Texas camps and drive away to the cities for five-day weekends. I took a thousand dollars from the pile of bills in my wallet and handed them to Jerry. He gave me the keys and the title of ownership. It was just that fast and simple. Later that afternoon we went to the parking lot and he pointed out my car, a handsome midnight blue job with only one real flaw, which Jerry had neglected to mention: the seat back, perhaps from excessive gymnastic action in the sexual antics department, was sprung back nearly parallel to the ground. Rushing down the Texas roads I lounged behind the wheel like a feasting Roman, my eyes just barely showing above the dash. Buying that car was another little minute I like to remember: we were so princely, so trusting, so grand about the way we took or spent money, so contemptuous of it.

I was sitting in a San Antonio movie house at three o'clock one afternoon when the screen suddenly went blank and the house lights went on. A man climbed onto the stage and in a voice that broke so that he could hardly speak, he announced the death of Roosevelt. After an awful amount of time, minutes that belonged to neither the past nor the present, the lights dimmed, the movie continued, and the theater gradually emptied. Outside in the late afternoon people wandered in the streets with stunned faces. Strangers talked with strangers, seeking solace or impelled to share themselves in this moment which was so clearly historic. For me, Roosevelt's death was the period at the end of a sentence which had begun the day that the Japanese had bombed Pearl Harbor.

Now, though here in Texas we had no sense of time's passing, the war rushed toward its ending. Russians, raping and implacable, sweeps through eastern Germany and enters the ruins of Berlin defended by fourteen-year-old members of the Hitler Youth. And Hitler, in an underground bunker, damning the German people for being unworthy of him, simultaneously bites down on a pellet of cyanide and blows his brains out. While he and his gasoline-soaked bride burn amid exploding artillery shells, I sit in a classroom and listen for the ninety-third time to a slow and careful reading of the articles of war. Germany surrenders unconditionally. Scarcely three months later Hiroshima disappears in a burst of light.

In Texas the headlines for Hiroshima read, "A bomb with the power of the sun." Since the sun, the source of all life, was employed, harnessed to annihilate our enemies, we tended to equate the atomic bomb with the cosmic powers of nature and to see the destruction of an entire city as a religious event in which God himself had now finally decided to take sides. The wholesale slaughter of entire cities meant only, to those of us sitting out the war in relocation camps, that the war was probably over, though with time a sense of guilt began to grow. But was it morally acceptable to kill ten thousand people with ordinary bombs and evil to kill eighty thousand with an improved product? Don't worry about it, certain members of the press explained. Everyone knew that Hiroshima was no ordinary city, but a rotten place full of whorehouses, low bars, and dimly lit dance halls. Wiping out sinful places improved a soldier's morale and turned whorehouses into grade A military targets. We wanted to believe this lie that Hiroshima was another Sodom, but on a deeper level we were not bothered by questions of morality. If Hiroshima had been nothing but Buddhist temples, tea gardens, university buildings, and boy scout encampments, and if the atomic bomb would end the war, then the bomb was a supernatural gift.

The war ended.

Tucked within those Texas months like beautiful and exotic blooms pressed between the pages of some book of horrors lay a couple of extended leaves; I mention them now slightly out of their proper chronology. They were times outside the banality of the military life that hinted at what being a civilian, that almost forgotten condition, might be like. Years ago when I decided to write these pages about what I remembered of my youth, the last pages of these memories formed easily in my mind. I didn't know how to begin this book, but I knew exactly how I wanted to end it. (I still haven't the beginning.) Let me go back to that first leave after coming home from England, to San Francisco where my wife had gone to live and then later, after I had proved myself, north to Seattle to stand in all my ribbons and bows before my father.

If I had been celibate in England I would probably have returned to my wife in a state of overwhelming nervous apprehension concerning the ability of my body to cooperate with my sexual anticipations. But I had discovered on a few sordid and lustful occasions that all that complicated machinery that had once betrayed me now worked with admirable efficiency. The women who worked the London streets had perfected a technique of appearing before you in the darkness of blackout and in a matter of seconds flipping open your overcoat, unzipping your trousers, and holding in their hands your already violently engorged penis. The only thing faster than their deftly moving fingers was the speed with which, being young and deprived, you could be brought to tumescence. A few blocks from the theater district around Piccadilly Circus was a street lined on both sides with great buildings that looked at night as though they had been carved from solid chunks of marble. They were government buildings, and after eleven o'clock when darkness finally fell, the street was deserted. It emptied into Trafalgar Square and had a couple of bright red telephone boxes sitting alone in a wide space. At night it looked as weirdly unreal as one of those empty paintings of De Chirico, isolation and perspective reduced to anguish. From time to time I would tell myself that I wanted to see again that curiously surreal street, but in truth it was the little band of women who hung around the telephone boxes that I hoped to encounter. And I usually did.

Standing up and screwing in a telephone booth was so quick, exotic, and degenerate, so absolutely devoid of any human tenderness, so essentially inhuman that I could never connect these infrequent and fugitive five-minute periods with myself or my emotions. They had nothing to do with me; they relieved an awful tension; they left me guiltless; they cost three pounds.

I have two vivid memories of Trafalgar Square: one, standing alone at midnight in the middle of that vast emptiness, fainting with terror as a shrieking buzz bomb, spouting a blowtorch of flame, slowly and at rooftop level crossed above me while I waited for the failure of its motor and the quick plunge and explosion. And the second — another buzz bomb on another night as I stand in a telephone booth rapidly reduced to another kind of innocence, less and less deeply involved with a sadly dressed but pleasant young woman who in that moment as we begin the serious but hopeless grinding, suddenly pushes me from her violently and disappears into the night, her hysterical screams scarcely heard through the obscene growling above us. Talk about coitus interruptus.

Dorothy was waiting for me in a San Francisco hotel. She had been living in Sausalito with my mother or with my sister, but I could not face this meeting with her, all mixed together with the complications of a family reunion. Things had to be simple; I could only handle things in a simple way, and had arranged this rendezvous from Texas with a long-distance call. We would spend a few nights alone together in the city. How did we feel about each other? About being married? By this time we had become complete strangers, for my own passions for over a year had been centered around statistics about being blown out of the sky.

The passage of more than forty years has dimmed the memory of the monumental physicality of those first ten minutes that began as, trembling, I knocked on her door, and as it slowly opened, and even before I saw her, heard her heavy breathing. We were both, of course, in a state of crisis. Thinking back to this meeting now, I tend to confuse it with the high jinks, the sexual hanky-panky of those later movies like *Tom Jones* or *Clockwork Orange* where the scenes of lovemaking are speeded up into incredibly fast, fast motion and the act becomes visually as exciting, and as grotesque, as the mating of salmon or praying mantis. Wham bam, shades being rapidly lowered, blankets zipped back, murky cries and fumblings, strange bird-like squawks, pantings and exclamations, clothes being ripped away, shirts and pants, socks and brassiere sailing through the air. Hands moving over the ecstasy of skin. It was certainly intense and some of the emotion was undoubtedly sincere and some of the wildness that Dorothy's mother had warned me about was greeted with an equal lack of restraint from this girl whom I had left in a state of incredible innocence and had returned to find managing the situation with a sophistication that set my imagination to reeling. It wasn't until we both lay spent and resting that I realized what a load of apprehension had been lifted from my mind and how much self-loathing and confusion I had lived with for over a year.

But in the three weeks that we spent together before I returned to Texas, the idea that lived for a very short time in both our minds, the idea that everything was now possible between us, slowly faded away. We had become different people, the strangeness grew, the awareness that hit us from time to time upon awakening or in moments of vacant musing (my God, I'm married) arrived with all the shock of a pie in the face. We could say it to each other — my God, we're married — and at first it would produce a few gasps of nervous laughter, but then later a sad, puzzled, lingering frown of bewilderment as we each contemplated without understanding them those events that had entrapped us and put us two naked strangers into the same bed.

How strange — after we had learned to enjoy one another, to move in freedom unafraid of our bodies' powers to betray us — that it was only for those few minutes in the darkness that we shared a sense of joy. That brief closeness, that desperate clinging, only accentuated the deep isolation in which each of us moved. It was a true wartime marriage, a union of strangers brought together by the fear of death and annihilation, a sad, embarrassed time as we secretly regretted how we had entangled ourselves in a relationship in which no hint of a common future revealed itself.

Combat had twisted or robbed me of my better qualities, had made me touchy, cynical, secretive. I was too tired to work at putting together something with subtle complications — the advancing and retreating forays into the territory of another human soul. What I discovered, or rather what I have discovered now, forty years later, thinking about it and trying to understand, is that I had been proved too weak to confront the senseless and obscene injustices of this awful century. What I wanted was to leave the stage, to move away, to observe without participation, like someone comfortably seated in a movie theater eating popcorn while the earth, falling into the sun, sizzles and blazes like a flaring match, like the falling body of an airman.

What I wanted was to be alone. Intimacy, even with members of my family, made me nervous. I was irritated by those who took it for granted that I needed them or assumed that I would learn to need them. I looked on kindness offered to me as a kind of offense, a technique to manipulate me, a scheme to patch me up, to destroy the only power I had now — the power to live alone in my own rage, despair, and disillusion. To move back into that society that could dance, sing, and rush into life with the enthusiasm of puppies seemed like a betrayal of the millions dead. The only decent response to the dead was like the response of the old who dress all in black and sit motionless for hours with vacant faces in the shade of trees — a state of perpetual mourning.

I could no longer play a part in anyone else's drama, could not mimic tenderness. I remember certain nights lying awake long after we had made love, wondering dumbly, "And what am I going to say if one day she should ask me if I love her?" She never did. I think she was not half so worried that I might not love her as to discover that she no longer loved me, or that looking into the future she could no longer automatically want to find me at her side. We never quarreled, never disagreed, never raised our voices. With shamed faces, but like six-year-olds playing house, we went through the motions for a while of what we figured marriage should be like, but in less than a year it all simply dissolved into smoke. We were too solemn to laugh at ourselves.

26

ONE MORNING IN MARCH of 1945, I turned and walked down the drive toward my father's house to stand before him after a two-year absence with my wings and bars and ribbons. I was in the last week of a thirty-day leave. If I was no longer particularly proud of the silken and pewter and tin-plated wings and ribbons, having seen them distributed by the truckload, I knew my father, a civilian subjugated by war propaganda, would be dazzled and awestruck. My quest for approval that morning certainly contained elements of a neurotic dependence that long before 1945, when I was twenty-nine, I should have outgrown. But it was a dependence so corrupt that in all my life I never completely conquered it, based as it was not on love or filial respect, but on my father's money. And so while I needed my father's admiration, more importantly, I wanted to soften him up to keep the promise he had made me on the day the Japanese bombed Pearl Harbor — that after the war he would help me buy three hundred white-faced cows and the winter and summer pastures to run them on. If he would have been unable at the beginning of the war to help me in such a generous way, by its end he had, he claimed, more than made back the million dollars he had lost in the early 1930s when the stock market collapsed and so many of his business friends began falling from office windows.

There was another selfish reason for my visit: before going overseas I had left a little red Dodge pickup truck in my father's care. Now due to report back in a few days to a Texas air base, I looked forward to the freedom and loneliness of driving across the western deserts through the memories of my youth.

Mainly, of course, I hoped that my return, which he might consider as miraculous as a rising up from the dead, and that my ribbons with their blatant and dishonest reference to my courage under fire, would disorient and weaken him and impel him to act toward me in a way that was foreign to his nature — with generosity. Looking back then (and now) I couldn't and can't remember much of anything I had ever done to make him proud of me, and in fact, couldn't remember a dozen times after the age of thirteen, say, when he had even seemed happy to have me around. One night at the dinner table when I was ten or thereabouts he had said absolutely gratuitously, "Some day someone is going to give you a million dollars for that smile." It was like being given a five-dollar bill for no reason, and I treasured that remark, and, since I still remember it, probably still do. I think it was the only loving remark he ever made to me.

It has been more than forty-two years since that morning when I came back from the war, and I no longer remember the day in any precise detail. If I had understood what happened, if I could have said to myself, This is the funniest thing that has ever happened to me in my life, or This is the ugliest thing I have ever seen, then, by characterizing the action I might have felt, perhaps falsely, that I understood it. But I didn't understand it, and forty-two years later still don't understand it, at least not well enough to worry out the proper voice, the tone appropriate to the telling of this story.

I remember walking down the drive toward the house, remember that I wanted to please him, that I wanted him, finally, to be proud of me. And one reason I remember this so clearly is that by early evening of that same day I didn't much give a shit what he thought of me, and the rest of his life I pretty much spent not giving a shit if he were proud of me or not. In fact, though finally there was a nearly two-million-dollar inheritance at stake, and though I am probably no more self-destructive than most, I began to take a certain pleasure in appearing before him in ragged Levis and dirty T-shirts, knowing that he judged people by the way they dressed, knowing that my work boots in his living room filled him with contempt. He had told me so many times that I was an idiot, that I was scatterbrained and irresponsible, that I had no business sense, that I disgraced him, that finally as the years passed, and though I saw him less and less, I began in his presence to act the part of an idiot, never speaking, staring at him with my mouth open and my eyes vacant, my lips curled in a kind of dreamy smile. A part of the imbecility that I paraded before my father was an attempt to turn our relationship into the high black comedy that would let him know how little I valued it. But another frightening part was a simple surrender to the pressures of his presence. Twenty-four hours in his house trying to half conceal myself behind the Christmas tree and listening to his judgments about the way I lived reduced me to a state of near catatonia.

Of all my faults and vices I willingly acknowledge, the worst of them was my cowardly and self-serving subservience to my father's tyranny in the hopes of one day inheriting his wealth. It certainly to some extent poisoned and diminished my life; it fed a self-loathing that I tried to rationalize away by telling myself that, by paying him an outward though minimal degree of respect that I didn't feel, by in fact conforming to the Biblical injunction, I was honestly earning wages that, no matter should they finally total millions, would not begin to pay me back for a lifetime's humiliation.

But our relations were not that simple, and there is no reason to paint myself blacker than I was. On that May morning in 1945 when I prepared to meet my father — dressed in the proofs of my gallantry, hung with the symbols of a manhood which he would no longer be able to deny — if a good part of my motivation was venal, so was there that other part, those awful bonds that tie families together, bonds that are stronger, more dangerous, more irrational than simple love or hate. He was a man for whom I had little respect; I scoffed at his standards of excellence, which were as childish as a boxer's; and the admiration I yearned for, though real enough, was perhaps no more than a manifestation of the neurotic dependence that any neurotic father will try to develop in his children — the only kind of castration that is legal under the law.

It was about ten-thirty when I walked into my father's house, and it was no later than seven o'clock on the evening of that same day that he made it quite clear, after rapidly downing three old-fashioneds to ignite and fan into flames a rage that would reflect what sober he didn't quite have the courage to reveal, that he would give me none of the things I had had the effrontery to expect — no cattle ranch, no white-faced cows, no pickup truck, no admiration or respect. "In all your life," he cried, "you've done one decent thing. Made captain. Why? Because you finally stepped into something you couldn't get out of." The years I had been gone, he said, had been calm and sunny, free of troubles, the happiest years of his life. "Get off my back," he yelled. "Leave me in peace;

make your own way, goddammit. Don't walk in here demanding this, demanding that, ruining my sunset years."

At five o'clock the next morning, without bothering to say good-bye, I quietly left the house for what I was sure would be the last time, and in a pre-dawn darkness darker than night while a heavy May dew began to drip from the trees at the road's edge, walked down the gravel road and across the bridge at the end of Lake Washington to the highway and the local Bothell bus. There are great blanknesses in my mind here, though I seem to remember that that same day, treated with the special considera- tion that was sometimes paid to soldiers on leave during wartime, I was, without a reservation, put on a train heading back to Texas by way of Chicago. The rails clicked out a rhythmic message to my father too ob- scene to record.

What makes funny stories funny is the sudden downward plunge of someone's fortunes or dignity, or their realization that God sees them far differently than they see themselves. Funny stories always have a victim; as human beings we have a built-in meanness that rejoices at other peo- ple's misadventures. In German there is even a special word to describe this little glow of joy that warms us when a friend is brought down. And so, just as in every funny story there is that one person who is hurt too much to laugh (the fat man spread flat on the sidewalk beside the banana peel that has broken his back, the society lady with the pie in her face and her bloomers showing), so it was a long time before I could laugh at the fool I had been to expect rewards and recognition from my father. It was years before I could laugh.

And then as I more carefully examined the components of that day it slowly dawned on me that, rather than my being the victim in this black family comedy, it was my father who couldn't have laughed, that all the time the joke had been on him, and that my coming back from a war that was supposed to have killed me was that final illumination of some brutal knowledge that probably had been, until he first saw me standing in the kitchen, even a secret from himself. Good-bye to his dreams of a peaceful old age during which he could mourn, and probably sincerely, the loss of his son, heroically dead in the full flower of his youth. Good- bye to the memorial drinking fountain which he had dreamed of presenting to my high school, and to the bronze plaque he might have had set in the trunk of the memorial plum tree. Good-bye to that sad and beautiful fantasy: sitting in the grape arbor in the long sunset of the thirty years still remaining to him and watching all his old rage and disgust for me turn to love. Instead of crying to his friends, "That boy of mine doesn't know shit from tar," he would find himself saying in all sincerity, "He died so young but with so much promise."

He wanted to love me and probably felt guilty because he couldn't, and he had discovered with the deaths of his father and his sisters that the one thing they had to do before he could really love them was to die.

And so finally it was my father who became the victim of this funny story. But now that I had made a kind of sense of my father's welcome, I had without knowing it constructed another joke, a new one, of which this time surely nothing was at point except my own stupidity — the thirty years it had taken me to catch my breath and begin to understand.

At six o'clock my father yelled up the back steps to my room where I was sitting on the bed in a state of anger. He told me he was mixing me a drink and that dinner was almost ready.

I had spent the morning and most of the afternoon with him driving around the farm, mailing off some packages of blueberry jam that he cooked and advertised in *House Beautiful*, inspecting the crazy little factory he had built out of junk for canning blueberries, admiring the ton of sugar he had lied out of the war board, plus a small pile of rationed tires, plus ration books for God knows how many gallons of gasoline. He showed me the site of last year's Victory garden where everything he had planted with a small group of friends from the city (I was amazed to find out he had friends) grew insanely out of control like a science fiction story of pure horror; his squash when he weighed them were heavier than sacks of wheat and required a crew of men to load them onto trucks; his rows of spinach grew into small trees like windbrakes; and from a dozen tomato plants he harvested a crop that had to be measured in tons. His four or five acres of blueberries were planted on bottom land, pure peat, so rich in organic material that a chunk of it, tossed in water, would float. The war, looked at coolly, had been wonderful and something he could turn to his own advantage; he had seen it as a dirty plot of Roosevelt's to communize the world and, since it was corrupt, his duty had been to circumvent the war's restrictions and refuse to become involved in the sacrifice of his little pleasures.

He was rich again. He had built apartment houses near the naval air station at Sand Point, sixty units, and hadn't had a vacancy for years. He was building more apartments and talking to a wrecking firm about the millions that could be made buying up Army and Navy installations when the war was over.

He told me about a particular day just a few months past when his wife had started ringing the emergency iron triangle summoning him home from the cannery, and how, when he had driven up expecting something awful — some news from the air force, perhaps — she met him in the drive, grinning, and said, "Pardon my French, precious, but the son of a bitch is dead." (This, I realized later, would not necessarily have ruled out the arrival of that telegram from the air force.) "And now," she went on, "that crooked crony of Pendergast, that failed necktie salesman is going to be president." They had called their friends and invited them all to a party; they were good loyal Americans, good decent Republicans who would soon have a martyr, young John Birch, to rally around; and all night long they danced and drank and celebrated that death they had waited for for so long, all of them carried away with joy.

But it hadn't all been wonderful; he had suffered too. He told me about locking himself by mistake in the basement quick-freeze room he had had built and that he had filled with meat — beef steaks and pork sausage, a year's supply all cut up and packaged. The room was kept at some extreme of freezing temperature, twenty or thirty degrees below zero, and he had been trapped down there for hours, screaming for help, cursing his stupid wife, and battering at the door — running against it with his shoulder, not feeling the cold at all but steaming with sweat as he ran at the door again and again through the late afternoon and early evening until, though it was a foot thick and heavily built, he knocked the door off its hinges and more dead than alive, sobbing and bleeding, crawled up into the kitchen on his hands and knees. Being wartime, he constructed his story as a war story. A newspaper reporter had written up the experience, not as my father might have wished — his semi-heroic victory over death — but as a joke, the first sentence of his article reading, "Charles Thomsen, Seattle businessman, may be the only person in the world who knows if, when you close the refrigerator door, the light goes off."

"Well," I asked, "does it?" But the question may have struck him as flippant. I don't believe he answered me.

That all-day conversation had been a typical family production, a monologue that I had allowed him to dominate and direct, not only because he was the top banana but because, wanting things from him and thinking I knew how to manage him, I was waiting for the proper psychological moment to strike. Besides, he had scarcely mentioned the war, and certainly not with curiosity; a relief because I had nothing to say about the war. All day I had been looking surreptitiously in his warehouses and garages for my truck, without luck. I had said nothing, however. Now, as I sat in my room and he called up to me and I found myself trembling with outrage, I realized that the moment had come; a couple of very suspicious things had come to my attention:

About noontime, while my father made sandwiches in the kitchen and told me how he had eaten dog food by mistake out of the refrigerator for a week and, in fact, enjoyed its honest meaty flavor, I had idly opened a drawer by the kitchen table directly under a large banner that hung in the window — a nylon or rayon five-and-ten-cent store purchase with a single blue star in a white field announcing to the public that a family member was serving in the armed forces. What I had found in the drawer, rolled up but instantly identifiable, was part two of the blue-starred announcement in the window, another almost identical banner differing only in the star's color, now gold. A gold star in your window was a real feather in your cap; it announced to the public that your son (or your brother, husband, uncle — you name it) was dead.

The sight of the banner embarrassed me; it was a violation of my father's privacy and, just as years before I had shuddered upon opening a drawer in my father's dressing room to discover a loose pile of condoms scattered among his pill bottles, I shuddered now. Buying that gold star while I was still alive struck me as grossly sentimental and in extremely bad taste.

Late in the afternoon my father went to his room to lie down for a half hour before dinner. He suggested I do the same. And so it was past five when I carried my musette bag upstairs and went into my bedroom for the first time. It seemed unchanged at first, as though it had been no more than a day or two since I had left, and not two years. Then I went to the clothes closet and slid its door back on its rollers to reveal a hundred empty coat hangers, and alone in this emptiness a single black suit I had worn on formal occasions and perhaps no more than a half dozen times — the tails now eaten through in a hundred places by moths; holes as big as nickels; ten dollars in nickels' worth of holes. Everything else had vanished: suits, tweed jackets, flannel shirts, skis and ski pants, golf clubs, tennis rackets — everything. I walked down the hall and went through the closets there, into the guest room with its closet, and into the closet of my sister's bedroom, unused for years. In the hall closet where my father changed his farm clothes I found one pair of pants that were mine; they were made of heavy material, were cuffless, and had enormous pockets, and I had bought them for deer and elk hunting in those foolish days when I thought it was fun to shoot at animals.

One pair of pants. That was all that was left of me, the pants and the star in the window which apparently was the wrong color. They wouldn't have put my things in the attic, but I went looking anyway, opening trunks, old dresser drawers, a row of suitcases. Nothing.

And now my father called to me to come and have a drink with him, and I went down through the kitchen where my stepmother was doing something at the stove and through the pantry and into the little sitting room that they used now instead of the living room and — my God, how can I have forgotten to put his dog, Missy, into the center of this memorable homecoming, Missy, the creature he loved most in the world? A large purebred collie with a nose as long and thin as an anteater's, little rheumy eyes set very close together, and in repose, which was ninety percent of the time, as shapeless as the swept up pile of hair around a busy barber's chair; and just about as intelligent; and just about as appealing. She was a dog driven insane by baby talk, close confinement, and the loss of all usefulness. Just as people who live emotionally derivative lives will grow to resemble their pets, in the same way the pets enslaved by eccentrics will become as crazy as their masters. This mountain of black hair called Missy, in May of 1945, was one of five dogs that lived in the house from 1927 until 1969: five identical collies, all named

Missy, all of them driven insane, and all but the first one (who had been sadistically murdered) extravagantly loved and buried when they died at seven or eight years of age beneath bronze plaques in a neat row like a military cemetery at the edge of the rose garden — Missy Two, Three, Four, Five.

One of those interchangeable creatures was lying at my father's feet as I entered the room. "Your drink," my father said, pointing to it on a coffee table by the couch. "Skoal."

"Cheers," I said. It was very strong and brutal, a cheap whiskey badly disguised with sugar and angostura bitters and loaded with memories of this house. "Good," I said. I believe that for the last fifty years of my father's life, until he was no longer able to get out of bed, he drank one of these explosive black draughts every evening except when he was upset or planning to be, and then he drank two and very occasionally three. Three old-fashioneds produced a temporary but violent insanity.

The evening paper lay before him on a footstool and he bent over it, glancing at the headlines and burying one hand in Missy's thick coat. "I heard you up in the attic," he said. "Looking for something, need a suitcase or something?"

"Not something; I'm looking for everything. Everything's gone out of my room, all my clothes, shoes, shirts, the tweed jackets, my ski clothes. Did you put them someplace?"

"I haven't touched your things," my father said. He bent closer to the dog. "Yeah, the sweet Missy, oh the sweet dog."

"Skis, guns, tennis rackets, fly rods." I waited for some kind of an answer and waiting, drank. "It's a very strange feeling to come back to a room stripped of all the things that prove you exist. Like being erased, like being scissored out of a family photo. All I found were those pants I bought when I went elk hunting; they were in your closet."

"Ah yes, I did take those. Wonderful pants for the farm, great for the cold weather. You don't begrudge me the pants, do you?"

"No. On the contrary. I'm glad you took them, or rather, glad to think I had bought something you liked well enough to want to use."

"If you want them, take them back," my father said. He had lost his pleasant relaxed look, and he looked into his glass and then drank from it. "They were just hanging there year after year; a terrible waste; it seemed a shame."

"Yes, well, keep them; a present. My hunting days are over anyway. But what about the other things?"

My father shrugged but didn't answer, and I took a drink of the whiskey, good now, bright and hot, a knife blade sharp with the promise of real anger and the strength to reveal it. "My pants, what happened to all my pants? You didn't farm in my ski pants, did you? And the pickup, what about the truck? I didn't see it any place. I want to drive it back to Texas when I go."

"Oh, the truck," he said. He straightened up in his chair, looked at me briefly, frowning, and drained his glass.

"I don't understand," I said. "Is this some kind of a game? Why don't you talk? Have you stored the truck someplace? Can't you tell me?"

"The truck was worn out, a pile of junk."

"It wasn't when I left it with you, and what do you mean *was*?"

"*Was* means *was*, goddammit. It means I had a chance to sell it, and I sold it."

"Well, thanks a lot. Without asking me, without even telling me. Were you so goddamn sure I wasn't coming back?"

"That's a hell of a thing to say," my father said angrily. "There wasn't a day I didn't pray for your safe return, not a day I didn't sit here dreading that telegram from the War Department. All you can ever see is your side of things."

"I come back, the closets are empty, you've sold my car, my clothes have disappeared. Your side of things, hell, you don't open your mouth."

"I'm not accountable to anybody, goddammit," my father yelled. "This is my house, I'm master here."

We sat without speaking, glaring at one another with hatred. "How could you sell my truck?" I asked finally. "I never signed the title of ownership. You must have forged my name; they call that grand larceny, don't they?"

"Throw me in jail then," my father cried. "Like the commies do, teaching children to turn on their own parents, denounce them to the police, my God, what a world." He pushed himself to his feet, stepped over the dog, and left the room; the dog, in a parody of his master, struggled up and, lightly weaving, followed him. From the pantry the click of glasses, the scent of bitters; from the kitchen the clicking of my stepmother's high heels, the opening and closing of cupboard doors — every sound familiar and depressing, never-to-be-forgotten family sounds as sad for their banality as old screams. And it was the strong antiseptic perfume of the angostura, as threatening as a whiff of chloroform, that made me feel for the first time that I was really back and that I would still be unable to function in this madhouse.

When my father returned he carried two drinks, one he set beside my still half-filled one. And apparently he had allowed himself an extra slug in the pantry: his face was flushed, his eyes shining, his step heavy. He sank into his armchair and sipped his drink.

The dog like a doppelganger appeared in the doorway, weaved across the room, gave a series of little yippy barks, and collapsed at my father's feet. "I take one step, she takes one step, I take two steps, she takes two steps," my father said, bending down to the dog.

After a long, uncomfortable silence I asked, "How much did you get for my pickup?"

And after another long moment, "Oh shit, I don't remember; more than it was worth."

"If you think I have a right to know, do me a big favor and concentrate, huh?"

"All right, then; nine hundred dollars," my father said.

"I just don't understand. You're so proud to be Republican, so proud, so *proud* of that. And what's the difference between a Republican and a Democrat? Mainly their attitude toward private property. Republicans think there is something sacred about the things they own, ownership more sacred than human rights. Hang the son of a bitch that steals my bread to keep from starving."

"I worked and slaved; the bread is mine," my father said. "If he wants bread let him work for it; let him beg for it."

"What I started to say is, I think you're a lousy Republican, a real lousy one. Or maybe your property is sacred and everyone else's is up for grabs."

"Because I sold that pile of junk? You calling me a thief?" my father yelled. " All the money you've had from me, all the cars I've paid for, violin lessons, private school, a trip around the world, that what-do-you-call-it, that starvation trip around the world, and not a word of thanks. So what do you do first thing, when we haven't seen you for years? You head for California. Well, let that woman take care of your things then if that's the way you want it."

"That woman" was my mother, but in twenty-five years he had never referred to her as "your mother." And when carried away, he would call her names so rough that at age fifteen I had threatened to fight him, and out of my mind with rage had called him a son of a bitch, the first of the two or three times I lost control, felt my father's blood rushing through me, felt the high intense joy of going crazy, of saying anything, ready to kill.

"Sorry, I don't know what the hell you're talking about. I doubt if you do either."

"You could hardly wait to go and stay with that woman in Sausalito. This is your home here, but oh no, after two years you choose to go first to that woman. It looks like everything you do — like voting for that son of a bitch Rosenfeld, voting Democratic just because I hate those commie bastards — is designed to hurt me."

"Listen," I began. "With all due respect . . ."

"All due respect, my ass," my father cried. "Don't all-due-respect me."

"O.K., with all due disrespect — this whole conversation is absolutely unbelievable. You're purposely getting drunk, like you always do so you can pick a fight; you're going ten miles out of your way to pick a fight. Old times, old times."

"Don't tell me how to act in my own house, goddammit," my father said, trying to lower his voice a little, like a driver letting up on the gas with the knowledge that he may be about to spin out of control.

"Now about going to California, I went to San Francisco because that's where my wife is. I wanted to see Dorothy. Now how is that designed to hurt you?"

"Hell, it's always the same old thing; I don't know, I don't know. The way you walk in here, that arrogant way of yours, demanding this, demanding that, ruffling my feathers the wrong way."

"But what arrogant way, and aren't you responsible for the things you do? My God, in three months I'll be thirty, I'm not a little boy anymore to be kicked around. I don't need your permission to go visit my wife, and what am I asking that isn't mine to ask about? Where are my grey flannel trousers, my shirts, where's my fucking underwear?"

"All right, goddammit, we'll have none of that gutter talk around here."

"Yeah, excuse me, five years in the army and that's how you talk."

"Well, keep it in the barracks."

We sat and silently drank. My father had begun to wheeze in one of his mini-asthma attacks as though he were allergic to me, as though my presence in the same room were suffocating him. "Will you give me a check for the pickup, for the nine hundred dollars that you got?" I asked finally.

The question obviously irritated him. He growled something, a kind of dog growl, and then, except for his wheezing, remained silent. "With the money maybe I can buy an old clunk that will get me back to Texas. That's too far to go on a bus and these days the train's almost as bad." I was sitting on thousands of dollars, piles of one-hundred and five-hundred-dollar bills jammed into my wallet — flight pay, combat pay, the better part of almost a year's earnings. It was money that I had suddenly decided not to mention.

My father continued to sit without speaking: an old trick, the dead calm before the storm, and recognizing it I felt both anticipation and dread. I knew now that for a time, or for always, he had decided to wipe me out of his life, and knowing that he was about to demonstrate his absolute power gave me a cleansing feeling of freedom — the freedom to goad him, to tell him to go to hell. "Well," I said finally, "it's absolutely great to be back in the warm heart of the old family circle; everything's the same, isn't it, that old black magic? And how nice to have the same old friendly conversations. Of course, I'm sad you've got so hard of hearing, but I guess that just means I have to talk louder." I waited a few seconds and asked in a strong voice, "That truck of mine you sold, will you give me the money so I can buy a new one?"

"All the cars, all the clothes, a college education," he yelled. "Make no demands on me; I'll give you nothing." He drained his glass, fought his way out of the chair, and clumped out of the room — the man, then the dog.

While he rattled glasses and bottles together and muttered to himself in the pantry my stepmother came to the doorway. "Come please. Now. Dinner's on the table." She waited, her face closed, until I got up and, half drunk, went in to that invariable meal she had prepared and divided on three plates — a small steak, a baked potato, a leaf of lettuce holding afloat a square of strawberry Jell-O below a dollop of cottage cheese. A niggard meal that, along with her eccentric habit of hiding food and filling secret closets with tinned goods, seemed to illuminate a childhood of poverty and terrible insecurity. I estimate now that before she died she had half filled twenty thousand dinner plates in this identical way. We sat at our places. "What have you done to upset your father?" my step-mother asked me.

"I'm upset because all my clothes have disappeared — tennis rackets, golf clubs, skis, everything. Everything I left here in your care. And he's mad because I'm upset. Can you believe it?"

She didn't say anything and then called into the pantry, "Hurry, sweet-heart, we're waiting for you, and it's getting cold."

"He sold my little truck on me, *my* truck, can you believe it?"

"Well, he's your father, and everything he does is for your own good, I'm sure." She picked up her fork. "Let's not wait."

"What about my things? The closet's empty except for my tails, and they're completely eaten by moths. But why, tell me? Couldn't you have had the kindness to dump a nickel's worth of mothballs in that closet?"

"I am not the upstairs maid," my stepmother said. "And after all it *has* been five years."

"Did *you* sell my clothes?"

"Certainly not. How can you say such a thing?"

"Well, then, to the Good Will, to the Orthopedic, the Salvation Army?"

But before she answered man and dog appeared, man with hair di-sheveled as though he had been passing his hands through it. He bent and said something sweetly secret to the dog and walked around the table to his place at its head. Whiskey spilled from his glass as he set it down. "Why can't you be like Missy?" he asked me accusingly. "She gives me nothing but happiness. I take one step, she takes one step, I take two steps, she takes two steps."

As the dog passed my stepmother's chair she restrained her by the col-lar. "Issums, duzzums, wussums?" she asked. The dog stared, with a terrible patience, at an empty space floating just before her eyes.

"I take three steps, she takes three steps," my father said.

"Right," I said, "and so on. Great story; right out of Arabian Nights." I drained my drink, pushed the plate away from me with its silly food that I'd never be able to swallow, and smiling brightly studied my father's dark face. There was no sense in continuing this hateful soap opera. "But tell me this: when you've taken twenty-six thousand, seven hundred and forty-two steps, how many steps has the dog taken? . . . And how do you know?"

"My God," my father said with disgust, "you're crazy."

"And I certainly agree with you that in this house at least, you and I would both be happier if I were a dog. What a tragedy for you that you had two children instead of what you really wanted — dogs. Boy, wouldn't that have been perfect, me one step behind you year after year, red ribbons on my ears, a kiss for me in the dark, baby necktie, little dog galoshes, a plaid raincoat. I'd be called Pissy. Old Missy and Pissy, what a combo, your two dogs one step behind, little dogs doing tricks — sit up, roll over, stand." I snapped my fingers at each command, feeling wonderful, curing myself of the war, and feeling the anger growing up in me almost like a sexual arousal. My father stared at me in dull drunken amazement, for this was one of the few times I had ever goaded him toward irrationality, had ever seen myself as a kind of Toscanini directing and encouraging my father to plunge into his apocalyptic mode. Now, flourishing an imaginary whip, I snapped my fingers again and cried in a loud, harsh voice that mocked his voice when drunk, "Down, boy, down. Play dead."

Just possibly it was the word "dead" that triggered my father's fall into the next, the final stage of his rage. But it was not whatever complicated feelings he may have had about *my* death that jabbed at his psyche; it was the resurrection in his mind of Missy number one who, hidden now within my role as dog in the mocking farce, may have come to life to remind him of that other death that he would never come to terms with, the unforgivable death of that first collie, that original Missy who lived on within all the other identical dogs he owned.

My father, redder in the face now, gulped his drink and began to speak in a voice that grew louder and more intense — like the second movement of the Shostakovich Seventh Symphony, where above a constantly repeated theme the airplanes arrive, and then the tanks, and then the heavy artillery, and then the women dying in the snow, their screams almost obliterating the sound of machine guns: banal art turned into grandeur through repetition and cacophony.

"All right, now," my father began, "you listen to me. In all your life you've had just one success, made captain. And why? Because you volunteered for something you couldn't get out of, couldn't give up on. You're like a fart in a skillet, jumping around from one thing to another. You never did want to make your living like anybody else. Business? Oh no, that's too common. Spoiled rotten by your grandmother, God rest her soul, that's your problem. You think money grows on trees."

My stepmother, that evil witch of a stepmother out of childhood fairy tales, picking delicately at the food on her plate, listened quietly, vaguely smiling. She reminded me of a voice coach approving a well-rehearsed performance whose points she may even have inspired. My father drank again, and his voice strengthened. "They fired you out of the mill; you were a bad influence they said. My God, we *owned* the mill, and they fired you out of it. And you went back to college. First, it was journalism, wasn't it? For about a year. Then you decided journalism was corrupt. You couldn't dirty your hands. What was it next? Oh yes, the movies. You were going to write for the movies. But you failed at that like you fail at everything, and then it was stories and books. You're going to be an *artiste* and write for the commie press, *Atlantic* and *Harper's*, magazines I wouldn't have in my house. Now if you want my opinion, you couldn't write your way out of a paper bag, all that childish stuff, all those dirty words, not one decent person in all those stories. Working stiffs, hitchhikers, runaways, bums. But we went along with you, shelling out the money to send you to college year after year. So now you have this first-rate education, Oregon, Columbia, and where do you end up? Underneath a forty-nine-cent straw hat, up to your knees in cowshit on a dry land pasture that wouldn't keep a dozen cows in grass, starvation acres, and you with your college education, an out-at-the-knees, checker-necked Okie.

"I thought the war would make a man of you, knock all that foolishness out of you, but no, everything's just the same. For five years you left me alone, left me to enjoy my life, five calm and sunny years, the happiest I've ever had, you in England or Texas or Fort Lewis, and that sister of yours married to a Mexican abstract artist in San Francisco, and don't tell me he isn't a card-carrying member of the Communist Party. And now you're back, you walk in here demanding this, demanding that, ordering me around in my own house, ruining my sunset years. Well, I won't have it. Leave me in peace; make your own way, goddammit. Get off my back."

Halfway through this tirade — parts of which I had heard many times before, parts of which I would hear many times again — I had been unable to keep my face decently solemn; a wide grin, so wide it made my mouth ache as though I sat in a dentist's chair, took possession of me. Actually, it was a grin as painful as a scream for what it hid — my despair at knowing that I had lost that fifty thousand dollars he had promised me on the day Pearl Harbor was attacked. My own personal money tree, twisted and stunted as it was, had lost its leaves, the ice age had swept over money tree country. Now I began to choke back great hoots of furious and derisive laughter that burst out as he finished speaking. How skimpy the little ways, out of our ape's past, that we are given to express emotion when laughter can so closely mimic sobs. I was standing behind my chair, not knowing how I had gotten there or when I had left the table, drunk I suppose, or at any rate numbed by the old eloquence, like a hypnotized chicken on a chalk-line, into a kind of semiconsciousness. The laughter erupted in waves, my stomach nauseated and convulsed so that the laughter came surging up like vomit. I stared at my father, at the malice in his face, at the little froth of spit-bubbles that had collected at the corners of his lips, at his wild tortured eyes; thinking with the beginnings of relief that would now steadily grow, "Well, there is nothing that he can do to me now, or rather, there is only one thing left that he can do to me now. Kill me."

And something new had struck me as I had listened: that he saw me in the same non-chronological way that I saw him, and that his angers at what I had done at the age of eighteen or ten or twenty-five or five still burned in his memory with the original heat, each separate memory of equal importance — unforgotten, unforgiven. Looking at me he could not see a thirty-year-old man, a soldier back from the war, but a hundred different aspects of that same man: the terrified screamer crouched in his crib under the power of a monstrous dream, the bed-wetting twelve-year-old, the petty thief, the masturbator, the awkward liar, the lazy daydreaming yokel, the sarcastic student arrogant in the certainty of his own cleverness and the boundless ignorance of his father.

Like him as he stared at me, I see him now, outside of time, the whole album of his life portrayed on a flat plane like a Warhol painting, fifty silk screens of Jackie Onassis framed together, except I see him simultaneously at all the different ages of his life — as farmer, child, dying veteran, man of business, recluse, bankrupt failure deserted by his wife into a temporary paralysis of the will. Strangely enough, I see him most clearly through the eyes of others, doing violent things in his youth and early manhood, acting out his obsessions years before I was born.

What I have tried to do when writing about my father has proved to be impossible: to put him there before the reader in one great flash of comprehension, like the ten-second earthquake that brings the house down around you — the whole man as I see him, seeing him in all his roles at once. This may be one of the miracles of painting or music; I have read of certain composers who can, before setting pen to paper, hear in all its intricacy an entire work in a single moment of time. And if the work is great enough it will leave the listener with the feeling that the impossible has been achieved, time itself obliterated, as the whole form of the symphony lives in the mind like an abstract work of art that one sees and can almost, but not quite, draw.

At the same time, among the hundreds of pictures that live simultaneously in my mind when I think of my father, his face that May evening in 1945 (helpless, furious, distraught, accusing, drunken, and yes, guilty) sits at the very center of my idea of him. And leaks its poison over all the others.

One very short last paragraph will bring this episode to an end and get me out of the dining room.

For a time I couldn't speak, but when I could I asked, "You got it all off your chest, you finished?" and then after a sulky silence, "Well, then, if you'll excuse me." I left the room and was halfway up the front stairs when my father yelled after me in typically brilliant recapitulation, "You don't know shit from tar." It was the last time I would hear his voice for almost two years.

27

FOR A TIME I BELIEVED that the shameful secrets that passed between a patient and his psychiatrist were as sacredly inviolate as what one might confess to a priest or a lawyer. My father's psychiatrist, however, the one who put him in the rest home for six months after Grandfather died in the early 1930s, was a man who did not strictly guard his patient's secrets. His daughter, a classmate of my sister's in high school, was a close friend; she picked up weird medical gossip at her father's dinner table and passed it on to us. She was a girl at the age to be disenchanted with her parents and like us willing to mock her father's eccentricities. "He's as crazy as your dad," she told us. "He has this thing about bath towels." We were convinced, of course, but not too impressed, since even in 1934 it was common knowledge that psychiatrists were people who should have their heads examined.

The doctor was a big, soft, stylishly sloppy man who, the few times I saw him, was dressed in the same loosely fitting black suit that matched his dark, intense, loose, unhappy face. In size he reminded me of Thomas Wolfe, whom he had treated in Seattle for exhaustion and a pulmonary infection and, though now I am imagining instead of knowing, sent him east by train (or allowed him to go) to his death. I resented and distrusted him for that. I had had the luck to read Wolfe at the age of eighteen, the perfect age to be swept away into adulation by his passion and his rhetoric. But even before Wolfe's death I had been suspicious of the doctor's competence, ever since he had stopped me on the stairs one afternoon as I was climbing up to my father's sickroom, to ask without even a greeting, "Do you hate your father?" I resented the question and the way it was asked, thinking, "Hell, I'm not the patient; don't third-degree me." And when I said "Yes" and he fell back against the wall with the stunned look of a man hit full in the face with a baseball bat, I found his reaction to be so timid and shocked that I doubted his courage to go scampering around into the nasty quarters of people's minds, wondered even if he were tough enough to read Freud. I was certainly convinced that he was neither tough nor cunning enough to force my father to reveal certain traumatic moments in his life. Knowing that I knew things about my father that lay on his soul heavier and deeper than any sexual guilt, things his psychiatrist would never know, gave me a proud little feeling of superiority.

All of the secrets that the doctor's daughter passed on to me and my sister must have been, I realize now, the silly or amusing razzmatazz that a respectable doctor might decently let drop within the family circle. And so I remember only one thing that was leaked out to us, a kind of summing up concerning his children as the treatment began to slow down and my father prepared to step out into the world again. "Charlie," the doctor had said, "listen to me now. Let go of your children. Let them go, let them go."

It was good advice addressing that part of his wounded self that had been bloodied by his children. But his real despairs were centered around the loss of his wife and his money, and how could he, having lost both, freely lose his children too? He couldn't of course, neither then nor later; never; though why did it never occur to him as we grew to maturity that giving us up would have been like freeing himself (and us) from some painful and crippling disease?

He was a man who never let go of anything, the extreme example of an anal type, if I understand Freud. He must have been reluctant to flush away his wastes, a speculation reinforced by knowing that for fifteen years before his death he took an enema almost daily. His attic was full of the past's garbage: old furniture, locked trunks, torn and faded World War One posters, a dismantled pool table, the front pages of old newspapers, a battered bugle, a battered mandolin, and among a hundred other things, the socks Grandmother was knitting when she died. With me, who enflamed and complicated and fully engaged his emotions, he had the yearly double satisfaction of throwing me out of his life and then, a few days or months or years later, of drawing me back into his opera — exactly as a fisherman will endlessly release and draw in a well-hooked trout for the pleasure of working it, aware of the artistry and the control of his performance. But on a deeper level he was like that Jimmy Durante who sang "Have you ever had the feeling that you wanted to go and still had the feeling that you wanted to stay?" a victim of contradictory passions.

Basically he saw both my sister and me as simply things he owned. We belonged to him in the same way as his Rainier beer stock, his little blueberry farm that lost him thousands every year in tax deductions, or that eternal, that replaceable Missy who took one step when he did. And so on second thought I want to soften that accusation I made against myself because never in my life, as I should have done, did I simply tell him to go to hell and walk out of his life. While I was always happy to regard his repudiations as being as final as he said they were, I was always, God help me, an exhausted trout on a million-dollar hook, willing to come back when he reeled me in. So this being booted out of his house just before the war ended was not the first nor the last time, but simply the most outrageously designed, the most senselessly motivated, the most vividly remembered.

For almost two years I lived in the freedom of what more and more looked like a permanent rupture. I bought a farm in California with that fifty percent of my inheritance that my father hadn't stolen and began the long slow descent into bankruptcy that took twenty years. But one day early in 1947, smiling as though everything were fine, my father arrived for a two-day surprise visit. Before leaving — and I believe he left in a rage, though I don't remember why — he wrote me out a check for three hundred dollars with the understanding that I was to buy a cow. So at the end he was only two hundred and ninety-nine cows short of keeping his promise. And, as we used to say in the army, that's better than a jab in the ass with a sharp stick.

Fantasies that grow out of our own shortcomings or our inability to control a hostile world are usually secret. Certainly the death my father needed (mine) so that he could grow heroically in the eyes of the world by the noble, extreme, and expensive way he mourned and memorialized me, was something he never discussed, at least to my knowledge. Perhaps he was unaware of his feelings and only mentioned the expensive memorials he would erect in my honor because, capable of unlimited self-delusion, he imagined his response to my death as an anticipated grief rather than an anticipated release. Then shortly before his own death twenty-five years after the end of the war, far gone in senile dreams that were much more real than anything around him, he gave himself away and dreamed me dead. Out loud this time.

My father was seventy-nine years old that year; he was very ill and failing fast and needed constant attention and had been persuaded to commit himself to a nursing home. Much of the time he was strapped into his bed, for he had taken it into his head that he was being held prisoner and had several times run out and hidden in the bushes in his hospital gown. Much of the time he was disoriented, hounded in his dreams by his daughter who tortured him with raging screams; tormented by the barbarity and venality of the only friends he had now — lawyers and doctors — all planning in the super-clarity of his hallucinations to rob him of his millions. In early summer I came back from four years in South America where I had gone as a Peace Corps volunteer. Joining that organization had been a mild act of courage, for my father was convinced that it was a communist club inspired by that well known communist, John Kennedy; he had threatened to disinherit me. Then toward the end of those four years he had begun to write me again. I went to Seattle to make whatever kind of peace he wanted; this sounds rather grand when the truth is that I went there mainly to kill time for a month, and to put the final touches to a book I had written. After that I would work as a Peace Corps trainer for a couple months and then return to South America — as an immigrant.

As it turned out, what he wanted from me was not a peace treaty but a forgiveness I couldn't give him, a forgiveness that I took a kind of pleasure in denying him. It was out of my department and in the hands of that God he tended to believe in when things got rough. In June of 1969 things for him were very rough; he was getting ready to die.

For the month I spent in Seattle I visited him almost every day; I drove his car. It was no more than five minutes to that awful place of green lawns and trees, of long halls and rows of rooms painted in happy candy colors, and full of old and senile people. Finally, when it was time to go to the Peace Corps training program, I took his car for three months. I knew he would never drive again; still I had taken it without asking, an action known as stealing. For once I got away with it; it was a crime without penalty since he never missed it, he was obsessed with graver matters.

In September his doctor called me in Montana. My father, he said, vividly remembered having read in the newspaper that I was dead. He had awakened in the morning with all the details alive in his mind. He had read it in both the Seattle *Post Intelligencer* and the *Times*. They had printed my picture, an old photograph sent out by the War Department in 1943. I had been out in a rowboat with a friend. In the middle of Lake Washington a squall of wind had struck the boat; it capsized; we had both drowned. "Call him up," the doctor said. "Relieve his mind; tell him it was a bad dream." I called him, and called him again a week later, trying with the sound of my voice to prove that he was deluded. I realize now that this was not a kind thing to do, though he never quite believed me, half convinced that I was tricking him with taped voices and the new technology that he had grown to hate. The newspapers didn't make mistakes like that. How could it be a lie when the details had been so precise? He told me again how it had happened. His description of my death was so immediate and vivid that, vacantly thinking about this grotesque episode almost twenty years later, I will, until I pull myself together, remember it as having happened . . . It was a cool grey day of low clouds, but to the south the bulk of Mount Rainier loomed up in a space of blue sky.

While in South America, I had written articles about the Peace Corps and about my friendship with a poor black fisherman for a San Francisco newspaper. Someone had sent a pile of these articles to my father. I don't know why he had such strong feelings about race. Aside from a very few phonograph records that he bought for his children — "Barney Google," "Yes, we have no bananas," "The Sheik of Araby," to name the greater part of them — the only record he had ever bought for himself was a disk of black patter, four minutes of not very funny jokes called "The Old Black Crows." It had been immensely popular in the late twenties. Each time my father heard it, and for a period that spanned months, he laughed until he cried. Later he was excessively fond of *Amos and Andy*, a benignly racist radio show that anchored America to its seats every weekday evening all through the first years of the Depression. My father was offensively friendly with the aging black men who shined shoes in the stand outside his barber shop, and at Christmas gave them five-dollar bills or bottles of cheap whiskey; he had been on decent terms with one of my grandmother's chauffeurs, a great black giant of a man. But he saw all black people only as entertainers; they were not wholly human. When my sister insisted that if she loved him she would marry a black, my father, after 1939 when she married, would scream in rage that she had done the next best thing, she had hooked up with a Mexican; and then to infuriate us would boast that while he had done some pretty bad things in his life, at least he had never eaten at the same table with a Negro.

And now my father read the newspaper articles in the *Chronicle*. The shock of seeing what I had publicly confessed — that my best friend was poor and black — was too much for him; there was nothing left to do but kill me off. He put me in a very small rowboat with a man of color, he pushed us out into the deep water, he conjured up a wind, he tipped us into the depths.

In a sense it was his final triumph over me. He died three weeks later thinking he had outlived me.

A NOTE ON THE AUTHOR

MORITZ THOMSEN was born in Hollywood, California. He was the author of *Living Poor, The Farm on the River of Emeralds,* and *The Saddest Pleasure.* He died in Guayaquil, Ecuador in 1991.

A NOTE ON THE BOOK

This book was composed by Steerforth Press using a digital version of Bembo, a typeface produced by Monotype in 1929 and based on the designs of Francesco Griffo, Venice, 1499. The book was printed on acid free papers and bound by Quebecor Printing ~ Book Press Inc. of North Brattleboro, Vermont.

AUG 1 2 1999			